With best wishes
for the success of the Bengal War Fund

A. W. Ward.

——

THE

ELECTRESS SOPHIA

AND THE

HANOVERIAN SUCCESSION

THE
ELECTRESS SOPHIA
AND THE
HANOVERIAN SUCCESSION

BY

ADOLPHUS WILLIAM WARD

LITT.D., HON. LL.D., F.B.A., MASTER OF PETERHOUSE

SECOND EDITION, REVISED AND ENLARGED

LONGMANS, GREEN, AND CO.

39 PATERNOSTER ROW, LONDON

NEW YORK, BOMBAY, AND CALCUTTA

1909

BIBLIOGRAPHICAL NOTE

*First published with numerous illustrations by
Messrs. Goupil & Co. in October 1903*

*Second Edition, Revised and Enlarged, cr. 8vo.
published by Messrs. Longmans, Green & Co.
in October 1909*

PREFACE

SECOND EDITION

THE long and eventful life of the Electress Sophia
admits of being treated from various points of view,
each of which possesses an interest of its own. A
Stewart by descent and breeding, and naturally
enough in a large measure by sentiment also, she
likewise, by reason of her birth and through the
traditions and experiences of her youth, had an
immediate part in the declining fortunes of the
Palatine House. The title acquired by her, for
herself and her descendants, to the succession to the
throne of her maternal ancestors, was a Parliamentary title ; but it rested ultimately on the relation of
herself and the House of Brunswick-Lüneburg to the
political and religious conflicts—the struggle against
France and the resistance to Rome—on whose issue
the future of Europe, and that of England in particular, mainly depended. Personally, thanks to the
unflagging vivacity and unfailing candour of her
mind, fostered by an education carried on by her
through life, she became one of the foremost feminine
representatives of the intellectual liberalism of her
age.

In the succeeding pages, the aspect of the
Electress Sophia's career to which prominence has
been designedly given, is the part played by her,
on her own behalf and on that of her descendants,
in the history of the question of the British Succession.   To this one aspect it has been necessary to
subordinate the rest, without, it is hoped, unduly
neglecting any one of them.   It has not been easy
to refrain from dwelling at some length on the story,
often but never yet quite adequately told, of the
Queen of Bohemia, with its alternations of light and
shadow.   And it would have been an interesting task
to seek to put into shape all that we know as to the
extraordinarily varied experiences, in Court and
camp, and in the contiguous spheres of religious and
intellectual activity, of Sophia's brothers and sisters.
But, with her marriage, there opens the period of
her life at the close of which, as the ancestress and
the source of the Hanoverian dynasty of British
sovereigns, she stands forth by herself as an important historical figure ; and it was her connexion with the House of Brunswick-Lüneburg
that moulded her own future and rendered it propitious for the destinies of Great Britain.   In the
present narrative, there has accordingly been included an account of so much of the history of that
House in the period preceding Sophia's marriage as
might suffice to indicate, not only its main dynastic
purposes and principles of policy, but also the

share which it had come to take in the general progress of European affairs.   On this there follows a more special consideration of the attitude consistently maintained by the Hanoverian family, as the representative branch of the whole House, towards the question of the British Succession, which gradually became one of the chief questions of European politics at large.   In these transactions the chief responsibility, on the Hanoverian side, necessarily devolved upon the Electress Sophia, though her eldest son pursued his own course, in general but not in invariable conformity with her own.   And thus, both the House of Hanover and Sophia herself contributed directly to a result of high historical significance.

In describing the ambitions, the achievements, and the experiences, good or evil, of the House of Brunswick-Lüneburg, in the period more immediately preceding its accession to the British throne, I have not thought it right to draw a veil over episodes which have often been intentionally slurred over or misrepresented.   On one of these episodes, the most vexed and the most painful among them, fresh light, but not such as to disturb conclusions already to all intents and purposes established, is thrown, in an Appendix to the present volume, by a supplementary series of documents now (with two exceptions) for the first time made public. Such episodes a truthful narrator cannot pass by ;

but they should not be allowed to affect his judgment on questions connected with his story which possess a far higher historical interest.   In my opinion, the debt of the British nation to the House of Hanover, from the times of the Electress Sophia to those of Queen Victoria, is one to which no conscientious student of the history of the dynasty, in both the one and the other period, ought to refuse to bear witness.

The materials for a history of the Electress Sophia, in its connexion with the Hanoverian Succession, are so abundant that they could only be satisfactorily enumerated in an elaborate bibliography, for which room could hardly be found in the present volume.   A succinct bibliography of the history of the Succession, so far as it enters into the general course of European history, will be found in Vols. v. and vi. of the *Cambridge Modern History*, in connexion with the chapter on *Party Government under Queen Anne* and the section on the *Hanoverian Succession*, by Mr. H. W. V. Temperley and by the author of the present work respectively.   The materials in question may be summarised as follows.   They consist primarily of Sophia's own *Memoirs* (which, however, only reach the beginning of the year 1681) and of her voluminous correspondence, preserved in the State Archives at Hanover.   Among her letters, the collections of those addressed to her mother, to the Elector Palatine Charles Lewis, to her nephews and nieces, the Raugraves and Raugravines, and to her

Mistress of the Robes, Frau von Harling, have been admirably edited by Dr. E. Bodemann, and that of her letters to her son-in-law, King Frederick I. of Prussia, by Professor E. Berner ; and to these has recently been added a very interesting collection of her (and her daughter's) letters to Hanoverian diplomats (more especially the younger Schütz and Bothmer). None of these collections, however, equals in general interest the correspondence of the Electress Sophia with Leibniz, published several years ago by the late Onno Klopp, the author of the monumental *Fall of the House of Stuart*. Besides her own letters, we have many from the hand of her mother, the Queen of Bohemia. So much of her correspondence as was in her hands at her death, went to her son Prince Rupert, and was published, in whole or in part, by Sir George Bromley, Bart., the great-grandson of Prince Rupert's illegitimate daughter Ruperta, under the title of *A Collection of Original Letters* (1787). Some of her letters to Sir Edward Nicholas in 1654-5 were printed by Mr. J. Evans for the Society of Antiquaries, and another set appeared with the private correspondence of Charles I. and Sir Edward Nicholas appended to Wheatley's edition of Bray's *Diary and Correspondence*. Many of the Queen's letters are, of course, to be found in the late Mrs. Everett Green's *Life of Elizabeth*, a work which has long held its own and is on the point of being republished in a new edition, carefully revised by the expert hand of Mrs. Lomas, of the Record Office, and provided by her with an admirable Introduction. In this Mrs. Lomas refers to a very interesting set of Elizabeth's letters, addressed by the Queen to her son, the Elector Charles Lewis, accompanied by a few drafts of his replies, which was a few years ago edited by Miss Anna Wendland for the Stuttgart Literary Society.[1] The letters of Charles Lewis himself and his family have been edited by Dr. W. L. Holland for the Stuttgart Literary Society; and there is, in addition, the inimitable and endless series of letters by Charles Lewis' daughter, Sophia's beloved niece and second self, Elizabeth Charlotte Duchess of Orleans, among which mention need only be made of the selection of letters to her aunt, edited in two volumes by Dr. Bodemann. The letters addressed by Sophia's youngest son, Prince Ernest Augustus (afterwards Bishop of Osnabrück and Duke of York), to his friend J. F. D. von Wendt, edited by Count Erich Kielmannsegg, together with the editor's notes, throw much light on certain passages and personages

---

[1] The reader may like to be referred to certain contributions to the biography of the Queen of Bohemia, besides Häusser and Söltl's well-known *Elizabeth Stuart*; viz. J. O. Opel, *Elizabeth Stuart von der Pfalz* (*Histor. Zeitschrift*, Vol. xxiii.); K. Hauck, *Elizabeth, Königin von Böhmen, Kurfürstin von der Pfalz, in ihren letzten Lebensjahren* (*Kleine Schriften zur Geschichte der Pfalz I*); A. Wendland, *Hannoverische Erinnerungen an die Winterkönigin* (*Zeitschrift d. histor. Vereins für Niedersachsen*, Jahrg. 1903). The last named contains some notes on portraits.

of Hanoverian history ; unfortunately, their continuous sequence breaks off in November, 1713.
To these may be added the letters and memoranda
of Ilten, Schulenburg and other Hanoverian politicians and courtiers, including Bernstorff's correspondence and autobiographical fragment ; the
numerous contributions of Leibniz, in the historical
section of Pertz's edition of his *Collected Works*,
to the politics and later history of the House of
Brunswick-Lüneburg ; and Toland's account of his
visit to Hanover, told well if not too wisely. Of
the despatches of our envoys and residents
preserved in the Record Office and elsewhere,
part only have been given to the world by J. M.
Kemble and others ; while a vast amount of matter
of this kind, especially from the despatches of the
Imperial envoys and residents in London, preserved
in the Vienna Archives, is embedded in Onno
Klopp's *magnum opus*. A very useful guide to
the *personnel* of the diplomatic representation
of England and the North German Governments
at the respective courts is furnished by the *List of
Diplomatic Representatives and Agents, England and
North Germany*, 1689–1727, contributed by Mr.
J. F. Chance to Professor Firth's *Notes on the
Diplomatic Relations of England and Germany*. The
Memoirs of de Gourville have not been lost sight of ;
and the records of the court of Hanover, selected
for publication by the experienced hand of C. E.

von Malortie, and illustrated by him with much
additional matter, have been of occasional use.

There seems no necessity for referring in this
place to the secondary authorities to which, as a
matter of course, I have made more or less frequent
reference—from Spittler to Havemann and O. von
Heinemann and to the late Professor Adolf Köcher's
standard *History of Hanover and Brunswick, from* 1648
to 1674, beyond which date the author unfortunately
did not live to carry his invaluable work. Häusser's
History of the Rhenish Palatinate, a work which
satisfied the requirements of its day, and is most
readable into the bargain, has been in constant
use. Among earlier biographical sketches of the
Electress Sophia I may mention, besides J. G. H.
Feder's and W. Nöldeke's monographs, Dr. E.
Bodemann's account of her in the *Historische
Taschenbuch* for 1888 ; H. Forst's article on *Sophie
Herzogin von Braunschweig Lüneburg, Frau von Osnabrück*, 1661–1679, in the 1889 *Jahrgang* of the *Mittheilungen of the Osnabrück Historical Society* (kindly made
accessible to me by Mr. S. Jaffé of Sandfort), in which,
however, there is little as to her life at Osnabrück
and Iburg, of which one would gladly know more,
besides what is to be found in her correspondence ;
and R. Fester's and H. Schmidt's biographical essays,
to the latter of which is appended a contribution by
Professor A. Haupt on *Art (plastic and pictorial) at
Hanover in the times of the Electress Sophia*. The

masterly chapters in the late Kuno Fischer's great book on Leibniz which deal with his political and religious activity, and with his relations to the Electress Sophia and her family, are certain to be consulted by serious students ; nor will the late M. Foucher de Careil's *Leibniz et les deux Sophies* be overlooked. Of Sophia's brothers, Charles Lewis has found a careful as well as sympathetic biographer in Dr. K. Hauck, who has printed a large number of the Palatine family letters in the *Neue Heidelberger Jahrbücher ;* and Miss Eva Scott has recently published a useful *Life of Prince Rupert.* The Princess Palatine Elizabeth would no doubt have preferred to live in her correspondence with her great friend Descartes, which will be found in Victor Cousin's edition, and in Vols. iii., iv., and v. of the definitive edition of the philosopher's works by C. Adam and P. Tannery. Several attempts have, however, been made to put the materials for the biography of this fair sage—and saint—into form. Among these are G. E. Guhrauer's exhaustive essay in the *Historische Taschenbuch* for 1850 and 1851 ; the admirable monograph by Foucher de Careil, *Descartes et la Princesse Palatine*, and M. V. de Swarte's *Descartes Directeur Spirituel*, which contains a commentary on his correspondence with both the Princess Elizabeth and Queen Christina. The reader should not fail to consult Miss E. S. Haldane's *Descartes, His Life and Times.* I may also mention M. J. Bertrand's paper *Une Amie de Descartes* in the *Revue des Deux Mondes*, Vol. cii., and another contributed by the present writer to *Owens College Historical Essays* (1901). I have not seen an essay on the Princess by Dr. J. Witte in the *Neue Heidelberger Jahrbücher* (1901), which is described as very attractive. A biography of the Princess has quite recently been published by Miss Elizabeth Godfrey, under the title of *A Sister of Prince Rupert*. I am not aware of any attempt to put together in more than outline the curious life's story of another member of the family—the Princess Louisa Hollandina; the source of most of what I have been able to add to details generally accessible on the subject is acknowledged below. I have, of course, used Guhrauer, Varnhagen, and the later memoir writers for various kinds of collateral information ; and on the Succession question I have, besides the works mentioned above, consulted divers essays as to special points by A. Schaumann, O. Meinardus, Reinhold Pauli, and others. It has not been part of my design to trace the way in which the progress of the Succession question was affected by the course of English party history on the one hand, or on the other by the action of the exiled Stewarts, and of the Jacobite interest at home and abroad. But I have endeavoured to keep both influences in view, noticing any Parliamentary transactions of importance, and attempting to utilise such

information as is afforded by the Reports of the
Royal Historical MSS. Commission, including those
on the Stuart Papers at Windsor, and on the Harley
MSS. Among recent secondary works on the
subject, I am greatly indebted to Dr. F. Salomon's
extremely valuable research relating to the history
of the last four years of Queen Anne ; I have also
referred to Mr. W. Sichel's *Bolingbroke*, Mr. E. S.
Roscoe's *Oxford*, and Mr. Percy M. Thornton's useful
Brunswick Succession. I may take this opportunity
of noting the fairness of tone which characterises
Mr. Lewis Melville's now completed book, *The
First George in Hanover and England*. Finally,
I have sought to keep abreast of the learning
which, I am glad to say, continues to stream into
the exemplary *Journal of the Historical Society for
Lower Saxony*.

I have to thank Mr. John Murray and Messrs.
Longmans, Green & Co., as well as the Editors of the
Quarterly, Edinburgh, and *English Historical Reviews*,
and of the *Owens College Historical Essays*, for
allowing me to make use of various articles by me
which have appeared in these quarters on subjects
treated in this volume. For a remarkably full
account of the Abbey of Maubuisson and of the
connexion with it of the Princess Louise Hollandina,
its twenty-sixth Abbess—many details of which I
have reproduced—I am indebted to the excerpts
made by M. L. Toyant from the *History and*

Cartulary of the Abbey, edited from original documents by MM. A. Dutilleux and J. Depoin for
the Societé Historique du Vexin Français (1882).
M. Toyant rendered me this service at the request
of Mr. H. Tinson (late of Messrs. Goupil & Co.),
without whose skilled assistance, most readily and
courteously given, the first (illustrated) edition of
the present work could not have been produced.
In revising the last chapter of the present edition,
I had the advantage of utilising some notes kindly
made by Mr. J. F. Chance on the section entitled
The Hanoverian Succession contributed by me to
Vol. vi. of the *Cambridge Modern History*, which
volume also contains a most valuable section
by Mr. Chance on the earlier foreign policy of
George I — a subject closely connected with that
of his European policy before his accession to
the English throne, which is discussed in the
present volume. Mr. R. W. Goulding, Librarian
to the Duke of Portland, was so kind as to
communicate to me in 1903 extracts from three
letters from the Electress Sophia to the Earl of
Portland, dating from the years 1703–4, preserved,
together with eight others, at Welbeck Abbey. Of
these extracts I have in my last chapter taken the
liberty of translating that which has reference to the
death of King William III. I desire also to thank
Miss A. D. Greenwood (who has just published a work,
based on careful research, dealing with parts of

the subject treated in this volume), and Mr. A. T. Bartholomew, M.A., of Peterhouse, and the Cambridge University Library, for aid given in the preparation of one of the Appendices to the present edition.

In this Appendix will, as already indicated, be found, a series of letters between the Electoral Princess Sophia Dorothea and Count Philip Christopher in Königsmarck. This correspondence, which supplements the much longer series deposited in the University of Lund, is preserved in the Royal Secret Archives of State at Berlin, and is now (with the exception of two letters forming part of it) printed for the first time. I have to offer special thanks to the authorities of these Archives for allowing this correspondence to be transcribed for me. I request the eminent historian, Geh. Oberregierungs-rath Dr. Koser, who holds the office of Director of the Archives, to accept the expression of my sincere obligations; and I desire very particularly to thank the Second Director, Geh. Archivrath Dr. Bailleu, to whose historical works I owe a debt which the present is not the occasion for recording at length, for his courtesy in arranging for the transcription of these letters and thereby facilitating the execution of my task. For the translation of the letters I am myself responsible, as well as for some elucidatory remarks concerning these documents. The Appendix on the Religious Situation in Scotland, as it affected the Hanoverian Succession, I owe to Mr. R. S. Rait, of New College, Oxford, whose command of Scottish history is well known.

The present edition of this book necessarily appears without the illustrations which adorned the first. In the Preface to that edition I expressed my own gratitude and that of my publishers (Messrs. Goupil & Co.) for services rendered in many quarters both at home and abroad, towards the collection and reproduction of the illustrations in question. More especially, I asked leave to offer the respectful thanks of publishers and author to the present Head of the House of Hanover, His Royal Highness the Duke of Cumberland and Teviotdale, K.G., who had, through Privy Councillor and Chamberlain von der Weise, kindly granted permission for the reproduction of a series of family portraits preserved at Herrenhausen and in the Fideicommiss. Gallery in the Provinzial-Museum at Hanover. I expressed at the same time our gratitude to the Right Hon. the Earl of Craven for allowing the reproduction of several of the pictures forming the unique collection at Combe Abbey, which contains so many of the portraits of the Queen of Bohemia.[1] Next to the collection of Palatine portraits at

---

[1] I may perhaps take this opportunity of observing that the many portraits of the Queen of Bohemia which I have seen at Combe Abbey, at Herrenhausen, in the National Portrait Gallery, in Corpus Christi College Lodge, Cambridge, and elsewhere, do not all agree in details of feature, or, of course,

Combe Abbey, the most interesting is that at Blair Castle, of the existence of which Miss Haldane, the translator of Descartes, was so good as to apprise me. His Grace the Duke of Athol, whom the Marchioness of Tullibardine had, at the instance of Miss Haldane, informed of my interest in the pictures, kindly wrote to me that there are at present in Blair Castle original portraits in panel by Gerard Honthorst of the Princess Palatine Elizabeth, Louisa Hollandina and Henrietta Maria

of costume, though in most of them the Queen wears one of those mighty farthingales which her father (poor man !) in vain attempted to moderate. In most of her portraits her eyes are dark, in one at least they are slate-grey. In a contemporary account of her wedding special mention is made of the long flow of her amber-coloured hair, which descended to her waist ; and I notice that Miss Wendland speaks of her children as ' fair' (*blond*) ' like their beautiful mother.' But of her appearance in later life we have a different account from the trustworthy hand of the Duchess of Orleans, who says that she remembered her grandmother as if she had been in her presence on the day of writing, and who notes her black hair, long face, and powerful nose. Elizabeth Charlotte adds that there was a great likeness between the Queen and her eldest son, of whom, as of her second, she was in his early days fond of speaking to the King, his father, as her ' petit black babie.' Altogether there can be no doubt that she was one of the ' dark ladies ' to whom Shakespeare and others have attributed so peculiar a fascination, and for whom Goethe had so marked a preference. The other feature noted by the Duchess of Orleans was inherited by all of Elizabeth's children whose portraits are accessible— notably by Prince Rupert and the Princesses Elizabeth and Sophia and her family, including numerous Honthorsts and some works ascribed, I suppose traditionally, to Louisa Hollandina's active brush. More than a quarter of a century has passed since I had the privilege of paying a visit to Combe Abbey; but the memory of it has never left me.

(married to Prince Sigismund of Transylvania). These portraits, together with two of the Queen of Bohemia and Prince Rupert, likewise by Honthorst, and 'head and shoulders' portraits on panel, belonged to John, first Duke of Athol, who probably inherited them from his mother, daughter of James, seventh Earl of Derby. At the Duke's death in 1724 he left the furniture of Huntingtower to his widow (who had been his second wife) ; and the last-named two pictures being there, were after her death removed to England by her eldest son, Lord John Murray, from whom they descended to W. H. G. Bagshawe, Esq., of Ford Hall, Chapel-in-the-Frith, Derbyshire ; but the portraits of the three Princesses, being at Dunkeld, went to the Duke's heir and successor. Mr. Bagshawe (who informs me that the portrait of the Queen is extremely like that of her in the National Portrait Gallery) in 1886 allowed copies of these two portraits to be made for the Duke of Athol, which are now with the three originals of the three Princesses at Blair Castle. I recollect seeing a charming portrait of at least one of the Palatine Princes at Ford Castle, Northumberland.

M. Toyant's researches, communicated to me by Mr. Tinson, showed that, besides the portraits of the Princess Louise Hollandina at Combe Abbey, Hanover, and Herrenhausen (to which has to be added that at Blair Castle), there exists one at Wilton House, the Earl of Pembroke's seat near Salisbury.

Of the Electress Sophia herself, one of the two portraits by Gerard Honthorst at Combe Abbey served as the frontispiece to the first edition of this book. The other, and a third of her and her daughter, Sophia Charlotte, said to be the work of the Princess Louisa Hollandina, were reproduced at later points in the volume; in which also appeared engravings of Engelhard's statue of the Electress, in a sitting position, in the gardens at Herrenhausen, and of a gold medal in her honour designed by Lambelet, of which a plaster cast is in the British Museum. Other medals struck in her honour are depicted in Rehtmeier's *Hannöverische Chronik*. On the occasion of the serious illness, in October, 1701, of an old and confidential friend, the Electress Sophia wrote that ' if she was to have her medal made of her portrait, she ought to do it now; for, should Frau von Harling recover, she would not allow me to spend so much on *ma vieille trogne*.' Personal vanity, or personal self-consciousness of any kind, was not among the shortcomings traceable in the character of the brave and high-minded Princess of whose life I have attempted to trace the unblemished record.

A. W. WARD.

Peterhouse Lodge, Cambridge.
April, 1909.

CONTENTS

APPENDICES

Corrigenda.

Page 21, *line* 7 from bottom : *for* Henry Frederick *read* Frederick Henry.

,, 71 ,, 15 : *for* his *read* her.

,, 97 ,, 10 : *for* Tarento *read* Taranto.

,, 141, note, *line* 12 : *for* Scroope Emmanuel *read* Emmanuel Scroope.

,, 151, *line* 15 : *for* Charles *read* Christian.

,, 164, note, *line* 4 from bottom : *for* Court *read* Coat.

,, 195, *line* 23 : *for* 1685 *read* 1687.

,, 224 ,, 7 *et al* : *for* Cressett *read* Cresset.

,, 224 ,, 6 from bottom : *for* 1696 *read* 1694.

,, 292 ,, 4 from bottom : *for* his *read* this.

,, 333 ,, 11 : *dele* better.

,, 371 ,, 8 from bottom : *for* 1694 *read* 1704.

,, 371, note, *line* 2 from bottom : *for* 1902 *read* 1702.

,, 392 ,, ,, 4 from bottom : *after* Howes *read* (or Hughes).

,, 393, *line* 5 : *after* clause *read* as.

Additional Corrigenda.

Page xvii, *line* 9 : *for* in *read* von.

  ,, 10   ,, 11 : *for* 1712 *read* 1714.

  ,, 11   ,, 6 : *for* 1640 *read* 1630.

  ,, 16   ,, 6 from bottom : *for* fourteenth *read* fifteenth.

  ,, 26   ,, 3 *for* 1617 *read* 1614.

  ,, 148   ,, 5 from bottom : *for* 1634 *read* 1635.

  ,, 179   note, *line* 2 : *read* the late ' Arvède Barine ' (Mme. Charles Vincens).

  ,, 445   ,, 2 : *for* 1632 *read* 1662.

THE

ELECTRESS SOPHIA

AND THE

HANOVERIAN SUCCESSION

INTRODUCTORY

In the burial-vault of the Guelfs, at Hanover, stands a coffin enclosing the remains of the Electress Sophia, and bearing the inscription : *Magnæ Britanniæ Hæres.* These words sum up her story as that of a great hope, long cherished but never fulfilled. Yet a biography of this Princess, who died, though herself uncrowned, the ' mother of our Kings to be,' will, if truthful, be found to treat a nobler theme than a personal ambition born of chance upon chance, vexed by prolonged delays, and doomed to final disappointment. The Electress Sophia was in herself worthy to be the source of a dynasty whose last and most august member left to her successor a throne far securer than that which was mounted by Sophia's eldest son. But the nation, of whose institutions a limited monarchy has long formed an integral part, also owes a debt to the very fact

B

of the accession of the House of Hanover, and therefore to the insight and self-control exhibited by that House, and conspicuously by the Electress Sophia, during the entire preceding period of uncertainty. At a highly critical date in the course of those years, when the Electress and her family were most anxious to avoid any rash or false step on their own part, she told a correspondent that, at the English Court, it was held indispensable to pretend to wish for the succession of the Electoral line—*because of the people*. Although there were, in those days, Jacobites enough and to spare in London and other parts of the kingdom, and although the stolidity of our first Hanoverian King, and the self-conceit of his successor, retarded the growth of personal sympathy between monarch and subjects, yet the perception, in both dynasty and nation, of a definite community of interests formed a sufficient beginning for the growth of a close mutual attachment. To this the Electress Sophia contributed, it is not too much to say, both by the circumstances of her birth and by the conduct of her life. She was the daughter of a Stewart Princess, on whose Protestant marriage the nation had set its hopes, and whom it had seen condemned, because of her husband's youthful venture in the cause of militant Protestantism, to long years of exile and privation. In her own conduct Sophia displayed a prudence, a dignity, and a sincerity, which have rarely, under conditions so trying, been so consistently combined. The legend, indeed, of her having often declared that she would die content if those other words, ' Sophia, Queen of Great Britain,' could be inscribed on her tomb, is irreconcileable with the whole tenor of her known private thoughts, as well as of her public acts. She was far from indifferent to the greatness that might be in store for her, or to the necessity, in the interests of her House, of constant vigilance, promptitude, and tact. But she deemed it enough to be found, at no stage of her career, either unequal to her present fortunes or unready for those responsibilities of a greater future which cast their shadow before them. Thus it is largely due to her, and, as it is but just to acknowledge, with her and after her, to the next heir to her expectations, that, so far as the House of Hanover is concerned, the history of its succession to the British throne may be reviewed without the feelings of humiliation too often aroused by narratives of disputed inheritances. At the same time, the essential significance of that history would, in any case, have to be sought deeper than in the vicissitudes of personal ambitions or the machinations of families or factions. The Hanoverian Succession was, in fact, only another name for the Protestant Succession in flesh and blood, and, as such, represented the principal gain which most Englishmen and Scotchmen were intent upon bringing home out of the long struggle against the

Stewart monarchy. Not that the disputes and efforts connected with the Hanoverian Succession throughout, or, at times, mainly addressed themselves to the religious issue ; but it would be futile to ignore, or to seek to obscure, the origin and basis of the great political transaction in which the Electress Sophia was called upon to play so prominent a part. She was fitted to play it, alike by the circumstances of her descent and marriage, and by the qualities of her character and intellect, and above all by a perfect self-control, joined to a freedom of spirit in which, during the efforts and trials of her life, she found encouragement and consolation.

From the relation in which the Electress Sophia stood to the question of the British Succession, that loomed so large on the political horizon during her later years, the story of her life derives its paramount interest. Even on the experiences of her earlier years, whose memories carry us back to the time of the Thirty Years' War and of the great Civil Conflict in this island, it is impossible to dwell without thinking of the great destiny reserved for her line, and of the many helps and hindrances which were to facilitate or to impede its accomplishment. But in the semi-obscurity of her youth, as under the gaze of inquisitive eyes to which her maturity was exposed, she remains true to herself ; and few biographical records could prove more fascinating than one covering her fourscore years, were it but possible to depict her from first to last in the same life-like colours in which she has portrayed herself in her *Memoirs*, and in which she reappears on almost every page of her correspondence. Unfortunately, it is difficult to convey by extracts, and impossible to preserve in translation, the constant alertness of thought, and refreshing vivacity of expression, frequently touched by real humour, and, at all times, free from any tinge of affectation, which are not less characteristic of her letters than they must have been of her conversation. As for her autobiography, it breaks off as early as 1681, and thus fails to cover that longer half of her life in which she was to become a figure of importance in European affairs. For it was the ' abdication ' by flight of King James II and the subsequent passing of the Bill of Rights which brought about and established the restriction of the English Succession to Protestants, and which first placed Sophia and her line, though not as yet by name, in direct relation to that Succession as a question of practical politics.

It is accordingly proposed, in the following pages, to speak, in the first instance, of Sophia's descent and parentage ; of her mother, who, while remaining, even throughout the woful sequel of her Bohemian Queenship, conscious of her position as a Stewart Princess, never faltered in her adherence to the Protestantism for whose sake her husband had cast a long blight upon the fortunes of the

Palatine House ; and of her brothers and sisters, Princes and Princesses of that House, not one of whom, in spite of their many distinctions and qualities, brilliant or solid, succeeded altogether in rising above the depression which had fastened upon the family, as Sophia herself rose in the eyes both of her contemporaries and of posterity. The task will thus become easier of describing, in turn, the three stages of that part of her life which preceded the acquisition by her and her House of a definite expectation of the succession to the British throne. During her childhood and girlhood she was virtually confined to the refugee Court of her parents, afterwards that of her widowed mother, in the Netherlands. She next passed some years at Heidelberg, in the land of her forefathers, then restored in part to the Palatine rule. The earlier years of her married life, divided between Osnabrück and Hanover, introduced her to new personal relations and to new political interests ; but, though these at times conflicted with each other, she learnt how to identify herself more and more with the dynastic policy of the House, to the fortunes of whose future head she had united her own. A second period of her life may be said to open when the question of the British Succession unexpectedly comes into the foreground of European political life ; and in this period, again, two stages are very clearly distinguishable. The earlier of these extends from the passing

of the Bill of Rights (1689), with its strict limitation
of the Crown to Protestants, up to the Act of Settlement (1701). Within these years the House of
Hanover, while actually or in prospect consolidating
the various territorial interests of the Brunswick-
Lüneburg line, firmly established its position as an
electorate in the Empire, and began to be taken
into account by the ambition of France, the chronic
disturber of the peace of Europe. Incidentally,
the skilful management and the stern resolution by
which this advance of the House was effected, led
to unhappy consequences; and no narration of
its history in this period can pass by the catastrophe
of one of Sophia's sons, or pretend to ignore the
tragic story of her daughter-in-law, Sophia Dorothea.
In the second stage of this period we recognise, in the
Electress Sophia, a personage of importance in the
great theatre of general European history, but
calmly standing back herself from the glare of the
footlights. By the Act of Settlement the Succession
was settled upon her and the heirs of her body, being
Protestants. She thus obtained a Parliamentary
title for herself and for her descendants.

Before this point is reached in our narrative,
it will have shown how largely fortune had contributed to the genesis of this title. Of James I's
two sons, the elder, Henry, had died in the early
flower of his youth. Charles I left three sons, of
whom the third, another Henry, also died young

and unmarried. Since Charles II left no lawful issue, the Crown fell to James II, and, having been transferred from him to his son-in-law, William of Orange, and to his elder Protestant daughter, Mary, passed in turn to his second Protestant daughter, Anne. Mary had left no issue, and her widowed husband, on whose issue by another wife the Crown had been eventually settled, should Anne die childless, declined to marry again. Of Anne's numerous progeny, none survived their infancy except the Duke of Gloucester, and he died in 1700. Nor could there be any question of the conversion to Protestantism of any child of James II by his second, Catholic, wife except the Prince afterwards known as the Old Pretender ; for all the others died in their infancy, with the exception of Marie Louise, who survived into her twelfth year. The chance passed away of finding a Protestant successor to the Crown among the grandchildren of Charles I's youngest daughter, Henrietta, Duchess of Orleans, in the House of Savoy and it was therefore necessary to turn to the offspring of James I's only daughter, Elizabeth, the Protestant consort of a Protestant prince. But of the sons born from this union who survived to maturity, the eldest, Charles Lewis, died in 1680 ; his only legitimate son, Charles, died without issue in 1685 ; his only daughter, Elizabeth Charlotte, became a Catholic on her marriage to the Duke of Orleans. Of the others who

remained Protestants, Rupert persistently refused
to marry, and died in 1682 ; Maurice and Philip,
both of them homeless wanderers, had perished in
1654 and 1650 respectively. Edward, alone among
the younger brothers, married and became the
father of a family ; but he had been carried away
from the traditions of his House by the wave of
Catholic propaganda, of which this biography will
repeatedly have to take note ; and his three daughters all became the wives of Catholic husbands.
Of Sophia's elder sisters, one, Louisa Hollandina,
fell under the same religious influence, and became
the Abbess of a Catholic convent; another, the
eldest of the sisterhood, who came to hold the same
position in a Protestantised foundation, likewise
elected to remain the votaress of an unmarried life ;
a third, Henrietta Maria, died in 1652, soon after
she had been wedded to a Transylvanian prince.
No other personage possessed a claim of birth equal
to Sophia's, yet even of pretensions palpably inferior
to her own on this score, fortune, which seemed in
this question always on her side, disposed in her
favour.

The Electress Sophia's later years were chiefly
spent in the tranquillity of Herrenhausen, more
especially after she had become a widow in 1698 ;
and here she held intellectual intercourse with
Leibniz, her own and her daughter's friend, and with
other fit companions of her solitude, while keeping

up her voluminous correspondence with her favourites of heart and mind, among them her inimitable
niece, the Duchess of Orleans. She lived to see the
territorial power of the House of Hanover fully
established at home, and its foreign policy completely
merged into that of the Grand Alliance against
France ; and there remained now nothing but the
consummation of the British Succession. This she
was not destined to see accomplished in her own
person ; but less than two months after her death, on
June 8th, 1712, her eldest son, the Elector George
Lewis of Hanover, was proclaimed King George I of
Great Britain and Ireland.

I

DESCENT AND PARENTAGE; CHILD-HOOD AND GIRLHOOD

(LEYDEN, THE HAGUE, AND RHEENEN, 1630-1650)

SOPHIA, the youngest daughter and the youngest but one of the thirteen children of Frederick, sometime Elector Palatine and King of Bohemia, and of his wife Elizabeth, the eldest daughter of King James I of England, was born at the Hague on October 14th, 1640 (N.S.). She was thus, by only a few months, the junior of her first cousin Charles, afterwards King Charles II, whose ' star ' was so long to remain under a cloud in the period of her youth, and who was himself in those dubious days to play a transient part in her personal history; while the date of her birth was preceded, at a not much longer interval, by that of the landing of Gustavus Adolphus in Pomerania, the turning-point of the Thirty Years' War, although not, as her family had hoped, also that of their fortunes. Her baptismal name of Sophia she doubtless owed to the remembrance of her mother's youngest sister, buried in Westminster Abbey in 1607, the ephemeral flight of whose earthly existence strangely contrasts with the long life in store for the younger Sophia.

It was by her marriage to Frederick V, Elector Palatine, on St. Valentine's Day, 1613, that James I's only surviving daughter Elizabeth was first brought into contact with the political problems that were agitating Europe. The bridegroom, it is true, was only a boy of sixteen, who would not till August, 1614, be entitled to assume the government of his paternal inheritance. Elizabeth was only a year older than he, and her previous life had been marked by but one personal experience of general interest. As early as 1603 she was consigned to the care of Lord and Lady Harington, and with them she soon took up her residence at Combe Abbey, near Coventry, in Warwickshire—the lordly castellated mansion which, whether or not she re-visited its moated solitude towards the close of her life, still remains as it were consecrated to her royal memory.[1]

[1] Lord and Lady Harington, as will be seen, accompanied Elizabeth after her marriage to Heidelberg. From them Combe Abbey descended to their daughter Lucia, Countess of Bedford, Drayton's ' sweet nymph of Ankor ' (on whose banks the Abbey is situated) and earlier ' Idea,' and the recipient of other poetic tributes from Ben Jonson and Donne. (See Courthope's *History of English Poetry*, Vol. iii. pp. 29 *sqq.*) It was her prodigal tastes which made it necessary to sell Combe Abbey, which was finally purchased by the Earl of Craven. (See the notes to *Combe Abbey*, a historical tale of the reign of James I, by Selina Bunbury (Dublin, 1843)—the first work of the authoress, written in an ardently Protestant spirit. In this novel are cited the stanzas, ' This is a joye, This is true pleasure,' said to have been composed by the Princess Elizabeth in her childhood.)

King James, in the early years of his English reign, had good reason for dreading the designs of some of his Roman Catholic subjects, and Elizabeth's mother, Queen Anne, the sister of Christian IV of Denmark, had not yet given way to the influences which (as is now ascertained beyond all doubt) afterwards caused her to become a secret convert to the Church of Rome. The sound Protestantism, of the Puritanising type, but probably intermingled on both sides with strains of literary sentiment, that had marked out Lord and Lady Harington for this charge, was unmistakably the primary source of those feelings of attachment to the Reformed religion from which in times both fierce and fickle Elizabeth never swerved a hair's breadth. In her childhood the country round Combe Abbey was full of more or less open adherents of the Church of Rome ; and by some of these a conspiracy was hatched, which was to co-operate with, and supplement, the Gunpowder Plot. On the day at last fixed for the demonstration in chief at Westminster, the eight-year-old Princess at Combe Abbey was to be seized by a body of gentlemen who had agreed to assemble for the purpose on the pretext of a meet of hounds, and so soon as the throne became vacant she was to be proclaimed Queen, professing herself at the same time a member of the unreformed Church. But *non tali auxilio* was this future ancestress of our sovereigns herself to ascend a throne.   Combe Abbey was warned, the moat was drawn up, and the towers were manned, and the Princess was conveyed in safety to the loyal town of Coventry, where the townsmen armed in her defence. As fate would have it, John Digby, the young Warwickshire gentleman who bore to King James I the tidings of his daughter's peril and preservation, was afterwards to be the most prominent agent of the royal policy which, with admirable intentions, only served to thwart the English nation's hope of helping to restore, at least in part, the fortunes of Elizabeth and her children.

The political significance of the marriage, which in 1613 brought the Princess Palatine Elizabeth's girlhood to a close, was perfectly patent alike to James I's subjects and to those Powers which more or less benevolently interested themselves in his foreign policy.   In 1612, when the marriage was arranged, that policy had not yet fully revealed its visionary purpose and its shifty methods ; while at home his quarrels with his Parliaments had scarcely more than begun.   Three years earlier the affairs of Europe had, with the death of Henry IV of France, assumed a wholly new aspect, and it had become evident that the struggle between the House of Habsburg and its adversaries, in which James I had long hoped to play the august part of a pacificator, must take place under quite new conditions.   This aspiration, together with a pride of descent natural to a

Stewart and a Scot, had led him to scheme marriages for his children with half the chief reigning houses in Europe, including those of France, Spain, and Sweden (whose youthful King, Gustavus II Adolphus, was, however, soon put aside as unequal to a match with a daughter of the House of Stewart). But when, in 1610, friendly relations, soon to be sealed by a double marriage, had set in between the French and Spanish Courts, James I was not slow in perceiving how this turn of affairs must affect the political prospects of his own kingdom. On the outbreak of the European conflict which was expected on all sides, it would go hard with the Protestant interest, unless it contrived to consolidate itself into an alliance capable of confronting the great Catholic Powers.   When, in March, 1611, the Count of Cartignano arrived in England as a special ambassador from Duke Charles Emmanuel of Savoy to negotiate a double marriage between the Houses of Savoy and England, James, though he refused to enter into this scheme, seemed willing to approve of the marriage of his daughter to the Prince of Piedmont. In November, Cartignano reappeared with fresh instructions, and at the audience in which he asked Elizabeth's hand for the Prince Sir Henry Wotton, who had had a hand in the negotiations, was present. But the King had practically already decided how to dispose of his daughter's hand, and the Savoyard returned

home in dudgeon.   The step which was now taken
by James I, and by means of which a Protestant
Succession was ultimately to be secured to the
English throne, was in full accordance with the
identification of England with militant Protestantism, which had been accomplished as a matter of
fact rather than of deliberate purpose in the great
age of Queen Elizabeth.   After, in March, 1612,
concluding an alliance with the Union of German
Protestant Princes, of which the Palatine House
had from the first assumed the leadership, James,
to the delight of the large majority of his subjects,
resolved upon the marriage of his only surviving
daughter to the young ' Palsgrave,' as he was called
in England, Frederick V.

The line of the Electors Palatine boasted a high
antiquity and dignity ; and though it would take
us too far to account for the claims maintained
by them to the first place among the temporal
Electors, the familiar fact may be recalled that
early in the fourteenth century the Elector Rupert
III, of the older Electoral line of the Wittelsbach
House to which the Simmern line had since succeeded, had worthily held the high dignity of German
King.[1]   It is after him that Elizabeth is supposed to
have named her third son, whose name of Prince

---

[1] In the fifteenth and the sixteenth centuries respectively,
two Palatine Electors, Frederick II and Frederick III, aspired
to the German Kingship.

Rupert is so familiar to our ears; but she may also have been aware that an earlier English Princess who had become Electress Palatine—Blanche, daughter of King Henry IV and wife of the Elector Palatine Louis II—had named her son Rupert, and that during his short life he bore the cognomen 'England.' Though portions of the Palatine territory had from time to time been split off in accordance with the German tendency to subdivision which no systematic effort was made to repress till after the times of the Thirty Years' War, the electorate about the time of the opening of that war extended far on both banks of the Rhine, being on one side contiguous with the kingdom of Bohemia. If not equal in size to any of the other temporal electorates, it was not far inferior to Saxony, and hardly at all to Brandenburg, in territorial importance, being largely composed of districts peerless among the German lands in beauty and productivity—amidst whose orchards and vineyards throve a busy and light-hearted population. The religious sympathies of the electorate were in so far divided, that the Upper Palatinate (on the left bank of the Rhine) adhered to Lutheranism, while the inhabitants of the Lower or Rhenish were, like the dynasty, Calvinists. The electoral residence was Heidelberg, whose castle and its treasures were reckoned among the wonders of the Western world. To its graceful earlier buildings, the florid taste of the Elector Frederick IV

c

had added the splendid but pretentious structure, in the artificial style of the latest Renascence, of which a characteristic remnant is the inner side, decorated, something after the manner of Alnwick, with statues of defunct Palsgraves. The outside commands the wondrous view over the valley of the Neckar, to which nothing but the genius of a Turner could have imparted an additional charm. The choicest possession of the castle was the electoral Library, the finest collection of books in Germany and far beyond, thrown open with rare liberality to the use of all qualified comers. And the pride of both court and town was the University, now again, as it had been under the single-minded rule of the Elector Frederick III, the foremost Calvinist seminary of higher learning in Europe.

But though the Electoral Palatine House honoured learning, and, as both the bringing-up of Frederick V and that bestowed by him on his own children showed, set a high value upon a many-sided intellectual as well as upon a careful religious and moral education, its interests had in the early years of the seventeenth century become engrossed by public affairs, and it had acquired a political importance out of proportion to its territorial power. Partly by force of circumstances and because of the situation of the Palatinate, on the confines of France and on the water-way to the Netherlands, but still more by their own zeal and ambition, its Princes and certain of their statesmen stood in the front of that active party in the Empire which might be termed the advanced, or militant, Protestant Opposition. This party, among whose other members Landgrave Maurice of Hesse and Count Christian of Anhalt are pre-eminent, derived its impulse entirely from Calvinist sources. Palatine blood had been shed and treasure spent under the Elector Frederick III and the Administrator John Casimir on behalf of the Revolt of the Netherlands and the cause of the French Huguenots; and under his successor, Frederick IV, these designs had taken a wider range. He was a man of great intellectual force; and, more especially in connexion with the later history of his dynasty, it is interesting to note that in the later years of his life he was much occupied with the scheme of a union, on a broad basis, between all Protestant confessions.[1] But the young Elector Frederick V had probably been more especially influenced by the pure Calvinism of his mother the Electress Dowager Louisa Juliana, the daughter of William the Silent and of Charlotte de Montpensier, who had taken refuge at the Palatine Court for the sake of the Religion. Louisa Juliana, though at the crisis of the Palatine fortunes her judgment was not obscured by her sympathies, was one of those women the fervour of whose religious convictions communicates itself as a legacy of faith

[1] See Häusser, *Geschichte der Rhein-Pfalz*, Vol. ii. pp. 243-4.

and love to the minds of their descendants for generation upon generation.[1] Maurice of Hesse-Cassel also had a Nassau Juliana to wife, so that the three Houses at the head of the Calvinistic movement were closely linked together by inter-marriage. In his father's lifetime, the young Frederick had been placed at the Court of the Calvinist Henry Duke of Bouillon, whose second wife was likewise a daughter of the great William of Orange, and to Sedan he afterwards returned, with fit diplomatic and theological counsellors by his side, for a second sojourn till the year before his marriage. To these multiplied influences the Princess Elizabeth's husband may in part have owed the fortitude of spirit which, although not naturally a man of strong character, he exhibited under a long and heavy pressure of trouble ; while to the liberality of his education may fairly be ascribed something of the refined and lovable gentleness which he preserved to the last.

Under the Elector Frederick IV, the first head of the Union, vast designs had been set on foot against the Catholicising policy of the House of Habsburg, and for a dismemberment of its domi-nions. In 1612, the hopes of the Palatine House and its counsellors were already directed towards the

[1] A memoir of her was published in 1645 by the scholar and diplomatist Ezechiel Spanheim, of whom Sophia frequently makes respectful mention in her correspondence with her brother Charles Lewis.

attainment of the Bohemian Crown ; moreover, as the Spanish ambassador, Don Alonso de Velasca, informed the Spanish Council early in 1613, James I was then of opinion that in a few years Frederick V would be King of Bohemia. Thus, the expectation of the Bohemian Crown unmistakably contributed to bring about the marriage which determined the course of Elizabeth's life.[1] To the English public, of course, ' the Palsgrave ' was a handsome and courtly Prince, the nephew of Maurice of Orange, heroic father's heroic son,[2] and in their eyes his union with the Princess Elizabeth promised to connect the royal family not only with the great Protestant Houses already mentioned, but with the Protestant interest at large.[3] As a matter of fact, English royalty was thus to become connected with the dynasties of Brandenburg, Sweden, and Transylvania.

[1] See Gindely, *Geschichte des dreissigjähr. Krieges*, Vol. i. p. 186, and note.   It may perhaps be added, by way of a *curiosum*, that at this time there survived in England the lineal descendant of a declared heir to the Bohemian Crown in the person of Humphrey Tyndall, Dean of Ely, who died in 1614 and whose brass still remains in Ely Cathedral.   See Bentham's *History and Antiquities of the Conventual and Cathedral Church of Ely*.

[2] On his visit to England in 1612 Frederick was accompanied by Count Henry of Nassau (who in 1625 became Henry Frederick Prince of Orange).   His companion duly fell in love with a daughter of the Duke of Northumberland.   (*Letters of George Lord Carew*.)

[3] A Count Palatine Frederick (Frederick II of the old line) had visited England early in the sixteenth century; but he had come in the service of the House of Habsburg.

The young Elector Frederick V had hardly presented himself at the English Court, when a deep shadow passed over the sunny prospect seemingly opening before Elizabeth, and she and her possible descendants were suddenly brought nearer to a Succession undreamt of by her for them.   In November, 1612, Henry Prince of Wales, whose heart was entirely with his sister's in her Protestant preferences as in other matters, died suddenly of typhoid fever, though, in accordance with the evil fashion of the age, credulous or clamorous Protestants, perhaps not quite inexcusably, attributed his death to poison. At the Court of James and Anne, or in its vicinity, for which the Princess had since 1608 exchanged the retirement of Combe Abbey, she had continued to carry on her studies, which were specially directed to the French and Italian tongues and to the art of music, while the general guidance of Lord and Lady Harington still continued to sustain the serious impulses that contended with the frivolous in her receptive and responsive nature. As a matter of course, the brother and sister, who dearly loved one another, were companions in the elaborate enter_ tainments that absorbed so large a share of their royal parents' attention, and in the field-sports by which the masques and tilts were diversified, and in which Elizabeth long retained an eager interest. There is some evidence that she also shared the higher aspirations discernible in the many-sided and ambitious activity of the brother who was taken so suddenly from her side.[1] But youth and the exigencies of her position exercised their effacing powers ; and thus, within little more than three months, the brother's funeral was followed by the sister's wedding. Indeed, while the echoes of both events are loud in the literature of the time, the same poetic voices occasionally attune themselves in turn to condolence and to congratulation. But, though the show was great that carnival week, and though besides so much of the powder as would go off for the fireworks, plenty of incense was burnt on the occasion by Chapman, Beaumont, Thomas Heywood, Campion,[2] Francis Bacon, Taylor the Water-poet, and the rest, an undertone of doubt or apprehension was audible among the rejoicings. The bride laughed too much at the wedding, and her father yawned too soon in the course of the ensuing festivities, which he finally felt obliged

[1] The theatrical company (formerly the Lord Admiral's) which had been under the patronage of the Prince of Wales, sought and, on January 4th, obtained that of the Palsgrave, the Fortune continuing to be their playhouse. After 1625, they appear to have ceased to be under the Elector's ' patronage.' (*Henslowe's Diary*, ed. Greg, Part ii. pp. 98–9.)

[2] Part of a stanza in a song in *The Lords' Masque*, accompanying a dance of stars, may be quoted, if only to suggest the contemporary pronunciation of the King's name :

' So bravely crown it [the night] with your beams,
    That it may live in fame
As long as Rhenus or the Thames
    Are known by either name.'

to cut short in fear of the bill and of the House of Commons. And most ill-omened of all was the fact that among the representatives of foreign Powers bidden to the solemnity the Spanish ambassador remained away. Count Gondomar 'was, or would be, sick.'

It was not till after Easter that the young Electress and her husband were allowed to take their departure from London, nor till the beginning of June that, after a semi-royal progress from Holland up the Rhine, they at last set foot in Heidelberg. The greater part of the Electress' English suite, which included Francis Quarles and Nicolas Ferrar, soon afterwards left her—Lord Harington, by a pathetic fate, dying on the way at Worms, so that his wife returned home a widow. Elizabeth's life in her new home was for many a day much what it had latterly been in her old—a round of Court festivities, banquets, and hunting-expeditions. Nor does she, after the protracted honeymoon was over, seem to have ceased to be preoccupied with the trivialities of her daily life. We may discount the report of a divine who visited her husband's Court, that 'she is not often heard to speak of God . . . she is fond of grandeur and the precedence of rank.' And we may excuse her for not allowing the ascendancy of the Court-preacher, Abraham Scultetus, to dominate her thoughts and conduct, in spite of the potent authority exercised by this divine, afterwards one of the most vigorous of the anti-Remonstrants at Dort (where he had the satisfaction of seeing that Heidelberg Catechism, which Sophia was so ruefully to remember as the religious *pabulum* of her youth, adopted as the symbol of the Dutch Church). At Heidelberg she had her own English Chaplain.[1] For the rest, it seems to have been the use of her horse and gun which, on the occasion of the death of her firstborn child, assuaged the first sharp sorrow of her married life. While the high state kept by King James' daughter—with her army of ladies-in-waiting, chamberlains, chaplains, and the rest—could not fail to heighten the splendour and swell the outlay of the Palatine Court, her influence must have helped to soften and refine its tone, though in neither respect was the ground unprepared. It may safely be ascribed to Elizabeth and to her bringing-up that the place of German was taken by French as the Court tongue at Heidelberg. Her husband, whose favourite extravagance was that of building, was much engaged at this time in perfecting the Castle gardens in the most approved

[1] Alexander Chapman, Fellow of Corpus Christi College, Cambridge, D.D. 1610, and Archdeacon of Stow and Prebendary of Lincoln in the same year. In 1618 he was appointed Prebendary of Canterbury, where, on his death in 1629, ' an elegant Monument of blue and white Marble, with a demy Effigie of him thereon, was erected to his memory by his Brother.' See R. Masters' *History of C.C.C.*, pp. 264–5. He was possibly the donor of the speaking likeness of Elizabeth which hangs in the Master's Lodge at Corpus.

French style, and in adding a new ' English wing '
to the Electoral residence itself.   On January 1st,
1617, she gave birth to her eldest son, and half the
Protestant Powers of Europe were represented round
the baptismal font.   The fortunes of the family had
sunk low, when, fifteen years later, this Prince—
Henry Frederick—was, in his unhappy father's sight,
drowned off Haarlem.   On December 22nd, 1617,
another son was born to the Electoral couple, Charles
Lewis, afterwards Elector Palatine ; and on December
26th, 1618, followed the birth of their eldest
daughter, Elizabeth.

There were, however, certain drawbacks to the
perfect contentment of Elizabeth in the ' merry '
Heidelberg days, which readily revealed themselves
to the eye of the sympathising observer.   Even at a
distance she dwelt as it were in the shadow of the
paternal throne ; and the pride of her father, to
which her own seems to have very readily responded,
obliged her to assert extravagant claims in matters
of precedence.   As to these pretensions full information is furnished by the communicative pen of Sir
Henry Wotton, who in April, 1616, when on his way
to Turin and Venice, spent six days in the Electoral
Court at Heidelberg.   He had some public business
of moment to transact with the Elector, to whom he
submitted a plan for a league with Savoy, which
Frederick approved and promised to lay before the
Princes of the Union.   But it was his chief duty

to give some account to the King of the Court of Heidelberg, and of the treatment there extended to the King's daughter in those matters which her father had so much at heart. Sir Henry Wotton, whose deep admiration for Elizabeth, expressed in undying verse, has indissolubly linked his name with her own, addressed himself to his task with even more than his usual diligence. He describes the Electoral Court as one 'of great sobriety,' and very well attended. The Elector he found '*par boutades* merry, but for the most part cogitative, or, as they here call it, melancolique ; his chiefest object was money, and his principal delight architecture.' The Electress, although already at that time ' the mother of one of the sweetest children,' still retained ' her former virginal verdure in her complexion and features.' Very manifestly, though the ambassador approaches the subject with many courtly involutions, things had not at first, and did not even now, run quite smoothly between the Elector and his consort. At first, some trouble was caused by the ' emulation ' of servants—in other words, rubs between the English and the German members of the Court ; and now there remained the cardinal difficulty about ' placing her Highness.' The claim which James I had set up before his daughter's departure from England, and which Frederick had then promised to allow, that she should have precedence in her husband's and other

non-royal Courts, had proved one which Frederick
found it impossible in practice to reconcile with
self-respect ; and Wotton hardly bettered the
situation by trying to prove too much.[1]   The problem was ultimately settled in no very satisfactory
fashion ; the Electoral pair decided to pay no further visits to other Courts ; and Louisa Juliana,
the Electress Dowager, whom Elizabeth had expected to give her the *pas*, withdrew for some time
from her son's Court.

Wotton had judiciously recommended the
Elector to state his case to the King through
a nobleman particularly valued by the Electress—
Hans Meinhard von Schönberg (Schombergh),
Marshal of the Palatinate. Schönberg had, in March,
1615, married Anne Sutton, daughter of Lord
Dudley, a favourite lady-in-waiting of Elizabeth,
with whom she had remained after Lady Harington's departure ; but she had been taken from
him by death in the following December.   Schönberg's advice, the Electress informed Wotton, had
been of the utmost value to her, ' though by divers
provocations and offences, of the greatest part for
her sake, he had been moved and had himself
resolved to be gone.'   (He was now serving as a
colonel under Maurice of Nassau.)   She also spoke
with gratitude of the attentions of Frau von Pless

[1] ' My Lady,' he argued, ' was not to be considered only
as the daughter of a King, like the daughters of France, but did
carry in her person the possibility of succession to three Crowns.'

(who had been her husband's governess), though she desiderated the company of another English lady of Anne Sutton's age. With the services of the English secretary, Albertus Morton (Wotton's nephew), whom her father had sent to her, Elizabeth was well content.

We must conclude from this report that the English-born Electress had to bear at Heidelberg some of the unpopularity incurred by her countrymen who, in search of amusement or employment, swelled her Court without being attached to it ; and that she had also to suffer from the consequences of a self-consciousness fostered by her father. It is further clear that, in one way or another, she came at this early period of her career to be oppressed by a burden of debt which it was not easy, with or without good advice, to shake off. Perhaps these features of her life as Electress Palatine should be called to mind, before the customary version of her conduct at the crisis of her consort's destinies and her own is unhesitatingly followed. In 1619, the great opportunity for which the Palatine diplomatists had been so long scheming arrived at last. It has been seen that the idea of the Bohemian Crown had been present to them for some time ; probably, the first suggestion of it arose in the course of the negotiations carried on by the Palatine Government in 1605–7, the chief advocate of the notion being Lösenius, while it was actively supported by Chris-

tian of Anhalt.[1]   But, though the chance of carrying
it into execution was now before the Palatines, it
found them and their allies, great and small, unprepared. They had not succeeded in turning to
account the strong feeling which prevailed in many
quarters against the choice as Emperor of the
Archduke Ferdinand of Styria, the destined head
of the House of Austria, and the formally acknowledged successor to the Bohemian and Hungarian
thrones.   They had dallied with idle thoughts of the
King of France and the Duke of Lorraine, and had
then concentrated their efforts upon the paradoxical
device of securing as a candidate the head of the
Catholic branch of the House of Wittelsbach, Duke
Maximilian of Bavaria, who was also the head of the
Catholic League.   But Maximilian, though by the
tradition of his House jealous of Habsburg, better
knew his own mind and his own interests.   Thus,
when (in March, 1619) the Emperor Matthias passed
away, the Elector Palatine wasted the little time
remaining in protests ; and, when the day of election arrived (August 28), after some empty words
accepted the predetermined vote in favour of
Ferdinand of Styria.   The pupil of the Jesuits was
seated on the Imperial throne ; but, on the very
evening when this defeat of the Palatine policy
was proclaimed at Frankfort, the news arrived that

[1] See M. Ritter, *Deutsche Geschichte in der Zeit d. dreissigjähr.
Krieges*, Vol. ii. p. 201.

it had scored a victory at Prague. Here, only a year previously (1618), the troubles between the government and the Utraquists had come to an outbreak, and on the Hradschin had been perpetrated the *defenestration* (ejection through the window) of certain Ministers of the Crown, which it is usual to regard as the opening of the Thirty Years' War. Quite unable to establish his authority in Bohemia, Ferdinand had been actually menaced in his palace at Vienna by the Utraquist chiefs, with an army at their back. And now it was announced that, after deposing Ferdinand, the Bohemian Estates had elected Frederick V Elector Palatine King of Bohemia in his stead.

' Thou hast it now.' After a few diplomatic operations by Achatius von Dohna, the Elector Palatine had only to stretch his hand from Amberg across the Bohemian frontier, and a great historic throne was his,[1] with its large territorial dependencies, and with a second electoral vote ensuring the majority in the College to the Protestant interest. He was Calvinist enough in his habits of mind to be able afterwards to declare conscientiously that, in accepting this Crown, he obeyed an inner voice, which he thought spoke the will of God. And, certainly, there was no pressure of advice to urge him in this direction. His Council, setting

[1] ' Then County Palatine, and now a King.' (*Tamburlaine*, Part II, Act 1, Sc. i. l. 103.)

forth the *pros* and *cons* in the argumentative fashion
of the day, could only find six reasons in favour of
acceptance to balance fourteen against ; and the
gist of their opinion was after all that everything
depended on the support the Elector would receive
in a forward policy. But at most of the friendly
Courts opinion was found to be adverse ; and while
Maurice of Orange and others eagerly advised
acceptance, Maximilian of Bavaria with honourable
candour raised a clear voice of warning. As for
Frederick's father-in-law King James, he was not
at present prepared to depart from his masterly
attitude of declining to pronounce against acceptance, while desiring not to be supposed to have
advised in favour of it. Whether or not a strong
protest from James before Frederick's formal
acceptance of the Crown might have arrested that
final step, no such protest was made.

Frederick's mother, Louisa Juliana, though a
woman cast in no ignoble mould, is said to have
burst into tears and fallen ill on hearing of her son's
election to the Bohemian throne. On the other hand,
it has again and again been asserted, or at least
represented as highly probable, that it was the urgent
representations of the Electress Elizabeth which
determined her consort to cast the die ; and everybody has heard the anecdote of her taunting him
with the avowal that she would rather partake
of sour-krout with a King, than of a joint of roast

meat with an Elector. Elizabeth is unlikely either to have forgotten herself so far, or to have sought for any analogy between her own position and that of the Bohemian Princess who shortly after Wyclif's death had mounted the English throne. Moreover, we have the statement of her grand-daughter, the free-spoken Duchess of Orleans, that at the time of the Bohemian offer the Electress knew nothing at all about the matter, her thoughts being in those days entirely absorbed by plays, masquerades, and the reading of romances. No doubt the Duchess, though deeply attached to her father's house, is not to be absolutely trusted in her statements as to all the members of her father's family ; but her account of the condition of Elizabeth's mind at the time when she was first brought face to face with the chief problem of her life, harmonises with all we know as to its previous current. After all, however, the point is not very material. Even before her husband had actually decided to become a King, she stood forth every inch a Queen ; nor was it with a light heart, or in a spirit inflated with vanity or ambition, that at the last she left the decision in his hands. She was, in her own words, prepared to bow to the will of God, and, if need were, to suffer what He should see fit to ordain. Of her worldly goods she at the same time declared herself ready to make any reasonable sacrifice, by pledging her jewels, or whatever else of value she possessed.

D

Early in October (1619) the last bridge had been burnt.

From this time forward, Elizabeth's troubles came thick upon her ; and indeed, but for a very imperfect return of prosperity towards the close of her life, they may be said never to have ceased again on earth. When, with Frederick, she quitted the Palatinate for Bohemia towards the end of October, they left behind them at Heidelberg, in the care of the Electress Dowager Louisa Juliana, their two children Charles Lewis and Elizabeth ; but, though the former was long his mother's favourite, it was hardly in her way to be deeply affected by a separation from her babes. The part which the new King and Queen were called upon to play during the twelve-month of their residence at Prague was from the outset the reverse of easy. The self-conscious and stiff-necked Bohemian Estates had not the least intention of being ruled in fact as well as in name by the sovereign of their making ; while part at least of the population was steeped in ignorance like the peasants who welcomed his entry with shouts of ' Vivat rex *Ferdinandus !* ' [1] In Frederick's mistake of importing and maintaining among Utraquist (i.e. Lutheran) surroundings, a rigid and aggressive Calvinism, incarnate in the

---

[1] The entry of Frederick into Prague, and his handsome reception by the three Estates ' after the manner of our ancient Kings,' was witnessed by Jacob Böhme.

iconoclastic Scultetus, Elizabeth probably had no share ; for, as is worth remembering in connexion with the rather complicated religious history of her children, she never became a Calvinist herself or displayed any liking for Calvinistic ways. She did her best to gain popularity for herself and her consort, checking the insolence provoked among her courtiers by the uncouth manners and customs of her new subjects, and delighting all and sundry by pleasant English 'hand-shakes.' Now and then, offence was given by such innovations as the holding of Court balls on great Church holidays, and by the fashions of the attire worn on these occasions by the Queen and her ladies ; and more serious umbrage was taken at the King's conclusion of an alliance with the Calvinist Transylvanian, and at the project of another with the Sultan himself. Finally, there was the eternal difficulty as to ways and means, alike in Silesia (where the royal pair had been received with great rejoicing) and in Bohemia itself. Among all these agitations Elizabeth's spirits from time to time flagged, both before and after the birth of her third son ; for the changeful story of Prince Rupert's life began at Prague in December, 1619.

Within less than a year from this date the brief glories of her Bohemian royalty had ' turned to coal.' In July King James, while sending Sir Edward Conway and Sir Richard Weston to Prague, ordered Sir Henry Wotton to repair to Vienna, where,

if the King of Bohemia consented, he was to propose
the settlement of the difficulty by means of an Imperial Diet; while to all Princes visited by him on the
way he was to protest his master's abstinence from
any participation in the election to the Bohemian
Crown. The choice of Wotton for this singularly futile
mission was in itself extraordinarily infelicitous; very
naturally, however, his task impressed itself at once
upon the chosen ambassador's vivid imagination.
For it was on the eve of his departure for Vienna that
Wotton,' being in Greenwitche Parke, made a sonnet
to the Queen of Bohemia,' of which he sent copies
to Lady Wotton and Lord Zouche, and as to which
Wotton's latest biographer remarks, with perfect
truth, that 'such is the magic of art, these verses
have done more than anything else, perhaps, to
make both' Ambassador and Queen 'remembered.'[1]
Neither the Prague nor the Vienna mission had any
effect whatever; indeed, before Conway and Weston's reply reached Wotton, all was over. Early
in September the Leaguers under Maximilian of
Bavaria, the head of the rival Wittelsbach line, had
joined their forces against him, while Spinola's
Spaniards were approaching the Palatinate. Soon
the enemies of the new Bohemian monarchy had
closed in upon it. The battle of the White Hill was
waged and lost in an hour (November 8th); and,

[1] See L. Pearsall Smith, *Life and Letters of Sir Henry Wotton*,
Vol. i. p. 171.

though Frederick can hardly be blamed for the actual loss of the battle, in his accidental absence from
which there was nothing disgraceful,[1] he had entirely
failed to take precautions for the event of such a
catastrophe, and lacked the self-confidence which
alone could have made possible further resistance
on the spot.   Thus, though he did not at first quite
understand the full significance of his overthrow,
Bohemia had passed for ever out of the weak hands
of the Winter—or Twelfth Night—King.   When,
on the evening of the rout, the long stream of
vehicles, headed by Queen Elizabeth's coach,
ebbed out of Prague, bearing with it whatsoever
was portable of the Protestant interest, no hopes
remained except such as were wholly illusory.
But Elizabeth intended that, even though Bohemia
was lost and the Palatinate, which, as Louisa Juliana
had formerly lamented, had 'gone into Bohemia,'
might prove to be lost with it, the drama so swiftly
played out should have no ignoble epilogue.   She
had resolved—in her own words—' not to desert her
husband, and, if he was to perish, to perish by his
side.'   Fate dealt with her after no such sudden
fashion ; but she was true to the spirit of her vow.

From Prague Frederick and Elizabeth first
made their way into Silesia, then still a dependency
of Bohemia ; but soon Frederick, though, owing

[1] The *Mercure Français* stated that he took part in the
battle, and lost his ribbon of the Garter on the occasion !
(Charvériat, *Histoire de la Guerre de Trente Ans*, Vol. i. p. 235, note.)

to Wotton's protest against the invasion of the
Palatinate, the ban of the Empire did not descend
on him till the following January, had to realise
the position to which he was reduced.   He sent on
his wife before him, to seek shelter in the dominions
of his brother-in-law, the Elector George William
of Brandenburg.   This Prince, a Calvinist and one
of those who had advised the acceptance of the
Bohemian Crown, was afraid at the same time of the
Swedes and of the Emperor, to whose policy he had
not yet rallied ; and in after days the great Elector's
sister, the brave Duchess Louisa Charlotte of Courland, recognising in the experiences of her own
married life some analogy to those of her Aunt
Elizabeth's, recalled as memorable the impunity
with which her father had afforded a passing refuge
to his unfortunate relatives.[1] The intimacy between the two Calvinist Electoral Houses was to
survive backslidings on the part of Brandenburg
in the course of the great War, and was at a later
date to be very notably renewed, in spite of
the perennial jealousy between the two dynasties
and governments, by the marriage of Elizabeth's
grand-daughter Sophia Charlotte with the future
first Prussian King.   But, in these early days, the
welcome extended by the Elector George William to
his fugitive kinsfolk was limited to the coldest

[1] See A. Seraphim, *Eine Schwester des grossen Kurfürsten*, &c.
(*Quellen und Untersuchungen zur Gesch. d. Hauses Hohenzollern II.*).
Berlin, 1901.

courtesies. At Küstrin, where on Christmas Day,
1620, Elizabeth gave birth to her fifth child, the Prince
Maurice to be known in later life as Rupert's *fidus
Achates*, the royal mother and her attendants are
said to have hardly had enough to eat, and, when
in January, 1621, they were joined by her husband
from Breslau, he brought no good tidings with him.
The Union was on the eve of dissolution ; an offer
of aid from the Sultan, so at least it was rumoured,
had been refused by Frederick ; and the vacillations
of King James were more hopeless than ever. At
Berlin, where the fugitives were received by Frederick's sister, the Electress Elizabeth Charlotte, they
were glad to leave behind them the infant Maurice
in the faithful charge of his grandmother Louisa
Juliana, who, with his elder brother and sister
in her care, had taken her departure from Heidelberg
even before the battle of Prague. Her own estates,
together with those of her second son Lewis Philip,
long remained sequestrated ; though neither of them
had taken any part in the Bohemian business.
The boys were afterwards removed to Holland ;
but the young Princess Elizabeth continued under
her grandmother's care till her ninth year, chiefly
at Krossen in Silesia. This early training and the
closer connexion into which it brought her with the
Brandenburg Electoral family, were to exercise a
notable influence upon her character and upon her
later personal history.

→

From Berlin her parents, luckless emigrants, had still been obliged to move on, Queen Elizabeth journeying to Wolfenbüttel, the residence of the elder branch of the House of Brunswick, Frederick roaming about the Lower Saxon Circle in quest of military or other aid. Finally, they entered the Netherlands together by way of the Rhine. Everywhere in the Low Countries they were warmly welcomed, not only as kinsfolk of the House of Orange, but also as fellow-martyrs of those Protestant refugees to whom, in the Elector Frederick III's days, the Palatinate had accorded so hospitable a reception. On April 14th, 1621, they were received with the utmost cordiality by the great Stadholder, Maurice of Orange, in the midst of a large assemblage of princes, nobles, and foreign ambassadors ; and soon the States-General of the United Provinces, and the States of Holland and Friesland in particular, gave substantial expression to the universal warmth of the public welcome.

But the arm of the young Dutch Republic, though strenuous, was not long enough to reach effectively into the heart of the Empire. In the previous autumn, Frederick Henry of Nassau, the Stadholder's brother, had made a show of protecting the Palatinate with a couple of thousand men, among whom there was an English contingent ; but the effort had come to nothing. Already in 1620 the greater part of the Lower Palatinate had been occupied by the Spaniards; and in 1621, after Frederick had been placed under the ban of the Empire and the execution of the sentence had been entrusted to the expectant Duke of Bavaria, the inhabitants of the Upper Palatinate were called upon to forswear their allegiance. Frederick's cause was upheld only by the English volunteers under Sir Horace Vere and by Mansfeld's mercenaries. The Union had dissolved itself in the spring, and after midsummer James, while still cherishing the hope of bringing to pass a friendly intervention by Spain, was attempting through his ambassador Digby to obtain favourable terms at Vienna. Before the year was out, Maximilian of Bavaria had, with the aid of Rome, obtained an imperial promise of the reversion of the forfeited Electorate; and the future, as well as the present, seemed wholly dark for the Electoral couple and their children. Near or far, no ally seemed prepared to strike a blow in their interests, except that already, in 1621, the Queen of Hearts—as she came to be called in the days when she exercised no other sovereignty[1]—had found a true knight neither anxious, like King James, about probabilities of failure, nor, like the great *condottiere* Mansfeld,

[1] The origin of the application of this title seems unknown. It had been formerly connected in a peculiar fashion with Elizabeth's august godmother. (See the weird story in H. Clifford's *Life of Jane Dormer*, how not long before Queen Elizabeth's death a playing-card, the Queen of Hearts, with an iron nail knocked through the head, was found at the bottom of her chair. Soon afterwards all hopes of her recovery were abandoned.)

solely intent upon the main chance. This was Duke
Christian of Brunswick, the administrator or (as
an English letter of the time aptly calls him) the
' temporal bishop' of the see of Halberstadt.[1]
There is no evidence of his having ever met, or so
much as corresponded with, the Queen ; but Sir
Thomas Roe distinctly states that it was only for
her sake that he had engaged in the war, and he
made much the same confession himself to his
mother ; while the story of his having worn in his
helmet a glove belonging to the Queen, which he
had vowed to restore to her in reconquered Prague,
can be traced back as far as 1646. After losing an
arm, he rode forth in 1624 with a substitute made of
iron. Though a poet's son, he was as rough a cam-
paigner as any of the captains of the age ; and in
1625 a flagrant act of violence placed him under a
cloud. In the following year a fever ended the
excesses of his military career, his wild defiances
of Spain and the League, and his romantic passion,
which, as we know from a letter written by his
sister, Sophia of Nassau-Dietz, pined almost to the
last for some mark of recognition by its object.[2]

[1] Halberstadt was one of those sees which had by special
treaties with the Chapters been made hereditary in particular
Protestant princely families. (Opel, *Niedersächs. Krieg*, Vol. i.
p. 193.)

[2] It must at the same time be allowed that the epithets
applied to James I by Christian after the breakdown of the
scheme of 1623 could hardly under any circumstances have
been condoned by the King's daughter. (See Ritter, *Deutsche
Geschichte*, &c., Vol. iii. p. 253.)

Elizabeth's power of attracting the sympathy of soldiers, which had been so conspicuously exhibited in the case of Christian of Halberstadt, and to which afterwards Lord Craven's life-long devotion was to testify, was further exemplified by the goodwill shown to her in these times of distress by her martial kinsmen of the House of Orange. The readiness of the great captain Maurice of Nassau to further her interests so far as in him lay was shared by his younger brother, Prince Frederick Henry, who, in 1625, succeeded him in the stadholdership, and between whom and one of Elizabeth's ladies-in-waiting, attached to her person since her Heidelberg days, Maurice a few weeks before his death arranged a marriage. But the new Princess of Orange proved to be as proud as the beautiful Countess Amalia von Solms had been poor ; and, before long, her desire of furthering the interests of the House into which she had been admitted made her hostile to those of the family of her former mistress.

The charm of Elizabeth's beauty, and the stimulus of her high spirit, also inspired with a warm personal concern in her affairs, those of her father's numerous diplomatists who were or became known to her. Sir Henry Wotton seems never to have seen her again after their 'merry hour' of meeting at Heidelberg ; but he remained stedfast in his admiration for his 'Royal Mistress,' and among the

intimate letters of the days of his retirement at
Eton are those which he addressed to her, then a half-
forgotten exile at the Hague. In his will he left
to the Prince of Wales her picture, with an inscription [1]
which reappears, with slight modifications, in two
of his published pieces. Wotton's successor at
Venice, Sir Dudley Carleton (afterwards Viscount
Dorchester), who had likewise been received by the
Electoral pair at Heidelberg, and who was English
ambassador at the Hague when the fugitives
arrived there, cheerfully gave up his house for their
use ; besides judiciously exerting himself in their
interest both in this and in his second embassy to
the United Provinces. Lord Herbert of Cherbury
was warmly thanked by Elizabeth for his exertions
at Paris ; and Lord Conway did his best for her
cause with the Emperor at Prague. Lord Doncaster
(afterwards Earl of Carlisle) had, during his futile
mission before the Bohemian crisis, gained her goodwill in such a degree as to be honoured by her with
the intimate nickname of ' camel-face ' ; and it
was through him that his eloquent chaplain Donne
was privileged to ' deliver mesages ' to the Queen
when in sore straits. More to the purpose were
the active services of Sir Thomas Roe, the ' honest
fatt Thom ' of her correspondence ; but, although
these had begun before this diplomatist's return
from Eastern Europe, he does not seem to have come

---

[1] '*Inter Fortunæ sortem, extra Imperium.*' (See L. Pearsall
Smith, *u.s.*, Vol. i. p. 297, note.)

into much personal contact with her before 1628.

Only a few brief indications can be given here of the general course of the exiled family's fortunes during the quarter of a century which elapsed, before a definitive settlement of the Palatinate problem was at last reached in the Peace of Westphalia. Negotiations were at first carried on in Sweden, through Ludwig Camerarius, who from 1623 directed the diplomacy of the Palatine House, with the purpose of engaging King Gustavus Adolphus in offensive operations, in the course of which the latter intended that Frederick should appear in the Palatinate at the head of an army ; but the perennial Danish jealousy of Sweden put a stop to the plan. About the same time (1623–4) the faithful Rusdorf sought, by negotiations in London, to obtain fair terms for his master at Vienna, Frederick signifying his willingness to allow his eldest son (Frederick Henry) to be educated at Vienna, with a view to his marriage with an Imperial Princess ; but the overtures came to nothing, as did the specious offers of the disguised Capuchin della Rota. These latter proved, in truth, to be mere pretences on the part of Maximilian of Bavaria, who, in 1624, was received into the College of Electors in Frederick's place. Towards the close of 1623, King James I, who earlier in the year had broken off negotiations with Mansfeld and Christian of Halberstadt and concluded a truce with the Infanta at Brussels, which Frederick was obliged to ratify, had at last been undeceived as to the intentions of Spain. He saw at last how during the Spanish marriage negotiations he had been tricked into the false hope that good terms would be obtained by Spanish mediation for the Palatines ; and, during the last year of his reign, when war with Spain was becoming more and more imminent, a treaty promising an English army for the recovery of the Palatinate was concluded with Mansfeld, who was for the moment the lion of London, whither he was soon followed on a similar errand by Christian of Halberstadt. Thus, when in March, 1625, James I was succeeded on the English throne by Charles I, Elizabeth's hopes rallied with pathetic buoyancy, and she cherished the hope that her brother's approaching French marriage would further advance the interests of her family. There can be no doubt of Charles I's intention to serve his sister and her children ; and his wishes on this head were shared by Buckingham. The Duke is even said, when visiting the Palatine family at Leyden, not long before his assassination in January, 1629, to have had in his head a scheme—which, if fate had so willed it, might have had strange consequences for the British Succession—of a marriage between his daughter Lady Mary Villiers and Elizabeth's eldest son, Prince Frederick Henry. But, as is well known, the history of Charles I's foreign policy during the first part of his reign, in which the question of the recovery of the Palatinate could not possibly hold the central place as it had in his father's, had, as Eliot summed it up in his scathing speech, been one of constant and utter failure. Afterwards, of course, the King was so hopelessly at issue with his Parliament, that all chance of effective intervention had come to an end. Mansfeld's army at first remained inactive in the Low Countries, where it was not increased, except by fragments of the levies of Christian of Halberstadt, which a tempest had scattered at sea. Instead of reinforcing the mercenary troops, the English expedition which sailed under Lord Wimbledon in October, 1625, had orders for Cadiz. When, in 1625, Elizabeth's uncle, Christian IV of Denmark, at last took the field as chief of the Lower Saxon Circle, the death of his namesake soon deprived him of his best commander ; and, in 1626, Mansfeld, after being defeated by Wallenstein at Dessau, was ' chased ' by him into Hungary, whence, after making over his army to Bethlen Gabor, he took his departure only to die. In August of the same year, Tilly entirely overcame Christian IV at Lutter, and the ' Danish War ' was virtually at an end. Henceforth, no further intention was entertained either at Vienna or at Munich of granting any terms to Frederick, although, on Cardinal Khlesl's principle of never either dropping negotiations or concluding them, conditions were still offered him. In return for the restoration of part of his paternal dominions, he was, while renouncing both the Bohemian Crown and the Electoral dignity, to pay the costs of the war, and to consent to bring up his children as Catholics; but the former condition he could not, and the latter he would not, accept. It is said that, at this very time (1627), the unhappy ex-Elector paid a secret visit to the Palatinate, whose fate seemed sealed for ever by the Austro-Bavarian treaty of the following year. The Spaniards held the left bank of the Rhine and the Bavarians the right; conversion was forced upon the inhabitants, who began to emigrate rather than submit to it; and, when, in June, 1630, Rusdorf presented a letter from his master at Ratisbon, where the Bavarian policy was conspicuously to the front, the Emperor had no answer to return except a demand of unconditional submission. Had the Palatine family yielded to this demand, and accepted the further condition of conversion to the Church of Rome, they might perhaps have been allowed some sort of domicile in the Empire. But they were of a different metal, and held out, though their prospects had never been gloomier; for, in the same year, peace was concluded between England and Spain, and whatever hopes had been placed upon King Charles' anti-Spanish policy were thus brought to nought.

Yet, soon after these events—in July, 1630—
Gustavus Adolphus landed on the Pomeranian coast,
and in him the Palatine family hoped to find both
an avenger and a deliverer. The Electress Dowager
Louisa Juliana met him at Berlin, and after his
great victory at Breitenfeld he approached the
Palatinate. Before the end of 1631 most of it had
been recaptured and re-Protestantised ; and early
in the following year Frederick was on his way
to meet the conquering hero. Frederick's Dutch
hosts had furnished him forth with great liberality,
and the number of state coaches with which he
arrived at Frankfort, in February, 1632, had been
increased to two score by Gustavus Adolphus
himself, who treated him with great courtesy as
King of Bohemia. But the future of the Palatinate
was left undiscussed between the two Kings ; nor
was it till after Gustavus had continued his vic-
torious progress through Bavaria, that he proposed
a settlement. It showed unmistakably that the
treatment of the Palatinate formed but a subsidiary part of his great design, and filled Frederick,
who was looking for restoration to his patrimony,
with alarm. For, besides other onerous conditions,
there were imposed on him the admission of Swedish
garrisons to some of his chief towns, the concession
of the supreme military command to Gustavus,
and the grant of equal rights to the Lutherans in
the Calvinistic half of the Palatinate. Hard as

E

these terms seemed to Frederick, amicable negotiations were still in progress between him and the great Swedish King, when the awful news arrived of the death of Gustavus on the field of Lützen. Frederick had a little before this fallen ill of a fever ; but, as if driven by his doom, he once more began to wander from town to town, till, on November 29th, 1632, thirteen days after the death of Gustavus, he breathed his last at Mainz. The homeless wanderer's heart was buried in the church at Oppenheim, in his own Palatinate ; his corpse was hurriedly borne hither and thither—being carried off from Frankenthal by Bernhard of Weimar on his retreat in 1635, to preserve it from desecration—till it was at last composed in peace within the walls of Metz.[1]

After Frederick's death, the regency of the Palatinate was assumed by his brother Louis Philip, who was married to a Brandenburg Princess (Maria Eleonora) ; but though under his rule Heidelberg was recovered, and with the aid of foreign (especially Scottish) beneficence the prosperity of

[1] Elizabeth bore no love to the Swedish royal family, partly because of these memories, partly perhaps because of the Danish blood in her. (' The States,' she writes on one occasion, ' are justly punished for assisting the Queen of Sweden against my uncle' (Christian IV). She detested Gustavus' daughter Christina. On the death of the Queen Dowager Maria Eleonora, she writes : ' Queen Mother is dead, which makes her rap out with many an oth.' (*Unpublished Letters of the Queen of Bohemia to Sir Edward Nicholas, Antiq. Soc. Publ.* 1857 (xvi).)

the Palatinate began to revive, the fatal day of Nördlingen (September 6th, 1634) undid all the work of the previous two years, and the sufferings of the Palatinate from both ' friends ' and foes—from Swedes and Bavarians—began afresh. After the Peace of Prague, in 1635, the Swedes fell back upon the Main, and after Heidelberg had been once more occupied by the Imperialists, the Palatinate remained for some five years under the government of the Emperor, which banished all Calvinist and Lutheran preachers with their families and households, and in every way promoted the decay of University and schools. It cannot be said that the general condition of the population, whose sufferings were of the most heartrending description, and productive of that awful brutalisation which is so characteristic of the later period of the Thirty Years' War, was much affected by changes in the occupation of the country.[1] The renewal of warfare in these parts, in 1640 and again in 1644, brought in the French and their German allies and the Bavarians to augment these troubles. It will be noted below how the dispossessed heir of the Palatinate bore himself in these evil years, and what he finally saved for his House out of so pitiful a wreck. The Bohemian Crown was, of course, a

---

[1] The project of despatching a Scottish army in 1639 to occupy the Palatinate broke down because of a disagreement between Leslie and the Covenanters.

thing of the past, though to the end Elizabeth retained the royal title.[1]

The birth at the Hague, on October 14th, 1630, of Sophia, the youngest of the children of Frederick and Elizabeth, had preceded the death of her father by very little more than two years. Her mother, it must be remembered, was then still in the full flower of her womanhood—in the thirty-fifth year of her age—an eager horsewoman and fond of the pleasures of the chase ; and in mind she remained not less vigorous than in body, venting her wrath freely on both enemies and neutrals—on that ' devil ' the Emperor and that ' beast ' the Elector of Saxony, just as at a later date she had to search in the Book of *Revelation* for analogues fitly expressing her sentiments concerning Oliver Cromwell. Yet private as well as public griefs had helped to sadden her heart as well as to sober her spirit even before the death of her husband, whose affection towards her had remained unchanged, showing itself in little expressions of care and tenderness such as abound

[1] It would seem as if after her husband's death she had for a time approved the style of ' the King's only sister.' (See Wotton's letter *ap.* L. P. Smith, *u.s.*, Vol. ii. p. 342.) When, on the marriage of her daughter Princess Henrietta in 1651, her son Charles Lewis took exception to the title ' Queen of Bohemia,' Elizabeth wrote to him indignantly that ' leauing it you doe me so much wrong as to the memorie of your dead father, as if you disapproved his actions ' ; and declared that whatever public instrument she might at any time have to sign, she would never sign it without the royal style. *Letters*, &c., ed. by A. Wendland, p. 16.

in his letters almost to the day of his death. In
1624, they had lost an infant son, Lewis; and, in
January, 1629, their first-born, Frederick Henry,
a boy of fifteen, was (as already noted) drowned off
Haarlem as he was travelling back in the common
passengers' boat with his father from Amsterdam,
whither Frederick had gone to collect the share of
the profits from a captured Spanish treasure-fleet
assigned to him by Maurice of Nassau. The infant
Princess Charlotte was laid in the grave by her
brother's side only three days before the christening
of Sophia. But, as there survived five brothers
(to whom a sixth, significantly named Gustavus,
was added two years after Sophia's birth), the statement may perhaps be credited with which her
Memoirs open, that her arrival in this world caused
no excess of joy to her parents. She relates that her
name—the name which narrowly missed marking
the beginning of a new English dynasty, and which,
in token of its popularity in this country, was
bestowed upon his heroine by the author of one
of the masterpieces of our literature—was drawn
by lot out of several written for the purpose on slips
of paper, because of the small choice of godmothers
remaining in the case of so large a family. Sophia's
destinies were not encumbered by a second name
like that which her sister Louisa Hollandina bore
in honour of her godfathers; although the States
of Friesland, who undertook the same responsibility

for the infant Sophia, presented her with a pension
of forty pounds for life and handsome supplementary gifts. So soon as it was possible to transport her,
she was sent to Leyden by her mother, who preferred
that her children should be brought up at a distance
from herself, 'since,' says Sophia, 'the sight of her
monkeys and dogs was more pleasing to her than
that of ourselves.'   At Leyden, therefore, Sophia
spent her early childhood, chiefly in the company
of her youngest brother Gustavus, who died nine
years after his birth. Her graphic reminiscences
of her tender years chiefly turn on the cumbrous
etiquette (*tout à fait à l'allemande*) by which she
was environed, and on the lessons in the Heidelberg
Catechism (which she 'knew by heart without
understanding it') imparted by her venerable
governess, Frau von Pless, with the assistance of
her two daughters, ladies of 'awe-inspiring' presence, whose age seemed to the child almost equal
to her own. 'Their ways were straight in the eyes
of Heaven as before men.' The good ex-Elector
had been consistently careful as to providing sound
Calvinistic instruction for his children, and Frau von
Pless had been his own instructress in his infancy;
but his English wife, at least during part of her
residence in the Netherlands, continued to employ
the services of a Church of England chaplain.   In
general, it is clear that at Leyden, and afterwards
at the Hague, Sophia, while her wits quickly opened

to the demands of life, passed, like the rest of her brothers and sisters, through a training which equipped them more or less efficiently for the struggle before them. In her case, it must also have helped to regulate the remarkable intellectual curiosity with which she was naturally endowed, and which, though it cannot be shown to have carried her to great heights or depths of study or thought, at least enabled her in later life to rise serene above the troubles and trials of the hour. The usual training of the Palatine Princes and Princesses, while including some mathematics, history, and law, appears to have been based in the main upon the study of languages, of which most of them came to have several at command. Their mother they always addressed in English, but among themselves they used French, as had been the custom of their father in his letters to his wife, and as continued to be the practice of Sophia's son and grandson in domestic conversation, even when they had become British sovereigns.

On Prince Gustavus' death, in 1641, Sophia, who was herself suffering from illness, quitted Leyden for the Hague, bidding farewell to her *bonnes vieilles*, whom she said she had loved from gratitude and habit, ' for sympathy rarely exists between old age and youth '—a maxim to be flatly contradicted by the experience of her own later years. At the Hague, where, during the rule of Frederick Henry, his consort Amalia strained every nerve to prove the authority of the House of Orange equal to that of a royal dynasty, the Queen of Bohemia was beginning to find some of the conditions of her life oppressive, and, worst of all, the continuous pressure of debt unbearable. Already in her husband's time, the generosity of Maurice had furnished them with a pleasant summer retreat at Rheenen, in the wooded country on the Rhine, not far below Arnhem, described by Evelyn as 'a neate palace or country house, built after the Italian manner, as I remember.'[1] But Sophia, on first arriving at the Hague, found the change so delightful as to make her think that she was 'enjoying the pleasures of Paradise.' This early glamour must, however, have soon passed off ; for, though blessed with good spirits even in her later years, Sophia was without that gift—sometimes enviable, sometimes dangerous—of seeing things rather as one wishes them to be than as they are, which her brother Charles Lewis described himself as having inherited from their mother. And it was this mother herself to the flaws in whose brilliant and in many respects noble personality

[1] As to Rheenen, the best account appears to be contained in J. Kretzschmar, *Mittheilungen zur Geschichte des Heidelberger Schlosses*, pp. 96–132, which I have not seen. There seems at one time to have been a notion of making it over to Prince Rupert ; but it afterwards became the property of Sophia, who says that it had cost 40,000 crowns to build (*Briefe an Hannov. Diplomaten*, p. 229). The Electress Sophia, not being able to sell the property at its estimated value, made it over to her son Ernest Augustus.

Sophia seems to have been from the first unable to shut her eyes. It cannot have been only her love of horses and dogs, or her *penchant* for what may be called the pleasures of the toilet which affected both Sophia and her eldest sister Elizabeth unsympathetically ; there seems to have been in the Queen a vein of frivolity, inherited perhaps from her own mother, which estranged from her these and perhaps some other of her children, though they could not fail to recognise that her life was devoted to the interests of her family as a whole. It must, however, have been to his sister Elizabeth, and not to Sophia, that their brother Charles Lewis refers in expressing a hope that their mother may not find reason ' to use her with the former coolness.'

Of her eldest brother, Charles Lewis himself, Sophia can have seen but little in the days of the family life at the Hague and Rheenen, although she afterwards grew warmly attached to him and came to regard him, as she says, in the light of a father rather than of an elder brother. He was a prince of remarkable intellectual gifts, which, till on his father's death he by his mother's wish took service under William II, Prince of Orange, he had cultivated to so much purpose at the University of Leyden, that he was afterwards credited with a share in the writings of Pufendorf, the chief glory of the restored University of Heidelberg. His disposition resembled his youngest sister's in not a few points, as their

correspondence shows. His nature, like hers, was
at bottom both kindly and humorous, and, while
both had a turn for sarcastic wit, there was, one
must confess, a coarse fibre in both for which the
habits and traditions of Palatinate life are not to be
held altogether responsible. It must have been
because of this natural wit, rather than because
of the avarice born of necessity which Charles Lewis
displayed in later passages of his career, that he
was called *Timon* by his brothers and sisters, to
whom Shakespeare, with whose plays Charles Lewis
was not unacquainted, is quite as likely as Lucian
to have suggested the nickname. He was through
life a friend of English literature, and, so late as 1674,
John Philpot's edition of Camden's *Remains* was
dedicated to him. There is evidence of his having
had other literary tastes—among the nicknames
which he gave to his eldest son by Louisa von
Degenfeld were those of ' Pantagruel' and ' Lance-
lot du Lac.' But his favourite book was the Bible
('*meinliebotes Evangelium*'). At the same time he
was, like his sister Sophia, free-spoken on all subjects ; though, on occasion, as is not wonderful when
his experiences are remembered, a pathos welled up
in him which she, not so much from cynicism
as from habitual self-control, steadily repressed.[1]

[1] See his extraordinary outburst of passionate woe on
receiving the news of the death of a daughter (in 1674) in *Briefe
des Kurfürsten Karl Ludwig an die Seinen*, pp. 234–5: ' I do not
know, why the Lord God seeks to try me so—when I have but a

Nor was he free-spoken only ; he might be called a free-thinker but for that aforesaid love of the Bible which, together with a double share of his intellectual alertness, he bequeathed to his daughter Elizabeth Charlotte, Duchess of Orleans.

After his father's death, Charles Lewis had been acknowledged as Elector Palatine by King Charles I and some of the German Protestant Princes ; and his mother, though he was and always remained the darling of her heart, would have urged him to assume his place in the Palatinate, had not the battle of Nördlingen placed any such attempt out of the question.   Charles Lewis and his brother Rupert were accordingly sent to England (1635).   Here for two or three years they led a life of gaiety and dissipation ; but they could hardly, in any case, have effected anything to the purpose, even had the young ' Elector ' devised some more practical scheme than that of asking the hand of the young Queen Christina of Sweden.   After their return to Holland, however, the two Princes were, in 1638, stirred to a more vigorous activity on their own account.   They began badly by the loss of all their stores at Meppen in Frisia ; but they, notwithstanding, resolved to make an armed attempt upon the Palatinate, of which the cost was defrayed by Lord Craven, who himself held a command in it.   They were supported

few years more to live, and after all did not create myself, and have no conscious desire of committing any sin,' &c.

by a Swedish force under Major-General King (the Lord Eythin of Marston Moor) ; but, after siege had been laid to Lemgo, the gallant raid came to an unfortunate end at Vlotho on the Weser, both Rupert and Craven remaining behind in captivity. Hereupon, Charles Lewis, in 1639, once more set forth from Holland with the design of placing himself at the head of the army left without a leader by the death of Duke Bernhard of Weimar ; but Cardinal Richelieu, whose schemes the success of the adventure would have thwarted, gave it an unexpected turn by causing Charles Lewis to be arrested and detaining him, for the most part in prison, during several months. In 1640, he used the freedom which he had regained for new efforts, first in Denmark, and then at the Diet of Ratisbon, upon whose walls Swedish guns were playing. Once more, there was much excitement in the ' Palsgrave's ' favour in both England and Scotland—it was in fact the last occasion on which King and Parliament might have united in a policy approved by the nation at large ; and when, in 1642, the Emperor Ferdinand III propounded a settlement which would, on stringent terms, have restored a portion of the Palatinate, the English ambassador (Sir Thomas Roe) joined the agents of Charles Lewis in protesting against its inadequacy. The horrors of war were renewed in the exhausted Palatinate, and Charles Lewis once more betook himself to England (1644), where he presented a memorandum to Parliament, which allowed him £30 a day for his stay in London, but limited it in the first instance to a fortnight. Early in this year, Louisa Juliana had died, and it almost seemed as if the hopes of her descendants were to be buried with her ; for, though a dim prospect of a general peace was opening, there seemed little hope that, in the conflict between the great Crowns, thought would be taken of the Palatinate. In England, the Civil War had been for nearly two years in progress ; both Rupert and Maurice had, to their brother's actual or pretended displeasure, taken service under the King ; and it is hardly possible that, at such a time, Charles Lewis could have reckoned on obtaining military or pecuniary support for his schemes for the recovery of his patrimony. He has, accordingly, been supposed to have harboured deeper designs, and these have been connected with Sir Harry Vane's proposal, rather earlier in the year, of dethroning King Charles I. But whether or not the idea of supplanting his uncle had entered into Charles Lewis' mind—and Sophia's mention in her *Memoirs* of Vane's previous visit to the Hague lends some colour to the conjecture (she calls him Vain and speaks of him and his large chin without seriousness)—it is certain that the Prince was well received by the Parliamentary

leaders.[1] In return for his supposed goodwill to
their cause, to which he is stated to have testified
even by taking the Covenant and sitting in the
Assembly of Divines at Westminster, he was granted
an annual allowance of £8,000 and assigned the
Deanery at Windsor as a residence, where he thought
it most prudent for the time to give himself up to his
scientific studies.[2]

The career of Prince Rupert, whose personal
attractions had eclipsed those of his elder brother
during their former joint visit to England, was
widely to diverge from Charles Lewis', now that
they both found themselves once more in the land
of their maternal ancestry. In those earlier days,
Sir Thomas Roe had informed Elizabeth how the
King took pleasure in the sprightliness of her second
son, from whom, in her fondness for his senior, she
had expected so little ; and Charles Lewis himself
reported to his mother his dismay that *Rupert le
Diable* was always in the company of Queen Henrietta Maria, her ladies, and the Papists. At the

[1] As to the possibility of an offer of the Crown to Charles
Lewis by the Parliamentary leaders, see W. Michael, *Englische
Geschichte*, &c., Vol. i. p. 282.

[2] It should be remembered that in this morigeration Charles
Lewis had the support, up to a certain point, of his mother, who
in the days of the Civil War blamed Queen Henrietta Maria for
opposing the attempts of Charles Lewis to bring about a reconciliation between his uncle and the Parliament. Gradually, however, all that the King did seemed right to his sister, and she blamed
Charles Lewis for remaining on good terms with the Parliament. See
K. Hauck, *Elizabeth, Königin von Böhmen* (Heidelberg, 1905).

same time, Prince Rupert was understood to be engaged in discussing with his uncle the King wild schemes for the foundation of a colony in Madagascar. The Princes were recalled home ; the Madagascar scheme collapsed ; and Rupert's Protestantism henceforth stood firm. It has been already seen how he was taken prisoner in the fight at Vlotho (1638). The offer of Lord Craven, who had paid £20,000 for his own ransom, to increase this sum, were he allowed to share Prince Rupert's captivity, was refused, and the Prince was lodged in captivity at Linz under the care of Count Kufstein. He came forth from it, having resisted all attempts to lure him from his religious belief and into the Emperor's service ; neither, however, was he inclined to avail himself of the prospects of a wealthy Huguenot marriage held out to him in Paris. With his faithful brother Maurice, he hereupon betook himself to England, where they devoted themselves to the cause of the King in his struggle against Parliament, and became the very types and exemplars of the Cavaliers. Across the seas, in New England, the good old Puritan minister Nathaniel Ward, who had held Rupert in his arms as a child, ' when, if I mistake not, he promised to be a good Prince,' prayed that even now he might be turned into ' a right Roundhead, a wise-hearted Palatine, a thankful man to the English,' and that his soul might be saved, ' notwithstanding all his God-damn-me's.'

But the ordinary picture of Prince Rupert as general of the horse, impetuous even to fool-hardiness, and as a passionate partisan who could not restrain his vehemence even in the presence of the King himself, conveys no complete view either of his services in the Civil War, or of his character. As to the former, neither the calamity of Marston Moor, for which he was not responsible, as he certainly was for that of Naseby, nor perhaps even the surrender of Bristol, should have been allowed to obscure their lustre. As to his character, he was not less humane than resolute, and self-reliance was combined in him with the nobler kind of self-respect. His intellectual curiosity was a genuine family characteristic, though it happened in him to take a peculiar turn towards applied science and the technicalities of art.[1] After the fall of Oxford, in 1646, the Princes Rupert and Maurice left England, the former to hold a command in France ; but, in the year before the execution of King Charles, he once more came forward to serve the sinking cause of the English monarchy, and took charge of the royal fleet. Maurice was, of course, once more found by his side, and, after the King's death,

[1] The honour of having discovered the art of engraving in mezzotint, frequently claimed for Prince Rupert, seems due to a Hessian officer named Ludwig von Siegen, who, meeting the Prince at Brussels about 1654, taught him the new process. See Cyril Davenport, *Mezzotints* (' The Connoisseur's Library,') pp. 52–65.

they engaged in those remote maritime adventures in the course of which the younger brother met his death.   Rupert's earlier naval—or buccaneering— career continued till 1653, when he returned to France, creating a considerable sensation by his entry into Paris ' like an old Spanish *conquistador*, with Indians, apes and parrots.'[1]

Sophia's third brother Maurice was, as has been seen, an all but inseparable follower of his elder Rupert, whose equal he can have been neither in military genius nor in general intellectual ability and personal charm—' he never,' says Clarendon, who resented the pride of the Palatines, ' sacrificed to the Graces, nor conversed amongst men of quality, but had most used the company of ordinary and inferior men, with whom he loved to be very familiar.' Sophia writes to him as to one little interested in intrigues of State, and his preference through life seems to have been for the camp rather than the Court.[2]   But, whatever other abatement should be made from the censures with which, like the brother of his heart, he was visited by both Puritan animosity

----

[1] See K. Hauck, *Karl Ludwig, Kurfürst von der Pfalz* (Leipzig, 1903), p. 252.

[2] His mother's coolness towards him is curious.   She communicated the news of his disappearance to Charles Lewis without a word of sympathy, and advised that, should he really be at Algiers, no ' great inquierie' should be made, lest his ransom should be fixed at a quite inordinate height, or Cromwell should purchase him from the corsairs.   *Letters*, &c., ed. A. Wendland, p. 43.

and Royalist spite, he most certainly possessed in a rare degree the soldier's cardinal virtue of fidelity. Thus we may fain hope that, in accordance with the most trustworthy account, his fate overtook him, whelmed beneath the deep gulf of the Atlantic, and that he was not, as a different tradition would have it, carried off by corsairs to Algiers, there to linger out a forgotten existence.

The sixth and seventh brothers, Edward and Philip, had been brought up in common; but in their later lives they were much divided. About 1637, they had, with their brother Maurice, been sent to school in Paris, whither, as has been seen, the Palatine family long looked for political succour; and here they remained after Maurice had taken his departure, with a view to beginning his military career. In 1645 the elder of the pair took a step which estranged him not only from his brother Philip, but from the whole of the Palatine family, and which, together with a similar proceeding at a later date on the part of Princess Louisa Hollandina, stands in direct contrast to the general tenour of the family history. Anne of Gonzaga, second daughter of the Duke Charles of Gonzaga-Nevers, afterwards Duke of Mantua, was already a celebrity in French society, when, her amour with Henry of Guise having come to an end which wounded her self-esteem, she in 1645 secretly gave her hand to the Prince Palatine Edward, and henceforth became the ‘ *Princesse*

Palatine,' under which name she plays a conspicuous part in the literature of contemporary French memoirs. We have, however, no concern here with her share in public affairs at a rather later time, when (in 1650) she effected a union between the two branches of the Fronde and thus drove Mazarin into temporary exile, and when, after being herself persuaded by the Cardinal to 'rally' to Anne of Austria, she (in 1651–2) succeeded in bringing over to the same side the Duke of Bouillon and the great general Turenne.[1] Mazarin, when indicating the price (a great Court office) at which her support might be gained, described her as a *femme intéressée ;* but, as M. Chéruel observes, it was not this aspect of her character which was in the mind of Bossuet when, in a funeral discourse, he dwelt on her great qualities of head and heart. In an age of confessional propaganda she was a great proselytiser in high places ; and it was a signal instance of her activity in this direction, that she should have exacted Prince Edward's conversion to the Church of Rome as the condition of her acceptance of his hand. For she thus secured to herself a claim for direct interference in the affairs of the Palatine House, which still possessed a certain importance and might again acquire a greater. Her foresight

---

[1] See A. Chéruel, *Le rôle politique de la Princesse Palatine pendant la Fronde en* 1651. (*Séances de l'Acad. des Sc. Mor. et Pol.*, January–February, 1888.)

was justified ; for, in course of time, there can be
no doubt that she contrived to have a hand in the
conversion of Princess Louisa Hollandina, as
well as in yet another conversion, which made it
possible for Charles Lewis' daughter Elizabeth
Charlotte to become the wife of Louis XIV's
brother, Philip Duke of Orleans.   Although the new
Princess Palatine had retained her share of the wealth
of the Gonzaga, notwithstanding the efforts of her
father to accumulate the whole for bestowal on his
eldest daughter Marie, who in this same year 1645
became Queen of Poland, the agitation of Edward's
mother at the news of his change of religion was
extreme, and was shared by most of her children.
Charles Lewis besought his mother ' with her
blessings to lay her curse ' upon Prince Philip, who
was about to quit Paris for the Netherlands, should
he too ' change the religion he had been bred in.'
As for Prince Edward, his fortunes were henceforth
more or less severed from those of the family,
though we find him, in 1651, at the Hague, as he
passed the ambassadors of the English Commonwealth in the streets, calling them ' rogues ' to their
faces, and thus doing his best to embroil the United
Provinces with the enemies of the House of Stewart.[1]

[1] His mother seems to have been pleased with this outburst,
and to have testified to her gratification by presenting to Edward
certain family articles of value—more in number than was agreeable to Charles Lewis.   Edward, who certainly seems to have

With Edward's daughter, Benedicta Henrietta, born in 1652, we shall meet again as the wife of John Frederick, Duke of Hanover, Sophia's brother-in-law. In her the Palatine type, of which Sophia herself and her niece Elizabeth Charlotte were such striking examples, was well-nigh effaced; but it will not be overlooked that by descent she stood nearer to the English Succession than her father's youngest sister.

Of Prince Philip's fateful conduct at the Hague immediately. While, before his return to her mother's little Court, Sophia had necessarily seen little of him or of her brothers there or at Rheenen, she was, as a matter of course, much thrown into the society of her three sisters. At first, as she tells us, she was by no means troubled to find them handsomer and more accomplished than herself, and admired by everybody; and she was perfectly contented that her juvenile gaiety and *railleries* should help to amuse them. 'Even the Queen took pleasure in my fun'; for she was gratified to see the child tormented, so that her wits might be sharpened by the process of being put on her defence. It became the established practice for her to 'rally' any and everybody;

had in most things an eye to the main chance, had a cynical vein in him, like some of his brothers and sisters. When he came to Heidelberg in 1658, accompanied by a facetious M. de Jambonneau, Charles Lewis writes to his 'second' wife: ' He turns everything into a joke, so that I cannot bring him on with me.'

the clever people were delighted by it, and the others were made afraid of her. Gradually, however, Sophia's quick ears heard the ' milords ' at her mother's Court say to one another that, when she had finished growing, she would surpass all her sisters. And the remark inspired her with an affection for the whole English nation ; ' so greatly is one pleased, when young, to be thought good-looking.'

Elizabeth, the eldest of the Palatine Princesses, though by no means indifferent to the family interests, or without sympathy at any time of her life with the troubles either of her father's or her mother's House, was of an introspective turn of mind, grave and thoughtful, and little inclined by nature to the levity inborn in most of her brothers and sisters. Both as imbued with the Calvinism in which she had been so carefully nurtured by her grandmother amidst the congenial Brandenburg surroundings, and perhaps also because, though an accomplished linguist, she alone of the sisterhood had no occasion to learn to speak Dutch, she already as a girl fell into a way of leading much of her life to herself. At the same time, she was always interested in public affairs, and more especially in marriage projects, which in those times formed an important part in politics ; and it is noticeable that she continued fond of match-making even after she had herself settled down to a single life. Among the suitors for her hand was the young King Wladislaw IV of Poland, a tolerant and liberal-minded Prince.[1] But the marriage fell through, because the Diet would not hear of their King marrying an ' English ' Protestant ; and Elizabeth, of whose noble character perfect veracity formed one of the noblest traits, refused in her turn to listen to a diplomatic suggestion that she should become a convert to Rome. In January, 1639, there was a notion of making a match between her and Bernhard of Weimar. We are not told that the Electoral Prince Frederick William of Brandenburg—afterwards known as the Great Elector—between whom and Princess Louisa Hollandina a marriage was at one time projected, had ever thought of asking the hand of his elder sister. But he may have met Elizabeth in 1638 at Königsberg, when, after the Peace of Prague, George William was induced by troubles in his Margravate to send his whole family into Prussia, whither some of their Palatine kinsfolk also came ; and he was in these years much at Rheenen, where he cannot but have been attracted by the Princess Elizabeth, whose unflinching Protestant sentiment resembled his own, which formed a constant factor in his shifting system of policy. She was afterwards a visitor to Berlin, where, in 1646,

---

[1] This was at the time (1636) when Charles I was very active in his negotiations on behalf of the Palatine House, sending Lord Arundel on a special mission to Vienna, projecting an alliance with the States-General and France, and scheming the Polish match mentioned in the text. Everything failed.

Princess Louisa Henrietta of Orange, whose spirit was akin to hers, held her entry as Electress, and at Krossen, where the Dowager Electress (Frederick V's sister) kept a Court of her own, and where Elizabeth is said to have specially interested herself in the instruction of the Elector Frederick William's sister Hedwig Sophia, afterwards Landgravine of Hesse-Cassel. We shall see in what fashion the Great Elector ultimately succeeded in providing for the peace and comfort of his kinswoman. Before this time, owing chiefly to her friendship with Descartes, by which she is probably now chiefly remembered, Elizabeth's mental horizon had unmistakably widened ; and, though she retained to the last a sincere piety and (a trace or so of pride of birth apart) a touching modesty of spirit, her growing familiarity with broader philosophical principles gradually freed her from some of the narrowing influences of Calvinism. Descartes' intimacy with the Princess Palatine, against whose family he had, curiously enough, in former days borne arms in Bohemia, was during her absence from the Hague maintained by an exchange of letters between them, of which the artless Sophia contrived the conveyance.[1] Although the relations between the great

[1] The correspondence of the Princess Elizabeth and Descartes extends over the years 1643 to 1649. Comte Foucher de Careil, after publishing his *Descartes et la Princesse Palatine* in 1862, was enabled to supplement the letters of Descartes by those of

thinker and his matchless pupil were not in the
least of a kind to suggest clandestine methods,
Elizabeth was not, like Queen Christina, independent
of control ; and Sophia's services in screening the
correspondence from her mother's unsympathetic
notice, while they earned her the gratitude of the
first philosopher with whom she was brought into
personal relations, show that, notwithstanding her
raillery and ridicule of her eldest sister's moments
of distraction, kindly feelings prevailed between
them. Elizabeth's refined beauty, though it was
hardly in reference to this that her sisters nicknamed
her *la Grecque*, is described by Sophia in her *Memoirs*
very vividly, but not without an admixture of spite.

The second of the sisterhood, Louisa Hollandina,
is stated by Sophia not to have been so beautiful
in the days of the Hague and Rheenen as Elizabeth,
but, as it seemed to the young critic, of a more
pleasing disposition. ' She applied herself entirely
to painting, and her love of this art was so strong,
that she made likenesses of people without having
ever cast her eyes upon them.' This master-passion
possessed her to the last, although, perhaps, it was
only when Honthorst touched up her pictures that
they did full justice to his teaching. Some of her

the Princess in a second volume, published in 1879. A most
interesting summary is furnished by V. de Swarte's attractive
*Descartes Directeur Spirituel : Correspondance avec la Princesse
Palatine et la Reine Cristine de Suède* (Paris, 1904).

handiwork is to be found in the galleries containing portraits of her family ; an Annunciation was painted by her at the age of seventy-three, and several other pictures from her hands were bestowed by her upon the parish churches in the vicinity of Maubuisson during the period of her rule there as an Abbess. In her younger days, as we learn from the observant Sophia, Louisa Hollandina, while intent upon painting the portraits of her friends and acquaintances, was too neglectful of her own personal appearance. On the other hand, it seems wholly unjust to infer from the ripple of unaffected gaiety which overspread the calm of her maturer years, that her nature was essentially frivolous.   While her life, as we shall see, was one of piety and unselfishness, we may conclude her to have possessed in her youth what she preserved in her old age— much of her youngest sister's intellectual alertness and vivacity, and perhaps also something of her humorous turn of mind, without attaining to the depth of thought, any more than she had passed through the intellectual training, that distinguished their elder, Elizabeth.

Of Sophia's third sister, the Princess Henrietta Maria (so named after Charles I's charming but ill-starred Queen), a portrait is drawn in the *Memoirs* hardly less attractive than that which pictures her on canvas.   But of the younger Henrietta Maria's disposition and character nothing is recorded, except that she cared only for needlework and preserves, by which latter taste of her sister's Sophia declares herself to have been the principal gainer. She must, however, have had her share of the delightful vivacity which marked her sisters Louisa Hollandina and Sophia—for the Queen of Bohemia was afterwards vividly reminded of her ways by the irresistible *espièglerie* of the little Elizabeth Charlotte. Largely through the match-making activity and Protestant sympathies of her sister Elizabeth, a marriage was, in 1651, brought about between Henrietta Maria and Prince Sigismund, a younger son of Prince George I of Transylvania, who had died in 1648, after carrying his throne and country safe through eighteen years of peril, first as the ally of Sweden and France, and then under Turkish pressure in friendly relations with Austria. But she died a few months after her outlandish marriage, and was soon followed to the grave by her husband, who did not live to witness the troubles which in the end overwhelmed his brother, the reigning Prince George II.

Such were the brothers and sisters who were the objects of Sophia's unstinted affection in the youthful years of which she has drawn so pleasant a picture and which to her were beyond all doubt the happiest of her life. Nor has she refrained from drawing her own portrait as a young girl, with light-brown hair naturally falling into curls, of gay and unembarrassed manners, of a well-shaped but

not very tall figure, and with the bearing of a
princess. Like most of her family, and especially
like her favourite brother Charles Lewis, whom their
mother the Queen had been wont to call her 'little
black baby,' she had the complexion of a *brunette*.
Even more than by their royal mien and handsome
features, these Palatines were distinguished among
other men and women by the *vis vivida* with which
they were hereditarily endowed. Although, however,
to their mother display was second nature, and
although during her residence in the United Provinces she was in the long run most fortunate in the
bounty, interested or other, of her hosts, yet the
time came when she could not keep more than the
ghost of a Court, and as a matter of fact frequently
found herself in sore straits. In 1645 one of her
sons describes her Court as worried by rats and
mice, but most of all by creditors. And Sophia, who
was still young enough to find even financial difficulties good fun, writes that her mother's banquets
were more sumptuous than Cleopatra's, since in
order to provide them she had sacrificed not only
pearls but diamonds. Yet even the poorest of
royal exiles are rarely left without hangers-on,
moved by the remembrance of past kindness or by
the expectation of favours to come ; and such
Court followers as 'Tom Killigrew,'[1] 'the elder,' as

[1] 'Tom Killigrew is here, who makes a rare relation of the
Queen of Sweden.' (Elizabeth to Sir Edward Nicholas, in

he is usually called, and the ' reverent Dick Harding,'
of whom she often makes humorous mention in her
letters, appear to have clung to the Queen's skirts till
the end of her exile was at hand. But she and her
family had other friends, or at least one other friend,
Lord Craven, whose attachment and devotion were of
the sort that gives rather than takes, so much so that
one can hardly imagine how but for him she would
have tided over her troubles. Of little body, but
with a soul full of generosity, he had gone forth in
1631 to serve under the Swedish deliverer ; and
very soon he had begun to identify himself with the
cause of Elizabeth, and to lay at her feet what he
had saved of the great fortune bequeathed to him
by his father, the Lord Mayor of London.[1] It has
been seen how his sword had been drawn and his
treasure spent in the futile raid upon the Palatinate ;

Evelyn's *Diary and Correspondence*, Vol. iv. p. 216.) Not long
afterwards, in January, 1655, moved perhaps by the remembrance of the sport made by him of Christina, she makes a
humble suit on his behalf to her royal nephew. As late as 1705
Sophia (then Electress Dowager) is found speaking with scant
respect of this ancient and faithful, but somewhat volatile,
Cornish family, the remembrance of whom still survives at
Falmouth. ' Tom Killigrew's' son Robert was anxious to commend himself to the favour of the Electress ; but she left it to her
' posterity ' to attend to his claims. (*Briefe an Hannoverische
Diplomaten*, p. 195.)

[1] The Earl of Craven took his title from the deanery of that
name in Yorkshire, of which his father (Sir William Craven) was
a native. See D. Whitaker, *History and Antiquities of the
Deanery of Craven*, 3rd edn., by A. W. Mount, Leeds and London,
1878.

and now he was back at the Hague paying the homage
of his service to the unfortunate Queen. But Lord
Craven, though at the time little more than forty
years of age and destined to outlive by some thirty-
five the loved Queen of whom an unauthenticated
tradition persists in asserting him to have finally
become the clandestine husband, seemed to Sophia's
disrespectful young eyes merely a kind old gentleman
with a purse full of money, and with a quantity of
little trinkets to bestow upon the young folk. She
appears not to have thought him quite so brilliant
a member of society as it was his wish to be, although
among other things which she heard him say purely
for the sake of effect was the assertion that, when he
chose, it was in his power to think of nothing at all.
Perhaps she shrewdly suspected the *vieux milord*,
as she calls him, of a tender sentiment for her mother ;
perhaps she could not help looking down upon him
as, with all his munificence, a new man ; for the
Palatines were as proud as they were poor.

Of their pride—or at least of that of some of the
members of the family—a lurid illustration is to be
found in an episode of the year 1646 which, tragical
in its results, went far towards creating a permanent
breach between the Queen of Bohemia and some
of her children. Colonel de L'Épinay, formerly a
favourite of the Duke of Orleans, had brought with
him from France to the Hague the reputation of an
homme à bonnes fortunes or lady-killer, something

in the style of the Königsmarck to be mentioned
on a later page of this biography. He had gained
a footing at the Queen of Bohemia's Court, where
probably no very rigorous rules were observed as to
affairs of gallantry ; and here rumour was once more
busy with his supposed triumphs. The Queen of
Bohemia herself was said—it does not appear on
what authority, but the laws of evidence are not
much studied in schools for scandal—to have
looked on him with favour. Her daughter Louisa
Hollandina was, so far as we know, only connected
with de L'Épinay through the malicious pen of
Madame de Longueville, who, on her return from
a visit to Holland, declared that, after casting eyes
on the Princess, she no longer thought that anyone
would envy him his crown of martyrdom. In any
case, the pride of Prince Philip, who may have
known something in France about the earlier adventures of this squire of dames, had taken umbrage
at his actual or rumoured proceedings at the Hague.
A quarrel ensued between the Prince and de L'Épinay;
of which the end was that one evening in June,
Prince Philip, returning home late with a single companion, was assaulted by two Frenchmen, and that,
while defending himself against them, he recognised
de L'Épinay as one of his assailants, and called out
his name. De L'Épinay took to flight ; but meeting
him on the following day in the market-place, Philip
rushed upon him and engaged him in a hand-to-hand

struggle. In this de L'Épinay lost his life. The deed, possibly for more reasons than one, roused the anger of the Queen of Bohemia against her son Philip ; he fled from Holland, and, though Charles Lewis pleaded for him with his mother, she never seems to have been reconciled to him. He was one of the most luckless of the brotherhood. On his leaving Paris, his eldest brother had sought to obtain employment for him under the English Parliament ; but the attempt, doubtless made with the view of strengthening Charles Lewis' own interest in that quarter, proved futile, and the unfortunate Philip was left to his own devices. In 1649, we find him in the company of Charles Lewis (who seems to have had a special kindness for him), on the occasion of the entry of the Elector into the capital town of his diminished patrimony. Philip met with his death in the battle of Rethel in 1650, fighting among the French royalists against Turenne and the Spaniards. On the occasion of the killing of de L'Épinay the Princess Elizabeth appears to have taken her brother Philip's side ; indeed, according to one version of the matter, it was she who had instigated him to commit the fatal deed. In any case, she in 1646 absented herself from her mother's Court and the Low Countries for more than a year ; and, though she seems afterwards to have returned thither for a time and certainly to have been again on good terms with the Queen, her life was henceforth generally led apart from her mother. No deeper sympathy can at any time have existed between them. Princess Louisa Hollandina remained at her mother's Court for eleven years after the de L'Épinay affair, leading, it is stated, an exemplary life, and gradually falling more and more under the dominion of religious ideas very far removed from the sphere of those which came home to her sister Elizabeth.

Not very long after Sophia's introduction to her mother's Court a succession of English visitors were attracted to it, whom the troubles that had broken out on this side of the sea had driven across.[1] In 1642 came Queen Henrietta Maria, to ask assistance from the States-General for King Charles I, and bringing with her the Princess Royal, Mary, the youthful wife of the heir of the House of Orange, upon whom was afterwards to be thrust so important a part in the affairs of her adopted country. By discovering in Sophia a slight resemblance to her own daughter, Madame, Henrietta Maria gratified the authoress of the *Memoirs* so sincerely as to induce her to revise her first criticism of the little Queen of England's charms. More direct compliments were before long paid to Sophia by some of the English

---

[1] One of the members of the Queen of Bohemia's Court in Holland was James Harrington, the author of *Oceana*, a relative of her former guardian, Lord Harington. He had just left Oxford, and afterwards took service under Lord Craven.

lords and gentlemen ; and, as time went on, the English residents at the Hague began to speculate very eagerly upon her chances of securing the hand of no less a personage than her cousin the Prince of Wales, who at the time of his father's confinement in the Isle of Wight (which she spells *Weit*) was about to seek a refuge in Holland. But this scheme, or rumour of a scheme, was strongly resented by the Princess of Orange (Amalia von Solms), whose soaring ambition was intent upon gaining the valuable but not very easily negotiable prize for one of her own daughters. While to Mary, the future Princess of Orange, the Queen of Bohemia's heart seems to have opened with a warmth of feeling which she was not in the habit of manifesting towards her own daughters, a very different sentiment had come to animate her towards Prince Frederick Henry's consort. Upon the favour of her former dependant, who aspired to be in everything but name a Queen, Elizabeth now herself in a sense depended. We cannot, therefore, place implicit trust in the account of the intrigue the *Memoirs* state to have been set on foot by Amalia. If the back-stairs information received by Sophia was correct, the Princess of Orange sought to ruin her young kinswoman's reputation by causing an unmarried son of her own to compromise her by his advances. Though this trick fell through, yet, when the Prince of Wales had reached the Hague in 1648, it soon became evident to the Queen of Bohemia and her daughter that there would not and could not for the present be on his part any question of marriage.

Charles remained in Holland after to him, in his turn, a barren royal title had accrued. When the terrible news of the execution of King Charles I arrived in Holland, it came home with the utmost poignancy to his sister and her family. The younger Elizabeth in particular was almost overwhelmed, physically and mentally, by the catastrophe; and for once the philosophical reflexions of Descartes, which certainly fell short of the occasion, afforded her little or no comfort. The time had of course long passed when any service could be rendered to the Palatine family by the King to whose good offices it had of old looked forward so hopefully; and, in this very year 1648, after two years of weary negotiations, which had almost taken the heart out of the efforts of Charles Lewis and his agents, the Peace of Westphalia had at last restored to him part of his patrimony, with the dignity of Elector. The Lower Palatinate with the fair town of Heidelberg was his once more; but the Upper remained with Bavaria, whose Duke retained the first temporal Electorate, while to the Elector Palatine fell only a newly created eighth. Alike for the Palatine House, and for the Electorate recovered by it, the conditions of the Peace were full of disappointment and humiliation ; but the worst, at all events, had not happened, when there was some danger of its happening ; and Descartes could impress upon his friend and pupil the expediency of her brother's accepting the half-loaf which Fate had bestowed upon him.

In the meantime, the thoughts of Sophia—and perhaps not hers alone in the family—were still turned chiefly in a different direction. When the most enterprising of the followers of ' King Charles II,' the gallant Montrose, early in 1650 started for Scotland with a royal commission, he had, Sophia tells us, resolved on demanding from the King, should the enterprise prove successful, the hand of her sister Louisa Hollandina. Sophia's own chances of securing her royal cousin's hand still formed a subject of speculation ; and, on his return from France in 1650, the Princess of Orange still thought it worth while to influence the Presbyterian leaders among the King's suite (Hamilton and Lauderdale) against Sophia, on the ground that she was a bad Presbyterian and in the habit of accompanying his Majesty to Common Prayer. Sophia was with her mother at Breda, when Charles agreed to take the Covenant. This, she writes, was not the only weakness she observed in him. From the first he had shown her pleasant cousinly attentions ; but of a sudden, at the instigation of certain of his followers who had designs upon Lord Craven's purse and took this roundabout way of seeking to

open its strings, these attentions developed rather
alarmingly.   After some extravagant compliments to
her charms, which he pronounced superior to those of
'Mistress Berlo' (a misspelt *alias* of Lucy Waters), he
informed Sophia that he hoped to see her in England.
But, with the same circumspection in dangerous
situations which she displayed in later years, she
preserved her name free from taint on the occasion
of this trying adventure.   She had, as she says,
wit enough to perceive that this was not the way
in which the marriages of great princes are made,
more especially as at Breda she noticed that 'the
King,' who had previously sought opportunities
of conversing with her, avoided them in the presence
of the Scottish Commissioners.   Thus she in her
turn sagaciously contrived to keep out of his way ;
and this first brief vision of an English throne, which
had probably excited those around her more than it
had moved herself, came to an end.   'King Charles II'
passed out of the horizon of Sophia's hopes and
calculations ; and, when afterwards he returned to
Holland, his prospects were much darker, and she
was no longer resident at her mother's court.

It could hardly be but that this episode, although
it had touched neither her honour nor her heart,
should have made Sophia all the more ready to
quit her mother's court, in which of late years new
troubles had begun to add themselves to old sorrows,
and which was now no longer the centre of the life

of the Palatine family. In 1650 she was evidently
rather tired and out of harmony with a sphere of
existence in which at the outset she had taken so
much pleasure ; and this not so much for any
special reason as because it was gradually borne in
upon her that 'her joy could not endure there.'
Thus it was settled between her and two ladies
in her particular confidence, whom she calls the
Ladies Carray (Carr ?) and Withypol (the latter is
mentioned under the name of ' fraw Wittepole '
as residing in Heidelberg Castle in 1658), and the
good Lord Craven, that she should try a change
of scene and life by starting in their company to pay
a visit to her brother, the restored Elector Palatine,
at Heidelberg. At first her mother the Queen
objected, still clinging to the fancy of a match
between her youngest daughter and the head of the
House of Stewart. At last, however, she acquiesced
on being assured that this consummation would not
be prevented by the proposed journey ; and so,
borrowing a vessel from the friendly States of
Holland, Sophia, who was now in her twentieth
year, and whose travels had hitherto not extended
beyond an occasional jaunt to Leyden, Delft, or
Rheenen, in the summer of 1650 set forth on her
voyage up the Rhine towards Heidelberg and the
unknown.

II

EARLY WOMANHOOD AND MARRIAGE

A HOME, to which Elizabeth of Bohemia was
fated never to return, was opened to her daughter
Sophia. For eight years—from 1650 to 1658—
she was the guest of her beloved brother Charles
Lewis in that part of the Palatinate which had been
at last restored to the family in his person. To
these congenial surroundings she easily acclimatised
herself; nor did she ever afterwards forget how,
before her destiny at last bore her away from Heidelberg and its familiar neighbourhood, the interests
of her maiden life had long centred in the affairs of her
brother, in his troubles both public and private,
and in his children, for whom her large heart never
ceased to cherish a peculiar tenderness, even after
the welfare of her own numerous family had become
the chief anxiety of her existence. She was not at
first aware that her departure from Holland had
been against her mother's wish—a fact which she
discreetly passes over in her *Memoirs*.[1] After telling

[1] Charles Lewis wrote to his mother in much trouble on the

of her leisurely journey along the route formerly
followed by her parents on their wedding journey
home, she graphically describes the forlorn poverty
which stared her in the face, when she first
entered her brother's shrunken dominions. He and
his Electress met her at Mannheim and took her
on with them to Heidelberg, where the castle still
lay in ruins, and they had to lodge in the town.

In truth, the Lower Palatinate had barely begun
to recover from the tribulations which it had undergone both in the earlier and in the later periods
of the Thirty Years' War; and the population was
literally the merest fragment of what it had been
before the outbreak of the conflict—one-fiftieth
part of it, according to a calculation which it seems
almost impossible to accept. Moreover, Charles
Lewis only gradually recovered possession even of
the moiety of his patrimony allotted to him, nor
was it till 1652 that the last Spaniard quitted the
land. It is all the more to the honour of this Prince,
and in a measure atones for the grievous aberrations
of his private life, that after his restoration he should
have held his head high in the Electoral College,
to which, as his father's son, he had been so
grudgingly readmitted; and still more, that during
the whole of his rule—which lasted till 1680—he

subject, only eliciting the reply that ' as for Sophia's journey,
I will never keep anie that has a minde to leave me, for I shall
never care for anie bodies companie that does not care for
mine.' *Letters*, &c., ed. A. Wendland, p. 9.

should have spared neither thought nor effort for the welfare of his sorely tried subjects.

It was not his fault that, while engaged in these beneficent labours, he had again and again to turn the pruning-hook back into a sword.[1] In 1666, he maintained a brave heart through his weary campaigning against French and Lorrainers, although he met with little luck under arms and suffered severely in health. Five years later, he sacrificed the happiness of his daughter Elizabeth Charlotte by yielding to the French demand for her hand, and went near to sacrificing his honour by allowing her, against her own wish or disposition, to be converted to the Church of Rome. When, in 1674, the first of the wars between the Empire and France broke out, Charles Lewis may have indulged in some passing dreams of an Austrasian kingdom under French supremacy ; as a matter of fact, he found that neither the Orleans marriage nor his exertions to remain neutral protected his unhappy lands

---

[1] The celebrated *Wildfangsstreit*, which was carried on by Charles Lewis in the years 1665 and 1666, is passed by in the text, where few readers would probably care to find it discussed. This strange dispute turned on the rights of the Electors Palatine over bastards and aliens (*Wilden*) in their own and *adjoining* territories, and troubles which had thence arisen between Charles Lewis and his neighbours, in which the Great Elector of Brandenburg was involved through his alliance of May, 1661, with the Elector Palatine. The Great Elector's efforts brought about a settlement on the whole favourable to his ally. (See *Urkunden und Aktenstücke zur Gesch. d. Grossen Kurfürsten Friedrich Wilhelm von Brandenburg*, Vol. xi. (*Polit. Verhandl.* Vol. vii.). Ed. F. Hirsch, Berlin, 1887).

from invasion and its attendant horrors. Things
went better when, in 1675, he had thrown in his
lot with the Empire; for there can have been no
truth in the rumours which made themselves heard
in the city of gossip, Venice, that his father's son
was aiming at the Bohemian Crown. The troubles
of the Palatinate recommenced when, in 1679–80,
the French added to pretended reprisals the monstrous mockery of the so-called *réunions;* but of
these Charles Lewis only survived to see the beginnings, and he was spared the bitterness of witnessing
the devastation of his beloved Palatinate in the
so-called Orleans War, of which his own daughter's
supposed claims were, to her unspeakable anguish,
made the pretext. For the rest, the Elector Charles
Lewis was a genuine son of the Palatinate, to which
he devoted so much care and labour; he loved its
good things, including the Bacharach wine, whose
praises he sang in homely dithyrambs, and the
wealth of choice fruit, mindful of which he denounced
the sour pears and bullet grapes outside his own
promised land. Like his daughter after him, he was
nowhere so happy as in the midst of it, and his very
diction is coloured with a proverbial phraseology
of native Palatinate growth. As late as 1665, he is
found declaring that if ten years more of life were
granted him, and no war or pestilence came in
the way, he would, *en despit de l'envie,* turn Mannheim into a second Rome. Nor were his thoughts

only set upon material things ; whether justly or
not, he was regarded as one of the most learned
princes of his age ; he was consistently anxious to
revive the prosperity of the University of Heidelberg, and had nearly crowned his efforts on its
behalf by securing Spinoza as one of its teachers.
The education of his own children was to him a
subject of anxious and minute care.[1] In his youth,
the evil times on which Charles Lewis had fallen had
(it is not uncharitable to assume) taught him to
dissimulate ; but in his later years he had retained
little of the Puritan associations of his earlier manhood except a love of the Bible and a hatred of
Rome, and of priests and priestcraft in general.
He was, in short, a most liberal-minded and tolerant
Prince, who found satisfaction in the *Imitatio Christi*
as well as in the New Testament, who would gladly
have made his Palatinate a refuge for persecuted
adherents of any religious creed, and whose dedica-
tion, not long before his death, of a church (at
Mannheim) to *Sancta Concordia* was far from being

---

[1] He drew up elaborate instructions for the tutors and
governesses of the Electoral Prince Charles and Princess
Elizabeth Charlotte. One of the former was Ezechiel Spanheim,
who had accompanied his father, a rigid Calvinist, when the
latter had been summoned to Leyden by Elizabeth and the
States-General. Ezechiel was himself called from Geneva in
1656 to Heidelberg, where he afterwards passed from theology
to diplomacy. It was in the Brandenburg service, which he had
entered in 1680, that he was accredited to the English Court,
of which he wrote an *Account* (1706). He was buried in Westminster Abbey.

an empty pretence. He had, moreover, inherited his mother's taste for poetry, and during his sojourn in England had acquired considerable familiarity with its literature, and its drama in particular. In a way it brings Sophia herself nearer to us that her favourite brother freely quoted Shakespeare, that a version by him of Ben Jonson's *Sejanus* was acted at Heidelberg, and that he was so sturdy a critic as to pronounce the Spanish drama superior to the French, but the English best of all.

But, heavy as were the burdens laid upon the head of the Palatine House after Charles Lewis' partial restoration, the troubles that came nearest home to him, and that in the end infected the whole atmosphere of his court, were of his own making. He cannot be held accountable for the financial difficulties which obliged him to discourage his mother's desire to return to the Palatinate ; and, even before the troubles in question broke out, more general considerations may have rendered him the reverse of eager for her presence. His policy was to bury the past, which she in a sense typified ; and he may have feared her extravagant ways, and thus preferred to lighten her expenditure by inviting his sisters Elizabeth and Sophia to his capital. His offer of some rooms in the *Ottheinrichs-bau* of Heidelberg Castle, which he could not afford to furnish, failed to attract, and the hope which she had cherished, that she might end her days in her

own good dowry town of Frankenthal, it was not in
his power to fulfil. Meanwhile, the compensation
for the temporary occupation of the place by the
Spaniards, which had been promised in the Nürnberg
settlement of 1651, supplementary to the Peace of
Westphalia, remained unpaid by the Emperor.
Charles Lewis, who had in the first instance to think
of his Electorate and its defences, was without
resources enabling him to respond to his mother's
requirements ; and the recriminations which followed on her part left the situation unaltered. Even
before mother and son had been at odds on this
subject, there was a dispute between them as to
various heirlooms at the Hague and at Rheenen,
which she refused to give up to him as he demanded.
In short, their correspondence had reached a most
painful stage, and it is pitiful to read the description
of the sore straits to which she found herself reduced,
just when the cloud seemed to be at last lifting from
the fortunes of their House. She was, she wrote,
entirely dependent upon the monthly allowance of
the States-General ; it amounted only to a thousand
florins, and was not made for more than a single
year, and she had only accepted it as a *pis aller*
when she found it out of the question that her claims
on payments from England should be made part
of the Anglo-Dutch treaty concluded in 1654. As a
matter of fact, her case was a very hard one ; for her
creditors had never been so pressing as now, when

there seemed a chance of payment; the very heirs
of the faithful Ludwig Camerarius demanded
the redemption of a favourite jewel which she had
pawned to them; all her children were in debt
like herself, from the high-minded Elizabeth to the
volatile Edward; and it is touching to find her
entreating a loan of a thousand pounds for the purpose, because the jewel 'was my brother Prince
Henry's.' At an earlier date, Charles Lewis had
suggested to an agent that it would be desirable
for her to approach Cromwell as to the relief of her
creditors, but was told in reply that she would
certainly never do this, ' but only break into passion
against those that should give such advice.' So
matters went on till other reasons came to a head
which made the Elector undesirous of receiving her
at his Court; and his seeming ingratitude infused
another drop of bitterness in her cup.

The quarrel between Charles Lewis and his
brother Rupert, which became mixed up with the
cardinal trouble of the elder brother's later years,
and caused great sorrow to their mother, had its
origin in the financial difficulties which beset them all.
In 1653, the Elector had settled a modest allowance
on his brother Edward, and in 1654 he made a
similar arrangement with Rupert, who on his
arrival in Paris had entered into negotiations on the
subject through the Palatine envoy, Pawel von
Rammingen. Rupert was to be allowed 2,500

dollars *per annum*, to rise after five years to 4,000,
while the Emperor agreed to pay him a substantial
sum under the Nürnberg settlement. But Rupert
could not sit down contented with this compact,
and, quite in the spirit still prevailing in many of the
princely Houses of Germany, demanded a share of
the Palatinate territory as his younger brother's
portion. Charles Lewis at first dallied with the
proposal, which, however, could not be to his mind,
more especially as he had no wish for introducing
into his Electorate the permanent influence of so
martial and combative a spirit as his brother's.
Rupert, however, insisted on his demand, and in
1656, after refusing to receive any further payments
of his allowance, asked for an immediate interview.
The Elector having declined to receive him at Heidelberg, but offered to meet him at Neustadt, and in
the meantime to increase his allowance, the fiery
Prince repaired uninvited to the capital, and, having
been refused admittance to the castle by the colonel
in command, swore an angry oath that he would
never return to the Palatinate, and passed on to
Mainz. Here he proceeded to lay his grievances
before the Arch-Chancellor of the Empire, and then
offered his sword to the Emperor. But, though he
seems to have actually entered into the Imperial
service, he found its atmosphere uncongenial, and,
when in 1661 he made another attempt to obtain a
high command (in the Turkish War) and at the same

time to obtain payment of the sums promised him under the Nürnberg settlement, he was unsuccessful. This failure he ascribed to the intrigues of his brother the Elector, and he now settled down after a fashion in England, whither he had betaken himself on the Restoration. Though it was not till later that the brothers were again on good terms, the dispute between them was settled in 1670, when the arrangement of 1654 was put into force again, Rupert's allowance being, however, raised from 4,000 to 6,000 dollars, the balance of the Nürnberg compensation paid over, and the Rheenen property being given up to him—an old notion of his mother's, which he had formerly rejected.[1]

At the time when Charles Lewis' quarrel with Rupert broke out, the elder brother was in the midst of a difficulty which, unlike those just described, was essentially of his own making. Of this trouble Sophia's quick wit had, already on arrival at Mannheim, and first meeting with her brother the Elector and his bride, detected the germs. She had perceived at once that all was not well between the pair. While her brother met her with his usual geniality of manner, the Electress,

---

[1] In 1655 she writes to Charles Lewis that she had sent him all that she could spare in the house there, and entreats him at the same time to dismiss the concierge, 'for he is the veriest beast in the world and knave besides.' See *Letters*, &c., ed. A. Wendland, p. 67.—J have revised my account of the dispute between Charles Lewis and Rupert with the aid of K. Hauck, *Karl Ludwig, Kurfürst von der Pfalz*, pp. 251 *sqq.*

whose mien was *fort dolente,* said very little.   When
the party proceeded to Heidelberg, where Sophia
had the satisfaction of seating herself in the best-
appointed carriage on which she had cast eyes since
her departure from the Hague, she found that her
praise of this vehicle gave offence to her sister-in-law,
to whom it had been presented as her wedding-
coach, and in whose opinion it was vastly inferior
to one presented to her sister for her marriage with
the Prince of Tarento.   This afflicting comparison
was, however, only the first and slightest clause in
her long litany of grievances.

Charlotte Elizabeth, daughter of Landgrave
William V of Hesse-Cassel, and his wife, Amalia
Elizabeth, seemed marked out by descent as a most
fitting consort for the restored Elector Palatine.
Her grandfather, Landgrave Maurice, had in his day
been one of the foremost representatives of militant
Calvinism, and at once the boldest and the most
steadfast of all the Princes of the Union.   Her
mother, the Landgravine Amalia, deserves lasting
remembrance as one of the most remarkable Princesses of her age, by whose exertions Hesse-Cassel was
preserved from ruin in the Thirty Years' War, and
to whom more than to anyone German Calvinism
owed the rights of parity at last secured to it in the
Peace of Westphalia.   But her married life with the
Elector Charles Lewis, which began in February, 1650,
proved a singularly unhappy one ; nor can there

H

be any pretence but that she was made to suffer grievous and intolerable wrong. It is at the same time undeniable that the aggravating elements in her character—to Sophia's critical eye there seemed to be such even in her beauty—contributed to the beginning of the end. Sophia rapidly arrived at her own conclusions as to the intellectual capacity of her sister-in-law—what with her love of dress and her stories of Duke Frederick of Würtemberg-Neustadt, not to mention the Brunswick-Lüneburg Dukes, George William and Ernest Augustus, and several other admirers, to whom she had been forced by her mother to prefer her present jealous ' old ' husband. In his turn, Charles Lewis, although he far too demonstratively adored his handsome wife, confessed that there were defects in her education, which he entreated his shrewd youngest sister to correct. Very soon, however, Sophia perceived that the comedy was taking a serious turn. The quarrel between the pair began with an outburst of jealousy on the part of the Elector, followed, in more violent fashion, by another from the Electress. Charles Lewis hereupon became violently estranged from his consort ; and his aversion was deepened by a passion which he conceived for one of his wife's maids-of-honour, Baroness Louisa von Degenfeld. Perhaps this more decorous Anne Boleyn was rendered all the more attractive in his eyes by her literary turn of mind, if we may judge from their initial correspondence under names borrowed from an Italian novel,[1] and from the liking which she afterwards showed for such classics as Lucian, Corneille, and Molière. For some years or so, however, the husband and wife rubbed on together, two children being born to them. The elder, born 1651, was Charles, afterwards Elector Palatine, the last of the Simmern line, who died less than five years after his father (1685) ; had he survived, he must of course have stood before Sophia in the English Succession. In most respects he had little character of his own, perhaps partly because he had been over-educated ; but he was a devout Calvinist, and would probably have remained such had it been his fate to mount the throne to which, in earlier times, some of the English Parliamentary politicians may have thought of raising his father. The younger of the two children, born 1652, was Elizabeth Charlotte, the *Liselotte* of her father's affections and of those of her aunt Sophia, by whom she was partly brought up, and a darling of whose later years she became.

For a time the Elector contrived to conceal his amour from his wife ; but, in 1657, a letter addressed by Prince Rupert to the Elector's mistress, by whose

---

[1] This was quite in the style of the age, which loved the mystifications of pseudonyms, and of ciphers without much concealment. Elizabeth mentions that her daughter Sophia writes to her about Berenice's business (Sophia's own), and that they are discussing it with Tiribazus (Charles Lewis). *Letters*, &c., p. 91.

beauty and wit he seems to have been attracted on a previous visit, having fallen into the hands of the Electress, and the quarrel between the brothers having probably contributed to exacerbate matters, there was an end of the secret. Put on the track of her husband's infidelity, the Electress ruthlessly ran him and his mistress to earth ; and the result was a public scandal without an equal in the domestic annals of this anything but shamefaced age. The Elector having at last withdrawn from Heidelberg with Louisa von Degenfeld, whom he in the first instance settled with many precautions at Schwetzingen, there ensued a long and disgraceful series of proceedings which, to the unfortunate Electress, must have recalled a notorious episode of her native Hessian history in the days of Landgrave Philip the 'Magnanimous.' Salving his conscience as best he might with the obsequious assistance of his court divines, Charles Lewis, early in 1658, married Louisa von Degenfeld as his second wife. He had previously conferred upon her the ancient title of Raugravine Palatine, with a provision that a corresponding titulature was to be transmitted to their issue. From this abnormal union, which lasted till Louisa's decease, twenty years afterwards, there sprang not less than fourteen children, of whom eight survived their mother. The marriage—if marriage it may be called [1]—supplied

---

[1] It is, Elizabeth plainly told her son, ' both against God's law and man's law.' *Letters*, &c., p. 92.

him with the felicities of a tranquil home, though for some time he had to keep watch over it with an anxious care, of which the humorous aspect escaped him, against the evil designs imputed by him to ' X,' his repudiated wife, and though her Hessian relations long endeavoured to assert her rights. Latterly the ' second wife ' seems chiefly to have resided with her children at Frankenthal, where the proud Queen of Bohemia had hoped to find repose for her last years. The correspondence between Charles Lewis and Louisa shows him to have been entirely faithful to her, and to have passionately loved his children. But, though his fidelity to his chosen companion was unswerving, the relations between them were disturbed by occasional dissensions. On her death he put forth, together with an account of her Christian ending drawn up by the divine whom he had originally consulted as to his ' second marriage ' (Hiskias Eleazar Heiland), an elaborate analytical statement of her virtues and shortcomings during their union, for which, with a conscientiousness showing that there was still a drop of Calvinistic blood in his veins, he had himself contributed the most important materials. For his children, the surviving Raugraves and Raugravines, he had intended to make ample provision, but had perplexed himself so much about its conditions, that his legitimate son and successor, the Elector Charles, declared all his father's arrangements on the subject

invalid. Several of the sons afterwards distinguished themselves in the field. Charles Maurice,
who was till his death in 1702 a familiar figure at
Hanover, and who is the Trimalchio of the banquet
' after the manner of the ancients ' described in
Leibniz's correspondence with Sophia, drank away
his remarkable intellectual powers. But the children
of Louisa von Degenfeld were treated kindly by
the Dowager Electress Charlotte, and Sophia took
them one and all to her heart, more especially
the two sisters Louisa and Amalia, ' *les deux sibylles
de Francfort*.' Louisa was in later years at Hanover
appointed Mistress of the Robes; and it is said that
there was at one time some intention of entrusting her
with a confidential mission to England in connexion
with the Succession question.

After the death, in 1677, of Louisa von Degenfeld,
Charles Lewis, having in the first instance (with
Sophia's approval) taken to himself a mistress,
was desirous of inducing the Electress to consent
to a divorce, which would have enabled him by a
' third ' marriage to seek to secure the Succession of
his (the Simmern) line, resting as it did on the life
of his legitimate son Charles only.[1] But Charlotte Elizabeth was not found ready to oblige her
erratic husband thus far. Prince Rupert, with

---

[1] The Queen of Bohemia was very anxious about her grandson, in whose early days she had recorded with satisfaction
that the little Prince of Orange (William III) was a year older,
but considerably smaller in size.

whom Charles Lewis had gradually come to be on better terms, had already, in 1675, declined to come to the rescue. The match-making Princess Elizabeth had in vain desired a match between her brother Rupert and her young kinswoman Princess Charlotte Sophia of Courland.[1]   That young lady's aunt, Landgravine Hedwig Sophia of Mecklenburg-Schwerin, opined that nothing would come of the match, especially as Prince Rupert was on the lookout ' not only for beauty, but for means.' As a matter of fact, the ardour of Rupert's aspiring youth had by this time settled down into a sober though still singularly active maturity ; moreover, he had formed a connexion so close that it has been suspected to have amounted to a secret marriage, with Francesca Bard, an Irish Roman Catholic lady of good birth, with whom and their child, called ' Dodley ' (Dudley) by Sophia, the indulgent Palatine family were on friendly terms. But neither this boy nor, of course, Ruperta, Prince Rupert's daughter by the actress Margaret Hughes, was ever formally acknowledged by him ; and thus this brother, too, left no descendant who, when the time came, might have forestalled the claims of Sophia and her progeny to the English Succession.

Sophia's own life at Heidelberg, though much clouded by her brother's domestic troubles, of which more than enough has now been said, and towards

---

[1] She died at an advanced age as Abbess of Herford.

which, in its initial stages, she appears to have
borne herself with a discretion already habitual to
her, was by no means without its agreeable aspects.
It had at first been made uncomfortable by the
ways of the Electress Charlotte, whose favourite
amusements, field sports and the card-table, were
not much to Sophia's personal taste. Still, the life
of the Palatine court, though an economy little
dreamt of in former days now prevailed there, was
not without diversions in which she took pleasure—
among them those *Wirthschaften*, a fashionable
amusement half-way between a fancy fair and a
bal costumé, of which the Queen of Bohemia had
shared the vogue in Holland. Mention has already.
been made of Charles Lewis' familiarity with the
literature of the English stage ; and the English
comedians whom he saw at Frankfort possibly
also found their way to Heidelberg. But his sisters
had more direct opportunities for keeping up their
interest in England and things English, since
Charles Lewis seems to have entertained a good
many English gentlemen at his capital, where some
of them settled down as they have done in later
days. Among his English guests was the former
Parliamentary General, Sir William Waller, though
with the Restoration Charles Lewis became a good
Royalist again, and contrived to put himself on good
terms with Lord Chancellor Clarendon. We have
already seen how Prince Rupert himself was an

occasional visitor at Heidelberg, as was his younger
brother Edward—though the latter proved so full
of '*ralierie*' that Charles Lewis refused to take him
to visit the lady whom he wished to be regarded
as his wedded wife.   Before this, Princess Elizabeth had, in 1648 and again in 1651, arrived
as a visitor at the Electoral Court—much changed,
as on the latter occasion Sophia and Edward thought,
both in outward appearance and in tone of mind,
which Sophia expressly attributes to her recent
sojourn at Berlin, at the Court of the pious Electress
Louisa Henrietta.   Perhaps, too, she was saddened
by the death of Descartes (1650), and perhaps by a
growing estrangement from her mother ;   in any
case, her whole nature was more and more tending
towards that contemplative life whose attractiveness for some minds seems so incomprehensible
to others.   Unfortunately, as Sophia confesses,
she was weak enough to join her brother and sister-
in-law in rebelling against a certain air of superiority
which in their eyes Elizabeth seemed to assume.
She warmly interested herself in the Elector's
efforts to give a new life to the University of Heidelberg, where she is said to have acquired a personal
reputation by her exposition of the Cartesian
philosophy. Sophia's day for listening to the
conversation of philosophers had hardly yet arrived,
and she at no time aspired to place herself on what
may be called the professorial level.   There is no

appearance of the two sisters having been permanently alienated from one another; but mutual sympathy could not otherwise than dwindle between one who was preparing to bid farewell to the world, and one who was intent upon establishing her position in it.

The real reason of Sophia's quitting Holland had been her sense of the uncertainty of her own position there; yet, even had the prospect been wholly agreeable, she could not now look forward to a permanent residence at the strangely distracted Court of her eldest brother. As the solitude of a religious, or of a quasi-religious, life would not have been to her mind (though it was about this time that she sat for her portrait in the costume of a Vestal Virgin), a suitable marriage engagement had, in a word, become a necessity for her. So attractive and high-spirited a princess might fairly expect to find an acceptable husband without having, like her sister Henrietta Maria, to espouse a Transylvanian prince. Unluckily, in the latter part of 1651 or beginning of 1652, Sophia underwent an attack of small-pox, which, as she confesses, seriously impaired her beauty. But she had no mind to take whoever might be the first comer; and not long after her recovery she declined overtures made to her on behalf of the Portuguese Duke of Aveiro; 'having had thoughts of marrying a King she could not stoop to a subject.' In much the same mood she about this time broke off an innocent correspondence (on the subject of compositions for the guitar) into which she had entered with a prince with whom she had in her childhood made acquaintance in Holland, and who, when recently passing through Heidelberg on his way to Venice, had seemed to her more charming than ever. This prince, who ' pleased everybody,' was no other than her future husband, Duke Ernest Augustus of Brunswick-Lüneburg. Since, however, he was the youngest of four brothers and (as will be seen immediately) without any present prospect whatever of enjoying any territorial dominion of his own, he was clearly not *bon à marier ;* and it was best to avoid a kind of gossip of which Sophia had only too vivid an experience.

There appears to have been some talk of other matches for Sophia, and above all of a design of marrying her to a more important personage than the disinherited King of England—the young King of the Romans, who, as such, during the last year of his life bore the designation of Ferdinand IV.[1] It is true that, in 1652, the Elector Charles Lewis had, on the occasion of his being received by the Emperor Ferdinand III within the unconscious walls of Prague, established excellent relations between the Imperial House and himself. But it

---

[1] A match between his grandfather, afterwards Emperor Ferdinand II, and Sophia's great-aunt on the mother's side, Princess Hedwig of Denmark, had been suggested in 1617.

is difficult to suppose that anything could have come of this scheme, which would have involved as a preliminary transaction the conversion of Sophia to the Church of Rome ; and the statement that the young King of the Romans had fallen in love with Sophia, and intended to marry her, rests only on the authority of the Duchess of Orleans. Charles Lewis might, in the interests of the Palatinate, have assented to the match ; but Sophia would assuredly have refused it with more determination than was afterwards shown by her niece when the Orleans marriage proposal was pressed upon her. The earlier project, however, came to a speedy end with the death of the young Roman King in 1654.

Thus the first suitor proper of Sophia during her stay at her brother's Court was Prince Adolphus John, brother of the newly crowned King of Sweden, Charles X Gustavus, and like him a scion of the Zweibrücken line of the Palatine House. Though he had no prospects of the throne, he was, as his subsequent conduct at a critical moment after his great brother's death showed, an ambitious prince, and his suit was favoured by the Electress Charlotte, who would have been pleased to be rid of her sister-in-law. But Sophia looked very coolly on the negotiations that ensued ; for she had conceived an aversion to this suitor, which she declares could only have been conquered by a virtuous effort. He was a widower, and was said to have ill-treated his first wife. Fortunately for Sophia, the difficulty of marrying a princess who had been trained as a Calvinist into a rigidly Lutheran land, stood in the way of the proposal ; and, though the match was announced with much satisfaction to Secretary Nicholas by the Queen of Bohemia for the information of King Charles II, the negotiations were still incomplete, and the King of Sweden's approval of his brother's offer in doubt, when the likelihood of another proposal intervened. The House of Brunswick-Lüneburg, this time in the person of George William, the second of the brothers between whom its territorial inheritance was divided, now appeared upon the scene. It will be more convenient to review at a rather later point the general position and prospects of the House of Brunswick-Lüneburg at the time when Sophia definitively threw in her lot with its destinies, and when the first step was thus taken towards its acquiring an interest in the question of the English Succession. At the time of his visit to Heidelberg, in 1656, George William, afterwards the ruler of the Lüneburg-Celle portion of the paternal inheritance, held the Calenberg-Göttingen portion, and resided at Hanover. He had recently been urged to marry by his Estates, who were anxious to avert any likelihood of blending the several divisions of the family inheritance ; and, though he had always felt the strongest repugnance to any such step, much preferring to a married life the Venetian pleasures of bachelorhood, he now thought of giving way to the Estates, if they would in return vote an increase in his revenue. George William and his brother Ernest Augustus were united by an intimacy and affection as close as that which in the next generation tied the namesake of the latter to his eldest brother George Lewis (George I) ; and there is every probability that it was the report of Ernest Augustus after his earlier visit which induced George William to make preliminary enquiries through an agent, George Christopher von Hammerstein, who was much in the confidence of the dynasty. Hereupon he paid a visit to Heidelberg in person, but accompanied by his favourite youngest brother. George William's attentions to Sophia were well received ; and though (for the painful reasons to be indicated below) she could never have been brought to confess it in her *Memoirs*, her heart seems to have been really touched ; and it may be added that, through all the vicissitudes which ensued, she retained a kindly feeling towards him. As for the present, she allows that when at last he requested her permission to ask her hand from her brother, she failed to answer like a heroine in romance, ' for I did not hesitate to say Yes.' Probably what attracted her in George William, whose political principles must at the time have been a matter of indifference to her, while she could not, like King William III in later days, have much sympathised with his love of hunting and of a good glass of wine, was the comparative refinement of manners which distinguished both him and his younger brothers among the German princes of the day. Though two of the Brunswick-Lüneburg Dukes afterwards came to be known as resolute opponents of the political designs of France, yet George William and Ernest Augustus, as well as their brother John Frederick, belonged to the new school of German princes, who loved the society and cultivated the fashion and manners of Frenchmen, and who with more or less of success sought to model their Courts on Versailles. This fact should not be overlooked ; for patriotic Englishmen (especially when in Opposition) afterwards made a constant point of deriding the unrefined Teutonism of the Hanoverian Court. At the same time, George William's frequent visits to Italy, and especially to Venice, cost a great deal of money to the Estates of his principality ; and they were accordingly anxious that he should arrive at a settlement, while he, with a view to the bargain proving to his advantage, kept the engagement to which the Elector Palatine had assented as secret as possible. Of a sudden there came from Venice, whither the brothers had proceeded after their visit to Heidelberg, the unexpected and mortifying news that George William, who had been leading a loose life at Venice, had found it necessary to break off his engagement. Sophia, though 'too proud to be touched,' thus found herself placed in a most cruel position. Who can say what in these circumstances might have been the result of an offer made to her on behalf of Ranuccio II, Duke of Parma (dependent, of course, upon her previous conversion), had not her Hanoverian suitor shown himself most anxious to do what in him lay to remedy the wrong which he had inflicted on her? He now proposed that his youngest brother Ernest Augustus should marry her in his stead, taking over with her the principalities at present held by George William, and in return only promising to pay to the latter a comfortable pension. But to this arrangement the third of the four brothers, John Frederick, a prince of much ambition as well as obstinacy of character, very naturally objected as unfair to his own interests, and a serious illness which had befallen Ernest Augustus further delayed proceedings. Thus it was not till 1658 that the transaction was actually carried out, though on lines somewhat different from those first contemplated. Sophia's hand was transferred from Duke George William to Duke Ernest Augustus, the former undertaking to remain unmarried during the lifetime of his brother and his consort, and in that of any male heirs whom they might leave behind them. This renunciation, for which there were several precedents in the annals of the House of Brunswick-Lüneburg and doubtless

in that of other German princely houses also,[1] is
set forth at length in the original German in Sophia's
Memoirs, though even she could not when copying
it out be aware of the full significance which it
possessed for the future of the family. She knew,
however, that of her husband's three brothers the
eldest was childless and the third still unmarried,
while the second had renounced the prospect of
lawful issue. The possibilities of future importance
which her marriage now open to her husband and
herself were, therefore, wholly due to the arrangement by which this marriage was accompanied. The
renunciation of George William contained in it the
germ of the greatness which awaited the line founded
in his stead by his brother ; while the consequences
of the fact that his promise was half broken, half
kept, clouded the initial stage of that greatness with
the shame of a terrible family catastrophe. Sophia
dwells on the weakness and inconstancy of George
William in yielding to the demands of his councillors
that he should reduce the handsome yearly allowance
promised by him to his brother ; unhappily, as she
hints, the same defects were to be exhibited by him
in matters of far greater gravity.

Sophia's engagement to Ernest Augustus was for
a time kept secret from her mother ; but she seems
to have borne the pair no malice, and to have

---

[1] According to Spittler, not less than six of the uncles of
George William (brothers of Duke George) promised to remain
unmarried.

I

sent her blessing in due course, with congratulatory letters from King Charles, in English to the bride, and in Latin to the bridegroom.[1]

The Elector Charles Lewis, however, who acted in the place of a father to his sister, found the expenses of her marriage weigh heavily upon his reduced finances. ' Besides her due,' he wrote to the Queen, his mother, by way of excusing himself for being ' uncapable of what her Majesty was pleased to require of him,' ' I am bound to an extraordinary, more especially for the friendship she always shewed me, and because nobody else hath done anything for her.' Sophia tells us that on Ernest Augustus' arrival for the wedding she found him lovable, because she had made up her mind to love him ; and something of this resolute spirit of attachment may, in the face of many provocations to the contrary, be said to have characterised her relations to him through-out their married life. According to Leibniz, the wedding took place towards the end of September, 1658 ; but, according to a contemporary authority cited by Sophia's biographer, Feder, the date was October 17th of that year. She describes the wed-ding solemnities, which, if not so magnificent or appealing so persuasively to the imagination as those of her mother on the banks of the Thames, showed the Palatine House to be equal to itself in the maintenance of a stately etiquette. A few days

---

[1] *Letters*, &c., ed. A. Wendland, p. 100.

afterwards he posted back to Hanover, and she soon
followed, attended by an ample escort which he
had provided for her. The indispensable Hammerstein conducted the journey, on which her brother,
the Elector, accompanied her as far as Weinheim.
She held her entry into Hanover on November 19th,
being received by the whole family, her mother-
in-law, the Duchess Anna Eleonora (widow of
Duke George), at its head. On her wedding-day
Sophia had, like her niece Charlotte Elizabeth on
her subsequent marriage with the Duke of Orleans,
renounced any future claims to the Succession in the
Palatinate, unconscious of the remoter claims which
she was to owe indirectly to her Palatine, as well as
directly to her English, blood. But, though she
dearly loved her brother, and shed a few tears on
parting from him, they would, as she declares, have
flowed more abundantly had her heart not been
with her husband, and, as we may add, had not her
hopes rested on the future which she went forth
to meet by his side.

While to Sophia, at an age of life neither late
nor very early—for she was near concluding her
twenty-eighth year—married life thus opened with
its duties, cares, and consolations, it was otherwise
with the two sisters of whom she has told us most,
and whose life was likewise to be prolonged beyond
the period of early womanhood. (Her third sister,

Henrietta Maria, had died already in 1661.) Both of them, by a singular dispensation of fate, at a time not far removed from that of her marriage, embraced a religious life, though in two different communions ; each was to end her days as the abbess of a conventual establishment, revered and beloved in no ordinary measure by those around her. Since Sophia's marriage, though it cannot be said to have estranged her from either of these sisters, concentrated her interests upon spheres of activity from which theirs were in the main or altogether removed, the present may be the most appropriate place for recalling the twofold picture of their later lives, whose tranquillity contrasts so strangely with the agitations with which hers was necessarily filled.

The Princess Elizabeth, whom we have seen more or less absorbed in her own high thoughts and ennobling pursuits while still a resident at her mother's Court in Holland, and again actively interested in the learned studies for which the rule of her brother, the Elector, had once more provided a home at Heidelberg, remained behind in the Palatinate for some three or four years after Sophia's marriage. They cannot have been happy years, for the scandal of the Elector's second union was now at its height, and the Electress, on whose side, whatever Charlotte's faults of temper, her sister-in-law's high sense of moral rectitude could not fail to range her, still held out, perhaps chiefly for the sake of the

Electoral children.[1] When, in 1662, the Electress, her own efforts and those of her kinsfolk having proved vain, at last left Heidelberg for Cassel, Elizabeth followed her thither. In the preceding year her attached cousin, the Elector Frederick William, had named her Coadjutress of the Abbess of Herford, and her ultimate destiny was thus assured. The six years (or the greater part of them) which intervened before she succeeded the Countess Palatine Elizabeth Louisa as Abbess of the Westphalian convent were peacefully spent by her at Cassel, in the society of the Landgravine Hedwig Sophia, a daughter of her aunt, the Electress of Brandenburg, and herself a lady of strong religious feeling and, as her administration of her dower - estate of Schmalkalden showed, a determined Calvinist. Elizabeth's own Calvinism, it is interesting to note, had, already before she settled for the remainder of her days at Herford, assumed a peculiar hue. She seems

---

[1] In 1660 and the following year there is a good deal of talk and solemn banter between Dr. Worthington and his correspondent S. Hartlib as to the expected arrival in England of the Princess Elizabeth with her mother. Dr. (Henry) More is repeatedly referred to as specially interested in the hoped-for event. On May 28th, 1661, however, Hartlib reports a profane piece of gossip : ' I hear a secret of the Princess Elizabeth that Lord Craven is like to marry her. I wish she were in England, that she might marry Dr. More's Cartesian notions, which would beget a noble offspring of many excellent and fruitful truths.' (See *Diary and Correspondence of Dr. Worthington*, edited by J. R. Crossley for the Chetham Society, Vols. i. and ii. ; and cf. Crossley's note on the Princess in Vol. i. *s. d.* October 15, 1660. The Princess Elizabeth never came to England.

about this time to have been much impressed by the Dutch divine, Johannes Cocceius, professor at Leyden, whose personal acquaintance she had made on a visit to her aunt at Krossen. Cocceius, who played an important part in the religious movement known as Pietism, in so far as it affected the Reformed or Calvinistic Church, recalls to us other eminent religious teachers in whom the evangelical and the latitudinarian have been blended. The gist of this teaching was a direct appeal to Scripture and a deprecation of any insistence on the *formulæ* of dogma. Elizabeth, whose mind had expanded, and whose religious conceptions had deepened under influences very different from the rigid Calvinism of an earlier type, welcomed the simple and profound enthusiasm of Cocceius and of the so-called ' Lodensteyners,' whom the endeavour to bring home religion to the individual mind and conscience had all but led into secession or sectarianism. Thus it came to pass that, after Princess Elizabeth had, in 1667, become Abbess of Herford in her own right, her rule was signalised by her sympathetic relations with sectarian movements.

In the middle of the seventeenth century the prosperous Westphalian Hanse town of Herford which had always been Lutheran, had lost its position as a free imperial city, and had been finally annexed by the Elector of Brandenburg, as representing the former Protectors of the Abbey. This foundation had been Lutheranised rather less than a century before ; but since the time of the Thirty Years' War the Abbess might be either a Lutheran or a Calvinist, and the Brandenburg influence of course favoured the second alternative. Though she had lost her sovereign rights, she was still regarded as an Estate of the Empire, and as such represented at the Diet ; she had a Court of her own, with regular (even hereditary) officers, and a limited jurisdiction ; and with her and her Chapter was connected a foundation, which indeed outlasted them, for the education of young ladies of family. The position was thus one of considerable traditional dignity and actual influence ; and nothing of either was lost in the tenure of Elizabeth, a true princess as well as a genuine student. She was at the same time well aware that, as a matter of fact, the authority of the Abbess of Herford was dependent upon the stronger arm of the Elector of Brandenburg—in her case a dependence ungrateful neither to the protector nor to the protected.

Thus, when in 1670 she was asked to extend the hospitable shelter of Herford to Jean Labadie and his following of women and men, which from some fifty gradually rose to seven or eight times that number, her first step was to assure herself of the consent of the Great Elector. With him, as with her, religious tolerance was a constant principle ; nor is there any reason for assuming that the good-

will shown by her towards both Labadists and
Quakers had any other root than Christian humility,
wherein for such as she lies the beginning of wisdom.
It is of course easy to trace the more immediate
influences by which she was drawn to the founder
of the now half-forgotten sect of Labadists.   He
had begun his career as a Jesuit, and, after seeking
to set up a new congregation within the Church of
Rome, had become a convert to Calvinism, and in
this new sphere tried the experiment over again
with a freer hand, and with greater success.   At
Geneva he was assisted in his endeavours by the
brother of Anna Maria von Schurmann, whose
learning had made her the ' wonder of her age,'
but whose thoughts were now set on other things.
Soon afterwards, she permanently associated herself
with Labadie's attempt to realise without delay
his scheme of the true Church.   After ministering
to a small Walloon congregation at Middelburg in
Zeeland, he was duly excommunicated ; whereupon
he carried on his work at Amsterdam, in a small
community with peculiar institutions, as a declared
schismatic.   It was from the tyranny of the Amsterdam mob that, at her friend Anna Maria von Schurmann's request, the Abbess of Herford summoned.
them to take refuge in the ' liberties ' of her abbey.
Very soon, notwithstanding the Elector's approval
of her reception of the fugitives, the Lutheran
burghers of Herford raised a loud clamour against

the practices of the strangers, and then tried to starve them out, till a commission of enquiry, appointed by the Elector, arrived in the town. During the respite thus obtained another visitor, attracted by motives of curiosity, arrived at Herford in the person of the Abbess' sister Sophia. She brought with her no faith in supernatural gifts and a mocking tongue ; and the account of her visit admirably illustrates the innate difference between the two sisters. The report of the commission was on the whole favourable to the liberties of the strangers ; and, after Elizabeth had with much spirit refused to obey a mandate of the Imperial Aulic Tribunal at Speyer ordering their removal, and had journeyed in person to Berlin to bring about a decisive intervention on the part of the Elector, the question was solved in 1672 by the imminence of the French invasion of the Low Countries. This danger obliged Labadie and the majority of his followers to fly to Holstein, while the rest remained behind under the protection of the Abbess. Thus closed a noteworthy episode, in the course of which a high-minded and enlightened princess had, on behalf of a band of sectaries with whom her own sympathy can hardly have been other than imperfect, successfully upheld the cause of tolerance against both official and civic bigotry.[1]

[1] The Labadists seem to have ultimately taken refuge in Maryland, where the sect was gradually absorbed and is now almost forgotten. (See Bartlett B. James, *The Labadist Colony in Maryland*, John Hopkins Press, 1899.)

The last of the Labadists had not yet left Her_
ford, when Elizabeth began to hold intercourse
with a sect of greater significance than theirs in
modern religious history—the English Quakers,
or, as we find her brother Charles Lewis disguising
their name,' quaquors.'[1]   Three years later, in 1667,
she received two visits from William Penn and
Robert Barclay during their missionary journey in
Holland and Germany, including the Palatinate.
From Penn's account of these interviews, and the
letters exchanged between him and the Abbess,
it is clear that the latter, who was on both occasions
attended by her intimate friend, Countess Anna
Maria van Hoorn, a canoness of the Abbey, was
deeply moved by Penn's appeals to her heart and
conscience.   But it is equally clear that the humility
which bade her listen prevented her from accepting
the conclusion that she, too, was divinely called to
teach.   Her mind was equipped ; her soul alert ;
but she still waited.   Five years later, when she had
passed away from the religion of doubts and difficulties, Penn inserted in a new edition of his
treatise, *No Cross no Crown*, among the testimonies
to the significance of *Serious Dying as well as Living*,

----

[1] The passage (in *Schreiben das Kurfürsten Carl Ludwig*, &c.
must be quoted : ' To-day we have had in our presence an
English *quaquor* or trembler ; I repeatedly silenced him, for
his mind works very slowly indeed ; he never takes off his hat
and always calls me " thou " ; but he loses his temper if he
is contradicted.'

the following reminiscence of ' the late Princess Elizabeth of the Rhine ' :—

She chose a single life, as freest of care, and best suited to the study and meditation she always inclined to ; and the chiefest diversion she took, next the air, was in some such plain and housewifely entertainment as knitting, &c. She had a small territory, which she has governed so well, that she shewed herself fit for a greater. She would constantly, every Last-day in the week, sit in judgment, and hear and determine cases herself ; where her patience, justice, and mercy were admirable ; frequently remitting her forfeitures, where the party was poor, or otherwise meritorious. And, which was excellent, she would temper her discourse with Religion, and strongly draw concerned parties to submission and agreement ; exercising not so much the vigour of her power, as the power of her persuasion. Her meekness and humility appeared to me extraordinary. She never considered the quality, but the merits of the people she entertained. . . . Thus, though she kept no sumptuous table in her own Court, she spread the tables of the poor in their solitary cells. . . . Abstemious in herself, and in apparent void of all vain ornaments.

I must say her mind had a noble prospect. Her eye was to a better and moré lasting inheritance than can be found below, which made her often to despise the greatness of Courts, and the learning of the Schools, of which she was an extraordinary judge.

Then he gives instances, very simply put, of her way of deprecating too narrow an interpretation of the duty of paying respect to our betters ; of her distrust of her power to walk in the straight way she had chosen ; of her humility towards the humblest ; and he concludes :

I cannot forget her Last Words, when I took leave of her, ' Let me desire you to remember me, though I live at this distance, and that you should never see me more—I thank you for this good time ; and know and be assured, though my condition subject me to divers temptations, yet my soul hath strong desires after the best things.'

In view of this record of the eternal longings with which this beautiful soul was filled at the last, it seems vain to make any reference to the earthly cares which still from time to time occupied her, in connexion no doubt chiefly with the family history, or even to the intellectual occupations which continued to engage her interest to the last. She was a diligent collector of books and manuscripts, and the last great writers with whom she corresponded were Leibniz and Malebranche, the mystical and Christian follower of her former teacher, Descartes. Shortly before her death, Elizabeth sent for her sister Sophia to pay her a long visit, and received her, Sophia relates in her *Memoirs*, with a joyfulness as if an angel from Heaven had descended to heal her. She then notes that the Abbess had been surrounded by people whose melancholy notions of a religious life had made hers a martyrdom. Wasted away in body, she was, however, calm in spirit and prepared for death, though full of sympathy with her sister and with the troubles which might await Sophia out in the turbulent world. Elizabeth died in peace at Herford Abbey in February, 1680 ; a letter addressed by her to her sister Louisa Hollandina, Abbess of Maubuisson, shows that more than three months before she was already making herself ready for death.[1]

Not much is known as to the life of the Princess Louisa Hollandina herself during the years which followed on the occurrence of the de L'Épinay scandal, and which she quietly spent at her mother's

[1] I must take leave to insert here the inscription on her tomb in the Abbey Church, Herford, kindly copied for me by Miss A. D. Greenwood, who mentions that the name of the Princess Palatine is commemorated in that of the Elizabethstrasse, a curly old street near the Minster :

D. O. M.
H. S. E.
Serenissima Princeps et Antistita Herfordiensis
    ELISABETH
Electoribus Palatinis et Magnæ Britaniæ Regibus orta
    Regii prorsus animi Virgo
Invicta in rebus gerendis prudentia ac dexteritate
    Admirabili eruditione atque doctrinâ
Supra sexus et ævi conditionem celeberrima
    Regum studiis Principum amicitiis
Doctorum vivorum Literis ac monumentis
Omnium Christianorum gentium linguis ac plausibus
    Sed maxime propriâ virtute
Sui nominis immortalitatem adepta.
    Nata anno 1618, die 26 Decembris
    Denata anno 1680, die 8 Februarii
Vixit annos 61 mensem 1 et dies 16
Rexit annos 12 menses 10 et dies 2.

Court in Holland. Nothing seems to have been
bruited abroad concerning her except that she was
leading an exemplary life, and that she was very
intimate with a lady whose name is given as Madame
d'Oxsordre, and had frequent conversations with
her on the subject of ' the bases of the Protestant
religion.' In other words, a propagandist influence
was steadily at work upon her, and in the end she
made up her mind to become a convert to Rome.
Conversions to Roman Catholicism were common
during the whole of this period, and there can be
little doubt but that in this particular transaction
her brother Edward and his wife, the Princess
Palatine Anne (of Gonzaga), had an important
share. In December, 1657, Louisa Hollandina,
who had reason enough to fear the maternal
wrath should her intention become known, secretly
left the Hague at night-time in the habiliments of
a maid-servant, and made her way to Antwerp,
where, in January, 1658, she abjured Protestantism
for the Church of Rome. Her change of confession
was not the result of any sudden resolution, but
it could not fail to incense as well as grieve
her mother, whose wrath, however, fell upon
Princess Maria Elizabeth of Hohenzollern-Hechingen,
hitherto an intimate of her court. Whether or not
a letter from this lady to Princess Louisa Hollandina had finally determined her flight, further
letters from the same hand, which appear to have

been accompanied, or preceded, by the whisperings of verbal scandal, reflected in no measured terms on the Palatine *ménage*. Elizabeth hereupon insisted on the expulsion of the slanderer from her place of residence, Bergen-op-Zoom, pending further enquiry. The ' Princess of Zollern' hereupon entered into a series of further charges, culminating in the suggestion that Louisa had been obliged to fly in order to conceal her shame. The Queen behaved with prudence as well as dignity, counselling her son the Elector to contradict this calumny, but to do so quietly and civilly, without demanding proofs as if he had any doubts on the subject. In December, 1658, or thereabouts, Louisa Hollandina addressed a not undignified letter to her mother, in which she announced her admission into the Church of Rome, which the occasion of the Christmas Communion had made necessary to her conscience, and begged her mother's pardon for the trouble thus caused to her. About the same time the Princess made her way to Havre, having ascertained that she would be received with open arms by the French Court, which had formerly remained deaf to her mother's solicitations for support. Immediately after Louisa's arrival on French soil, she was welcomed by her brother, the Prince Palatine Edward, and conducted by him to the Abbey of Maubuisson, near the river Oise, and almost immediately facing Pontoise, the ancient capital of the Vexin. Edward's own daughters, Maria Anne and Benedicta, were being educated here, each receiving at the same time a handsome pension out of the Abbey funds. This ancient Benedictine nunnery (originally planted in a wooded part of the country infested by brigands ; whence the name *le buisson maudit*) dated from the middle of the thirteenth century, and the favour accorded to it by Queen Blanche, who was buried in the convent after assuming its habit on her deathbed, attracted to it the frequent presence of her son, St. Louis. His example was followed by other sovereigns of France, and the later history of the Abbey is full of interest. But here it must suffice to say that, in the second half of the sixteenth century, the prevalent decay of conventual life in France particularly affected Maubuisson, which had so long been connected with the Court, and lay so near to Paris, and that this corruption became complete under the reckless *régime* of Angélique d'Estrées, the sister of Henry IV's Fair Gabrielle, who was herself buried with one of her infants in the Abbey. After her death Henry IV came there no more; but this period of worldly misrule was not ended, till in the next reign Mère Angélique came from Port Royal to reform Maubuisson under the supervision of St. François de Sales, and after a hard struggle effected her purpose. Once more there was a terrible backsliding ; but better times returned in 1627 with the choice as Abbess of the worthy Mère des Anges (Marie Suireau) who was really a nominee of Mère Angélique's, and who brought with her a fresh infusion of religious zeal from Port Royal. Her twenty-three years of conscientious administration once more restored the convent to a well-ordered and pious life. On her return to Port Royal, the worthy abbess of Lieu Dieu became Abbess of Maubuisson, where in the course of her short rule she received Louis XIV ; and after her Louisa Hollandina's immediate predecessor, Catharine d'Orléans, an illegitimate daughter of the Duke de Longueville, against whom nothing remains on record except a series of unfortunate ' architectural improvements ' in the Abbey church. But these changes have long been obliterated, together with the church itself, which, after at the Revolution the Abbey had been taken over by the nation and sold, was in 1790 blown up by powder. At the present moment the traces of this notable historic monument are described as hardly discernible.

There can be little doubt that, probably owing to the efforts of Louisa Hollandina's powerful sister-in-law, the French ' *Princesse Palatine*,' it had been from the first determined to provide for this interesting princely convert at Maubuisson. No sooner had her foot touched the soil of France than the royal favour of Louis XIV, whose magnanimous hospitality never did things by halves,

K

shone upon her.   After her first visit to Maubuisson
she was taken to see her aunt, Queen Henrietta
Maria, who was at the time residing with the
Visitandines at Paris, and who, after vain attempts
to convert her sons Charles and James to the Church
of Rome, was engaged in a project for obtaining
the hand of the young French King for her daughter
Henrietta, brought up as a Roman Catholic.   Hereupon, Louisa was received at Court, and assigned
a liberal pension by the King ;   and thus she was
enabled, on terms befitting her position, to form a
definite connexion with the Maubuisson convent.
After a noviciate of eighteen months, she took the
vows on September 19th, 1660, in the presence
of a distinguished assembly, before whom the
Bishop of Amiens preached ' divinely.'   Happily
for her peace of mind; the kindness shown her by
the French Court had impressed itself upon her
mother, for whose forgiveness Queen Henrietta Maria
persistently sued.   In October, 1659, Elizabeth
informed her son Charles Lewis that this inter-
cession had prevailed with her, and that, in
obedience to the King and Queen's commands, she
had forgiven ' Louyse,' and prayed God also to
forgive her, ' which is all my letter in a few lines.' [1]
But Louisa Hollandina was the only one of her

[1] See *Letters*, &c., ed. A. Wendland, p. 118. These letters
at last throw a full light on this episode of the Palatine family
history.

mother's surviving children left without mention in her will.

The long evening— if it should be so called—of Louisa Hollandina's life, which lasted till 1709, was a peaceful one ; but it would be unjust to her, more especially in view of some misconceptions which have arisen on the subject, not to say a word as to the spirit in which she both entered upon this period of her existence, and to which she throughout remained true. Just before she took the vows, she is said to have been warned by one of the Maubuisson sisters, who belonged to a reactionary clique in the convent, desirous of obtaining a mitigation of the severer rule introduced from Port Royal, not to engage herself to observe any standard of discipline in excess of the proposed reduction, for which it was probably hoped to secure the requisite sanction with the aid of an Abbess in so much favour at Court. But she refused point-blank, and, during the few years which she spent at the convent as a simple religious, would not consent to be relieved from any one of the duties incumbent on her. When, in August, 1664, she was, on the death of the Abbess, named as her successor, her first act after accepting the office was to sell part of the silver plate which had been presented to her by the Queen of France in order to defray part of the debt pressing upon the convent. She abolished the practice of former abbesses of keeping up a retinue and footmen of

K 2

her own, saying that she had abandoned the world on purpose to see no more Courts ; and her niece, the Duchess of Orleans, in her humorous manner, describes her as going about the convent and garden all alone and with her skirts tucked up, and giving her orders in an authoritative tone that nobody ventured to disobey. She even—no insignificant sacrifice for a Palatine—ceased to use the arms of her House. This simplicity was partly natural to her, for even before her retirement it had been noted how careless she was as to matters of dress and outward appearance. Partly it was due to a resolute humility of spirit, and a determination to avoid any assumption of superiority on her own part over the sisters of the convent, to which Saint-Simon bears express testimony. She would not seat herself on the throne hitherto occupied by the Abbess in the convent church, and as a fitter object of reverence placed a statue of the Virgin there. On the other hand, she opposed a steadfast resistance to the tendency manifested by some of the nuns towards a relaxation of the conventual discipline ; she observed the entire seven months' fast imposed by the Cistercian rule, until at last she became as thin as a lath ; according to the account of her niece she never ate flesh except when ill, and slept on a mattress as hard as stone, with no other furniture in her chamber but a straw-chair ; and she rose every midnight for prayer.

Beneath her dress she wore an undergarment of hair-cloth. She was careful to obey the rule which, except in special circumstances, prohibited the religious of Maubuisson from leaving the convent, and absented herself from it only thrice in the forty-nine years of her residence. According to the Duchess of Orleans, who spoke on this subject with sympathetic insight, the good Abbess' tongue was her temptation ; and she always chose a deaf sister to live with her in her chamber, so as not to be seduced into conversation.

On the charitable activity of the good Abbess there is less necessity for dwelling, since it accorded with the habits that were natural to her, as well as with her Palatine warmth of heart. In her indefatigable activity she resembled her brother Charles Lewis, to whom in her later years she bore so striking an outward likeness. Idleness of any kind was impossible to her ; 'never,' writes a contemporary, 'was she without some virtuous and religious occupation ; either she was plying her brush or her needle, or reading or praying.' To her love of painting, an art which she is said to have practised from her eighth year to past her eightieth, reference has already been made. Though it would not appear that her artistic powers increased in her later years, she utilised them for the decoration not only of the Abbey, but of several churches of the neighbourhood, and even found time to paint

pictures for other recipients. Sacred subjects seem
to have chiefly occupied her in these days ; to the
Cour des Comptes at Paris, which had rendered an
efficient service to her Abbey, she presented an
elaborate pictorial allegory of Justice.[1] During her
administration the structural accommodation of
the Abbey was considerably enlarged, and, in the
centre of it, a handsome fountain was for the first
time erected.

Beneath all the other qualities of Louisa Hollandina and, one is tempted to say, at the root of them,
lay that cheerfulness of soul which is a blessing
to all who are brought into contact with its happy
possessor. The Duchess of Orleans, who had all
her aunt's vivacity of mind, but little of her tranquillity of spirit, refers again and again to the
delightfulness of her periodical visits to the dear
old lady ; and we may well believe that in their
intercourse the seasoning of *malice* (in the French
sense of the word) was not wanting. But Saint-
Simon, an observer not less keen, though the
satirical vein in him took a different turn, informs
us that the Abbess of Maubuisson was adored by all
the sisters of the convent, of which she had made
herself the very life and soul, because of her charity,
her sweetness, and her loving-kindness. From a
character so pure—or perhaps it should be said
so purified—the shafts of ill report glance off

[1] In 1871, this picture was consumed in the flames.

harmlessly; nor is it impossible that they had their origin in traditions with which the Palatine Princess had no concern, and which her rule as Abbess ought to have been allowed to extinguish. While she held sway at Maubuisson, it became a chosen place as a religious retreat by ladies of rank; among these was Madame de Brisson, *l'âme de Saint-Cyr*, as Madame de Sévigné calls her, soon after her dismissal from that seminary. In 1679, the good Abbess had the pleasure of a visit from the Duchess Sophia, who was delighted with the happy regularity of her sister's life, ' which would suit me quite well, had I no husband and children.' The Duchess of Orleans herself, though she would hardly have come in the character of a penitent, in one of the crises of her life at the French Court begged the King to allow her to finish her days at Maubuisson.

Some two years before her death, Louisa Hollandina, who had hitherto only been subject to the *migraine*—for the statement that she had died in 1704 to save herself the trouble of periodically reminding the States-General of the annuity granted to her at her baptism was only a friendly jest— had a paralytic stroke, and the remainder of her life was full of suffering. She took it all easily, saying that people would not desire life so much if they knew to what it amounted near the end. She died in February, 1709, eighty-six years of age ; the good Princess, wrote her heart-broken niece to

Louisa Hollandina's sister Sophia, ' is now where
she long was wished to be ' ; Sophia herself, in her
very direct way, observed that, as there was so little
besides life left in her sister, there was the less to
deplore in her loss.   She was buried by the nuns,
who had loved her dearly and nursed her tenderly,
in her abbey-church at Maubuisson, as her sister
Elizabeth had been buried in hers at Herford
twenty-nine years earlier ; and both the Catholic
and the Protestant Abbess deserve each, in her own
way, to be remembered among the good women
in whom their age, with all its shortcomings, was
so rich.

And here we must take leave of the Palatinate
family, except in so far as Sophia herself and those
younger members of it with whom in her married
life she came into personal contact are concerned.
Late in 1659, Queen Elizabeth had the pleasure of a
visit from Sophia at the Hague, having had to solicit
from Charles Lewis ' a little money in extraordi-
naire ' for the purposes of the meeting.   They seem to
have been happy together, and the Queen wrote that
she would be ill-natured had she failed to show ' kindness to Sophie, because she shows so much love
to me.'   The real success of the visit was, however,
Sophia's little Palatine niece Liselotte, of whom
more hereafter, who captured her grandmother's
heart, although ' you know I care not much for

children.'[1] Sophia remained in Holland till March,
1660, when her mother was so much hindered by
people coming in to tell the English news about
Monck that she could hardly find time for writing.[2]
Mother and daughter, however, met again in the
following year; and Sophia's last farewell to ' *cette
bonne princesse,*' her mother, took place on board
the vessel on which, in May, 1661, Queen Elizabeth
was about to sail from Rotterdam for England.
For the high-souled royal exile was not, at the
last, denied an honourable refuge in her native land,
though she arrived there without the special invitation which she had been led to expect, and an attempt
was even made to delay her on the way. What
could surpass in pathos the picture of her arriving in
London in the darkness, with hardly a friend but
the faithful Earl of Craven to guide her home from
the riverside ? At Craven House she resided till
she moved to the house in Leicester Fields successively occupied by her great namesake's two
favourites, the Earls of Leicester and Essex. She
had no intention, as she told Prince Rupert, of
playing the poor relation. The King, her nephew,

[1] *Letters,* &c., ed. A. Wendland, p. 122.

[2] *Ib.,* p. 136. It was about this time that Elizabeth was also
enjoying the company of the young Baron von Selz, an illegitimate
son of her son Charles Lewis from his London days. She was
warmly interested in him, and in 1660 induced King Charles II
to take the youth to London in the suite of Henry Duke of
Gloucester. But Selz died in London, much to Elizabeth's
grief, before his friend the Duke. (Hauck, *Elizabeth,* p. 53.)

showed much cordiality to her as well as to her sons ; but his courtesies were for the most part inexpensive, and she confessed that he owed her nothing, though the Parliament owed her much.[1] He promised, accordingly, to see if her debts could not be paid by Parliament, and it actually granted her certain sums, which she applied as fast as they came in to the redemption of her jewels, though she still had to appeal to Charles Lewis for assistance in the process. A series of unpleasant demands and counter-demands ensued between the King and the Elector, each calling upon the other to pay to the Queen the outstanding moneys lawfully due to her. In the end, King Charles II granted her a pension of a thousand pounds a month, of which she did not live to enjoy the first year's total, and offered her a residence (Exeter House), into which she had not time to move.[2]

The Queen of Bohemia, as she called herself to the last, was seen at times in public—at the theatres and elsewhere—with the court ; and much attention

[1] On another occasion she writes with generous frankness : ' The King is not bounde to doe for me but what he pleases, for being maried out of the house he might justly pretend not to be bound to give me anything, but he is kinder than many nephews would be, his income besides is not settled as you believe it is.' (*Letters*, &c., p. 207).

[2] She told her son that she would have to order ' states,' chairs, stools, and carpets all new for Exeter House, as ' that beast, your Castelin,' had allowed what ' stuff ' there was at Rheenen to go to ruin. (*Ib.*, p. 211.)

was shown to her by her son Prince Rupert, who
(as has been seen) had returned to England a few
months after the King. Pepys, whose mention of
Rupert's return is the first notice of this Prince in the
Diary, observes that he was ' welcome to nobody.'
Perhaps the diarist had a presentiment of the friction
which, sooner or later, could hardly fail to occur
between a budding official like himself and a man
of the sword with a popular reputation, whom he
appears to have throughout regarded as passionate
and self-willed. But Prince Rupert was well
received in England both by the Royal Family
and by the public at large, though it proved before
long that he, like others who had served the throne
in the days of stress, was out of touch with the
younger generation of courtiers and politicians.
He had not found congenial employment abroad ;
but his readiness for active work had not yet
passed. The proposed expedition under his command to the Guinea Coast was abandoned (1664),
partly because of an illness which had befallen
him ; but he was placed at the head of one of
the squadrons in the First Dutch War, and in
the Second superseded the Roman Catholic Duke
of York as commander-in-chief of the English fleet.
The breakdown of his plan of action by his want
of success in the last battle of this war (1673) was
attributed by him to the misconduct of the French
and the intrigues of the friends of the Duke of

York ; and thus it rather heightened than hurt his
popularity.   For a time he seemed to be cultivating
relations of intimacy with Shaftesbury and the
Opposition ; but he never harboured any disloyal
intentions, though his sympathy with the Protestant feeling in the country is of a piece with the
traditions of his family and with the whole of his
own career.   He now withdrew more and more into
a retirement which suited both his scientific pursuits
and his growing aversion from the hopeless frivolity
and viciousness of the Court.   Although he still
continued to take an occasional part in public
affairs, his time was chiefly spent among his chemical
apparatus and his pictures and curiosities in the
Round Town at Windsor Castle, of which he had
been named Constable in 1668.   He died in 1682,
and was buried in Westminster Abbey, the faithful Lord Craven acting as chief mourner on the
occasion.

His mother, to whom he had been a good son
to the last, had long before this passed to her rest.
Her correspondence with her son Charles Lewis had
in the last period of her life assumed a more painful
tone than ever, turning as it did upon a past that
could not be set right, whatever might happen
in the future.   In the contention as to whose fault
it had been that she had not temporarily taken up
her residence at Heidelberg he seems to have been
more in the right than she ; and it is satisfactory to

observe that, though in the very last letter preserved
from her hand, while she expresses a hope that his
anger will be now over, she begs that he will
add to what he is paying to her of the jointure
which is her due, his last letter to her, and the
draft of one dated in the month of her death,
end on a dutiful and even affectionate note.[1]
After her death, Charles Lewis, as her eldest—
he had once been her favourite—son, made a claim
for her jewels as heirlooms ; and once more a bitter
dispute ensued between the brothers.[2] The proposal
that her eldest daughter should cross the water to
see her had met with no response. Of Sophia's
seeming content with her lot the Queen had, shortly
before coming to England, heard with pleasure ;
but she could not shut her eyes to the changes

---

[1] *Letters*, &c., pp. 212–3.

[2] The Queen's last will and testament shows that she declared
Charles Lewis her heir, but left special legacies to Rupert—
jewels, plate, and furniture, with the papers of which the *Original
Royal Letters*, published by Sir George Bromley in 1787, passed
into the hands of his lineal ancestress Ruperta, daughter of Prince
Rupert and wife of Scroope Emmanuel Howe. To Edward the
Queen left a large diamond ; to Elizabeth emerald ear-rings ;
and to Sophia the string of pearls which her mother had ordinarily
worn. Probably the medallion with the lock of King Charles I's
hair, which was found on her breast after her death, was buried
with her. Many years later, when the death of the Abbess
of Herford was apprehended, Sophia wrote to Charles Lewis
that he would not find so much reason for discontent on this
occasion as on that of their mother's death—' for she seems to
bear no malice against you.' It is distressing that Sophia's want
of sympathy towards her mother, which may have been explicable enough in earlier days, should have lasted beyond the grave,

that fate brings ; ' for it is easier said then done
to care for nothing.' Still, wherever she might
find herself, the lonely woman kept a stout heart
and an unclouded front ; though, whether at
Whitehall or at Combe Abbey (if she visited it
again), she must have seemed to herself like a
revenante—a ghost of the past come back. She
died, at Leicester House, on February 13th, 1662—
a few hours before the dawn of what, had her husband still been by her side, would have been her
golden wedding day ; and, on a night as full of
storms as her life had been, she was buried in the
Abbey where so many of her descendants were
to be crowned with a crown less rapidly evanescent
than hers.

III

THE DUCHESS SOPHIA

ERNEST AUGUSTUS OF BRUNSWICK-LÜNEBURG was the youngest son of his House, as Sophia was the youngest daughter of the Palatine family; nor was the scion of the Guelfs, as such, unfitted to mate with one who could boast an ancestry illustrious like hers. Previously to the marriage conferring upon Sophia a right of partnership, of which time only could reveal the significance, in the fortunes of the German branch of the Guelfs, more than one great historic opportunity had occurred to that ancient House. Five centuries had passed since Henry the Lion had held sway over territories reaching from the shores of the German Ocean and the Baltic to those of the Adriatic. He had been the husband of an English princess—Matilda, daughter of King Henry II; nor was Sophia unmindful of this ancestral connexion. We cannot follow here the repeated dynastic changes, or the numberless partitions and transfers that succeeded each other in the hereditary lands between Elbe and Weser, saved out of the shipwreck of the great Guelfic dominion, and granted to Henry's grandson, Otto the Child, as an imperial fief under the designation of the Duchy of Brunswick.

The severance declared by Otto's eldest two sons, between the territories of which Brunswick and Lüneburg were respectively the original centres, was—the numerous shiftings of ownership between the representatives of the Old, Middle, and New Brunswick and Lüneburg lines notwithstanding—never undone, and continues in a sense to the present day. Thus, it was only within the limits of each main division that it proved possible in the course of time to assert those two principles upon which, repugnant though they were to the traditions of Germanic life, the political future of the princely Houses of the Empire depended—namely, that of indivisibility of tenure, and, more tardily, that of primogeniture. Nor was there any consistent endeavour to supply the want of a single dominant authority in the Brunswick and Lüneburg Houses (as they were generally called, their various subdivisions being further distinguished for the most part according to the names of their chief ' residences ') by an identity, or at least by an agreement, of policy. Thus the German Guelfs missed the great dynastic opportunity of the Reformation, although the populations over which they ruled were at one in their ready acceptance of Lutheranism, and although a series of wealthy ecclesiastical foundations fell into the laps of the princes. Duke Henry of Brunswick-Wolfenbüttel opposed the Reformation with so much vehemence as to be denounced by Luther in the character of bugbear-in-chief of the supporters of the national movement. Still, with their augmented territorial strength, the Guelfs might have played an important part in the critical period which preceded the long-expected outbreak of the great religious conflict, and perhaps, during its earlier stages, might have done much to resist the inroads of the Reaction. Instead of this, after the ' evil Harry's ' accomplished grandson, Duke Henry Julius, had applied his ability as a statesman wholly to the furtherance of the imperial interest, his timorous successor, Frederick Ulric, had failed to avert from the Lower Saxon Circle the fury of war, drawn down upon it by the passionate Protestant partisanship of his brother, Christian of Halberstadt, the champion of Elizabeth of Bohemia. A change of dynasty occurred at a highly critical epoch of the Thirty Years' War, when nearly all the Protestant estates adhered to the compromise of the Peace of Prague (1634) ; and the ' New ' House of Brunswick entered into possession at Wolfenbüttel in the person of Duke Augustus, a cautious ruler and a man of kindly disposition and of bookish tastes. At

L

the Peace of Westphalia the rich see of Hildesheim
had to be given up by the elder (Brunswick) branch ;
and for a time adversity seemed to have impressed
upon it the expediency of uniting its policy with that
of the younger, which had issued forth in a more
advantageous position from the Great War. During
this temporary accord between the two branches, the
ambitious Duke Rudolf Augustus of Brunswick-
Wolfenbüttel was assisted by his Brunswick-
Lüneburg kinsmen in the important achievement,
which the resolute Dukes of the Middle House of
Brunswick had essayed in vain, of permanently
subjecting to their territorial authority the proud
Hanseatic city of Brunswick. And, alike in the
war provoked by Louis XIV's invasion of the
United Provinces (in 1672), in the march against
the Swedes which was crowned by the victory of
Fehrbellin (1675), and in the campaign against the
Turks which ended with the recapture of Neuhäusel
(1685), the armed forces of the two Guelfic lines
fought side by side. But, while the New Lüneburg line was, by consolidation, preparing its future
greatness, the advancement of the New Brunswick
line, the repartitions of whose territories cannot
occupy us here, again came to a standstill. Duke
Rudolf Augustus survived till 1704, a prince whose
virtues were of the passive kind, and with whom his
ambitious younger brother, Antony Ulric, was associated in the government from 1685 onwards. In

order to ensure the Succession to the offspring of his brother, the good Duke Rudolf Augustus, after the death of his first wife, contracted a *mésalliance* with the daughter of a Brunswick barber-surgeon, who, as Madame Rudolfine, led a life of happy obscurity by his side at Brunswick. His brother, Duke Antony Ulric, held his Court at Wolfenbüttel, where he cherished the literary studies in which he had engaged in the University of Helmstedt, and successfully essayed his own powers as an author, both in the favourite contemporary species of historical romances *de longue haleine* and in psalmody. But the mental activity of Antony Ulric, who in 1704 succeeded to sole ducal authority at Brunswick, was far from being absorbed by his literary pursuits ; or rather, as we shall see, he contrived to make them subservient to the influences of dynastic ambition. He kept a jealous watch, now self-interested, now malevolent and revengeful, over the advance of the Lüneburg dynasty, so nearly akin to his own. And, in whatever measure the same jealousy may have been a factor in his own ultimate conversion to the Church of Rome, it certainly contributed to make him press on those splendid marriages of his grand-daughters with Emperor and Tsarevich, whereby he sought to redeem his own political insignificance.

Very different results attended the progress, in

and after the latter part of the Thirty Years' War, of
the New House of Lüneburg, as it was called. Duke
George was the sixth of seven brothers, of whom
it fell in turn to the eldest four to conduct the
government of the Lüneburg-Celle dominions. Here
the principle of indivisibility had been established
in 1592 and confirmed in 1610 ; but it did not
apply to acquisitions by the line accruing after
that date. In order to maintain this principle
intact, all the brothers, with the exception of Duke
George, remained unmarried, and, by a singularly
orderly disposition of fate, the second, third, and
fourth succeeded in due course, each on the demise
of his next elder brother. The fifth and seventh
died before the arrival of their respective turns,
and thus it was to the progeny of Duke George
that the lands and their government descended.
He was accounted one of the most capable com-
manders of the latter part of the war, and an ardent
supporter of the Protestant cause, with whose
great champion Gustavus Adolphus he had been
one of the earliest among the German Princes to
enter into an understanding. But he was so
unwilling to imperil the immediate interests of the
dynasty, that, in 1634, he gave in his adhesion to
the Peace of Prague. In 1635 he assumed the
government of the principality of Calenberg, which,
by the repartition made at that date, was transferred
to the Lüneburg line ; and in the following year he

laid the foundations, in the fortified town of Hanover, of the castle which was to be expanded, in after ages, into the palace of Electors and Kings. He died in 1641 ; but his principality was preserved to his dynasty in the settlement of the Peace of Westphalia, and they further secured a ' satisfaction,' though by no means an adequate one, for the losses or disappointments undergone by them, in the shape of the right of appointing a prince of their family to the see of Osnabrück on every alternate vacancy. Thus, with a territory whose resources seemed to have been hopelessly exhausted by the devastations of the War and by the exactions of both war and peace, whose social system had been dislocated, and whose life had been in various respects demoralised, the sons of Duke George of Lüneburg entered upon a period in the history of their dynasty which was to conduct it from petty beginnings to unforeseen greatness.

The family consisted of four brothers and three sisters, of which latter two died in infancy. The surviving sister, Sophia Amalia, had in 1643 married the future King Frederick III of Denmark, and took a notable part in the defence of Copenhagen against the Swedes (1658), as well as in the few despotic excesses to be charged against the absolute rule with which, at a time when the Danish power had been laid low, her consort had been suddenly entrusted. The Duchess Sophia, who by her marriage had become sister-in-law to Queen Sophia Amalia, met her at Altona in 1671, and paid her a visit at her dower-palace at Nykjöping in 1680. Sophia saw this redoubtable sovereign on her amiable side, and relates how, on the occasion of a *battue* of hares, the Queen encouraged her to fire the first shot that she, her mother's degenerate daughter, had ever discharged. Of the four brothers, the eldest, Duke Christian Lewis, had in 1641 succeeded to his father's principality of Calenberg; but in 1648, when he assumed the government of the Lüneburg-Celle dominions proper and took up his abode at Celle, Calenberg, with its residential town of Hanover, passed to the second brother, Duke George William. The third and fourth, Dukes John Frederick and Ernest Augustus, in accordance with their father's will, remained without territorial possessions (the reversion of the Osnabrück bishopric had not yet fallen in); and it was arranged that, in the first instance, John Frederick should reside at the Court of Celle, and Ernest Augustus at that of Hanover. The young Brunswick-Lüneburg Dukes were left without paternal control in the very period in their lives when it was most needed by them; for, at the time of his father's death in 1641, the eldest, Christian Lewis, was only nineteen, and the youngest, Ernest Augustus, eleven years of age. The brothers had been brought into little contact with the

old-fashioned academical training, of which the influence is recognisable in the Dukes of the elder
branch ; and Christian Lewis, whose years of rule
at Hanover left behind them the memory of a
prince of the Mohocks, was incapable of introducing
the refinements of the modern era at Celle. At
the same time he, in this larger sphere, did his duty,
as he understood it, in both Church and State ;
staunchly adhering to the Lutheranism of his line,
asserting his ducal authority against the recalci-
trance of the good town of Lüneburg, and providing
himself with the beginnings of a standing army
in defiance of his Estates. His best friend and ally
was the Great Elector of Brandenburg, who afterwards married, as his second wife, Charles Lewis'
widow, the Dowager Duchess Dorothea. This
princess, who by birth belonged to the House
of Schleswig-Holstein-Glucksburg, played an important part in the last years of her second husband,
and, according to the irreverent expression of his
descendant, Frederick the Great, ' ruled the hero ' ;
but her interference in the interest of her children
cannot be proved to have gone the length, or to
have produced the effects, frequently attributed to
it.[1] The second brother, George William, who was
to occupy so prominent a place in the history of

[1] According to the Duchess of Orleans (Elizabeth Charlotte),
the Duchess Dorothea presented her, as a child, with two parrots,
and the Duchess Sophia ordered her to give in return her dog
Fidel. ' This was, to the best of my belief, the only occasion in

his House and in that of the personal life of Sophia, was deficient neither in courage nor in insight, and the constant habit of foreign travel added the charm of agreeable manners to the attractiveness of an open and amiable nature.   But, after, in his youth, he had seen some service under Frederick Henry of Orange, he had cast to the winds military ambition and serious purpose of any kind, and, leaving his ministers, as best they might, to carry on his government and manage his Estates, had with his 'flying Court' (as Sophia calls it) frittered away his time in a series of visits to Holland and, more especially, to Venice.   During the intervals which he spent at home in Hanover, he pursued the same round of frivolous pleasures, intent upon nothing but 'going a-hunting and making love.'   Announcing a visit from him at Heidelberg to the Elector Palatine Charles Lewis, Sophia bids her brother 'retail the wicked doings of his own youth in England for the entertainment of his guest, but not touch on matters of State ; for, though George William has plenty of wit and judgment, he wastes them on his jests and trifling amusements.'   As he grew older, he came to be extolled both as a 'mighty Nimrod' and as a connoisseur in champagne ; but he also, as will be seen, subjected himself to influences which had the effect of refining his

my life on which I ever obeyed you reluctantly ; for my little dog was very near to my heart.'

personal tastes and habits, while his intimacy with King William III could not but impart strength of purpose to his political action. But the moral infirmity of the good easy man remained incurable, and proved a source of sorrow to others besides Sophia.

The third of the brothers, John Frederick, like George William, matured his mental powers by travel rather than by study. But this prince, whose highest honour it is to have introduced Leibniz into the service of the House of Guelf, was not wholly undeserving of the praise lavished on him after death by the courtly philosopher in both German prose and Latin verse.[1] John Frederick was at any rate possessed by an ardent ambition, besides being determined to think out his own salvation. During a visit to Rome, in the year of Jubilee, 1650, he was much impressed by the arguments of Count Christopher von Rantzau, who, after adopting the irenic ideals of the great Helmstedt theologian Calixtus, had at Rome been brought over to Catholicism through the influence of the eminent convert and convert-maker Holstenius. In February, 1651, Duke John Frederick was himself at Assisi received into the Catholic Church ; but it was not till several months later that his conversion became known. In December

---

[1] See *Leibnizens Geschichtl. Anpätze und Gedichte I.* (Vol. iv. of Pertz' collected edition).

of the same year, at the very time when commissioners sent by his elder brothers had arrived at Rome to dissuade him from such a step, he made a public profession of his change of faith. There is no reason for supposing that the wish for a Cardinal's hat was one of the motives that actually prompted his conversion, though he certainly was in the course of his life a man of many ambitions—including the High Mastership of the Germanic Order, and the Polish Crown. The Cardinalate desired for, if not by, John Frederick, was bestowed by Pope Innocent X upon a previous convert of Holstenius', Landgrave Frederick of Hesse-Darmstadt; and, after lengthy negotiations, it was settled that Duke John Frederick's *apanage* should be increased on condition of his not returning to Celle. But the good-natured George William gave him quarters at Hanover, and even provided for his private exercise of his religion in the Palace. This in turn alarmed the Calenberg Estates; and further difficulties threatened when the convert, well aware of the vantage-ground which he occupied by reason of these very difficulties, showed himself disposed to marry. It was the fear that, in this event, the House of Brunswick-Lüneburg would become a Catholic House, which impelled George William, after he had made up his mind to remain a bachelor himself, to hasten the marriage of Ernest Augustus. The religious question thus, already at this point, directly affected the determination of the future of the dynasty with whose fortunes Sophia was about to associate her own; nor is it astonishing that John Frederick should have bitterly resented the preferential position conceded to Ernest Augustus, the youngest of the brotherhood.

The future husband of Sophia had, as the youngest of the sons of his mother, the Duchess Anna Eleonora, been kept near home in his boyhood. He had even spent two years at the University of Marburg, where, in accordance with servile academic usage, he had filled the office of *Rector Magnificentissimus*, and he had afterwards been elected *Coadjutor* by the (Lutheran) Chapter of Magdeburg. This was a suitable preparation for the succession to the ' bishopric ' of Osnabrück, which, in accordance with the provision of the Peace of Westphalia, was reserved for Ernest Augustus on the occasion of the next vacancy in the see. The conduct of this prince was, from the first, marked by a circumspection which neglected no opportunity; he was on the best of terms with both the eldest two of his brothers, and was devotedly attached to the second, whose companion he was in a long series of journeys and sojourns on the Lagoons.[1] Thus there established itself

[1] In 1686 was published at Venice a folio, with nine plates, by G. M. Alberti, entitled *Giochi festivi e militari, danze, serenate, machine, boscareccia artificiosa, regatta solemne, e posti alla*

between George William and Ernest Augustus a brotherly intimacy — a *fratellanza*, to use an Italian term of almost technical significance— which goes some way towards explaining how Sophia's marriage had been finally brought about. Ernest Augustus' affection for his favourite brother may be regarded as the most attractive feature in his character ; on the whole, his personality was a stronger though a less pleasing one than that of George William.   Like many of his descendants, Sophia's husband had an insatiable liking for ceremonial and was a stickler for etiquette, albeit, in the early as well as in the later years of his married life, his manners appear to have been remarkably free from restraint in the privacy of domestic life.

Although Sophia's marriage had not been exactly a love-match, in the beginning, as she joyfully reported to her brother at Heidelberg, all was roses at Hanover ; her husband's behaviour made her feel assured that he would love her all the days of his life, and she idolised him so sincerely as to think herself lost when deprived of his company. The two good English ladies who had adhered to her since she left the Hague were in all kindness dismissed from her service ; one returning to Holland, and the other being provided with a

sodifattione . . . dell' Ernesto Aufsusto Duca di Brunswick e Luneburgo in Venetia.

settlement on the spot; henceforth, the life of Sophia's husband was to be her own life. Unluckily, however, this involved a constant intimate association with his brother George William, of which she soon perceived the inconveniences, and which, but for her sincerity and tact—for she was obliged to give proof of both qualities—might have placed her in the falsest of positions. After she had appeased her husband's jealous suspicions, the two brothers joined in pressing her to accompany them on one of their Italian journeys ; but she was quit for a trip to Holland in the company of her little niece Elizabeth Charlotte, whom, as will be seen, her brother had assigned to her care. After her return to Hanover she gave birth, on May 28th (O.S.), 1660, to her first-born child, George Lewis, afterwards King George I of Great Britain and Ireland. The following winter was spent by her husband in Italy with his brother, according to his custom ; but they accompanied her down the Rhine from Heidelberg, where she had been staying with her brother, to Rotterdam, where, as has been seen, she bade a last farewell to her mother, the Queen of Bohemia, then on the point of starting for England. The two Dukes and Sophia soon afterwards returned to Hanover, in time for the birth, on October 2nd, 1661, of her second son, Frederick Augustus. Two months afterwards, the see of Osnabrück at last fell vacant by the death

of the Catholic Bishop, Cardinal Francis William
von Wartenberg. The event (which had been
rumoured to have taken place already two years
earlier) must have been welcome to Sophia, as
relieving her from a position by no means free
from difficulty, although in her letters she makes
no reference to her husband's jealousy of his brother.
After Ernest Augustus had held his entry at Osnabrück as Bishop—a ceremony at which, as Sophia
remarks, she felt that her presence would be superfluous,—she joined him at the castle of Iburg,
which became her residence for many years. The
little Court moved about a good deal between
Osnabrück and Iburg, besides (after a time) occasionally staying at Celle and at Diepholz, the
former seat of the Counts and *Edelherren* of Diepholz,
whose line had become extinct in 1585.

The change from Hanover was a delightful
one for the Duchess Sophia ; for, apart from the
fact that the Old-town of Hanover, within whose
walls lay the ducal castle, was a sombre and crowded
enclosure very unlike what was destined to become
ultimately one of the most cheerful and attractive
of German capitals, she and her husband had
resided there in a position which, in spite of the
excess of affection surrounding them, remained
one of dependence. They now for the first time
tasted the pleasures, on however small a scale, of
sovereignty. She was, in German fashion, 'the

Bishopess ' ; when she travelled in France, her *incognita* designation was ' Madame d'Osnabrück.' As the old episcopal lodging at Osnabrück was found inadequate to the ample requirements and luxurious tastes of the new Bishop,[1] he at once set about buying land and house property of all kinds with a view to the erection of a suitable episcopal palace. The building of it seems to have been begun in 1665, and seriously taken in hand from 1668; but it was not ready till early in 1673, from which date Ernest Augustus and Sophia continuously resided there for the last five or six years before their removal to Hanover. The palace, which still stands (it was restored with quite unusual success by the last King of Hanover), bears the name of Ernest Augustus on its portal, with the Arcadian motto *Sola bona quæ honesta*. The building erected by Ernest Augustus seems to have been intended for a direct reminiscence of the Luxembourg, at a time when Versailles and the Louvre were only in course of construction, and was, like its prototype, surrounded by magnificent gardens, designed by the Bishop's own gardener, Martin Charbonnier, whom he had brought from Paris, and who seems to have been a pupil of Lenôtre.

[1] We have it on the authority of the Duchess of Orleans, that, when Ernest Augustus became Bishop of Osnabrück, he at once launched forth into so large an increase of his household, as to create in the child the impression that he had become the possessor of great wealth.

The castle at Iburg was of a similar type of architecture—heavy but not ineffective—and betrayed the same lack of finish, due to the inadequacy of the expenditure upon artistic work.[1] Meanwhile, on the breezy heights of Iburg, as is shown by the evidence of her own letters and those of the incomparable Palatine niece whom she carried thither from Hanover, Sophia spent the happiest if not the most exciting years of her life. After all, she writes in her favourite ironical vein, ' One cannot live more than once. Why vex one's soul, if one can eat, drink and sleep, sleep, drink and eat ? All is vanity. . . . Tranquillity of the spirit is lovely, since from it springs our bodily health. Those whom the Lord loves He blesses in their sleep. We play at nine-pins, breed young ducks, amuse ourselves with running at a ring or backgammon, talk every year of paying a visit to Italy ; and in the meantime things go quite as well as is to be expected for a petty bishop, who is able to live in peace and, in case of war, can depend upon the help of his brothers.' In the summer an annual visit was paid to the waters of Pyrmont, and gradually things became more lively at home—in 1663, we find a company of French musicians engaged for the pleasure of the Court. As a matter

[1] See A. Haupt, *Die bildende Kunst in Hannover zur Zeit der Kurfürstin Sophie*, Appendix to H. Schmidt, *Die Kurfürstin Sophie von Hannover*. Hanover, 1903.

of fact, Sophia, though she was very far from vege-
tating in either mental or bodily inactivity, visited
Italy but once, crossing the Alps for the first time in
April, 1664. Nor is there any better or more convincing proof of her rare powers of observation and
insight than that she should have learnt so much—
and not only as to the beauty of Italian gardens
and the charm of Italian manners—in the course of a
sojourn extending over little more than a twelve-
month. While by no means irresponsive to the
æsthetic attractions of Rome and Florence, she was
the last person to give way to the religious influences
in readiness to be exerted upon her. Loretto
annoyed her ; and at Rome, with a spirit which
Sir Henry Wotton would have applauded, she
refused an offering to the Blessed Mary of Victory,
to whom the Emperor Ferdinand II had dedicated
his sceptre in grateful remembrance of the battle
of Prague. At Venice, amidst whose gaieties and
gallantries she found herself altogether ' *depaisée*,'
though, nevertheless, by no means incapable of
amusing herself, it was brought home to her how
largely religion was used as a cloak in a society
where the nuns made themselves agreeable to
gentlemen and the very churches were used for
the purpose of assignations. Much in the cynical
tone which became habitual to Sophia and to her
intimates is attributable to experiences such as
these, rather than to natural irreverence. An

M

attempt made at Rome to 'save her soul' by
bringing her over to Catholicism was so feeble that
she had no difficulty in repelling it ; nor could anything have been better calculated to heighten
the repugnance with which such overtures inspired
her than the want of appreciation of the dignity
of the House of Brunswick-Lüneburg, which she
thought observable in the illustrious convert (almost
a *bête-noire* to some of the Palatines) Queen Christina
of Sweden, as well as in Pope Alexander VII.

By none of the family was this indifference more
keenly felt than by Sophia's brother-in-law, Duke
John Frederick, who showed no sign of any wish
that his conversion should remain its own reward.
Sophia was to have reason for congratulating
herself on her discretion in abstaining from receiving
an *incognito* visit from him at Rome, before he
left the city.   For hardly had her husband and she,
in the early spring in 1665, once more set foot in
Germany on their homeward journey, when they
learnt that the eldest of the brothers, Duke Christian Lewis, had died, and that John Frederick, having
returned from Rome just in time, had made forcible
entry into Celle and Lüneburg, to which he contended that George William, having once made his
choice of Calenberg-Göttingen, could no longer claim
any right of succession.   Inasmuch as the question
between George William and John Frederick, which
the latter thus proposed to settle by a *coup de main*,

turned on the interpretation of the will of their father, a bitter *Bruderstreit* seemed to be announcing itself; and John Frederick, in his usual sanguine way, boasted his hopes of both Imperial and French support for his efforts as a Catholic prince. On the other hand, the facile temper of George William, who, moreover, at the time of his more ardent brother's incursion, was occupied with his own private affairs in Holland, might have given John Frederick a chance, but for the exertions of Count George Frederick of Waldeck, afterwards celebrated as the right hand of William of Orange, and for the intervention of the Elector of Brandenburg. Several Catholic Estates, such as the Elector of Mainz and the Bishop of Münster, favoured John Frederick; on the other hand, Sophia had solicited the diplomatic intervention of her brother, the Elector Charles Lewis. After long and angry negotiations, in which the Scandinavian Powers as well as France took part, John Frederick had to rest satisfied with the addition of Grubenhagen to the territories transferred to his sway from that of George William, who in his turn entered into possession of the eldest brother's portion of Lüneburg-Celle. The energy of Ernest Augustus, which had been as conspicuous in these transactions as had George William's want of this quality, was rewarded by the transfer to the Bishop of Osnabrück of the Countship of Diepholz.

We are obliged to refrain from more than touching upon the remaining course of John Frederick's career, and the *régime* now established by him at Hanover—one of the most peculiar of the vicissitudes undergone by that capital in the course of its many and changeful experiences. Capuchin friars once more found a home at Hanover, which, in days of old, had been a town full of churches and cloisters ; a Vicar Apostolic and Bishop of Morocco *in partibus* resided there as the centre of a propaganda fostered alike by Pope and Emperor.[1] The Jesuits at the same time had a centre of activity at Hildesheim. But there was no interference either with the rights of the Lutheran establishments, or with the claims of free intellectual enquiry, as represented by those whom John Frederick's high-minded liberality drew to his

[1] This was the vivacious Valerio Maccioni, one of the pleasant Catholic ecclesiastics who were Sophia's familiar associates and correspondents in these kindly days. (Others were the Abbé (afterwards Count) Balati, a Florentine nobleman who was afterwards of service to Ernest Augustus as a diplomatist and to the ladies of his family in the matter of *chiffons* at Paris, and the Abbé Hortensio Mauro, Italian secretary, and afterwards attached to the Court at Celle.) Maccioni, after acting for some years as John Frederick's ecclesiastical adviser and as papal representative at Hanover, was episcopated in 1669, when about thirty-eight years of age. He died at Hanover in 1676. Sophia was on the easiest of terms with him, as is shown by the references, in her letters to him, to the Holy Court at 'Traive,' and to a prophetess with a magic mirror, whom she requested the Bishop to exorcise, should he opine that the devil had a hand in her manifestations.

Court, and, above all, by his librarian, Leibniz.
The political ambition of the Duke, who cherished
the design of securing a Ninth Electorate for the
House of Brunswick-Lüneburg a generation before
it was actually accomplished, ranged him on the
side of France in the chief political conflict of his
times, and thus led him to stand in opposition,
not only to the interests of the Empire, but also
to the policy, on which his brothers finally determined, of resisting the action of Louis XIV. On
the other hand, it was John Frederick who set his
younger brother the example of a firm monarchical
administration, and who took the all-important
step of providing this administration with the
support of a standing army (two-thirds of which
he was, however, pledged by a secret treaty to
hand over as auxiliaries to France). But, before
the issues of the great European contest in which
he was prepared to sustain the part chosen by him
finally declared themselves, he was overtaken
by death, on his last journey towards his beloved
Italy, in 1679. Many ambitions, as has been seen,
had fretted his (far from pygmy) body. It was
natural that, estranged as he was from his brothers,
he should have hoped himself to become the founder
of a dynasty ; and it was equally inevitable that
his brother Ernest Augustus and his sister-in-law
Sophia, who were already intent upon guarding in
every way the interests of their own descendants,

should have shown scant sympathy with his matrimonial projects, which were, as a matter of course, directed to securing the hand of a Catholic princess. Towards this end no aid could be more effective, as none was more ready, than that of Sophia's sister-in-law, the ' *Princesse Palatine* ' (Anne of Gonzaga), in whose dexterous hold were successively gathered the threads of so many marriage-schemes calculated to advance the interests of France, and approving themselves to the Church of Rome. The *Princesse Palatine* accordingly apprised John Frederick, whose ambition was at the time occupied with thoughts of the next vacancy on the Polish throne, that an alliance with one of her and Prince Edward's daughters might ease the way to such a goal :—' *pour cela, il faut commencer avec le mariage.*' The negotiations for the match were carried on by the busy French diplomatic agent de Gourville, who, during these years and again at a later date, was employed by the Government of Louis XIV in the task of trying to win over the Brunswick Dukes to the interests of France, and whose *Memoirs* are thus a notable source of information concerning their Courts and their policy.

The danger with which Sophia and her husband found themselves ' *toujours menassés* ' was realised, when, in 1667, John Frederick gave his hand to the youngest of Edward's daughters, Benedicta Henrica. But, though two daughters were born to John

Frederick (the elder of whom, Charlotte Felicitas, afterwards became Duchess of Modena, while the second, as the consort of Joseph I, attained to the dignity of Empress), his hopes were not crowned by the birth of a son. Of the Duchess Benedicta, who, as a Catholic, was excluded from the English Succession, to which, in her later years, she had the first claim by birth among the surviving descendants of the Queen of Bohemia, Sophia's correspondence contains occasional kindly mention ; though there was little trace of the high spirit of the Palatines in the gentle and sombre-featured widow of the massive John Frederick. His own soaring ambition and imperious will isolate his memory in the annals of his House, while the shadowy figure of his consort has come to be all but forgotten in the history of the English Succession.

It may be convenient to note in this place that, owing to the attack made by ' Münster's prelate,' as an ally of Charles II of England, upon the United Provinces, the States-General had appealed for aid to George William and Ernest Augustus, who duly arrived in their support. In return, the Bishop of Münster threatened the city of Osnabrück, where Sophia and her children accordingly had to take up their abode during the winter 1665-6, under the protection of the Bishop's troops, Iburg being too exposed to be safe. It would have been a curious accident if this Bishop's war had ended in

any mischance, by which the future Heiress of
Great Britain should have been taken prisoner by the
ally of its King.   In June, 1666, Sophia was enabled
to return to the 'delightful solitude' of Iburg.
The autumn and winter of 1666 she spent chiefly
at Osnabrück, while her husband and his brother
were carrying on operations against Sweden in
defence of the city of Bremen.

At the time of the negotiations which ended
in the establishment of Duke George William
at Celle, and of Duke John Frederick at Hanover,
their youngest brother, Ernest Augustus, and his
faithful Duchess were much exercised in spirit
by the beginnings of another family trouble, of
which the course was to be more protracted and the
consequences far more enduring. For some time
George William's brother and sister-in-law had been
disquieted by the attentions paid by the amorous
Duke to Mademoiselle Eleonora d'Olbreuze, who,
in 1665, when he first made her acquaintance at the
Hague, was lady-in-waiting to the Princess (Henry
Charles) of Taranto, by birth a Princess of Hesse-
Cassel. The *animus* of Sophia, which renders it
necessary to treat with the utmost caution any
statement made by her or hers in the present connexion, is evident from her earliest mention of
the lady who was to be the object of her long and
bitter hatred, as ' *une fille qui estoit à la princesse de
Tarente.*' Mademoiselle d'Olbreuze sprang from

an ancient Poitevin family which belonged to the minor nobility of a province long full of Huguenot sympathies, and which held a leading position in the oligarchy, as it has been called, that charged itself with the religious and intellectual interests of Protestantism in these regions.[1] That she was exceptionally endowed with an ability including a great deal besides tact, is abundantly clear not only from the success of her manœuvres for raising herself, and afterwards her child, to such greatness as was attainable by them, but also from her living to be chosen as the spokeswoman of the House of Brunswick-Lüneburg on a memorable occasion in its history. Nor can there be any doubt but that her intellectual influence was a refining one, while her personality must have possessed a charm which is hardly suggested by such portraiture of her as remains. Sophia, after having, apparently through Mademoiselle d'Olbreuze's own judicious prudence, been spared her company in Italy, had found herself constrained, by her husband's anxiety to please his brother, to bring her over almost in state from Hertogenbosch to Iburg; and, though the *Memoirs* refer with scorn to the Frenchwoman's real or pretended conquests before that of George William, Sophia is obliged to confess that she found the intruder both modest and pleasant of speech,

---

[1] This information I owe to Mr. H. H. Sturmer, author of *Some Poitevin Protestants in London* (London, 1896).

and altogether very amiable. Thus it is clear that she prepared with consummate skill the first upward step on which so much depended, and which she actually accomplished in November, 1665. On the solemn occasion of the funeral of Duke Christian Lewis, the whole family, including his widow, his brothers George William and Ernest Augustus, and Sophia, met at Celle; and to this august conclave the new 'Duke of Celle,' as he was now so usually called, made known what Sophia terms his 'anti-contract' of marriage with Eleonora d'Olbreuze, and what, in other words, was his recognition of her as his mistress *en titre*. In this document, signed by his brother and sister-in-law, as well as by his mistress and himself, George William repeated his promise to remain unmarried, which he declared to have been dictated by his affection for his brother, and by a desire to consult his interests and those of his children. Mademoiselle d'Olbreuze, who had innocently begged that she might henceforth bear the name of Madame de Celle, had instead to put up with that of Madame de Harburg, by which, as Sophia rather savagely adds, she continued to be known for the next ten years.

Sophia and her husband seem at first to have regarded this revised arrangement, which was substantially quite in accordance with German as well as Italian precedents, as on the whole likely to ensure what to them was naturally the main

point, the continuance of George William's bachelorhood. In September, 1666, his mistress bore him
a daughter, the ill-fated Sophia Dorothea. From
the same year onward, Ernest Augustus and his
wife's own family rapidly increased, by the birth,
in December, of their third son, impartially christened Maximilian William after the Catholic Elector
of Cologne and the Protestant Elector of Brandenburg, and the births of their daughter Sophia
Charlotte, in 1668, and of their sons Charles Philip,
Christian, and Ernest Augustus, in 1669, 1671, and
1674 respectively. Sophia's love for her children
forms, perhaps because of the perfectly natural
expression which she gives to so natural an affection,
a most delightful feature of her personality. This
love enveloped alike the more and the less gifted,
the successful and the unlucky, the phlegmatic
and mild-mannered, though ungainly ' Brunswicker '
(her eldest son, George Lewis), and the fearless little
spitfire of a 'Palatine' (her second son, Frederick
Augustus)—as she described them in their early
days. We shall see how her tenderly loved only
daughter's bright and enquiring spirit also commended her to her mother's intellectual sympathies ;
but her motherly heart flowed out towards all her
sons, and even the inexpansive nature of the eldest
seems to have in a measure warmed towards her.
But she could only with difficulty reconcile herself
to a policy which made it necessary to sacrifice

the interests of his younger brothers to his, or rather to those of the House as a whole ; and even among these younger brothers themselves, it would almost seem as if her anxiety, like a true mother's, had been deepest for those who most needed support. Thus we find her, when both Frederick Augustus and Charles Philip were serving the Emperor in arms, pitifully pointing out to Leibniz how the younger of the pair was not ' *si chiche de ses sollicitations* ' nor ' *si misanthrope* ' as his brother, and succeeded better accordingly. Yet his prosperity, too, she had at heart ; nor could she suppress the thought that the sum spent on the purchase of a regiment for him by his father was less than what the latter had on occasion been known to lose at the basset-table.

In these earlier years, however, before the deeper anxieties of her motherhood had yet come to Sophia, although the happiness of her life was already beginning to centre in her children, it owed much to the presence at Hanover and Iburg of the niece, who had become to all intents and purposes her adopted child. From her fourth to her eleventh year, Elizabeth Charlotte, the Elector Palatine's only daughter by his unhappy first marriage, was the constant companion of her aunt, to whom this joyous period of intimacy sufficed to bind her heart and soul during a long life of trials. It was in a happy moment that her father resolved upon sending

his child, in the company of her governess (afterwards, as Frau von Harling, one of the most
favoured recipients of Elizabeth Charlotte's flow
of confidences), to what became the home of her
heart, and was, in after days, the perennial refuge
of her thoughts. As a child ' Liselotte '—so she
was familiarly called—was the very incarnation of
high spirits and natural gaiety, delighting in air and
movement like the leaves which the wind drives
before its blast ; hence the sobriquet, untranslate-
able but conjuring up a world of fairies and imps of
mischief, by which she liked to speak of herself,
even when cribbed and confined amidst the royal
splendours of Versailles. *Rauschenblattenknecht-
chen* never forgot either the homely comforts of
Hanover in meat and drink, or the airy freedom
of the heights of Iburg ; and for its *châtelaine*,
for her virtues and her wisdom, for her high intellectual powers, and for the charm of her style,
she conceived a loving admiration, which long
outlived its object, and which found expression
in many volumes of letters, brimful, from the
first to the last, of quick observation, animated
comment, and a piquant or pleasantly malicious
wit, relieved here and there by touches of an equally
irresistible natural pathos. So early as 1663, Liselotte was, to her unfeigned sorrow, summoned back
to Heidelberg by her father, whom her mother's
departure to Cassel had at last enabled to arrange

his family life after his own fashion.   Sophia deeply
regretted her niece's departure from Iburg, where,
as she wrote, they had led a vagabond life together ;
but, with her usual common-sense and self-control,
she declared it quite in order that the Infanta of
the Palatinate should be brought up at a Court like
Heidelberg, rather than down in Westphalia, where
her kinsfolk had lived in simple *bourgeois* condition
and seen few people.   To her changed home
Elizabeth Charlotte's nature, readily susceptible to
kindness, without difficulty accommodated itself
during seven further happy years.   The moral
atmosphere in which they were spent was that of a
religious tolerance springing partly from kindliness
of disposition and partly from indifference ;   the
epoch of religious strife seemed over, and another
at hand, of less fettered thought and philosophic
speculation.   Into this new movement it was easy
to enter superficially, encouraged by the lofty
aspirations for a reunion of Christendom that
occupied some of the foremost among contemporary
thinkers.   From these influences, of whose effect
upon the Elector Palatine Charles Lewis and his
favourite sister Sophia note has already been taken,
so receptive a mind as that of his Elizabeth Charlotte
was not likely to escape ;   and they undoubtedly
help to account for the process of the conversion which
ominously preceded a marriage destined to alter
the whole course of her life.   To the ' *Princesse*

Palatine ' (Anne of Gonzaga) and her allies no path
seemed impracticable that led to Rome ; and, in
the case of the niece, no such apparatus of argument
was required as had to be set in motion when the
attempt was made at a later date to work upon
the mind of the Duchess Sophia and her husband
through the pertinacious fervour of Madame de
Brinon and the swooping condescension of the
' Eagle of Meaux.' For Elizabeth Charlotte was
constrained by the instinct of filial obedience, her
father having persuaded himself that the welfare
of the Palatinate necessitated, together with the
sacrifice of his daughter's happiness, the ignoring
of her conscience. That in this calculation he,
as was indicated above, terribly deceived himself,
and that the bond thus knit proved the ruin of
the land which it was intended to benefit, only
enhances and deepens the cruel irony of the whole
transaction. A marriage had been arranged between Elizabeth Charlotte and Louis XIV's brother, the Duke of Orleans (whose first consort,
Charles II's sister Henrietta, had died in 1670,
in circumstances long regarded as suspicious) ;
and, though no mention of the subject of religion
had been made in the contract, her conversion
to the Church of Rome was regarded as an indispensable preliminary step to its execution, and it
was necessary that this step should seem to have
been taken spontaneously. She was accordingly

prepared for it by her father's secretary,[1] to the diversity of whose historical and philosophical learning two volumes of *Chevreana* survive to testify. Hereupon she was taken to Strassburg, whither her aunt the Duchess Sophia also found her way to meet her and her father, but where also appeared the presiding genius of the whole business, the ' *Princesse Palatine.*' After the sojourn at Strassburg—where aunt and niece parted—Elizabeth Charlotte passed on to Metz, where she was received into the Church of Rome, and thence into her new married life. The religious comedy was completed by a letter from her to her father entreating his pardon for her change of faith, and by his reply, the really contemptible part of the process, making pretence of a virtuous indignation. Whatever Elizabeth Charlotte's feelings may have been at the time, she afterwards made no secret of the matter to her aunt Sophia, and frequently dwelt upon her aunt's share in the transaction. ' It was you,' she says on one occasion, ' who made me a Catholic ' ; and, when Duke Antony Ulric had gone over to Rome, 'Why,' she asks, 'should you be so sorry, when you are such a fine convert-maker yourself ? '[2] But, though the constraint which had

[1] Urban Chevreau accomplished the task of 'instructing' Elizabeth Charlotte in four weeks. It must have been about this time that the same *savant* induced her father to read a few pages of Spinoza, who was thereupon invited to Heidelberg.

[2] It should be noted that, at the time of Elizabeth Charlotte's

been put upon her never ceased to rankle in her mind, and though her conversion was not consummated without some rubs and some qualms, these feelings perhaps never went very deep. Her real grief, which made her 'cry all through the night from Strassburg to Chalons,' was at parting from her German home and its associations, in which her whole heart was wrapped up ; and of this parting the enforced change of religious profession was merely an incident. 'Between ourselves,' she afterwards wrote to her aunt, out of her gilded exile, ' I was stuck here against my will ; here I must live and here I must die, whether I like it or not.'

And so the genial daughter of the Palatinate, true of heart and sound in body and mind, became the wife of a feeble and effeminate voluptuary, devoid of all character or will of his own, and by him the mother of a prince who, though neither incapable nor ill-meaning, typified the decadence of that

change of confession, toleration still obtained in France. We have her own assurance that, had the persecutions of the Huguenots at that date already begun, she would have refused to be converted. In 1698, she writes to her aunt Sophia : ' At Court one never hears a word spoken on behalf of those of the Reformed faith. If they had been persecuted in this way twenty-six years since, when I was still at Heidelberg, you would never have succeeded in persuading me to turn Catholic.' Sophia herself, when replying to a renewed attempt upon her Protestantism by Mme. de Brinon, by the remark that she trusts in the goodness of God, who cannot have created her to see her lost, adds that she cannot reconcile herself to the persecution of the Protestants in France, who crowd England, the Netherlands, and Germany as refugees.

N

France which he was called to rule as Regent.
But with this long second stage of her life we cannot
concern ourselves here. About August, 1679, she
had the pleasure of a visit from the Duchess Sophia,
who, as already noted, came to France at that time
to see her sister at Maubuisson. The aunt found
her beloved niece stouter, but in excellent spirits.
On the invitation of the Duke of Orleans the
Duchess Sophia was present at Fontainebleau on
the occasion of the wedding of the Duke's daughter
by his first marriage to the King of Spain (Charles
II) ; and, though she kept up her *incognito*, King
Louis XIV called upon her, and charmed her by
his conversation, which he magnanimously turned
to the success of the Hanoverian arms at the bridge
of Conz, mentioned below. For the rest, the sacrifice
of which, for all her philosophy of good humour,
Elizabeth Charlotte was the conscious victim,
was, as we know, not only made in vain, but brought
upon her father's and her own beloved Palatinate,
in the shape of the so-called 'Orleans War' (1688-90),
consequences which were the direct opposite of those
intended by him, and which caused her many
days and nights of anguish. During the half-
century of her exile—for down to the day of her
death, in 1722, she never saw the Palatinate again
—though she held her head high, with eyes un-
dazzled even by the closest propinquity to the sun,
there was hardly an experience of bitterness and

disappointment which she was not fated to undergo ; and through all she had but one consolation,
which was her pen. She wrote because she loved
her correspondents, but also because she loved the
relief of writing, and the opportunities thus afforded
of self-expansion and of free expression for the
loves and hatreds of her soul. That—in the days
of Louis XIV — her letters would be opened,
so as to ascertain the working of her Protestant
sympathies, and perhaps of her interest in the
English Succession question, troubled her not a
whit ; if her insults to Madame de Maintenon
—apparently quite unprovoked, and certainly, in
a large measure, baseless—were made known to
their object, this was so much gain to their author.
Yet, after every deduction has been made on account of the pride, the jealousy, the personal and
other prejudices, and the perennial impatience
which weariness of heart had made second nature
to the kindly-hearted Palatine, her picture of the
Court of Louis XIV, in the latter half of his reign,
possesses a historical value which is only surpassed
by its general human interest.[1] It is, above all, in
Elizabeth Charlotte's letters to Sophia, and in the

---

[1] In a series of articles in the *Revue des Deux Mondes*, begin-
ning October 15th, 1906, entitled *Madame, Mère du Régent*, M.
Arvé de Barine takes great pains to show that in estimating the
Duchess of Orleans' censure of the state of morals at the French
Court we should remember that she might have found a good
deal to complain of nearer her parental home.

references to *ma tante* in those addressed to her
various other correspondents, that the pathetic
side of her humour asserts itself, together with the
malicious ; nor has the whole literature of confidences any second example quite comparable to
this, either in volume or in the directness of its
derivation from nature's self.

We return to Osnabrück and Iburg, whither
Elizabeth Charlotte longed to fly, tying herself to
the end of a ribbon transmitted by her as a sample
of the fashions of Versailles. So long as the relations between Duke George William and Madame
de Harburg remained unchanged, Ernest Augustus
or his descendants were assured of the Succession
in Celle and Lüneburg ; for it had been finally
settled with John Frederick that the right of further
option, against which he had formerly protested,
had now determined. John Frederick's marriage,
in 1668, seemed to cut off from Ernest Augustus and his line the prospect of succeeding in
Hanover likewise, until John Frederick, whose
hopes of a son and heir had been repeatedly
disappointed, died in 1679 without having seen
them fulfilled. Thus, during these years, it was upon
the Succession at Celle that the ambition of Ernest
Augustus and Sophia was concentrated ; nor had
they for some time any reason to fear that their
wishes would be thwarted by George William.

Indeed, his acceptance of the existing situation seemed clear from his endeavours to secure, by means of a series of treaty arrangements, a large private estate in land to his children by Madame de Harburg. The early death of all of these, with the sole exception of the eldest, Sophia Dorothea, born in September, 1666, eventually made her a wealthy heiress ; but some time passed before her father abandoned all expectation of a son, and a disquieting rumour reached Osnabrück that, if George William's mistress were to present him with the desired heir, it was his intention to marry her, his ' anti-contract ' notwithstanding. As there had been precedents in plenty for the promise,[1] so it might no doubt be possible to find others for setting it aside. Already, Eleonora was tactfully asserting herself at Celle, and her personality was becoming the dominant power in the ducal Court. Some of her Poitevin relations held high office there ; and, though the fact that other Frenchmen of family entered the military service both of George William and of his brother the Bishop was, at the time, by no means an exceptional

---

[1] One of these was the case of the Elector Palatine, Frederick I, just a century earlier (1472), who after, on his usurpation of his nephew's dominions, making a promise similar to George William's, twenty years afterwards married his mistress with his nephew's consent. Another instance is that of Henry of Dannenberg, who, notwithstanding a supposed promise, married, greatly to the vexation of his brother William the Younger, the founder of the New House of Lüneburg.

phenomenon, yet it added to the significance of an
influence which the policy of Louis XIV might
just then deem worth cultivating.[1]   For the Brunswick Dukes were, from the time of the Triple Alliance (1668) onwards, political personages of much
interest both to France and to her adversaries, and
had, two years earlier, even seemed to have some
chance of subsidies from a Government more in the
habit of receiving than granting them—the Government of Charles II.   After John Frederick of Hanover
had, as has been seen, decided finally to throw in
his lot with France, his brothers George William and
Ernest Augustus continued to be solicited by her
diplomacy; and it was with the palpable purpose of
gaining over the former and more important of the
pair, that, in 1671, de Gourville was instructed to
question him by presenting a royal ordinance,
naturalising his daughter by Madame de Harburg in
France as ' *Demoiselle Sophia-Dorothée de Brunswick
et de Lunebourg.*'   But the bait was too minute.[2]
Larger issues were involved, and, though in 1671,

---

[1] No doubt a less reputable class of French and Italian
adventurers also found their way to George William's court, which
in 1670 Sophia states ' under the roos ' to be called ' *le Royaume
de la Canalle,*' adding that the nobility is held of no account
there, and that cooks are probably better paid than Ministers
of State.

[2] According to another view, this naturalisation of her
daughter, together with permission to herself to return to France
in the event of danger, had been sought by Eleonora herself,
aware of the jealousy with which she was regarded by most of
her protector's relatives.

apprehensive of the consequences which a bolder policy might have for the safety of his bishopric, Ernest Augustus actually entered into a treaty of neutrality for two years with France, George William was by his far-sighted Chancellor, Baron Lewis Justus von Schütz,[1] prevailed upon to stand firm. When the invasion of the United Provinces of the Netherlands took place in 1672, Duke George William ranged himself on the side of the adversaries of the French invader, and very soon Ernest Augustus followed suit. In 1674, George William, accompanied by Ernest Augustus, was in command of the Brunswick-Lüneburg troops forming part of the imperial army opposed to Marshal Turenne, the devastator of the Palatinate, in Alsace; and, in the following year, the Bishop of Osnabrück and his eldest son George Lewis achieved a brilliant military success at the bridge of Conz, and followed it up by taking part in the recovery of Treves. Before leaving Osnabrück for this campaign, Ernest Augustus had handsomely raised his consort's dowry to an annual income of 16,000 dollars. ' I hope,' she wrote, ' that I shall never need it, and that the Parcæ

[1] The elder Schütz was sent to London in 1683, to congratulate Charles II on his escape from the Ryehouse Plot. His reports from London are preserved from 1689 to 1709, the year of his death; but his interesting correspondence with Sophia (recently edited with other letters from her and Queen Sophia Charlotte by Dr. R. Doebner) does not, with the exception of a single letter, include any letters dated before 1701.

will allow him to survive me.' On this occasion he returned wreathed in laurels. At Osnabrück an imposing triumphal arch was erected by ' the dancing-master Jemme,' and all the princes and princesses at the little Court joined in a dance given in his garden by the same public-spirited professor. In 1675, they took part in the war carried on by the Empire against Sweden, which they helped to oust for a time from the duchies of Bremen and Verden. To allies so loyal and so useful as the two Dukes, no reasonable favour could be refused by the Emperor Leopold, who was manifestly unaware of the conflict between the desires of the elder and the interests of the younger brother. (It is interesting, as an illustration of the consistent dynastic policy of Ernest Augustus, that, when in 1674, after some cautious hesitation, he had concluded a ten years' league with the Emperor, the United Provinces, and Spain, he procured the insertion in the compact of a clause binding the States-General to use their whole influence in the peace negotiations in favour of his bishopric of Osnabrück being turned into a secular principality.) In July, 1674, a patent issued from the Vienna Chancery, granting to Madame de Harburg, for herself and her children, the hereditary title of Countess of the Empire (*Reichsgräfin*) of Wilhelmsburg—the designation of the landed property between Hamburg and Harburg settled upon her and her descendants

by her protector. At the same time, the Empress
Eleonora, a scion of the Catholic Neuburg branch
of the Palatine House, conferred upon her namesake at Celle the Order of the Female Slaves of
Virtue, hitherto reserved for princesses. Soon
afterwards, the right was secured to Eleonora's
daughter Sophia Dorothea, in the event of her
marrying a prince, of bearing the arms of the
House of Brunswick and of being recognised as
herself belonging to that House. The name of the
prince who was to secure the prize of the heiress'
hand while thus raising her in advance of her
mother, to the coveted rank, was no longer a secret :
it was Augustus Frederick, the youthful eldest son
of Duke Antony Ulric of Brunswick-Wolfenbüttel.
Antony Ulric was at the time, though co-regent
with his elder brother, involved in debt and prepared to bring about a rise in the prospects of his
family, even by means of a matrimonial connexion
in other respects not a little dubious. For the
conclusion of this match Sophia Dorothea's legiti-
mation was indispensable ; but her aunt, the
Duchess Sophia, indignantly relates that a shorter
and readier way of reaching this end was suggested
to her brother-in-law by his Chancellor Schütz.
He advised the Duke to marry Sophia Dorothea's
mother. Schütz was the most capable politician
in his master's Court, and served him, as his son-
in-law Bernstorff afterwards served Ernest Augustus

and his son, with equal fidelity and distinction.
There is no reason for attributing sordid motives
to the advice which this petty Wolsey gave to his
easy despot—that he should take the course on
which his heart might not unnaturally be supposed
to be set. For the moment, the incomplete step
of securing a patent of legitimacy for his daughter
was deemed sufficient; but, very soon, Eleonora, or
Eleonora's ally, prompted by the restless Antony
Ulric, again entered into campaign. At first, a
morganatic marriage, with renewed safeguards
for Ernest Augustus and his line, was suggested;
then, a preliminary attempt was made to place the
lady on a level with her lord, by obtaining for her
the title of Princess. The Duchess Sophia was on
the alert, and cites at length a letter which she
wrote to her brother-in-law in order to avert the
impending thunderbolt, and his bland reply assuring
her that it would prove absolutely harmless to her
family. In April, 1676, the marriage of George
William and Eleonora, who still remained Countess
of Wilhelmsburg only, was celebrated at Celle;
and nothing could, on the face of it, be more reassur-
ing than the treaty which followed in May, and
which, while guaranteeing the Succession in George
William's dominions to his brother and his brother's
descendants, actually provided that the oaths of
allegiance taken by his subjects in future should
be sworn to his brother as well as to himself. It

seemed to Sophia that this procedure might opportunely have been set on foot when George William's wife was again expected to present him with a son. Meanwhile Eleonora speedily achieved the remainder of her ascent ; in April, 1676, Sophia had to learn that the Frenchwoman—in her intimate correspondence this designation would have been avoided as colourless—was prayed for in church at Celle, as if she were the reigning Duchess ; and, soon afterwards, the final blow descended, when it became known that the Emperor's envoy had saluted her by the title of Highness. Sophia expresses herself, with not undeserved contempt, as to the excuse preferred by George William, that he could not help obliging one whom others called his wife. From the silence which, in the remaining pages of Sophia's *Memoirs*, ensues on a topic which cannot fail to have continued to exercise her patience, we infer that, though it was very long before either she, or anyone who cared for her, had a good word for the Duchess of Celle, the common-sense which no kind of emotion ever extinguished in her induced her to abandon the struggle against the inevitable. She consoled herself, as she told her favourite niece, with the reflexion that, whatever title the intruder might herself bear, no son of hers could ever be more than a Count of Wilhelmsburg, and that George William might still be trusted, in the event of a son being born to him, to keep his promise to his brother.

The Duchess of Orleans did her best to promulgate this faith to unbelieving or indifferent listeners at Versailles ; but it was not in this way that Sophia's half-pathetic trust in her *çi-devant* lover was destined to be put to the proof.[1]

The influence of the Duchess of Celle upon her husband's mode of life, and upon the tone of his Court, was altogether so excellent that we may without much hesitation discredit her sister-in-law's insinuations as to the bringing-up of George William and Eleonora's only surviving child, the ill-fated Sophia Dorothea. The engagement which had

[1] It was a proud experience of the Duchess of Orleans (in 1717) to find that Louis XIV had observed her dislike of *mésalliances*, and more than one racy reference to a horrible occurrence of the kind might be cited from her letters. The Celle marriage she could never have forgiven, if only for her aunt's sake. Yet *mésalliances* were not altogether unknown in the House of Brunswick (see above as to ' Madame Rudolfine ')—perhaps for the very reason that it was formerly one of those ancient German princely Houses (i.e. Houses which had a seat and vote in the Diet before 1582) which sought to maintain the principle of *Ebenbürtigkeit*. It is only in the branch of the House which attained to a royal throne that a wise policy (embodied in the Act of 1772) substituted for a rigid rule a provision which has sufficiently protected the dignity of the royal family and the interests of the Empire. It may be added that, according to Lord Dover, the *mésalliance* with Eleonora d'Olbreuze prevents the British royal family from taking rank as what is called *chapitrale* in Germany. (See Horace Walpole's *Letters*, ed. Cunningham, Vol. ii. p. 251, note.) Concerning the *Ebenbürtigkeit* principle as recognised in the House of Hohenzollern, and the rights of the head of the House with regard to the marriages of its members, see an article by E. Berner in *Historische Zeitschrift*, 1884, 4, *Die Hausverfassung der Hohenzollern* (a review of H. Schulze, *Die Hausgesetze der reg. Deutschen Fürstenhäuser*).

actually been concluded between her and the youthful Prince Augustus Frederick of Brunswick-Wolfenbüttel came to a sudden end by his death in August, 1676, from wounds received at the siege of Philippsburg ; and the attempt of his father Duke Antony Ulric to secure the hand of the heiress for one of his younger sons met with no ready acceptance. Other suitors appeared or were spoken of : the young Hereditary Governor of Friesland, Henry Casimir of Nassau-Dietz, who was recommended to George William by his cousinhood with William III of Orange, and Prince George of Denmark, for whom fate had in store the splendid, if not in all respects enviable, position of consort to an English Queen. Curiously enough, the hand of the Princess Anne had at this time been also thought to be within reach of Ernest Augustus and Sophia's eldest son George Lewis, who paid a visit to England from December, 1680, to the following March. But for him, too, a different destiny was reserved ; nor, if the account of a most sagacious observer and true friend is to be trusted, had this particular honour ever been coveted either by the Prince himself or at Hanover—for this among other reasons, that Princess Anne's birth on the mother's side was from a very second-rate family. The Prince had, accordingly, taken very little trouble in the matter ; so that, when he left England, it was thought that the marriage would never take place

—all of which things Queen Anne never forgot.[1] Before long a project of dynastic ambition ripened, as we must conclude, in the minds of the brothers at Celle and Osnabrück, which, if carried out, besides serving the immediate end of replenishing the resources exhausted by the extravagant life of Ernest Augustus, would go far towards ensuring the ultimate union of all the dominions of the Brunswick-Lüneburg line. As to the former purpose, it probably weighed heavily with Sophia's husband, whose expenditure on travel abroad and on pomp and ceremony at home had long been excessive, and who had more recently added to his self-indulgences the costly luxury of a mistress *en titre*, in the person of Clara Elizabeth von Meysenbug, since 1673, by her marriage to one of Ernest Augustus' chief courtiers, Baroness von Platen.[2] It would not be easy to show from Sophia's letters how she was affected by a *liaison* which lasted during her husband's lifetime ; one quite welcomes the late

[1] See Ezechiel Spanheim's *Account of the English Court*, printed by Dr. R. Doebner in *English Historical Review*, Vol. ii. 1887, pp. 757 *sqq.* Spanheim's statement as to the scruples felt at Hanover is exactly borne out by an observation of Sophia, *à propos* of the proposed match between her son George Lewis and the Princess Sophia Dorothea, that the example of the Prince of Orange (William III) ' renders the notion more endurable.' In other words, the House of Hanover thought a marriage with a daughter of Anne Hyde a sort of *mésalliance*. (See *Briefwechsel d. Herzogin Sophie mit d. Kurfürsten Karl Ludwig*, p. 387.)

[2] The Meysenbug family makes its first appearance as residing at the Court of Osnabrück during Ernest Augustus' episcopate.

indication afforded by her remark, on the occasion
of the visit of the Tsar Peter the Great, in 1697,
that in Russia all women paint, and that this was
why Countess Platen so much charmed the Musco-
vites. Of her personal power over Ernest Augustus,
and of certain other features in her history and
that of her family, something will have to be said
below ; but it may be as well to point out that there
is no satisfactory evidence to show that she played
the part ascribed to her in the tragedy to be
noticed below. This was not Ernest Augustus'
only infidelity, for about the same date we hear
of a relation between him and one ' Esther,' a *femme
de chambre* in the service of his wife.[1] Sophia, from
whom her husband's affections were thus being
alienated, after she had borne him six children,
seems at first to have felt anything but satisfaction
at the project of a marriage between her eldest son,
George Lewis, and his cousin, Sophia Dorothea ;
indeed, in a letter of November, 1677, the Duchess
of Orleans, as her aunt's faithful echo, profanely
denounces the union of such a creature with so
worthy a young prince as a sin against the Holy
Ghost. In 1679, Sophia describes the pill as
difficult to swallow, though adequately gilded, and
adds that, for her part, she would have preferred

---

[1] An earlier *faiblesse* (1668) of Ernest Augustus for a French
lady, Susanne de la Manoelinière, had been treated by his wife
with great discretion and success.

a daughter of John Frederick of Hanover with a
third of the gilding.   But, three years later, in 1682,
the Duchess of Orleans treats the marriage as an
accomplished fact.   ' She will,' she observes, ' imitate the discretion of her aunt ; ' but ' like the parrot
of the Duke of Savoy, though she holds her tongue,
she thinks a great deal.'   A large amount of fiction,
the origin of which is traceable to the same tainted
source—a ' historical ' novel published, nearly a
generation afterwards, by the ingenious but far
from disinterested Duke Antony Ulric[1]—has accumulated round the supposed exertions of Sophia to
induce her brother-in-law, despite the reluctance
of his wife, to approve the sacrifice of their daughter.
All we know is that, by 1681, the tone of Ernest
Augustus and Sophia towards Eleonora had entirely
changed ; and it is clear what had made both the
parents of the ' worthy ' Prince George Lewis intent
upon bringing the matter to a conclusion.   About
this time, Ernest Augustus had conceived the design
of obtaining the Emperor's consent to the postula-
tion of one of his sons as his successor in the bishopric
of Osnabrück, notwithstanding the express provision of the Peace of Westphalia that it should
be alternately held by a Catholic and a Lutheran.
Sophia was quite prepared to drive a coach and
four through that settlement, and let the Catholics

[1] Vol. vi. of *The Roman Octavia*, a romance in the then
fashionable style of the *Grand Cyrus*.

afterwards appoint two bishops in succession if they
chose.   But this would have been a merely temporary gain for the House.   At the close of the year
1679, as has been seen, John Frederick of Hanover
had died without leaving a son ; and to Ernest
Augustus, on succeeding to his principality, the
prospect of an enduring greatness for himself and
his dynasty at last clearly opened.   If the cordial
relations between his surviving brother and himself
could be maintained, the actual union in his hands,
or in those of his descendants, of the entire territories
of the Brunswick-Lüneburg House, was now merely
a matter of time ; and on the possession of so ex-
tensive and solid a dominion his dynastic ambition
would be warranted in basing ulterior designs.
Already personages of the greatest political consequence in Europe began to interest themselves in
the fortunes of the House of Hanover, and in the
immediate scheme of a marriage promising results
of so high an importance.   Hardly had Ernest
Augustus and Sophia held their entry at Hanover,
when, by the express advice of William of Orange,
they at once recognised the ducal title of Eleonora.
In the same year the august counsel of Louis XIV,
still hopeful of conciliating the goodwill of the
Brunswick-Lüneburg Dukes, was bestowed in favour
of the match, through his minister at Celle, the
Marquis d'Arcy, to whom the Duchess Eleonora
spoke with gratification of the civilities of her

o

sister-in-law. The Estates of Celle-Lüneburg, on the one hand, and those of Calenberg (Hanover), on the other, with a docility surprising after their former insistence on continued separation, declared that, if the marriage was actually concluded, they would consent to the establishment of the principle of primogeniture ; and a law establishing this principle, the very coping-stone of Ernest Augustus' dynastic policy, received the Imperial sanction in 1683, though it was only promulgated in the Brunswick-Lüneburg dominions, as part of the will of Ernest Augustus, on his death fifteen years afterwards. This provision was to entail upon Sophia even more personal unhappiness than the marriage of her eldest son itself ; but a renunciation of her own wishes had by this time become a law of her life.

In September, 1682, the Duchess Sophia informed her ubiquitous correspondent, the Abbé Balati, that henceforth Hanover and Celle would reckon as a single State—a result so advantageous as to warrant defiance of the German genealogical scruple about being equally grand on both sides of the tree. Prince George Lewis had made up his mind, and his mother trusted that he had done so under a good constellation.[1] On November the 21st following, the wedding of George Lewis and Sophia

[1] ' *Il est à present*,' she adds, ' *avec sa maîtresse.*' It is to be feared that this should be translated literally.

Dorothea took place at Celle, and was celebrated by Leibniz (such are the vicissitudes of Court life) in indifferent French verse. Nothing is known as to the early married life of a husband and wife who were no better, though perhaps not much worse, assorted than most couples united under similar conditions. Sophia Dorothea's was an indolent and emotional nature; the habits of George Lewis were active; he was fond of the camp and the chase; and his bearing was character-ised by a reserve which afterwards became stolidity. But, in these years, he was much absent from home, continuing his military career in the Imperial service, taking an honourable part in the historic achievement of the rescue of Vienna by Sobiesky, in 1683, and distinguishing himself two years later at the capture of Neuhäusel in the Hungarian campaign of Duke Charles of Lorraine against the Turks. Sophia Dorothea bore her husband two children—George Augustus (afterwards King George II), in 1683, and Sophia Dorothea (afterwards Queen of Prussia and mother of Frederick the Great), in 1685. Some letters of her mother-in-law, in 1684 and the following year, show that Eleonora's daughter had not been successful in conciliating permanently the sympathies of Sophia, whose politeness towards the mother had not developed into any warm goodwill towards the daughter; but the complaints against Sophia Dorothea are not very serious, and rather suggest a spoilt child in the company of an unsympathetic but by no means stony-hearted relative.

The *Memoirs* of Sophia break off early in 1681, when, after a visit to the Queen of Denmark in the latter part of the preceding year, she was again left alone by her erratic husband, who had departed on one of his pilgrimages across the Alps, although she was plunged into grief by the news of the death of her beloved brother, the Elector Palatine. Her eldest sister, the good Abbess of Herford, had, as we saw, died a few months before their brother, and, in her solitary sorrow, Sophia wrote that it would not be long before she followed them. When, therefore, these *Memoirs* are made to serve as a principal source for her biography, the troubled circumstances of the time in which they were actually written should be taken into account. She little knew how soon a new epoch in her life was to begin, destined to impose upon her a responsibility as great as it was unexpected. With however prudent a self-restraint she might meet it, neither in her own eyes nor in those of the numerous observers who henceforth watched every one of her actions or movements, could it fail to add signally to her personal importance. And although, according to modern notions, the Hanover of the later seventeenth century might seem to differ but slightly, in its capacity to become a theatre of political transactions

of moment, from the neighbouring city of Osnabrück, yet it should be remembered how strenuously
the deceased Duke John Frederick had exerted
himself to make his capital one of those secondary
centres of political and general intellectual life
which, in this age, paid the homage of imitation to
Versailles. To him was owing the creation of a
library which, if it could not rival that for which
Sophia's paternal ancestors had found a home at
Heidelberg, was fostered by the care of Leibniz,
whose services were the noblest legacy left by his
first Hanoverian patron, John Frederick, to his
successor, Ernest Augustus—a legacy of which the
value was to be so fully recognised by Sophia. In
other respects, too—notably in that of the attention
now given at Hanover to the cultivation of the
dramatic and musical arts—court and town had been
transformed under John Frederick's liberal *régime ;*
and an impulse had been given which his younger
brother sought, after his own fashion, to sustain.
Leibniz, of course, remained in his service, and was
treated with a consideration which he owed to his
usefulness both as publicist and historiographer,
and which, thanks to the favour of Sophia, was
never discontinued during her husband's reign.
Relations with Italy and Italian musical art
were certain to be kept up under so constant a
lover of Venice as Ernest Augustus ; an Italian
opera was again established at Hanover under the

conduct of the distinguished Venetian composer, Agostino Steffani ; [1] and the Abbate Hortensio Mauro, who took up his residence at Hanover about 1681, maintained at the Court of Ernest Augustus and Sophia a lasting interest in the Italian language and in Italian art, while himself becoming a trusted servant and friend of the Electoral family.   The Court of Ernest Augustus and France were from the first mainly connected with his love of foreign luxury and elegance of all kinds.   So early as 1668, Baron Platen had secured for him a Parisian *maître d'hôtel ;* and, nearly every year, the Duke sent his *valet de chambre* to Paris, there to consult a resident agent as to the requisites of Sophia and her ladies. The Palace at Hanover was greatly 'beautified,' though a great deal more money was spent on decoration of one kind or another than on architecture proper.   It is reckoned that on the former Ernest Augustus expended nearly 25,000 dollars at Hanover. Tapestry and pictures were imported from Holland, and particular attention was given to stucco-work, under the direction of an Italian *maestro* named Sartorio.   In course of time, Sophia could summon French artists to conduct the weaving of a great

---

[1] Steffani, after being employed in other diplomatic business by the Hanoverian Court, was chosen to accompany the Princess Amalia, daughter of the late Duke John Frederick, on her journey to Modena, where she was married to the Roman King Joseph.   Pope Innocent XI hereupon created him Bishop of Spiga *in partibus.*

Gobelin tapestry, which was carried out in the
Reithaus at Hanover, and which represented scenes
from the life of Duke George of Brunswick-Lüneburg, the ancestor of the Hanoverian dynasty, and
from that of Sophia's mother, the Queen of Bohemia.
In 1695, the interior of the *Schlosskirche* was completely gilded. With the exception of the great
Rittersaal, however, a very pompous and heavy
structure, nearly all the renovated palace buildings
were destroyed by fire in 1741. Ernest Augustus
also built, in direct connexion with the Palace, a new
opera-house.[1]   From the year 1684 we have an
account—*merum mel*—of a visit paid to Hanover
(following on one to Celle) by the celebrated French
traveller Tavernier, whom Duke Ernest Augustus
came over (from Herrenhausen?) to welcome, together with visitors so august as the Duchess Dowager
of East Frisia and so distinguished as the celebrated
Brandenburg diplomatist and statesman, Paul Fuchs.
The old gentleman (Tavernier was then over eighty),
who mentions that the Duke spent Sunday morning
at the 'temple' and the afternoon at a performance
of his company of French comedians, was delighted
both by the agreeable turn which the conversation

---

[1] It was broken up in 1852. See A. Haupt, *u.s.*, where the
palace on the property of Count Alten, which was at the time
mortgaged to the Platens, is said to be the one important specimen
remaining of the Italian architecture in the Hanover of the
period. It was said to have been built by Ernest Augustus for
Countess Platen.

took at dinner—viz. the subject of his own travels in Persia and India—and by the general urbanity and courteous liberality of his reception.[1] There can be no doubt but that in these respects there were few contemporary courts which outshone those of the Lüneburg Dukes. We shall see how, as time went on, Sophia did what in her lay to maintain around her a culture both higher and wider than would have specially commended itself to the personal tastes of her husband, or of her eldest son.

For the present, everything at Hanover seemed shaping itself for the benefit of the Hereditary Prince George Lewis, as the representative of that principle of primogeniture which, in his father's eyes, was of paramount importance for the future of the Brunswick-Lüneburg line, but which brought many tears into the eyes of his mother. The principle in question was by no means a new one in the history of the House of Brunswick. It already obtained in the elder branch, and in the younger had been established for Lüneburg-Celle and for Calenberg-Göttingen individually. Unless it were secured, the Brunswick-Lüneburgers could never hope to hold a more than subordinate position among the Princes of the Empire ; no dream of a Ninth Electorate was worth dreaming ; and any

---

[1] *Jean-Baptiste Tavernier, Baron de l'Aubonne, Chambellan du Grand Électeur.* D'après des documents nouveaux et inédits, par Charles Joret, Paris, 1881, pp. 342 *sqq.*

calculation as to further possibilities would have been more baseless than a fabric of the air. But, while this was understood by Ernest Augustus, and doubtless also by his eldest son, it is not wonderful that the next brother, Frederick Augustus, should have bitterly resented the consequences which followed for himself, and that his mother Sophia should have been full of sympathy with his trouble. After obtaining legal advice, Prince Frederick Augustus communicated his grievance to the willing ears of his kinsman, Duke Antony Ulric, at Wolfenbüttel; and, in the same quarter, the Duchess Sophia was lamenting the quarrel which had already taken place between her husband and their second son. ' Poor Gussy ' (*Arm Gustchen*), she wrote in December, 1685, ' is altogether cast out; his father will no longer give him any maintenance. I cry about it all night long; for one child is as dear to me as another; I am the mother of them all, and I grieve most for those who are unhappy.' Finally, a protest on the part of Antony Ulric was presented to Sophia at Herrenhausen, and forwarded by her to her husband, who was, according to his wont, enjoying himself at Venice. The pressure was applied in vain; and, though ultimately, through the good offices of George William, an understanding was patched up between his brother and the hot-tempered Antony Ulric, Prince Frederick

Augustus was left to his own devices. He followed the example of his elder brother by taking service with the Emperor and fighting
against the Turks ; but he was still intending
to institute a suit at Vienna for the recovery
of his rights, when, in January, 1691, he fell
in a skirmish at Chemetzvar, near St. Giorgy,
in Transylvania. After a heroic struggle, the
fourth of Sophia's sons, Charles Philip, had likewise
fallen in battle against the Turks at Pristina, in
Albania, almost exactly a year before Frederick
Augustus. Charles Philip seems to have been his
mother's favourite boy—possibly because of a
natural disfigurement (of the head) which had from
the first aroused her loving pity ; and the tragic
details of his dying, covered with wounds, on the
battlefield, went to her heart. She fell seriously ill,
and even a visit to Carlsbad in the spring of the
year failed completely to restore her to health.
We may so far anticipate the chronological
sequence of events as to note that, after the
death of Frederick Augustus, the third brother,
Maximilian William, who had at first acknowledged the principle of primogeniture, entered
the lists against it. He was joined in his resistance by the fifth, Christian, who was likewise
in the Imperial service, and who afterwards (in
July, 1703), as Major-General in the Imperial
army, met with his death by being drowned

in the Danube near Ehingen. When the news of his death came, those around his mother feared for her health—as she could not find the relief of tears. In Maximilian's quarrel, his mother's sympathies were again on his side, though, to judge from passages in the correspondence of Sophia Dorothea, he was of a more or less flighty disposition; and, when his father had not unnaturally declined to pay him his appanage, she attempted to obtain some pecuniary support for him at the Danish or at the English Court. Like his brother, he took the officious Antony Ulric into his confidence, and communications were opened with Danckel-mann, the powerful Minister of the Elector of Brandenburg, who, with the distinct purpose of thwarting the designed consolidation of the Celle-Hanover dominions, kept up the tension existing between his and the Hanoverian court, and that not-withstanding the marriage, in 1684, of the daughter of Ernest Augustus, Sophia Charlotte to the Electoral Prince—from 1688, Elector Frederick III of Branden-burg. A plot was now hatched, of which the precise object remained in some measure obscure, but as to whose progress the quick-witted Sophia Charlotte contrived to send sufficient information to her father. On December 5th, 1691, Prince Maximilian William was arrested at Hanover, together with the chief agents of his design ; and one of these, the Master of the Hunt (*Oberjägermeister*), von Moltke, with whom Danckelmann had been in communication, had shortly afterwards to pay the penalty of death for the high treason laid to his charge. Prince Maximilian himself was allowed to depart unharmed, after renouncing all claims to the Succession, except in the case of his elder brother's dying without leaving a son. Although he did not keep his oath very scrupulously, he refrained from any open violation of it during the lifetime of his father, expending his energy in the military service of Venice and of the Emperor. He commanded the first line of cavalry at Blenheim, and survived till 1726, having missed the reversion of the see of Osnabrück by a late conversion to the Church of Rome.[1] Earlier rumours of a change of faith on his part had sorely vexed his mother, to the unconcealed amusement of her niece, the Duchess of Orleans ; but his letters to Sophia, and the references to him in hers to Leibniz, give a pleasing impression of his frank and open nature, although, impulsive as he was, he seems to have been deficient in filial piety as in other qualities showing moral depth.[2]

[1] Already, as a child of six, Maximilian (who seems to have been the survivor of a pair of twins) had displayed an unusual piety, and kept a prayer-book in his bed for matutinal use.

[2] The Duchess of Orleans, who had been informed that a complaint had been preferred to the Emperor by Maximilian, as to a sum of money demanded by him from his mother, the Electress Sophia, not having been sent to him by her, who had loved him so well, exclaims : ' This is abominable ; this Prince

Sophia's youngest son, Ernest Augustus, destined when the time came (1715) to succeed to the see of Osnabrück, formerly held by his father, and also to be created Duke of York and Albany, was still in his boyhood at the critical stage which we have now reached in the history of his House. His birth in 1674, which for a time endangered her life, had elicited from his mother the confession that she already had boys enough ; and, inasmuch as there was some difficulty in finding a godfather for him as the latest-born of so large a family, his eldest brother George Lewis was called upon to undertake the responsibilities of the office.   The special bond thus established between the two brothers held out firmly so long as their lives endured ; indeed, the Duchess of Orleans regrets that, instead of waiting upon his mother, the Prince followed about his elder brother ' like a spaniel ' (1707).   While it is impossible not to respect the loyal devotion of the younger of the pair, the affectionate return made to it on the part of the elder, ' serious ' as he always was in manner, should not be overlooked by those who desire to form a fair estimate of the character of George I.   Ernest Augustus' childhood was spent under his mother's eye ; and, in 1687, the good Duchess of Orleans

can never meet with any good fortune either in this world or in the next, after having done this abominable thing, which I can never forgive him.'

undertook to introduce his elder brother Christian
and himself at the French Court, where, for the better
part of two years, the two Princes, and Ernest
Augustus in particular, by his charming manners
and quickness, did credit to their descent. In 1689,
they started on the indispensable Italian tour;
and, in 1693, Prince Ernest Augustus received the
baptism of fire equally necessary to this masculine
brood in the battle of Neerwinden (Landen), where
three sons of the Duchess Sophia—George Lewis,
Christian, and Ernest Augustus—were engaged.
In August, 1714, the Duchess of Orleans makes a
very curious remark concerning him, which suggests
that there was a notion at the time of passing over
the Electoral Prince (afterwards George II) in the
English Succession.[1] The correspondence of Ernest
Augustus, which covers the years 1703 to 1726, re-
veals a simple and soldier-like character, thoroughly
loyal and singularly modest. His elder brother,
King George I, actually died in his arms at

---

[1] ' I do not know whether it is true, but it is said here ' [at
Versailles] ' that the English are ready to have the Elector of
Brunswick for their King, but that they will make it a condition,
that the Electoral Prince shall never succeed him on the throne.
Duke Maximilian I do not know, but, between ourselves, I would
rather it were Duke Ernest Augustus than the Electoral Prince;
for my cousin, Duke Ernest Augustus, has a good ancestry on
both sides and is of wholly German descent, whereas the Electoral
Prince has some very bad ancestors, and is described to me as
so mad that I have often heartily pitied his wife; of Duke Ernest
Augustus I have never heard anything but praise, and I have
therefore a hearty regard for him.'

Osnabrück, and Ernest Augustus, as Sir Henry Wotton might have written, 'liked it not, and died,' little more than a year later (August 14th, 1728).

Of Sophia Charlotte, her parents' only daughter, the '*Figuelotte*' of a delightful babyhood, and during life the darling and in many respects the semblance of her mother, it will be more convenient to speak in our next chapter. Her youth had been happier than Sophia's, from whom she had inherited, together with her black hair, to which her blue eyes offered a charming contrast, a rare healthiness of mind, as well as, seemingly, of body, inexhaustible high spirits, and a rapidity of apprehension which made her in her early girlhood a linguist such as her mother and her mother's brothers and sisters had been in their generation. In 1679, she accompanied her mother on a visit to the French Court, where her natural charms, and above all the brightness of her intelligence, made so pleasing an impression that it was at the time thought likely that she might return thither as the bride of one of the Princes of the House of France. But at Hanover she soon seemed intent upon very different interests; and she had become the pupil of Leibniz before her destiny called her to give her hand to the widowed Electoral Prince Frederick of Brandenburg (September, 1684). 'It is fortunate,' wrote her mother, ' that she does not care for externals.'

The parting went very near to the heart of the
Duchess Sophia, who was now, more than ever, left
alone to support the dynastic endeavours and
suffer from the domestic troubles of the House of
Hanover, while meeting the responsibilities of her
own title to the English Succession.

IV

THE ELECTORAL HOUSE OF HANOVER

(HANOVER AND HERRENHAUSEN, 1688–1701)

NONE of the varied experiences through which Sophia had passed during a life of nearly sixty years, had either made her forget her English descent, or led her to regard English interests as alien to her own. During the reign of Charles II her personal recollections of his years of vagrancy could not but render her discreetly indisposed to keep up by letter any direct intercourse with her royal cousin ; but she was not the less desirous of remaining in touch with the progress of events in her mother's first and final home. After her brother Rupert had at last settled down in England, she expressed a wish that he should be made a peer, and thus be enabled to attend in Parliament and keep her informed of the course of public business. She was naturally much interested in the marriage, in 1677, of William Prince of Orange to the Duke of York's elder daughter, the Princess Mary ; and, in 1680, she had the satisfaction of welcoming to Hanover the Prince who had thus become closely connected with the English royal family, and of receiving his assurances of his anxiety to render some substantial service to her husband's House. It has already been incidentally noted how, in 1681, her eldest son, George Lewis, had paid a visit to England, where he might, it was hoped, secure the hand of Mary's younger sister, the Princess Anne. This scheme was favoured by the Prince of Orange, whose own marriage had remained childless, and who could not ignore the fact that the design for excluding his Roman Catholic father-in-law from the English Succession had already assumed definite shape. In 1685, after King Charles II had passed away, ' unconcerned as became a good Christian '—or, in other words, after having received the last consolations of the Catholic faith—William expressed his conviction that Sophia would share both his sorrow for the late King's death, and his joy at hearing of the unhindered accession of ' *celluy d'apresent.*' And King James II himself could assure her that he would always ' continue the same good correspondence which she had with the late King his brother.' [1] James II, to judge from an extant

---

[1] It is interesting to find Queen Mary Beatrice thanking the Dowager Duchess Benedicta at Hanover for her congratulations on the same occasion, and referring to her constant interest in the royal family, and to the links between them.

series of letters to Sophia from his hand, proved as good as his word, and she answered him in the same spirit. A constant communication seems, moreover, to have been kept up between her and the English royal family, through the personal agency of the faithful Lord Craven, of whom in 1683 she writes as 'at present my sole correspondent in England.' James II had appointed him Lieutenant-General of the Forces, and he would have been quite ready, had it rested with him, to act a decisive part with his Coldstreams on the King's behalf in the closing hours of his reign. Thus, when, in July, 1688, on the occasion of what ought to have been the happiest event of that reign—the birth of an heir to the throne—Sophia gave expression to her pleasure, the King wrote in return that he could have expected nothing less from her ; ' for beside our being so near related, you have always upon all occasion expresst a concerne for me of which you shall always find me very sensible.' And, with the straightforwardness of character which was not less distinctive of her than was her intellectual *finesse*, she never, either by word or by deed, belied her goodwill to the unfortunate King, or allowed herself to be impressed by the *consensus* between blatant prejudice and more or less wilful blindness that ' doubted ' the genuineness of the Prince of Wales. She transmitted to the Emperor Leopold a letter in which

King James had reproduced, for her benefit, the
substance of the refutation of these calumnious
doubts laid by him before his Privy Council ; and,
so late as 1704, she is found reproaching Leibniz
for the courtier-like insinuations which he seems
to have hazarded as to the Prince's birth. Accordingly, at the time when the expedition of William
of Orange was preparing, King James wrote to
Sophia in a perfectly trustful tone ; he had heard
that, with the exception of her husband, all her
Protestant neighbours had contributed to the
armament ; but, if the wind continued, he hoped
nevertheless to be able to give a good account of it.
As a matter of fact, Ernest Augustus maintained a
neutral attitude so long as he could ; and, so late
as 1691, James II is again found applauding
Sophia's husband for declining to support the
' vemper ' (William of Orange). Early in the
next year, he continues to harp on the same string
to her, while avowing his confidence in the continuance of her good wishes and requesting her
to use no ceremony in writing to him. In 1693,
Lord Dartmouth, whom Sophia received at Hanover
with much distinction because of the kindness
shown by his grandfather to her brothers Rupert
and Maurice, was informed by her that she maintained a constant correspondence both with King
James and with his daughter Queen Mary. On
the death of Ernest Augustus, both King James

and Queen Mary Beatrice warmly condoled with
the widow, the former avowing his gratitude for
all the marks of esteem and kindness which she
had so frequently shown to him. It is interesting,
too, to observe how Sophia, in conjunction with her
second self, the Duchess of Orleans, used her best
endeavours to make peace between King James
and his eldest daughter, whose conduct towards
him he pardonably misjudged, but in whose sincerity of soul a sure instinct led Sophia to place
full trust. The two kinswomen had never met,
when, in June, 1689, Queen Mary wrote to Sophia
to complain of the harsh terms in which the
Electress Sophia Charlotte of Brandenburg was
reported to have spoken of her, and took occasion,
with her usual candour, to dwell upon the conflict
of feelings through which it was her duty to guide
her conduct. An active correspondence ensued
between the two women, who were truly worthy
of one another, and who had, moreover, some
experiences of wedlock in common ; and from
this it is clear that Queen Mary had, to her deep
satisfaction, found in Sophia a friend ready to
credit her with real filial affection for her father.
In return she writes to the Duchess with a frankness declared by her to be indigenous to Holland,
where she had herself so long lived and where
Sophia had been born—each of them, as she says,
having to bear her cross as best she could.

But, though Sophia was never willing to let
political considerations warp her natural affections
or suppress her natural sense of justice, she would
hardly, like Mary, have gone so far as to say of
herself that she was unfitted for politics. The
interests of her family and of the Hanoverian
dynasty were steadily kept in view by her, and it
was these, rather than any personal motives or
wishes of her own, which determined her conduct
at the critical epoch of the Revolution. The events
that cost James II his throne, as speedily became
clear to her, opened a new political future for
herself and her descendants. Before the sailing
of William's expedition, when engagements in
his favour were being entered into by the new
Elector (Frederick William) of Brandenburg, the
Landgrave (Charles) of Hesse-Cassel and the Duke
of Celle, Burnet, as he tells us, sent, from the Hague,
a messenger to the Duchess Sophia at Hanover.
This messenger, a French refugee named de Boncour,
was instructed to inform her of the design of the
Prince of Orange, and of the certainty that, should
the expedition prove successful, it would result
in the perpetual exclusion of Papists from the
English throne. If she could persuade her husband
Ernest Augustus to sever his interests definitively
from those of France, there was little doubt but
that, after the two daughters of King James and the
Prince of Orange, from none of whom any issue

was surviving, the Succession would be lodged in her person and posterity. Burnet, who asserts that, in making this communication, he acted entirely on his own responsibility, though his action afterwards gained him William's approval, adds that the message was warmly entertained by the Duchess Sophia, but that her husband let it pass by him. Ernest Augustus, not unnaturally, looked on the whole question with a self-control facilitated by the fact that, in any case, he could only benefit from the English Succession through his wife. Whatever may be the measure of truth in this story (which, curiously enough, is not to be found in Burnet's *Original Memoirs*), it is extremely improbable that the Duchess Sophia should have allowed Burnet's agent to ascertain her personal views concerning his suggestions. When the expedition was actually on its way, she wrote a letter to Leibniz from which nothing can be concluded as to her feelings in the matter, except that, as was but natural, she was very anxious to know what would come of it all, especially, as she writes in her customary half-ironical vein, ' inasmuch as the words " for religion and liberty " are to be read on all the banners of the Prince of Orange.' After the expedition had been carried to a successful issue, we find her addressing the same correspondent in much the same tone ; and, though her letter of congratulation to William III is perfectly cordial and contains a remarkably *à propos* reference to the Blatant Beast, she shows true dignity as a descendant of the Stewarts in avowing her sympathy for William's dethroned predecessor. But with the new King's reply, written from Hampton Court less than a fortnight after the Coronation, the relations of Sophia to himself, and to the throne occupied by him and his Queen, entered into a new stage, which may be called the business stage.

In this letter, King William, without any circumlocution, expresses his hope of finding good allies in the whole House of Lüneburg—that is to say, in Sophia's husband, as well as in her brother-in-law, on whom he could already securely count. On the other hand, he points out that Sophia has a very real interest in the welfare of his three kingdoms, inasmuch as, to all appearance, one of her sons would some day reign over them. Although Sophia still wrote to Leibniz (then at Modena) in her habitual half-jesting tone as to the chances now opening to her, there can be no doubt that she is correctly stated to have at once taken action on King William's hint, and to have requested several English politicians known to her to support the project of naming her in the Succession. The attempt made in this year (1689) to carry the project in question through Parliament proves that the appeal had not been made in vain.

On May 8th, 1689, the Bill of Rights and

Succession came up for its third reading in the House of Commons of the Convention Parliament. While otherwise conforming to the Declaration accepted by William and Mary earlier in the year, and containing a clause excluding Papists, it made no provision for the event of the death without issue of Queen Mary, the Princess Anne, and King William, upon whose issue the Succession was, in the above order of sequence, settled. Such an event was at the time far from improbable ; should it actually occur, there was considerable obscurity as to where the Crown would devolve. Would, for instance, an infant child of Popish parents be excluded ; [1] and—a far more momentous question—would the exclusion extend to a Popish prince who might have been converted to Protestantism in time to succeed ? Godolphin, a statesman not unnaturally suspected, at this season, of facing both ways, but perhaps more benignantly towards the *régime* under which he had risen so high than towards that in which his own place was still doubtful, proposed a rider guarding the rights of ' any Protestant prince or princess' as to his or her future hereditary succession to the Crown. The proviso, in which, to the mover's virtuous indignation, more than one member suspected the influence of a foreign Power, was rejected ; but it is notable that, in the course

---

[1] Macaulay, who mentions this doubt, illustrates it by the supposed case of an infant prince of Savoy. (See below.)

of the debate, Colonel Herbert stated that he had
' seen a letter of a sister of Prince Rupert's, wherein
she was complaining of great hardship done to her
children, that they were not regarded in the entail
of the crown ; ' he therefore moved that they
should be mentioned in the Bill. The proposal,
which may confidently be ascribed to the action of
Sophia adverted to above, fell to the ground, the
judicious opinion of Paul Foley prevailing, that it
was inexpedient suddenly to introduce any further
limitation of the Succession ; but it had not been
made wholly in vain. When the Bill of Rights and
Succession reached the House of Lords, after, on
the motion of the Bishop of Salisbury (Burnet),
a clause had been added extending the exclusion
of Papists from the Succession to princes or princesses married to Papists, the same useful henchman,
in accordance with the directions of the King,
proposed, as a further addition to the Bill, the naming, in the Succession, of the Duchess of Hanover
and her posterity. This amendment having been
adopted by the Lords without debate (which could
hardly have been the case had the ground not been
prepared there) was carried down to the Commons,
who, in a debate held on June 19th, treated it in a
very different spirit. One member (Sir John Low-
ther) dwelt on the inexpediency of attempting to
settle the Succession a long time beforehand, instead
of following the example of Queen Elizabeth, who

' was a wise Princess ' ; ' this Princess of Hanover,' he pointed out, might turn Catholic before the time for her succession had arrived. In the end, the amendment was rejected without a division, and, a conference between the two Houses having proved fruitless, the Bill was lost for the Session. The birth, on July 27th, of Princess Anne's son (afterwards Duke of Gloucester) took away from the proposed addition its immediate significance; but, whatever may have been the cause of the failure to give effect to the King's wish, the fault certainly did not lie with the Duchess Sophia. There were ' heats ' enough in the politics of the day, and in the relations between Lords and Commons in particular, to explain the incident ; nor is it surprising that, when Parliament reassembled in the autumn, the Bill of Rights and Succession which was now passed contained no mention of the Duchess of Hanover or her descendants. Burnet, ubiquitously assisting at every stage of every transaction with which, as narrated by himself, he had any connexion at all, says that by King William's wish he wrote to Sophia an account of the entire affair. We know, however, that Lord Craven was sent to Hanover to explain it or to soften any unpleasantness in the effect which it might produce ; and, in a letter to Sophia, dated December 10th, 1689, William himself explained to her that, though she had not been designated in the Bill, she might rest satisfied with things as they stood. She was Heiress Presumptive, in the event of claims beyond those named in the Bill coming into consideration ; and the suggestion of Burnet was quite superfluous, that ' if any in the line before her should pretend to change, as it was not very likely to happen, so it would not be easily believed.' Sophia's answer to King William, in which she cordially thanks him for his exertions on her behalf, closes the entire episode. She trusts that the expectation of heirs implied in the Bill may prove correct ; as for herself, her life will be at an end before the matter is decided. She was, at the time, close upon the sixtieth year of her life ; and a son had just been born to Princess Anne, who very possibly might yet have other children that would survive her.

After this negative, but in no sense final, result had been reached, the Succession question remained in abeyance for something like eleven years. It accords neither with the circumstances of the situation nor with the character of Sophia, to represent her as during this long interval sleeplessly intent upon an issue so remote, so precarious, and so unlikely to prove, in the strictest sense, personal to herself. But, on the one hand, her and her family's interest in the Succession question had once for all been brought directly home to her ; and, on the other, she had had reason to appreciate the *bona fides* and the genuine goodwill towards her own

contingent claim exhibited by King William III.
Already in 1689, primarily with a view to the
restoration of amity between Denmark and Holstein-
Gottorp, Sir William Dutton Colt was appointed
Envoy Extraordinary and Minister Plenipotentiary
to the Brunswick-Lüneburg Courts, being also
accredited to Brunswick-Wolfenbüttel and Hesse-
Cassel ; and in 1692 he was further formally instructed to treat for the entry of the Dukes of Celle
and Hanover into the Grand Alliance.[1]   He appears
to have contrived to gain the good graces
of the ducal families both at Hanover and at
Celle, and in 1693 he reports that the Platens
were jealous of his favour with the ' Electrisse ' ;[2]
for Sophia and Eleonora were godmothers to
his daughter, and bestowed upon her their united
names.   The personal relations between Sophia
and the King and Queen of England at the
same time grew more and more cordial.   William,
though not as a rule inclined to sentiment, early
in 1691 condoled with Sophia on the death, at the

[1] *Notes on the Diplomatic Relations between England and
Germany*, ed. C. H. Firth : *List of Diplomatic Representatives
and Agents, England and North Germany*, 1689–1727, contributed
by J. F. Chance, Oxford, 1907.

[2] As Colt died in 1693 (at Heilbronn), on a mission on which
he was sent to treat with the Elector of Saxony, to bring him
into the Grand Alliance, I cannot say what was the nature of the
series of holograph letters from the Electress Sophia to Lady
Colt, extending from 1681 (?) to 1714, reported in the *Times* of
April 14th, 1905, as sold by auction.

close of the previous year, of her son Frederick
Augustus, for whom he had cherished ' *une amitié
toute particulière* ' ; and early in the following
year Queen Mary delicately expressed her regret
at Sophia's fresh family troubles (the death of her
son Charles Philip, and perhaps the catastrophe
of his brother Maximilian). These kindly feelings
combined with political motives to induce King
William to contribute his good offices for bringing
to a successful end, in the same year (1692), the
endeavours to which, as we shall see immediately,
the main political energy of the House of Hanover
had long been devoted—for the attainment of the
Electoral dignity. He had his reward when, as
part of the bargain between Ernest Augustus
and the Emperor Leopold, the House of Hanover
definitively threw in its lot with the interests of the
Empire and the cause of the Grand Alliance. On
Sir William Colt's death in the following year (1693),
a new English Minister Plenipotentiary to the Courts
of Celle and Hanover was appointed in the person
of James Cressett,[1] who, though at first he represents
the Courts to which he was accredited as having
' gaped upon him like roaring lions ' (not feeling

---

[1] There seems good reason for believing that the foreign lady,
named Louise-Marie, married by Cressett in 1704, about the close
of his residence at the Court of Celle, was a kinswoman of the
Duchess Eleonora. Cf., as to a survival of this connexion with
the dynasty, H. Walpole's *Memoirs of the Last Ten Years of the
Reign of George II* (1822), Vol. i. p. 79.

quite certain about the British Parliament's earnest-
ness in the War), soon contrived to place himself on
a footing of intimacy there. Leibniz speedily fell into
a correspondence with him about the lead produce of
the Harz as compared with that of the English mines.
But less academic matters also occupied the attention of the new envoy ; for, in 1692, two treaties
had been concluded between the Ducal Government
and those of England and the United Provinces,
according to which Hanover was to furnish a force
of 7,000 men, and the two maritime Powers were to
pay respectively 20,000 and 10,000 dollars a month
for their support, besides defraying two-thirds of the
cost of their rations and forage. In December,
1693, these subsidy treaties were discussed in the
House of Commons, and though the ' Duke of Hanover ' was praised as a loyal ally, objection was
taken to the payment for bread and forage, on the
ground that he might well pay a larger proportion,
' now that he is Ninth Elector.' In return, it was
pointed out that, on the one hand, the Elector had to
pay his quota to the Empire, and that, on the other,
if these troops were not paid by England, they must
be by France—a comment not altogether unwarranted by the changes of Hanoverian policy.
Cressett remained the diplomatic representative
of Great Britain at the Lüneburg Courts till 1703.[1]

[1] In 1700 he was also accredited to Berlin, where already in
1702 Queen Sophia Charlotte thought him a trifle *passé*.

A time of trouble was imminent for the domestic
peace of the House of Hanover, and Sophia, as was
noted above, had not long before suffered a severe
shock in both mind and body by the death of her son
Charles Philip, soon followed by that of his brother
Frederick Augustus.   In the spring of 1694 she was
again seriously ill.   Cressett, while noting that ' her
credit is not good in affairs,' says that he ' should
be heartily sorry to lose her, for she loves England.'
She recovered her strength at Wiesbaden, and
we find the good Queen Mary returning fervent
thanks for her cousin's restoration to her usual
health.   She needed all her strength to carry her
through the painful experiences awaiting the
Electoral family—the tragedy of Sophia Dorothea,
and, after this, the long illness and death of the
Elector Ernest Augustus.   Amidst such anxieties we
may rest assured that, even had intrigue and manœuvring suited her disposition, she would have had
little leisure for engaging in them.   Her attitude
during this period towards the Succession question,
which few events on the great political theatre
were of a nature to affect (for even Queen Mary's
death in 1696 made no material change in the
situation), was one of quietude—no doubt a vigilant
quietude.   In 1694, Lord Lexington, a diplomatist
whom William III had good reason for trusting, and
who, together with a Dutch plenipotentiary, had
mediated in the quarrel between Denmark and the

Brunswick-Lüneburg Dukes concerning the Lauenburg Succession, passed through Hanover on his
way to his post at Vienna. And, in the following
year, we find Leibniz discussing with George Stepney, the brilliant English diplomatist who, in 1693,
was suddenly summoned into prominent activity
in several of the German Courts, the applicability
of the exclusion clause in the Bill of Rights to
children, whether Protestants or Papists, born of
papistical parents. William III has been said to
have formed the plan of placing in the Succession
the Prince expected to be born to Victor Amadeus
II, Duke of Savoy, by his Duchess Anna Maria,
and of educating him for the purpose in England
as a Protestant. The Duchess Anna Maria was a
daughter of the Duchess Henrietta of Orleans, and
thus a grand-daughter of King Charles I; so that
on the ground of descent pure and simple she would
have a claim to the English Succession before the
children of the Queen of Bohemia. But there is no
proof of any such design, or of any response to any
suggestion of the kind on the part of the Duke of
Savoy; and, at the most, the idea was quite transitory. If any hopes had been raised as to William's
intentions, Victor Amadeus effectively extinguished
them by abandoning the Grand Alliance in 1696.[1]

---

[1] In 1701, however, the Duchess Anna Maria protested
against the Act of Settlement, which limited the Succession to
Sophia and her issue, being Protestants. For an account of the

Of course, it by no means follows from the fact that Leibniz was, throughout, Sophia's chief counsellor with regard to the Succession, either that she uniformly took his advice, or that she was always desirous of being privy to the efforts in furtherance of the claims of herself and her descendants, which, at times with *trop de zèle*, came from his indefatigable publicistic pen. But it remains at all events a curious coincidence that, soon after the House of Savoy had, as it were, fallen out of the running, William III's interest in the House of Hanover—and perhaps in its claims concerning the Succession—should appear to have revived. We shall return to this date a little later ; for the moment we must make some reference to matters which seemed of far more importance to the House of Hanover than the remote chances of the English Succession.

The House of Hanover, apart from the interest which it had shown in the military system of the Empire,[1] had a very direct share in causing the declaration of war against that Empire, by which, in September, 1688, at the very time when he

reasons of Victor Amadeus' original estrangement from France, and a searching analysis of his character, see a remarkable *Relation de la Cour de Savoie*, July 15th, 1692, in Appendix to G. de Léris, *La Princesse de Virrue* [for a time the Duke's mistress] *et la Cour de Victor Amad. de Savoie*, Paris, 1881, pp. 238-9.

[1] See as to F. C. von Platen's mission on the subject in December, 1686, R. Fester, *Die Augsburger Allianz*, pp. 124 *sqq.*, 167 *sqq.*

was promising assistance to James II against the expedition of William of Orange, Louis XIV laid bare his own designs against the peace of Europe. According to the manifesto of the King of France, the successes of the Imperial arms in the east had obliged him to protect his western frontier by crossing it ; and, a little before or after this declaration, his armies had entered the Netherlands, and had invaded the Palatinate to enforce the claims shamelessly put forward by him in the name of the innocent Duchess of Orleans. In the Imperial advance in Hungary, and in the simultaneous reconquest of the Morea on behalf of the Venetian Republic, Hanoverian troops had borne a most distinguished part. It was therefore not unfitting that the counter-manifesto, in which the glove hurled down by Louis XIV was taken up, should have been composed by Leibniz, whose publicistic pen was at the disposal of the House of Hanover. And among the German princes who, in the October of this eventful year, at the instigation of the new Elector of Brandenburg, Ernest Augustus of Hanover's son-in-law, and through the exertions of his minister, Paul von Fuchs, met at Magdeburg to agree upon joint action against the assailant of the Empire, none was more prompt, either in promise or in action, than Ernest Augustus himself. While the Brandenburg troops covered the Lower Rhine, the Hanoverian, Saxon, and Hessian secured the line of the Main, by the occupation of Frankfort (November, 1688). In May, 1689, the Grand Alliance was concluded, and though the Palatinate could not be preserved from devastation, Frankfort was once more saved, being occupied by a Hanoverian force of 8,000 men under Duke Ernest Augustus and his eldest son, George Lewis. Under the command of their Hereditary Prince, of whom there remains at least one letter written, in the course of the campaign, with an afflatus of humour proving that his heart was in active warfare, the Hanoverians forced Marshal Boufleurs to relinquish the investment of Coblenz, and materially contributed to the recovery of Mainz (September 1st, 1689). They were then transferred to the Low Countries, where a series of campaigns was to ensue, contemporaneous with the continuance of the conflict with the Turks. We have seen how the sacrifices made by the House of Hanover within a twelvemonth (January, 1690, to January, 1691) included the heroic death of Prince Charles Philip in Albania, and that of his brother Frederick Augustus, hardly more than a boy in years, in Transylvania. It neither was, nor could be expected to be, the intention of Ernest Augustus, that his House, which had served the Empire so well in both west and east, should have so served it without reward. And the recompense desired by him—one which, while conferring upon himself, as the head of the House of Hanover, the highest dignity to which, as an Estate of the Empire, he could, within its boundaries, lay claim, would at the same time reflect lustre upon the Brunswick-Lüneburg line, whose future he had come to regard as absorbed in that of its Hanoverian branch— could be no other than the creation of a Ninth, that is to say Hanoverian, Electorate.

The desire or demand for this dignity was neither a sudden nor even a new one. It had been in the mind both of Duke John Frederick and of his librarian, Leibniz, though the latter, while giving utterance to it in his *Cæsarinus Fürstenerius* (1677), had at the same time delivered himself of an elaborate protest against the preeminence in rights and dignity claimed by the Electors over the other Princes of the Empire. Such a protest was of course quite compatible with lending a willing ear to any suggestion of conferring the Electoral dignity upon a representative branch of the Brunswick-Lüneburg line itself. And suggestions of the kind were inevitable, if only from the obvious point of view that the Peace of Westphalia had left the number of Protestant Electors in a disproportion of three to five, as against their Catholic colleagues. The Great Elector of Brandenburg, in the varying combinations of whose policy a single-minded care for the Protestant interest was perhaps the most constant factor, had already during the peace negotiations at Nimeguen expressed his willingness

to assist in bringing about the admission into the
Electoral College of the House of Brunswick–
Lüneburg—probably at that time in the person of
George William of Celle, as Ernest Augustus was
still merely Bishop of Osnabrück. But the argument from the Protestant point of view became
a much stronger one, when, in 1685, the death of
the last Elector Palatine of the Simmern line
(Sophia's nephew Charles) transferred the Eighth
Electorate to the Catholic (Neuburg) line. Nor
should it be forgotten that, although the political
jealousy between the Houses of Brandenburg and
Brunswick-Lüneburg had never ceased to exist and
to operate, and although the advantage of balancing
the growing power and influence of the former, by
adding to the *prestige* of the latter, was very distinctly perceived at Vienna, the two Houses were
since 1684 closely linked together by intermarriage.
Sophia Charlotte, the new Electoral Princess (from
1688 Electress) of Brandenburg, was never mistress
of the situation at Berlin, and, unlike her mother,
gave to matters political only just so much attention
as seemed absolutely necessary. On the other
hand, Hanoverian interests could not but benefit
from the presence at the Brandenburg Court of a
princess whose personality was not one to be
ignored, and who had in her mother a monitress
to whom the constant affection between them
always made her ready to listen. And the friend

whom both mother and daughter trusted above all others as an adviser, had in 1685 begun to devote his powers of argument to the cause which, to the head of the House of Hanover, had become of paramount importance.

But a long siege was needed before the *Hofburg* could be expected to yield.   The services and sacrifices which the Empire owed to the House of Hanover were indisputable, and the solidity of its dynastic future must have seemed beyond cavil, after the Duke of Celle had confirmed his renunciation of any transmission of his dominions to a possible son of his own, and had married his only daughter to the Hereditary Prince of Hanover, where the law of primogeniture had been established.   The meeting (1689–90) of a Diet at Augsburg for the election of a Roman King in the person of the future Emperor Joseph I, seemed a suitable opportunity for bringing forward the Hanoverian proposal of a Ninth Electorate through Ernest Augustus' plenipotentiary, Count Platen.   Yet, although it could not but be of great importance to the Emperor to make sure of the adherence of Hanover to the alliance against France, of which at this very Diet he impressed the necessity upon the Electors, the request of Ernest Augustus met with no acceptance either at Augsburg or in the course of the ensuing negotiations at Vienna.   So soon as the Emperor appeared to favour Hanover's desire for an Electoral hat,

Bamberg, Salzburg, Würzburg, Hesse-Cassel, and Pfalz-Sulzbach were immediately on the alert to try for the Ninth Electorate on their own account ; and this general eagerness conveniently supplied the Imperial Government with a new bait for gaining votes in the Council of Princes.[1] Moreover, the high-handed action of the Brunswick-Lüneburg brothers in the matter of the Lauenburg Succession (September, 1689) had exercised a retarding influence, by which so friendly a court as that of Brandenburg had been for a time affected. Even certain overtures made through his emissary by Ernest Augustus—we may venture to surmise without the privity of his wife—that, if such a concession would solve the difficulty, he might be found disposed to listen to suggestions as to his conversion to the Church of Rome, and his enumeration of the services which his House had rendered to that Church, proved in vain. Hanoverian diplomacy hereupon tried a different tack, and occupied itself with a scheme for bringing about a combination between Brandenburg, Saxony, and Hanover, which would put the requisite pressure upon the Emperor by standing neutral between him and France. The device, for which more than one historical precedent could have been found, produced its effect on this occasion also, after Saxony had been induced to fall

[1] Droysen, *Geschichte der Preussischen Politik*, Vol. iv. Part i. p. 87.

in with it.   According to the current account, the
eminent Hanoverian minister, Count Otto von
Grote (who like Leibniz had been introduced by
Duke John Frederick into the Hanoverian service,
in which he spent twenty-eight years, doing his
duty to the State in the very spirit of Frederick the
Great), forced the hand of the Emperor by exhibiting
to him at Vienna the compact with Saxony which
realised the menace of a Third Party in the European
conflict.   Even if this story is apocryphal, there can
be no doubt that the neutrality project furnished
a very powerful lever in the negotiations carried on
at the Imperial Court by Grote in conjunction with
the resident Hanoverian minister, President von
Limbach.   Their arguments were supported by
representations on the part of Great Britain, the
United Provinces, and Brandenburg ; but they were
still more effectively reinforced by the Emperor
Leopold's pressing requirements for his next campaign against the Turks.   Thus, then, early in 1692,
was concluded the Electoral Compact (*Kurtractat*),
in which the Dukes of Hanover and Celle undertook
to provide, in addition to subsidies, a force of 6,000
men in their own pay, to be employed in the first
instance against the Turks, and afterwards against
France, while a supplementary agreement bound
both sides to perpetual amity and military assistance, and assured to the House of Austria the
support of the House of Brunswick-Lüneburg in

future Imperial elections as well as in the matter of the coming Spanish Succession. Hereupon, on March 19th, 1692, the Imperial rescript conferring an Electoral hat upon the Duke of Hanover was placed in the hands of his representative at Vienna.

But, before this act of authority on the part of the Emperor could command the assent of the Estates of the Empire which he required in order to proceed to the investiture, much remained to be done at Vienna, where Grote was active in person during the latter half of the year; at Dresden, where Jobst von Ilten, another specially trusted servant of the Hanoverian dynasty, successfully exerted himself; and elsewhere. In the midst of these difficulties, the Duchess of Orleans wrote to her aunt that she was convinced as to the source of opposition being German Princes rather than France. As a matter of fact, not only the political but the religious interests were agitated with which the House of Hanover had been, or might hereafter be, in conflict; and Grote was informed that both the King of Denmark (Christian V) and the Pope (Innocent XII) were adverse to the desired investiture. The good offices of Brandenburg were, however, freely exerted in its favour, and the Elector Frederick III's envoy at Ratisbon, von Metternich, was instructed to tranquillise the Catholic Electors by undertaking that, in the event of the dying-out

of the Bavarian and Palatine lines, the establishment of a new Catholic Electorate should be
promoted by Brandenburg, Saxony, and Hanover.
Thus, by the middle of October, 1692, a majority
of the Electors had been secured for the investiture,
and it was possible to ignore the violent opposition
of Duke Antony Ulric of Wolfenbüttel, who, as
Elizabeth Charlotte had hinted, was irreconcilable
on this subject, and was calling out troops as if the
world were out of joint.[1]   On December 10th following, the investiture took place at Vienna, and Grote
received the coveted Electoral hat for his master.
Ernest Augustus and Sophia were at Berlin on a
visit to their daughter when the good news reached
them ; a series of brilliant festivities ensued as a
matter of course, since Frederick III was always
glad of a reason for display ; and, two days before
Christmas, a defensive alliance for three years was
concluded between the two Electors, to be followed
a month later by an ' everlasting league.'   This
alliance, to whatever other results it might or might
not lead, unmistakably signified the recognition
of an important success gained for the ' Evangelical '

---

[1] See as to his opposition Bodemann, *Anton Ulrich und
seine Correspondenz mit Leibniz*, in *Zeitschr. d. histor. Ver. für
Niedersachsen*, 1879.   It was largely from ambitious motives
that this Duke entered so zealously into the great scheme for
a reunion between Catholics and Protestants.   (See Clemens
Schwarte, *Die neunte Kur und Braunschweig-Wolfenbüttel*, in
Münstersche Beiträge zur Geschichtsforschung, Neue Folge,
Münster, 1905.)

cause in Germany. Brandenburg, which was so soon to merge in the Prussian Kingdom, and Hanover, whose heir was not long afterwards to mount the English throne, would, if they held together, suffice to defy any religious reaction in the Empire, and likewise be able to resist any attempt in any quarter at asserting a political domination.

Neither, however, had Grote's labours as yet come to an end—though they were a few months afterwards cut short by his death—nor were the aspirations of the House of Hanover within the Empire satisfied by the Electoral investiture of December, 1692. Brandenburg, Saxony, and most of the other German courts recognised the new Elector ; but the question of his introduction into the Electoral College, which implied his admission as Elector to his due share in the administration of the affairs of the Empire—the question *quo modo*—had still to be settled. The progress of its solution was delayed by a persistent opposition, of which the guiding spirit was once more Duke Antony Ulric of Brunswick-Wolfenbüttel, and which included the King of Denmark as Duke of Holstein, the Dukes of Mecklenburg, and a number of other princes, both temporal and spiritual, in the north and west of the Empire. In 1693, these formed an association which designated itself as that of the Princes ' corresponding ' against a Ninth Electorate,

thus, as was justly observed to the Emperor by the
Elector of Brandenburg, who continued loyally to
support the demand of his father-in-law, lowering
the Imperial authority by ' maintaining ' a resistance against a decision already announced by it.
The Elector of Saxony, John George IV, had been
likewise well disposed to the Hanoverian promotion ;
but, in 1694, he had been succeeded by his brother
Frederick Augustus (Augustus the Strong, the lover
of Aurora von Königsmarck), whom, as will be seen
in a different connexion, private as well as public
motives had estranged from the Hanoverian Court ;
and thus a fresh obstacle had been put in the way
of the admission of Ernest Augustus into the College
of Electors. The virulence of Antony Ulric's
jealous hatred, which, as we shall also see, was to
find in the Königsmarck catastrophe of 1694 and
its antecedents a most tempting opportunity for
damaging the reputation of the Hanoverian family,
suggested to him what the Hanoverian diplomatist
Ilten termed a *' projet d'alliance diabolique.'* Frederick Augustus was to be gained over to the association of ' Corresponding ' Princes by a surrender to
Saxony of the Brunswick-Wolfenbüttel claims to
part of the Duchy of Lauenburg, and he was to
cooperate with Denmark in dispossessing Hanover
and Celle, who had occupied other parts of the
duchy claimed by them. Ernest Augustus had to
appeal to King William III to put a stop to

manœuvres which threatened seriously to affect the general peace of Europe.

Although the machinations of Antony Ulric were thus frustrated, he succeeded in depriving his hitherto so fortunate kinsman, Ernest Augustus, of the satisfaction of attaining in person to the consummation of his chief dynastic ambition. Soon after the death of Ernest Augustus, in January, 1698, the insensate jealousy of Antony Ulric led him to make, with fresh assistance, an armed attack upon Hanover, which amounted to an act of hostility against the Empire, committed at a critical season in the affairs of Europe. The defeat of this attempt by the energetic action of the Elector George Lewis broke down the opposition of Antony Ulric in the matter of the Ninth Electorate (1702) ; and soon afterwards he acknowledged the Electoral dignity and the precedence of the Hanoverian Elector at the Diet (1703). Previously to these occurrences, the exertions of Frederick III of Brandenburg had succeeded in inducing the three Spiritual Electors to abandon their resistance to the new Protestant Electorate (1699) ; but the outbreak of the War of the Spanish Succession had thereupon caused further delays. Thus it was not till 1707 that the positive assent of all the Electors was secured, nor till September 7th, 1708, sixteen years after the investiture at Vienna, that the Hanoverian envoy, von Limbach, at last took his seat in the Electoral College at Ratisbon.

The marriage between Sophia Dorothea of Celle and her cousin George Lewis of Hanover, which was to end so disastrously, came as a matter of course to be represented as having been ill-omened at the outset. It is, however, impossible to trust either the account of the transactions that preceded this marriage, or that of the long train of events ending in its dissolution, to be found in a long series of versions of this pitiful story. In substance, if not in every detail, they all go back upon the parent romance compiled by Duke Antony Ulric, very probably with the aid of information furnished to him by the confidante of the unhappy heroine. An authority so signally untrustworthy is best ignored ; though it would be idle to pretend that the copious stream, which has flowed through all sorts of channels from this turbid source, is likely to be wholly devoid of some admixture of truth.[1]   In

[1] The supplementary (sixth) volume of the *Roman Octavia*, which contains the story of Sophia Dorothea under the title of the *History of the Princess Solane*, was first published in 1707, when Sophia Dorothea's lady-in-waiting, Fräulein Eleonora von dem Knesebeck, who had, from first to last, been in the secret of the Princess' relations with Count Königsmarck, either was or recently had been resident at Wolfenbüttel under the protection of Duke Antony Ulric after her escape from prison. In the revised edition of this ' historical novel,' published at Nürnberg in 1712 and dedicated to the ' *Hochlöbliche Nymfen-Gesellschaft an der Donau,* the name of *Solane* was altered to

point of fact, we cannot tell in what frame of mind Sophia Dorothea entered on her married life, or even what was her mother's view of the match. Eleonora, beyond all doubt, tenderly loved her daughter ; but Sophia Dorothea's nature was light and frivolous, and there had not, so far as is known, been anything in her life to incline her to resistance. The views of the Duchess Sophia on the subject of her eldest son's marriage it may seem easy to guess. But, though she had execrated the d'Olbreuze connexion in all its earlier stages, and though she seems at no time to have pretended to anything like affection for Eleonora's daughter, we may take it for granted that, so soon as the marriage-project had been formally adopted as a matter of court and state policy, the Duchess completely acquiesced in it. And, indeed, no doubt could exist as to the advantages of the arrangement, whether from the point of view of the political future of the dynasty, or from that of the present resources of the House. The marriage-contract

Rhodogune, and there were certain other changes. The derivation of the traditional narrative from Duke Antony Ulric's romance was convincingly traced by the late Professor Adolf Köcher, who, though disbelieving in the genuineness of the correspondence to be mentioned immediately, succeeded in throwing a flood of light upon the entire course of Sophia Dorothea's story.—Writing, in 1709, about the amour between the Landgrave Ernest Lewis of Hesse-Darmstadt and the (married) Countess von Sintzendorf, the Duchess of Orleans observes that, since the lady is quite ready to show the Prince's letters, it would be easy for Duke Antony Ulric to turn their affair into a romance.

gave to the Hereditary Prince the free use of his wife's income, though it secured her fortune—which was certain to be a very large one—to herself in the event of her husband's decease preceding her own. It was only at a later date, when a dissolution of her marriage seemed desirable to Sophia Dorothea, that she complained of the terms of this settlement. The great wealth of the bride might well be held to cover whatever minor disabilities might result to the possible issue of the marriage from the imperfection of her own descent.

Nothing, it may be added, could be more improbable than that either George Lewis or his mother should have been at the pains of considering how far Sophia Dorothea's character and disposition were suited to his own, or whether she would find any difficulty in accommodating herself to his way of life. The Duchess Sophia had learnt by long experience to bear with the open faithlessness of her husband, and with his frank neglect of herself, without forfeiting the influence which her intelligence had long assured to her over him and his affairs. How should she, with her shrewd apprehension of the ways of the world, have supposed that the same lesson would not be learnt by her new daughter-in-law ? And it may at once be stated that there is no indication of George Lewis having during the early years of his married life kept up any relation that would have been unbearable to his young wife. If there was any truth in the rumour that he had been on terms of intimacy with Countess Platen's younger sister, Frau von dem Bussche (*née* Marie von Meysenbug), the relation must have been broken off before his marriage, as indeed a further circumstantial piece of scandal asserted. She appears to have been a very pretty person, with plenty of admirers ; and she is said to have set the fashion of ' drinking tobacco ' among the ladies at Hanover.[1] For the rest, although George I was at no time in his life in the habit of seeking personal praise, and in truth cannot be said to have received an overflowing measure of it either from contemporaries or from posterity, yet he was not without qualities sure to impress themselves on anyone brought into close contact with him. His unflinching courage and military capacity were generally known ; and it may further be averred in his honour, that he was never found false to his word, and that he was unswervingly true to any attachment once formed by him. His manners may, in his younger days in particular, have had a smack of the camp, and they must at all times have given proof of the reserve which was part of his nature, and which bad and good fortune combined to harden into the stolidity of his later years. That he made no pretence to intellectual tastes (though he quarrelled with his illustrious

---

[1] See *Briefe des Herzogs Ernst August*, &c., p. 33, note.

historiographer's unpunctuality in fulfilling his engagement to digest the ancient records of the House of Guelf) may have disappointed his mother, but could hardly perturb Sophia Dorothea, who came of no lettered stock.   In general, she might well have been thought likely to suit her own fluid temperament to a character cast in a stronger and sterner mould.   The portraits which remain of her show her to have been graceful and pleasing beyond the common, and this impression is confirmed by notices of her personality dating from the early years of her married life.   Perhaps there may be perceptible in certain of her portraits (one of which reminded the ingenious Wraxall of Sterne's Eliza) a sentimentality of the superficial kind ; but nothing could be more cruelly unfair than to draw from these likenesses conclusions as to her levity of disposition.   On the other hand, the Duchess Sophia may be thought a prejudiced witness, when, in 1684 and 1685, she is found expressing distrust of both the smiles and the tears of her daughter-in-law, and setting her down as an unsatisfactory example for Sophia Charlotte, the apple of her mother's eye ; in truth, however, the Duchess' strictures cannot, in this instance, be said to be very serious.   The bad maternal bringing up of Sophia Dorothea, on which the same censor's faithful echo, the Duchess of Orleans, was afterwards fain to dwell as the original cause of the

Princess' misfortunes, has been waived aside as a mere invention of spite ; yet it should not be forgotten that both Sophia and her niece were, in their girlhood, carefully and even rigidly educated, and that to this training the unfaltering rectitude that marked the conduct of both is, in no small measure, attributable. At the same time, it is equally obvious that the kindly guidance by which the most perfect system of moral discipline needs at times to be supplemented, or by which the absence of such discipline may be in part redeemed, was wanting to Sophia Dorothea at Hanover. While there can be no reason for gainsaying this, and while it must be allowed to have been natural enough that those who had hated the mother should have treated the misconduct of the daughter as what might have been expected almost as a matter of course, yet the attempt to throw upon the Electress Sophia the responsibility of the catastrophe which we are about to narrate may be at once denounced as inherently absurd. Whether or not George Lewis cruelly illtreated his wife—and there is no trustworthy evidence to support any such supposition—the assumption is altogether unwarranted that either in his bearing towards her, or in any other important relation of his life, he allowed himself to be influenced by his mother.[1]   Least of all was he likely to be

[1] ' That the Elector is a dry and disagreeable gentleman,' writes the Duchess of Orleans in 1702, ' I had opportunity

amenable to her counsel at a stage of his career
when he must have known her to be at heart adverse
to his interest in the matter, all-important to himself, of the institution of primogeniture.   And as
for Sophia herself, though elaborate efforts have been
made to represent her as morally guilty of her
daughter-in-law's ruin, there is not a tittle of
evidence to support a conjecture in itself utterly
improbable.   For her frankness and sincerity are
never found belying themselves ; and intrigue of all
kinds, as both her public and her private conduct
show, was wholly foreign to her nature.   Moreover,
though, as will be noted, no letters from her hand
referring to the crisis in Sophia Dorothea's affairs
have been allowed to survive, the general tone of
her correspondence during these eventful years is
one of a serenity of mind unbroken, except by her
grief for her losses as a mother.

At first, things seem to have gone well with
Sophia Dorothea at Hanover.   The Hereditary
Prince (for he was, of course, not styled the Electoral
Prince till 1682) continued the military career which
best corresponded both to his aspirations and to his
habits—serving during a series of campaigns in the
Imperial army, and taking no part in the home
government till, about 1694, his father's health

enough to discern when he was here . . . but where he is entirely
in the wrong, is in his way of living with his mother, to whom he
is in duty bound to show nothing but respect.'

began to give way.   Doubtless George Lewis' long
and repeated absences must have contributed to
keep him estranged from the Princess, and, as already
observed, there were at Hanover no members of
the ducal family or court likely to aim at endearing
themselves to her.   The star of Countess Platen,
mistress *en titre*, remained steadily in the ascendant,
and her villa of Monplaisir, in the immediate neighbourhood of the capital, became the centre of its
fashionable dissipations.   Her sister, Frau von dem
Bussche, was likewise still to the front (she took
part in Ernest Augustus' farewell expedition of
pleasure to Italy, to be noticed immediately) ; but,
whether or not she had formerly been a recipient
of the Hereditary Prince's favours, they do not
appear to have continued to be bestowed upon her
either under her present name, or when, after her
husband's death (at Landen), she bestowed her hand
upon another gallant officer, General von Weyhe.[1]
When the exigencies of etiquette did not require her

[1] He served with distinction under Marlborough in Flanders.
The marriage took place in 1696, two years after the Königsmarck catastrophe.   Yet the late Mr. Wilkins makes Countess
Platen, 'with a refinement of cruelty,' try to induce Sophia
Dorothea to be present at the wedding.   This significant blunder,
repeated in the second edition of *The Love of an Uncrowned
Queen*, is exposed by Mr. Lewis Melville, *The First George*, Vol. i.
pp. 52–6.   A Fräulein von Weyhe was in Sophia Dorothea's
service.   The court of Hanover, after all, has much of the aspect
of a large family party.   In 1701, Sophia mentions a tour to the
Harz made by the Elector in a company which included three
ladies, ' the Schoulenburg, Madame Wey, and Ernhausen, the
Schoulenburg's sister.'

presence at the interminable court dinners and suppers, or at the operas in the new theatre, in which the heart of Ernest Augustus delighted, Sophia Dorothea may be concluded to have led a life as solitary as it was dull in her apartments in the Leine Palace at Hanover.[1] The favourite companion of her long hours of idleness was her lady-in-waiting, Fräulein Eleonora von dem Knesebeck, who had come with her from Celle, and whose devotion, self-sacrificing though by no means blind, was to involve her in the consequences of her mistress' aberrations.

In October, 1683, the Hereditary Princess gave birth to a son, who was named George Augustus, in honour of his father and grandfather respectively, and who was nearly half a century later to ascend the throne of Great Britain and Ireland as King George II. We may feel assured that an event so auspicious for the future of the dynasty, and so speedily fulfilling the hopes with which the marriage had been brought about, specially commended her to the favour of her father-in-law; and, that this favour continued, is shown by his consideration for her some two years afterwards. In 1684, Duke Ernest Augustus had undertaken his last journey to the beloved land of Italy, being accompanied on it

[1] The Palace was enlarged about this time, and entirely 'restored' in 1831–41. In Sophia Dorothea's days the bear at his chain and the lynx in his cage were still to be seen near the guard-house at the outer gate.

by an oddly composed company consisting, among others, of Count Platen and Major-General von dem Bussche and their wives. During this visit the Duchess remained behind, professedly *à son grand regret,* and Prince George Lewis was, for part of the time, engaged in one of his Hungarian campaigns against the Turks. But his Princess, at the particular request of her father-in-law, joined the ducal party at Venice, arriving there just before the opening of the carnival of 1686. ' I am delighted to hear,' writes the Duchess Sophia from Hanover in January, ' that my daughter-in-law and her following are in good condition.' Sophia Dorothea then accompanied the Duke for the Holy Week to Rome, where their sojourn cost the cruel sum of twenty thousand dollars ; but, though her husband had by this time finished his campaign, ceremonial difficulties (which one would have thought would have affected the father as much as the son) prevented him from coming to the papal city, and he amused himself with a trip to Florence and Naples on his own account. All these things are told without so much as a suggestion of untowardness ; nor was it till long afterwards that a scandal, promptly credited by the Duchess of Orleans, declared Sophia Dorothea to have consoled herself for her husband's absence by an amour carried on at Rome with a French marquis of the name of de Lassaye. But the story in question rests entirely

on the braggadocio to which this squire of dames
treated the Duchess, and on the still more doubtful
evidence of certain compromising letters purporting
to have been addressed by him to Sophia Dorothea
when at Rome, and printed by him in his old age—
as late as 1738.   Thus the shame of this denuncia-
tion lies entirely with its cowardly author.

There seems, however, little doubt but that,
after her return from Italy, Sophia Dorothea became
further estranged from her husband.   To this date
would have to be assigned, were it otherwise worth
noticing, the attraction said by the Duchess of
Orleans to have been exercised by Sophia Dorothea
upon the Raugrave Charles Lewis, one of the family
of nephews and nieces ' by the left hand ' to whom
the Duchess Sophia extended so benevolent and
almost maternal a protection.   According to the
same authority, it was to escape the wiles of the
light-hearted Princess that the Raugrave took service
against the Turks in the Morea, where he met with
his death in 1688 ; but there was very probably
more malice than truth in the story.   In March,
1687, Sophia Dorothea gave birth to a second child,
the daughter who was named after her, and who,
as the wife of King Frederick William I of Prussia,
was to become the mother of Frederick the Great
and of his brother Augustus William, the direct
ancestor of the subsequent Kings of Prussia and
of the German Emperors of our own times.   It

cannot have been till after this event that George
Lewis, who seems to have remained nearer home
after his campaign in 1685, began to follow his
father's example and give publicity to his preference
of other attractions to those of his wife.   But much
uncertainty exists as to the date at which this
infidelity began, and as to the extent to which it
was carried.   It has been widely assumed, and is
constantly repeated, that Countess Platen sought
to maintain the family influence over the Hereditary
Prince, after he had tired of her sister, through her
daughter ;   but this assumption, which, because
of its revolting character, was carefully kept alive
and cherished by the detractors of George I and
his dynasty, must be dismissed as baseless.   This
celebrated lady, who, like the Duchess Sophia's
own daughter, had been christened Sophia Charlotte, in 1701 became the wife of Baron von Kielmannsegg, a nobleman of honourable reputation,
who had for some years been attached to the
Hanoverian Court.   Here the pair lived in unbroken
union and enjoyed a distinguished position ;   their
villa of *Fantaisie* on the avenue to Herrenhausen
being regarded as a favourite resort of foreign
visitors to Hanover.   They afterwards followed
King George I to England, where, after the resignation of the Duke of Somerset, the high household
office of Master of the Horse was left vacant, in
order that its duties might be performed by the

Hanoverian *Oberstallmeister*, while his wife was created Countess of Leinster in the Irish and afterwards Countess of Darlington in the English peerage. Neither at Hanover nor in England had George I ever made any secret of the nature of the tie which he believed to exist between her and himself; he had consistently treated her as his half-sister, giving her at the Electoral Court precedence over the Raugraves and Raugravines, and, in the patent that conferred an Irish peerage upon her, causing her to be designated *consanguinea nostra*. So simple an explanation of the honour in which she continued to be held till her death in 1727 was of course insufficient for Jacobite spite, for anti-German prejudice, and for the love of scandal on its own account. On the other hand, the only personage whom, either before or after he mounted the English throne, George publicly recognised as mistress, was also the only lady at the Hanoverian Court who seems in the days of his married life to have exercised a strong fascination over him. Yet Melusina von der Schulenburg (afterwards Duchess of Kendal)[1] appears at this time to have refrained from thrusting herself into notice; and this agrees with the indications of refinement which it is

---

[1] Of the persistently repeated story of King George I's morganatic marriage to the Duchess of Kendal there appears to be no proof. The late Dr. Richard Garnett, who could hardly have failed to come across whatever evidence on the subject existed, assured me that he knew of none.

impossible to ignore in the portrait remaining of her in the period of her youth.

Thus, then, scarcely anything is ascertainable as to the beginnings and rise of the general sense of unhappiness which is known to have come over Sophia Dorothea during her life at Hanover, and to which—some time in 1692 or later—she gave *naïve* expression by the avowal, afterwards, with cruel ineptness, judicially quoted against her, that she would rather be a ' *marquise* in France ' than Electoral Princess of Brunswick-Lüneburg. Yet fixed antipathies of this kind are commonly of gradual growth, and it would have been difficult for a nature like Sophia Dorothea's, craving for impulse to meet impulse, and quite incapable of renunciation, to settle down into the dull acquiescence which, with so many women, has to do duty for contentment. The restraint of a monotonous existence and the petty rules of an elaborate etiquette, imposed upon her among surroundings in which there was so much to annoy her and so little to sustain her self-respect, must in any case have made her restive and unhappy. Least of all could she have felt any inclination to take an interest in the schemes of dynastic ambition to which she knew herself to have been sacrificed—perhaps against the wish of her best friend, her mother. The anecdote that it was attempted to implicate her in the plot hatched by Prince Maximilian—Moltke, who was to pay the penalty of the discovered design, being offered his release, if he would charge her with a guilty knowledge,—may be dismissed as fictitious.   And it may be observed, by the way, that, while there is no authority for connecting Countess Platen with the supposed offer, it could not possibly have been promoted by the Duchess Sophia, whose sympathies were on the side of Maximilian's revolt against the principle of primogeniture.   Sophia Dorothea was, no doubt, on pleasant terms with her high-spirited but flighty brother-in-law Maximilian, who, indeed, unmistakably oppressed her with his attentions ; but it is quite clear that, in no sense of the word, can there have been anything ' serious ' between them.   We do not know how Sophia Dorothea was affected by the rise in the family dignity which procured for her the title of Electoral Princess. But, in regard to a question of still greater importance for the future of the House, we have it on excellent authority that she took a line opposite to that adopted by her husband.   Sir William Dutton Colt, who, as was seen, had entered upon his duties as English Envoy Extraordinary and Minister Plenipotentiary at Hanover in 1689, while describing the Duchess Sophia as an incomparable person, full of charming wit, kindness, and civility, and speaking of the ' Princess of Hanover ' (Sophia Dorothea), for whom and her infant son, he says,

Duke Ernest Augustus showed great fondness, as beautiful, accomplished, and agreeable, notes (in 1691) that the Princess was distinctly anti-English in her sympathies. Her partiality for France might have found a sufficient explanation in her descent, and in the associations so long cherished by her mother at Celle ; but Sir William Colt assigns another reason that cannot be overlooked. The eldest son (George Lewis), the envoy reported, was not in the least French in his inclinations ; and the French party, discontented with this, paid all the court imaginable to the Princess—' and I fear not without success, for she has no great fondness for the Prince.'

It is, therefore, clear that, by this time (1691), Sophia Dorothea's feelings towards her husband had passed into a condition of more or less active antipathy. And there can no longer be any pretence of doubt that, whether or not the indifference of her husband towards herself had hardened into positive unkindness, and whether or not this unkindness (as there is absolutely nothing to prove) had shown itself in actual ill-treatment, Sophia Dorothea was already under the influence of a growing passion for another man. The story of the guilty loves of Sophia Dorothea and Königsmarck need not be related at length here, since large portions of their correspondence are generally accessible, at least in a translation from the French originals, while a supplementary part is for the first time (with the exception of two letters which have appeared elsewhere) printed in an Appendix to the present book. The evidence for the genuineness of this correspondence, in so far as the greater part of it is concerned, which covers 679 pages, and is now extant in the University Library at Lund, was practically irresistible as it stood, and is confirmed beyond the last shadow of doubt by the letters in the Royal Secret Archives of State at Berlin, which cover 65 pages, and which are seen at the first glance to belong to the same correspondence. They agree in the handwritings, and in the use of the same cipher, as well as in all the distinctive features of style ; they refer to numerous details mentioned in the Lund letters ; and to some of these certain of the Berlin documents stand in the relation of supplements or answers.   It is said—but on no stated authority—that to these letters might be added others, of contents unknown, in the possession of the present head of the House of Hanover. No part of Count Königsmarck's correspondence with the Princess Sophia Dorothea remains in the possession of the present representative of his family. As for the Lund documents, their history can be satisfactorily traced up to the direct descendants of Countess Lewenhaupt, the elder sister of Count Philip Christopher von Königsmarck. The younger sister, the famous Countess Aurora, as will be seen, actively intervened in the transactions that followed on its

discovery, at a time when both the sisters were residing at Hamburg.   It must be supposed that Aurora
at some time transferred the letters from her
custody into that of her elder sister; how they
came into her own, must remain matter of conjecture, though it is a not unnatural supposition
that they were entrusted to her by the recipients.
On the other hand, the evidence of handwriting
obtained by a comparison of these documents with
others of incontestable genuineness, from the hands
of Sophia Dorothea and Königsmarck respectively, is
entirely satisfactory—though this part of the subject is complicated by the fact (for as such it may
be set down) that the Princess possessed the art of
writing in two different hands, while portions of her
part of the love correspondence were dictated by her
to her confidante. (Königsmarck wrote his own love-
letters; but his official letters at Hanover are, except
the signatures, probably in the handwriting of his
private secretary.)   But it is the internal evidence
contained in the documents themselves, in face of
which the refusal to accept them, though maintained by at least one historian of high eminence to
whom this period of Brunswick-Lüneburg history
and this particular episode were familiar as to no
other among his contemporaries, must be said to
have broken down.   The internal evidence in the
present case consists mainly of a number of coin-
cidences of circumstance and date, such as it is

impossible to ascribe either to chance or to design, that have been proved to exist between incidental statements in these letters and in contemporary documents of unimpeachable authenticity. The most important of these are the letters and contemporary despatches of Sir William Dutton Colt, the envoy to the Courts of Hanover and Celle mentioned above, now preserved in our Record Office, and extending over the period from July, 1689, to December, 1692. (To these have, at all events, to be added passages in the correspondence of the Electress Sophia, and isolated statements as to the campaign in the Netherlands and the battle of Steenkirke in particular, in a military list cited by Havemann, and in a contemporary account of the battle in the *Theatrum Europæum*.) The credit of placing this investigation on lines which could not but lead up to an irrefutable issue belongs to the late Mrs. Everett Green, for whom a careful second transcript had been made of the letters of which a first, incomplete, transcript had been presented to her by the late Count Albert von der Schulenburg-Klosterrode. The second, complete, copy, carefully digested and arranged, was placed by Mrs. Green in the British Museum, after she had, for prudential reasons, abandoned the idea of embodying it in a published work. This task was accomplished by the late Mr. W. H. Wilkins, in his own way, in a book afterwards republished in a new and revised

s

edition ; but he did not live to carry out his contingent design of some day ' translating the whole correspondence at Lund, at Berlin, and at Gmünden, and arranging it in chronological order with the aid of first-hand documentary evidence drawn from other sources.' The corroboration of the genuineness and authenticity of the Lund documents furnished by those now printed from the originals in the Berlin Archives is, as observed, complete, and all the more convincing, inasmuch as they must have been separated from the rest at a very early date. It is stated in the Register of the Archives of State at Berlin that they were found among the papers of Frederick the Great at Sans Souci after his death ; and the superscription which they bear ('*Lettres d'Amour de la Duchesse D'allen au Comte Konigsmarc*') is in the King's own handwriting. How they came into his possession must remain a matter of conjecture, which will be more appropriately discussed elsewhere. It should perhaps be added that the whole problem of the genuineness of this correspondence is of very secondary historical significance ; but, apart from the human interest of the letters themselves, their whole story shows how difficult it is to find, and perhaps also how difficult it is to kill, the truth.[1]

[1] For an examination of the whole question of the genuineness of the Lund letters I must refer the reader to an article on the original edition of Mr. Wilkins' book, *The Love of an Uncrowned Queen*, contributed by me to the *Edinburgh Review* for January, 1901. I have since re-examined the cipher with the aid of the

Nothing indicates that Count Philip Christopher von Königsmarck, the ill-fated hero of the tragedy of Sophia Dorothea's life, made his appearance at Hanover before the month of March, 1688, when his presence at a court *fête* is accidentally mentioned —just a twelvemonth after the birth of the second and last of George Lewis' and Sophia Dorothea's children. Königsmarck was a member of a Swedish family of high position and great wealth, which had derived lustre from the important services of Field-Marshal von Königsmarck in the latter

key supplied by the late Count Schulenburg to the late Mrs. Everett Green ; and it certainly fills one with amazement that any rational human beings should have thought concealment attainable by so perfectly transparent a disguise. But the miserable folly of the whole business is at least consistent with itself.—As to the Berlin letters, Mr. Wilkins does not explicitly say that he had seen them; but it was unnecessary that he should do so, as an exhaustive account of them (with the text of two of them) was given by Dr. Robert Geerds in the *Beitlage* to the *Allgemeine Zeitung*, No. 77, Friday, April 4th, 1902. The eminent historian Dr. A. Köcher, after first directing attention to these letters in the *Allgemeine Deutsche Biographie*, Vol. xxxiv. (art. *Sophia Dorothea*), and declaring them an audacious forgery (he repeated this assertion privately to myself), deposited in the Royal Archives at Berlin a statement of his belief that a comparison of handwritings left him in no doubt as to the letters being spurious ; but Dr. Geerds' explanations on this head (see *Appendix B*) are to my mind perfectly satisfactory.—I should like to add that at my request Count Königsmarck, in December last, most kindly allowed the examination of his family archives at Plaue near Berlin on my behalf by Archivrath Dr. Paczkowski, but that no part of any correspondence between Sophia Dorothea and her lover was discovered there. Dr. Paczkowski carried out the task which he was so good as to undertake with a thoroughness and *savoir faire* reflecting the highest credit upon himself and the distinguished official body of which he forms part.

part of the Thirty Years' War, and which had, through him, acquired large estates in northern Germany. The branch of the family to which Philip Christopher belonged were citizens of the world; to set them down as adventurers argues an imperfect apprehension of the spirit of their age, and indeed of that of a great part of the following century also. Like the rest of them, Philip Christopher had seen many courts already in his youthful days ; and nothing could be more probable than that he should have found his way to Celle, especially as he had a family connexion with France, such as would always have ensured him a welcome at the court of George William and Eleonora. He may thus very well have formed a boy and girl acquaintance with their daughter ; but the statement said to have been afterwards made by him, that he had loved her from childhood, is insufficiently authenticated, and does not recur in any of his love-letters. He then accompanied his elder brother, Count Charles John, whose wanderings had been more widely varied than his own (and with whom he is confounded by Horace Walpole, in his careless way), on a visit to England. Here the elder brother was the principal figure in a *cause célèbre*, the trial of himself and others for the murder of the wealthy Thomas Thynne ('Tom of Ten Thousand'), of which crime an elaborate representation may to this day be seen carved in relief on the victim's

tomb in Westminster Abbey.[1]   Fortunately for himself, Count von Königsmarck escaped the gallows,
where the careers of his accomplices ended ; but
England was no longer an agreeable place of sojourn
for the two brothers, and their travels recommenced.
The elder died in the Morea in 1686 ; so that it was
the younger who, in 1688, inherited the wealth of
their uncle, on his death after a distinguished
career as a commander in the service of the Venetian
Republic.   Thus, when Königsmarck, after visiting
France and becoming acquainted with the Saxon
Prince afterwards known as Augustus the Strong,
King of Poland, in this same year, 1688, arrived at
Hanover, he was not only a nobleman of much knowledge and experience of the world, but a personage
of great wealth, and an extremely desirable acquisition for a court such as that of Hanover, where
there were excellent opportunities for spending
money as well as for encouraging its expenditure.
On his side, Königsmarck, as the head of his migra-
tory family, may have wished to further the settlement of his sisters ; and the elder, about this time,
married the Swedish Count Axel Lewenhaupt,
who two years later passed into the service of the
Duke of Celle.   The younger, Aurora, had not as
yet found at Dresden, where her brother was probably already well known, the sphere in which her

[1] See Evelyn's *Diary* as to the scandal which surrounded the
trial.

beauty and wit, after liberally diffusing their radiance in many regions, were for a time established as supreme ; at Hanover, so fixed a constellation as that of the Platen family was sure to regard this brilliant meteor with much displeasure. But Countess Platen could raise no objection to Ernest Augustus' offer of a commission to Königsmarck ; and this offer was certainly made and accepted. For he is soon found commanding a Hanoverian regiment, in frontier operations and in Flanders, and afterwards holding, in the same service, a colonelcy of dragoons.

So far we stand on solid ground ; but, as to the beginnings of the intimacy between Sophia Dorothea and Königsmarck, and as to the incidents that occurred in the period before the commencement of the extant correspondence between them, we possess no trustworthy account whatever. There is no evidence even to show the authenticity of the story, which has been used with much effect in a recent poetic drama (very different in conception from that imagined by Schiller on the same theme),[1] that Königsmarck accompanied Prince Charles Philip in the campaign in which the Duchess Sophia lost her favourite son, and that he shared the Prince's dangers, though escaping his doom.

[1] See Schiller's *Dramatischer Nachlass*, ed. G. Kettner, Vol. ii. pp. 220 *sqq.* (Weimar, 1825), and the references there given to articles by Kettner on the subject.—The play to which allusion is made in the text is Mrs. Woods' *The Princess of Hanover* (1902).

At the time when the correspondence between Sophia Dorothea and Königsmarck opens—at the beginning of July, 1691—he must at any rate have been for some time back in Hanover ; for he had started at the head of a regiment of foot in the ducal service on a march towards the Elbe, undertaken for the purpose of ensuring the safety of Hamburg. A few weeks later, he was himself sent to that city on a diplomatic mission for the conclusion of a treaty of alliance with Sweden,—a balancing operation on the part of Ernest Augustus, before he had made up his mind to join the Grand Alliance against France. That this charge, for which of course his Swedish descent rendered him particularly suitable, should have been given to Königsmarck, proves him to have been at this time in full favour at the Hanoverian court.

Inasmuch as, already in the earliest of his extant letters to Sophia Dorothea, Königsmarck describes himself as *in extremis*, though at the same time assuring her that his respect for her is as great as his love, we find the pair already on the brink of an abyss of passion, and understand why their correspondence was a clandestine one. Such, in fact, it was, from first to last, intended to be and to remain ; and all the usual devices of secrecy at the command of the writers of these letters were adopted for the purpose. Of course they were all—or nearly all—written in French, the language ordinarily

used at the Hanover as well as the Celle Court.
The communications from Königsmarck, which
may be said to form about two-thirds of the
whole series of letters or portions of letters, are,
when they bear any address at all, directed to
Fräulein von dem Knesebeck, either by name or
by some kind of designation under which she is
evidently intended. Part of the Princess' letters
are written in a hand differing so much from that
which wrote the remainder, and which a comparison with her undoubtedly genuine writing seems
to identify as her own, that it may be assumed to
be the hand of the confidante. In the actual composition of the letters, the writers had further
agreed to guard themselves by the adoption of a
twofold—or perhaps one should say threefold—
system of cipher, which it needs no Œdipus to
unriddle, at all events sufficiently for the purposes of detection.[1] Under such flimsy safeguards,

[1] First, they use pseudonyms of a more or less allusive nature
in lieu of proper names. Thus *Don Diego* and *la Romaine* signify
the Elector and the Electress (the former is not a flattering nickname in contemporary English literature ; it will be remembered
that the eldest of Sophia's sisters had in former days been called
la Grecque by the younger); *le Grondeur*, *la Pédagogue*, are farcical
names for the Duke and Duchess of Celle, while the Electoral
Prince, Sophia Dorothea's husband, is (not quite so intelligibly)
called *le Réformeur ;* Countess Platen (query with an allusion
to Monplaisir) *la Perspective*, and Sophia Dorothea herself goes
by the appellation of *la petite louche*, or of *le cœur gauche*, or of
Léonisse, a character in a romance of the times. Aurora von
Königsmarck is *l'Avanturière*, and Prince Ernest Augustus
l'Innocent. Secondly, the writers of these letters employ a

explicable in Sophia Dorothea's case only by her youth and utter inexperience, and in Königsmarck's by the habits of a roving life which had led him to cast himself recklessly into a whirlpool of excitement, the lovers gave full vent to their feelings of amorous and jealous passion. The voice of nature is audible in this correspondence, but it is singularly devoid of charm. Königsmarck's tone, as could hardly but be expected, has a general tendency to coarseness, and is at times very gross, calling to mind Stepney's description of the unfortunate man, after his catastrophe, as a loose fish whom he had long known and would always have avoided. No similar charge is to be brought against the letters of Sophia Dorothea, which are written in an easy and flowing style. But her letters, as well as Königsmarck's, contain passages irreconcilable with any conclusion except one—that theirs was a guilty love. For the rest, there is no straining of style in the correspondence, and those who regarded it

numerical cipher of a tolerably simple kind. Of this Professor Palmblad, who published a few of the letters (carefully selecting the worst), and who formed a monstrous hypothesis upon them, lacked the key; Mrs. Everett Green, who possessed it, was already able to decipher most of the names; Mr. Wilkins had not to leave much obscure. Thirdly, names, and occasionally other words, are spelt in figures, the chief difficulty of deciphering being in this case the phonetic spelling adopted by Königsmarck (*biljay = billet*, &c.). Finally, the lovers also resorted to an occasional cryptogram, which would not deceive a child. A name, such as Chauvet, is split up and interlarded with the letters '*illy*'—thus: '*illychauillyvetilly.*' The farce of insertion might have gone further. Cf. *Appendix B* as to the Berlin letters.

as fabricated might well describe it as a ' clumsy '
forgery ; for it omits to make certain points which a
forger could hardly have missed. In the Lund letters,
at all events, Königsmarck, except when calling up
the image of the Electoral Prince George Lewis in his
marital capacity, refers to him with good humour ;
and Sophia Dorothea gives quite a matter-of-fact
account of a quarrel between her parents.

It would be unprofitable to attempt here to
follow the course of this unhappy passion, of which
many incidents have now been verified as to time
and place, chiefly by means of the despatches of the
English envoy, while the main event of its catastrophe is lost in impenetrable gloom.   Königsmarck—who asserts that, had he proceeded from
Hamburg to Sweden, he would have readily been
admitted into the service of that monarchy, where,
on account of his numerous connexions in many
lands at many Courts, he might very possibly have
come to play a conspicuous part—chose, instead,
to return to Hanover, probably in consequence of
the favourable reception accorded by the Princess
to his still hesitating written advances.   His
letters now begin to assume a freer tone.   Temporary separations inevitably ensued.   He accom-
panies Duke Ernest Augustus to Wolfenbüttel,
while she remains behind ; she joins in a visit, in
which he is not included, to her father at his hunt-
ing-seat at Epsdorff, or at Wienhausen ; and he

has to swear eternal fidelity in a letter signed in his blood, and to protest that he will go to the Morea (whither Ernest Augustus' son Christian was at the time intent upon proceeding), in order to relieve her of his compromising presence. It seems to have been not long after this that Sophia Dorothea succumbed to her passion; and, early in 1692, fears were already pressing upon them of discovery —in the first instance through her mother; for Königsmarck had followed her to the Court of Celle. At last, in June, 1692, he was obliged to join the Hanoverian force under the command of Sophia Dorothea's husband in Flanders; for Ernest Augustus, resolved on striking a bargain for the Ninth Electorate, had now openly become a member of the Grand Alliance. With the opening of the Flemish campaign (during which Königsmarck took part in the battle of Steenkirke) begins the series of the Princess' letters, several of which are dated from Brockhausen, where Prince Maximilian had taken refuge with the Duke of Celle after his trouble at Hanover, while others are written from Wiesbaden, which later in the year she visited with her mother. Many of these letters contain details that admit of verification from Colt's despatches. The intrigue between Sophia Dorothea and Königsmarck had now passed into a phase in which expressions of love, jealousy, and haunting apprehensions, breathlessly crowd upon one another; and, after the Princess had returned to Hanover, it almost seemed as if she must listen to the advice which he had sent to her from the Low Countries, and cut the knot of their difficulties by flying with him.

We here touch one of the obscurest passages in this pitiful story, and one which must here be dealt with quite briefly. It was quite impossible that Königsmarck's devotion to the Princess before his departure to Flanders should have remained unnoticed at the Hanoverian court ; and nothing could have been more appropriate than that her mother-in-law, the Duchess Sophia, who, without at all suspecting the worst, must have been seriously annoyed by what she had observed—unless we are to adopt the absurd supposition that she was pleased to see her daughter-in-law beginning to go wrong—should have lectured the Princess on her want of *conduite*. But Sophia Dorothea was aware that there was at court another and a less straightforward influence, which she suspected would be adverse to her—that of the Countess Platen. From what followed, there can be no doubt that the Countess had reasons for bearing Königsmarck a grudge ; and it has been unhesitatingly assumed, in accordance with an unauthenticated tradition, that her motive was jealousy, and that he had formerly shared her favours. On the other hand, the Duchess of Orleans deliberately states that there is no *apparentz* of Countess Platen having sought to attract to herself so young a man, and that it is more likely that, as the Electress Sophia had been informed, the Countess cajoled Königsmarck in the hope of his marrying her daughter ; ' for he was a good match.' This story also long found acceptance ; but it does not very well suit either Königsmarck's account of his later meeting with Countess Platen, or the jealousy of her which this account unmistakably excited in the Princess. In any case, when it occurred to Sophia Dorothea to consult the Electress Sophia Charlotte of Brandenburg on the situation—a step which at all events shows her to have been without fear of any underhand action on the part of her cousin or her mother-in-law—Sophia Charlotte counselled her to conciliate the Countess Platen ; and this piece of advice was communicated by Sophia Dorothea to Königsmarck. On his return to Hanover, about November, he seems to have determined to contribute towards the appeasing of the powerful mistress ; but, whether in sheer recklessness, or because he considered himself safe with the Countess, who would assuredly remain silent on the subject towards her august protector, he clearly overdid his part. After this escapade, a sort of desperate rage seems to have seized upon him, and the correspondence of the year 1692 concludes with a brutally sarcastic tirade launched against the new ' Electoral Princess ' by her infuriated lover. It is, then, manifest that Sophia Dorothea had grounds for distrusting Countess Platen ; but, how far the double insult offered to the Elector's mistress by Königsmarck's conduct is to be connected with the terrible events that followed, no evidence exists to show, and the part of evil genius assigned to the Countess in the tragedy has had to be written up with the aid of conjecture and fiction.

The last chapter of the correspondence, which extends from the early summer to the close of the year 1693 (or thereabouts), shows the fatal passion of the pair still aflame, but the clouds of danger thickening around them. In the absence of her husband during the year's campaign in Flanders, the Electoral Princess continued to idle away her days with her parents-in-law at Luisburg, or with her own parents at Brockhausen, whither Königs-marck followed her. She took some comfort from the good humour of the Electress Sophia ; though, foreseeing that, if she came to know the truth, she would show no pity, Königsmarck warned the Princess that her mother-in-law would, sooner or later, be her ruin. At Brockhausen, a nocturnal meeting between the lovers was not wholly un-watched, and the letters afterwards interchanged by them show increasing apprehension. Countess Platen herself vaguely warned the Princess as to the risk she was running—an act which it must be conceded at least admits of a kindly explanation. In her last extant letter, Sophia Dorothea utters

what comes very near to a cry of hopeless despair.
In the course of the month in which this letter was
written (August, 1693) Königsmarck was obliged
to absent himself from Court, in order to take part
in a military movement intended to check a Danish
coup de main upon the contested duchy of Lauenburg.   When he returned to Hanover, fresh warnings reached him—from old Marshal von Podewils,[1]
under whom he had served, and from the youngest
of the Hanoverian Princes, Ernest Augustus, whose
devoted attachment to his brother, the Electoral
Prince, appears not to have prevented this act of
kindness.   These warnings themselves, together
with other indications, show that, although the
actual character of the intrigue between Sophia
Dorothea and Königsmarck may have remained
unknown—unless indeed some letters had already
fallen into the wrong hands—the *liaison* itself was,
as is, after all, usual in such cases, more or less of an
open secret, and that thus the pair were rushing
headlong to their ruin.   Quite at the end of the
year, Königsmarck had once more to go away from
Hanover ; and, at this point, the Lund correspondence comes to an end with a letter from him
evidently addressed to the confidante, and, through
her, assuring *Léonisse* that, whatever might befall,
he would not abandon her.

The cessation of the correspondence leaves us in

[1] ' *Le bonhomme* ' in the lovers' cipher.

some doubt as to the precise nature of the occurrences in Hanover in the earlier half of the year 1694, which was to see the end of this lamentable history. Königsmarck, who had returned to Hanover, quitted it again in April; and, without having resigned his Hanoverian commission, betook himself to the Court of the Elector Frederick Augustus of Saxony (Augustus the Strong) at Dresden. Here he undoubtedly behaved with an indiscretion beyond that habitual to him, and it is probable enough—though this again cannot be proved—that his vaunts included some reference to his successes with Countess Platen. However this may have been, Königsmarck, though he had not accepted a commission offered him in the Saxon army and still remained a Hanoverian officer, could hardly expect on his return to Hanover to carry on his amour as before. There had been indications of an uneasy feeling at Court, which explain themselves without the supposition that a combination was at work there to drive Sophia Dorothea to her ruin, and without the wholly gratuitous assumption that, in the front of that combination, stood the Electress Sophia. Attempts were afterwards said to have been made to provoke ill-will between the Electoral Prince and his wife through the agency of her lady-in-waiting, Fräulein von dem Knesebeck; and, though there is no reason for suspecting her of any interference of the kind, it is certain that, about the early part of June, Sophia Dorothea left the Electoral Court and repaired to her parents at Brockhausen. Once more, there is nothing to show that her departure had been caused by actual ill-treatment on the part of her husband. On her way home to Hanover, she refused to alight at Herrenhausen in order to pay her respects to the Elector and Electress; and, after ascertaining at Hanover that her husband was away at Berlin, she resolved once more to join her parents at Brockhausen. But they refused to receive her; and, on the fatal night of July 1st, 1694, she was still with her faithful lady-in-waiting in the Leineschloss at Hanover.

On the same night, Count Königsmarck left his house at Hanover, never to be seen again. That his intention was to enter the Leine Palace and the apartments of the Electoral Princess, there can be no doubt; but the actual purpose of their meeting, and the plan on which they then agreed or on which they had agreed before, remain unknown. They may have merely designed to contrive her escape with his help to Wolfenbüttel, where she might rely on a welcome from Duke Antony Ulric; or they may have intended to realise the dream to which their correspondence refers, and henceforth to belong wholly to one another. But, from Sophia Dorothea, no attempt was afterwards made to extract an avowal on this head; and the confidante, Eleonora von dem Knesebeck, persisted from first

to last, both during her imprisonment and after she
had effected her escape from it, in asserting the
innocency of her mistress. Yet Fräulein von dem
Knesebeck confessed to having known of a 'plot,'
and to having been so full of uneasiness that tears
and entreaties were needed to persuade her to
remain in the Princess' service.

Some days passed before the disappearance of
Königsmarck attracted public notice. The first
sign that there was something wrong appears to
have been the intimation, noticed in a despatch of
July 3rd from Cressett (Colt's successor), that, while
the Electoral Prince remained at Berlin, the Princess
was sick at Hanover. As a matter of fact, both she
and her confidante had been strictly confined to her
apartments ; whether any letters from Königsmarck had been discovered in her keeping, we do
not know. But there is evidence that, already in
May and June, hands had been laid on some of the
correspondence between the lovers ; and the knowledge of this had probably determined the Elector
Ernest Augustus to proceed against his daughter-
in-law. And it is certain that some of her letters
were sent by the authorities at Hanover to her
parents ; for Leibniz positively asserts that, had not
her letters been produced, they could not have
thought her so guilty at Celle. These letters must
have been found in Königsmarck's residence ; and
we have no reason for doubting the statement that

a thorough search was made in his cabinet, in the presence of officials only, although it is added that a packet of letters thought to be incriminating was sent by persons who had been in his confidence to Celle, where his sisters soon afterwards made their appearance. These latter, in all probability, formed the correspondence which ultimately found its way to Berlin.

Both the Elector Ernest Augustus and Sophia Dorothea's father, the Duke of Celle, considering her guilt to be established, the question next arose as to the way in which her case should be treated. In the first instance she was taken to Ahlden, a magistrate's house or 'castle'—no one who has cast eyes on it could ever think of it as anything but a 'moated grange'—situate in a lonely marshland corner of her father's territory, at some twenty miles' distance from Hanover. While she was detained here in strict custody, the mode of procedure against her was arranged. It was resolved, for the honour of the House—which, for good or ill, was the dominant motive in the whole of this melancholy business—to keep the name and person of Königsmarck out of the affair altogether, and to make the desertion of her husband by the Princess the ground of a suit of divorce before a specially constituted Consistorial tribunal. This course, which could hardly have succeeded but for the attitude maintained by her, was carried through with a completeness which must have surpassed the

anticipations of the astute minds that had devised it.
Throughout the enquiry, the Princess made no confession whatever of any act of infidelity, adhering
to the instructions conveyed to her by her father's
ministers, Bernstorff and Bülow, who, in an interview at Ahlden, had informed her that ' everything
was discovered '—manifestly another reference to
the evidence of part of her correspondence with
Königsmarck. Accordingly, notwithstanding the
representations of the honest counsel with whom
she had been provided—and to whose dissatisfaction
with the proceedings and desire to preserve the
proofs of his not having been responsible for their
result is due the private preservation, at least in
part, of the documents of the divorce-suit—she
refused to swerve from her declared resolution no
longer to live with the Electoral Prince as her
husband. After some attempts on the part of
the Duke of Celle to mitigate the rigour of the
expected result, which were successfully resisted
on the part of the Hanoverian Government, the
sentence of the Consistorial tribunal was pronounced
on December 28th, 1694, and delivered to the Princess
at Lauenau, whither she had been temporarily removed, on the last day of the year. It dissolved
the marriage between her and the Electoral Prince,
granting him, as the innocent party, permission
to remarry, but withholding this from her as the
guilty party. She at once accepted the sentence ;

a few days later her confessor informed her father that she acknowledged ' *sa faute,*' and the justice of the punishment inflicted upon her ; and, in 1698, on the occasion of the death of the Elector Ernest Augustus, she wrote to her former husband and to his mother, the Electress Sophia, beseeching them to pardon her faults of the past, and entreating the favour of being allowed to see her children. This favour was never granted to her.

The Hanoverian court and Government had, as has been seen, persistently striven to dissociate the disappearance of Königsmarck from the disgrace of the Princess. In the first instance, this disappearance had been simply ignored, while a circular had been issued to foreign courts, drawn up in this sense, and attributing the alienation of the Princess from her husband to the machinations of Fräulein von dem Knesebeck, who was soon afterwards clapped into a dungeon at Scharzfels in the Harz, from which she did not make her escape till four years afterwards.[1] As to the vanished Königsmarck, it had been easy to stifle the anxieties of the unhappy Sophia Dorothea, who, before she was effectually silenced, had written a letter expressive of her fear that he had fallen into the hands of a certain lady, and that his life might be in danger. There can hardly be any doubt

[1] Of this castle little or nothing remains at the present day but a ' restored ' gate and staircase.

but that this referred to Countess Platen, although it merely proves Sophia Dorothea to have been afraid of the consequences of the Countess' anger. Nor could it be impossible to baffle the curiosity of the world at large—represented by no less august an enquirer than Louis XIV—in the assurance that the mystery would in due course be forgotten as a nine days' wonder. But it proved a serious task to meet the pertinacious efforts of Königsmarck's sister Aurora, who, adopting a rumour which for some time found an extraordinary amount of credit, insisted that her brother was still alive, and, while demanding that the truth should be revealed, pursued Countess Platen (with whom she had a quarrel of old standing) with special animosity. It is noteworthy that the Electress Sophia should be found taking the side of Countess Platen, who, she writes, is not accustomed to be spoken of in the terms applied to her by the Countess *Orrore*. Having been forbidden to show herself in Hanover, Königsmarck's dauntless sister betook herself to Dresden, in order to secure the assistance of the Elector Frederick Augustus in her quest. It was on this occasion that she conquered that potentate altogether ; and he espoused her cause so heartily as to send Colonel Bannier to Hanover, there to demand that Königsmarck, as an officer in the Saxon service, should be given up to him. As late as December, 1694, Bannier remained convinced that the Count was still alive, and detained as a prisoner somewhere in the Palace. Not until after some months had passed was the tempest raised by Aurora allayed, largely through the diplomatic skill of the Hanoverian minister at Dresden, Jobst von Ilten. But her passionate activity, and the widespread interest excited by so impenetrable a mystery, already in 1695 led to the publication of a narrative purporting to have been sent from Hamburg to the French minister at the Danish court, which the Duchess of Orleans characterised as impertinent and mendacious, and to which Leibniz was instructed to supply a corrective commentary. Meanwhile the Electoral Government had not only maintained an absolute silence as to the Königsmarck affair, but had resorted to the expedient of systematically destroying all evidence concerning it or in any way connected with it. This policy was carried through with extraordinary vigilance and consistency, as might be shown in various instances, of which some reach down to our own times. Above all, a systematic destruction took place of all the documents, whether public or private, at Hanover, in London— and even in Ahlden—which might have thrown light on the episode. Among the rest, the letters of the Electress Sophia bearing on it were destroyed. This was in accordance with the wish of the Duchess of Orleans, whose sagacity apprised her that there was something in the rumours which had reached her, although the excellent Frau von Harling had declared them to be all lies.[1] It would, however, appear that, whether because of a desire on the part of the Duke of Celle that some evidence should be procured which would justify his assent to the severe treatment of his daughter,[2] or because of the Electress' own wish not to annihilate all proof, certain incriminating portions of the correspondence remained undestroyed ; and these were perhaps the letters which are supposed to have been afterwards sent to Berlin, in order to remove the doubts of Sophia Dorothea's daughter and namesake as to the misconduct of her mother, to whom she always behaved with kindness—and which, afterwards, certainly found their way into the hands of Frederick the Great and thence into the Secret Archives of State. So far as Königsmarck is concerned, the current story as to his death, and as to the horrible part played in it by the Countess Platen, still remains unauthenticated. Horace Walpole, the author of *Historic Doubts on the Life and Reign of King Richard III*, was prepared to believe a story which he professed to have derived from George II, through Queen

[1] According to W. H. Wilkins, *A Queen of Tears*, George III similarly ordered the destruction of the entire correspondence with Copenhagen occasioned by the catastrophe of his daughter Caroline Matilda of Denmark and Struensee.

[2] In the spring of 1695, Cresset reports that the Duke and Duchess of Celle feel some distaste, now, for the company of the Electress, on account of the divorce proceedings.

Caroline and Sir Robert Walpole, according to which, on the occasion of some repairs in the Leine Palace, the remains of Königsmarck were discovered under the floor of Sophia Dorothea's dressing-room ; and, of the assassins rumoured to have been hired by Countess Platen, one at least is said to have been enabled by his crime to found a family of much respectability at Hanover.

Sophia Dorothea herself was henceforth lost to the history of her House, and almost fell out of the remembrance of the world in which she might have played so prominent a part. She was now officially styled the Duchess of Ahlden, the village on the Aller over whose immediate district a certain petty jurisdiction was given to the prisoner, together with a few shadowy rights of honour. During a period of thirty-two years she lingered out here her life of durance—never being allowed to quit Ahlden, with the single exception, when a movement of Saxon-Polish troops seemed to render her place of detention unsafe, of a brief visit to Celle, where, however, her father declined to see her. Neither was she at any time permitted to go forth from her castle beyond a distance of six miles ; and her carriage, closely attended by a guard of honour, had always to drive along the same road.[1] She had the occasional consolation of a visit from her mother till

---

[1] Her habit of driving along it at a furious pace recalls the practice of a very different captive—Napoleon at St. Helena.

the Duchess Eleonora's death in 1722 ; for the
mother's love never waned, and her will contributed
to make the prisoner nominally the possessor of
great wealth. On the other hand, she was, as
already noted, never allowed to see her children.
She occupied herself much with works of charity
and piety. She presented an organ and candelabra
to the parish church where during part of her imprisonment she worshipped—and was extremely
popular in the village, which she rebuilt at her own
cost after a fire in 1715 ; and she gave much attention to the affairs in the neighbourhood, receiving
formal visits, and bestowing great care upon her
personal adornment. She never quite abandoned the
hope of a change in her condition, until shortly
before her death she discovered that her interests
had been betrayed, and (it is said) most of her large
accumulated capital made away with, by an agent
(a certain von Bahr), in whom she had reposed confidence. The records of the poor woman's life
during the long years of her confinement do not
change our notions of her character ; but the story
of her solitary woe needs no deepening.

George Lewis has met with nothing but blame
for his share in the whole story of Sophia Dorothea's
misfortunes. Our age happily refuses to accept
the view that what is unpardonable in a wife is
venial in a husband ; but such was not the opinion
of George Lewis' contemporaries. On returning to

Hanover, he had found the relations between his wife and Königsmarck very much of an open secret at court ; and, when proofs were in his hands, a divorce was the only course open to him, if the honour of his House was to be vindicated. There was afterwards a rumour, mentioned by Elizabeth Charlotte to her aunt, that he would take back his wife on his accession to the Electorship at his father's death ; and, in 1704, a report was again current at Paris, that the Duke of Marlborough hoped to effect a reconciliation between the Elector and his discarded consort. But, as a matter of fact, he never varied his attitude towards her of absolute and immutable estrangement ; and least of all did he show any inclination to invite her to share the glories of the English throne, though it is probable that he might, by such a step, have diminished the prejudices to which he was exposed in his new kingdom.[1]   On the occurrence of her death on November 13th, 1726 (which, as is known, preceded

---

[1] It is a curious instance of a certain cynical hauteur in George Lewis (which, however, contains an element of manly self-possession) that he should have supplied the Duchess of Orleans with a key to the characters of the Supplement to the *Roman Octavia*, in which Duke Antony Ulric had taken the opportunity, perhaps with the help of Fräulein von dem Knesebeck's reminiscences, of giving to the world a version of the whole story of the Duchess of Ahlden.—A French MS., *Histoire de Frédegonde, Princesse de Chérusque, Duchesse d'Hanovre, Épouse de George, Roi de la Grande Bretagne*, proposing to give an account, *inter alia*, of ' *sa Prison au Chateau d'Alhen, où elle a fini ses jours*,' supposed to date from about 1740, was not long since advertised for sale.

his own by but a few months), he prohibited a general mourning in the Electorate, and she was buried without ceremony in the family vault at Celle, after her interment at Ahlden had proved impracticable. There can be no doubt that the bitter resentment with which her conduct had inspired him was, in a measure, continued in his feelings towards his son, the future King George II ; but, though the accounts on this head are contradictory, it is at least doubtful whether Sophia Dorothea's son ever exhibited any active sympathy for his unfortunate mother.[1] Sophia Dorothea the younger, who, in 1706, married the Crown Prince of Prussia (afterwards King Frederick William I), kept up some communication with her mother, and, after she became Queen, took Eleonora von dem Knesebeck into her service, besides entering into a more frequent correspondence with the prisoner. But mother and daughter never met ; and, finally, there seems to have been a marked difference of opinion between them as to the famous Double Marriage Project between the courts of Great Britain and Prussia.

That the unfortunate prisoner should have gained the active goodwill, which the fair young Princess had never conciliated, of her mother-in-law,

[1] Lord Hervey's story of his having preserved his mother's picture may be true ; but the further statement that he proposed, if she had survived, to have brought her over and declared her Queen, needs a stronger qualification than the ' it was said,' by which it is accompanied. (*Memoirs*, Vol. iii. pp. 348–9.)

the Electress Sophia, was hardly to be expected. Such advances as were made to her by the Duchess of Ahlden seem to have been coldly rejected ; and the tone in which the Duchess of Orleans continues occasionally to speak of her ill-fated relative no doubt reflects, with tolerable accuracy, that adopted by her aunt in her non-extant letters. The Electress, as we now know, had verified the conclusion of Elizabeth Charlotte, that Sophia Dorothea's case exemplified the proverb as to there being no smoke without fire ; and, while we may regret that the charity which, in the matter of morals, the Electress Sophia readily showed to the shortcomings of the men of her family, was never extended by her to the daughter of Eleonora d'Olbreuze, there is in this rigour nothing unnatural or incompatible with the rules of life which she consistently observed. To argue, however, from this severity back to the unproved supposition of an active cooperation on the part of Sophia towards the ruin of her daughter-in-law, is palpably unjust. And it should always be borne in mind that the sympathy of posterity was secured to Sophia Dorothea by her misfortunes, not by her character, in which there is little or nothing to admire, while much in it may have justly repelled the sound and self-controlled nature of her mother-in-law ; and that the Electress was more impressed by the Princess' fall than by what might seem its legitimate consequences.

There seems no reason for attributing to the painful experiences through which the House of Hanover had recently passed the decline which, about this time, set in in the health of the Elector Ernest Augustus. His illness (which Cressett thought in a large measure imaginary) has quite gratuitously been brought into connexion with Sophia Dorothea's catastrophe, the suggestion being that the wife and the mistress of the Elector had conspired to avert the consequences which might ensue, in the event of his death and the accession of a new Electress. In June, 1697, the Electress Sophia informs the Raugravine Louisa that, though the other symptoms in the Elector's condition are good, his nervous debility is great, and that it has been resolved to try the skill of a Dutch empiric, with whose '*charlattaneri*' she characteristically expresses impatience. Towards the end of the year the course of his malady seemed to have been in a measure arrested ; but the decay of his powers soon set in again with alarming rapidity. His life of constant self-indulgence ended very miserably ; for some time loss of sight in one eye was feared, and after this he was all but deprived of the use of speech. The Electress Sophia faithfully nursed him to the last. Even in the days of his health she had bravely accustomed herself to his habits ; and she afterwards humorously related that she had made a point, in the hour of domesticity, of filling his pipe

with the tobacco which she loathed. In his last
illness she, during many months, never left his side,
except when he was asleep. The end came on
January 24th, 1698 ; and a letter written by Sophia
a few months later shows her still in a condition
of deep and unaffected grief—hopeful only '*que
le bon Dieu me fera bientost rejoindre ce cher Électeur
en l'autre monde*,' but consoled by the attentions
of her children and her brother-in-law. Ernest
Augustus had well played his part as a ruler, not
only providing a sure basis for the progress of his
dynasty to augmented power and influence, but also
strengthening and consolidating the civil as well as
the military administration of the Electorate established in his person. His extravagant expenditure on
himself and on his court, though no doubt largely
occasioned by habits of self-indulgence and a profli-
gate temperament, seemed in consonance with what
was probably a well-merited reputation for liberality
of conduct and feeling towards those who served him
well. Thus he proved, in his way, an apt imitator of
the great French prototype whom he, not less than his
brother John Frederick, kept before his eyes ; and the
style in which he lived and reigned suited the interest
of the dynasty as well as his own tastes. At the same
time, he knew how to combine with his magnificence
and generosity a self-restraint that enabled him in
his will to dispose of an unencumbered personal
estate. To Sophia his death, in more respects than

one, brought a considerable change.   She had never
ruled him, not even controlled him by her influence,
as Eleonora of Celle long controlled her Duke, or as,
in another generation, Sophia's favourite Caroline
of Ansbach was to control King George II.   But the
aid of her counsel had been of great value to Ernest
Augustus, both in the ordinary business of government and in great questions of state policy ; and
much of the authority which thus accrued to her
passed away with him.   George Lewis was not of a
disposition likely to induce him, from motives of
piety, to show to his mother a deference beyond that
of ordinary custom.   On the other hand, the death
of Sophia's husband gave to her more of that freedom which no princess ever used less ostentatiously
or more nobly ; it made her, in certain respects,
more distinctly the centre of the intellectual life of
the Hanoverian Court than she had cared to be, or
at all events to seem, in the lifetime of Ernest
Augustus ; it probably brought her closer to her
daughter, and certainly allowed her a fuller enjoyment of the friendship of Leibniz.

No sooner had the reign of Ernest Augustus
come to an end, than his sons Maximilian and
Christian renewed their protest against the principle of primogeniture which he had so persistently
maintained ;[1] and the sympathy with Maximilian

---

[1] Early in 1694, Cresset reports him as ' moving heaven and
earth ' on the subject.

displayed by his sister, the Electress Sophia Charlotte of Brandenburg, can hardly have failed to find a secret response in the maternal heart of the Electress Dowager Sophia herself. But, though there was some talk of her paying a visit at this season to Berlin, she had learnt to tutor her own wishes, and was well aware how much depended upon the maintenance of the good understanding between the two Electoral Governments, which was at the time endangered by certain territorial questions that may here be passed by. Thus George Lewis succeeded without let or hindrance to the whole of the paternal inheritance and expectancies; and, as was noted above, Hanover and Brandenburg were united by a close and 'perpetual' alliance at the very period when the dynastic ambition of the one seemed on the point of consummation, and that of the other was near achieving its absorbing object—the acquisition of a royal (Prussian) crown. That the Hanoverian court was filled with joy by the success of the operations which ended, early in 1701, with the coronation of the first Prussian King, Frederick I, would be an unnatural supposition. The event had, however, been rendered virtually inevitable by the accession, in 1697, of the Elector Frederick Augustus of Saxony to the Polish throne; and the Elector George Lewis was personally not so constituted as to be impelled, even by jealousy, to an eagerness to follow suit. As for the Dowager Electress Sophia, there was, to her, something more than compensation in the thought that a royal crown now surmounted the brow of her favourite child.

Sophia Charlotte, her parents' only daughter, had grown up in a long and unbroken intimacy with her mother. With that mother, as already noted, she had in common a clear and penetrating intelligence, a charm of manner irresistible to anyone whom she chose to admit to familiar intercourse, and a self-possession against which scandal waged war in vain. She also had her mother's intellectual curiosity and general love of knowledge ; but she must have approached more nearly to her aunt Elizabeth in her power of entering into problems of philosophy, though it is only with a grain of salt that the assertion can be accepted as to the conferences between her and Leibniz having originated his *Théodicée*. On the other hand, what little remains from her hand in the way of familiar correspondence, can scarcely be said to be lit up with the natural humour that her mother and the Duchess of Orleans always had at command. Notwithstanding her power of delighting those admitted to her society by the sunny brightness of her manner, when she was so disposed, or when she was stimulated by intellectual interest, her nature seems from early years to have possessed the tranquillity which reason and resignation enabled her mother more gradually to acquire. Probably a certain physical indolence, or phlegma, may have contributed to this result, together with a calm determination to please herself—a luxury in which her mother had rarely or never enjoyed opportunities of indulging.

Already in her childhood, benefiting by the traditions in her mother's family as to the necessity of a good education based on linguistic knowledge, she had exhibited signs of talent ; while her character probably owed much to the training of Frau von Harling (who was also Elizabeth Charlotte's governess), one of those teachers whose destiny it is to be loved for their administration of the rule of law by pupils who, under a less vigorous influence, would certainly be inclined to remain a law to themselves. In the eleventh year of her age, Sophia Charlotte, as we saw, accompanied her mother on a visit to the French Court, while her father was recruiting his health at Ems. It was a delightful visit—perhaps one of the happiest episodes of Sophia's life—in the mixture which it offered of pleasant retrospect under the caresses of the faithful Duchess of Orleans, and of still earlier reminiscences in the genial company of the Abbess of Maubuisson, with a hopeful looking-forward to the future in store for her charming daughter. King Louis XIV himself was the perfection of magnificent courtesy, requesting his brother, the Duke of Orleans, not to

whisper in Sophia's presence, and taking magnanimous notice of her daughter. Sophia's quick wit
helped her through every difficulty, and enabled
her to avoid any mistake—even that of accepting
a *tabouret* when self-respect bade her take a *fauteuil*,
or not sit at all. She knew how to meet both the
stiffness of the French Queen (a Spanish princess)
and the effusiveness of the Spanish Queen (a
French princess); nor was her self-possession
disturbed even by the splendour of Versailles, for
which, as she justly observed, art had done more
than nature. As for Sophia Charlotte, the impression created, both by her beauty and by the extent
of her knowledge, was such as to suggest to Louis
XIV the idea of a match between her and one of
his princes. Nothing, however, came of the notion
except, perhaps, an accentuation of the diplomatic
activity of de Gourville at the Lüneburg courts.
Sophia Charlotte's quiet life continued; and,
though there was some talk of a Bavarian suit for
her hand, it gradually became known that her
destiny was shaping itself nearer home. The establishment of relations of intimacy between the
Courts of Brandenburg at Hanover had become
a political necessity, and Sophia had recognised
the expediency of promoting his object with the
aid of her daughter's hand. When, in 1683, the
Electoral Prince Frederick of Brandenburg became
a childless widower, these speculations at once

assumed a practical aspect. The obstacles which had to be surmounted did not include a religious difficulty, inasmuch as the Reformed (Calvinist) faith, of which Sophia Charlotte made public profession shortly before her marriage, was a form of religion always favoured, though never actually professed, by her mother.[1] There is no reason for crediting the story (which rests only on the gossip of Pöllnitz) that it had been thought unnecessary to anticipate Sophia Charlotte's own choice of a form of Protestantism till it was known whom she was to marry. But, whatever the daughter's religious profession, tolerance would always have formed part of her creed, as it did of her mother's. The marriage was celebrated at Herrenhausen on September 28th, 1684.

From the first, Sophia Charlotte displayed that indifference to playing any part in politics which seemed so strange in her, considering the capacity which she indisputably possessed for exerting influence alike by her personal charms and by her

---

[1] ' I used,' she writes to the elder Schütz in 1703, ' to know all the common prayers, practically, by heart, but I was never taught that our religion much differed from the reformed religion of France and Germany, and I have communicated in this also ; ' and, again : ' I have had prayers offered for the Queen ' [Anne] ' in both the German and the French reformed churches here ' [at Hanover], ' with the permission of the Elector.'—Erman, preacher at the French Reformed church in Berlin, subsequently wrote *Mémoires pour servir à l'histoire de Sophie Charlotte, Reine de Prusse.*

intellectual powers. But, during the few remaining years of the Great Elector's life, the Electoral
Prince Frederick was under a cloud ; and, in 1686,
he had to withdraw with his consort to Halle.   In
1688 he succeeded his father as Elector, and a few
months later his consort presented him with an
heir to his honours (the future King Frederick
William I). She continued, however, to show
little disposition to assert the authority and influence which had now accrued to her ; and, though,
during the ensuing decade, so eventful in the
history of the relations between the Houses of
Hanover and Brandenburg, she was always happy
to exchange visits with her parents and to listen to
the advice bestowed on her by her mother, she
cannot be said to have taken much trouble to use,
either directly or indirectly, the power which she
can hardly have lacked aught but the will to
exercise.   It was not that she had to contend against
any great strength of character in her husband,
who, if humoured in a few things, could without
much difficulty be ruled in the rest. But she did
not care to stoop even to the level of his rather
commonplace and formal nature, in order to conquer for herself an all-controlling influence in both
public and private affairs. She preferred to create
a sphere or circle of her own, into which only those
were admitted who approved themselves to her,
more especially by their intellectual gifts. Here

simplicity, typified by black dress, was the rule. The colony of French refugees, which was in these years establishing itself at Berlin and Brandenburg, was largely represented in her intimate social circle. Sophia Charlotte appreciated those gifts of conversation, of which, in her age, Frenchmen and Frenchwomen possessed, if not the monopoly, at least a predominant share ; and she seems herself to have become mistress of an art which is always more easily described than reproduced.   She was fond of theatrical entertainments of many kinds, and probably gave more offence to the pietism prevailing around her by these, for the most part, innocuous tastes than by her philosophising tendencies.   Toland amused her, and she was not, like her mother, obliged to respect British prejudices about his views or principles, though she was indignant to have been supposed to have gone so far as to ask a man without birth or official position to dine at her table.   In general, she was, no doubt, very much *sans gêne* in her relations with persons whom she liked ; but, though scandal was busy with these freedoms, she never compromised herself by indulging in them too far. The height of her personal influence seems to have been reached when, by 1696, the Elector Frederick III had fulfilled her heart's desire by building for her a country residence in the village of Lützen on the pleasant declivities of the Spree.   She had never been willing to sojourn in the castle of Copenick, where her predecessor, Frederick's first wife, had pined away her days ; and the ample gardens .at Berlin, which he had presented to his Electress, she had, with intelligent philanthropy, mainly distributed in allotments among the townsfolk, with whom, for this reason, and perhaps also because of a sympathetic quickness of wit indigenous among the inhabitants of the growing capital, her reputation always stood high. Lützenburg, as the Italian villa, which gradually grew into a palace, was called, became Sophia Charlotte's chosen abode, although the magnificence with which it was in course of time adorned, both inside and out, had not received its final touches before her death, when this famous royal residence was, in remembrance of her, rechristened Charlottenburg.

The death of Ernest Augustus, in 1698, as we saw, drew mother and daughter more closely together ; and, in the same year, a very important ministerial change at Berlin, the circumstances of which to this day occupy the attention of historical students, greatly increased Sophia Charlotte's opportunities of exercising a personal influence upon the government and policy of her husband. The fall of the hitherto omnipotent minister, Eberhard von Danckelmann, which was speedily followed by his incarceration, affords a most striking instance of the uncertainty of princely favour, and a cruel illustration of the recompense that may await great political services.[1] Here it must suffice to say, that Sophia Charlotte had certainly been jealous of Danckelmann's influence, and that his downfall was regarded by her mother and her friends, even more decidedly than by herself, as an epoch in her personal career.   Leibniz wrote to her, with rather exasperating *aplomb*, surmising that, since she had now secured the entire confidence of the Elector her husband, she would recognise the necessity of taking advantage of the situation (*ménager la conjoncture*).   As there was, he continued, an identity of interest between her and her mother, it was to be hoped that they would find consolation for the evils that had befallen them (the death of Ernest Augustus) in employing their gifts so as to bring about a complete union between Sophia Charlotte's brother and her husband.   (It may perhaps be noted that the sorrow afterwards shown by George Lewis on his sister's death indicates the existence of a genuine affection between them.)   Leibniz could not think of anyone likely to manage so effectively the requisite communications between the two Electresses as it would be within his own power to do ;   and he suggested that this purpose would be most easily accomplished if he were to be appointed

---

[1] See H. Breslau, *Der Fall des Oberpräsidenten E. von Danckelmann*, 1692 (H. Breslau and S. Isaacsohn, *Der Fall zweier Preuss. Minister*).   Berlin, 1878.

to some supervising post connected with science and art at Berlin, and thus supplied with a ready reason for occasional visits to that capital. As a matter of fact, Sophia Charlotte used her best endeavours to induce Frederick III to call into life a (prospectively) Royal Society or Academy of Science, which, as the Elector was quick to perceive, would conspicuously add to the reputation of his court and to the glory of the monarchy of which he was ambitious to become the founder; and, after Leibniz had spent several months at Berlin, and conducted the deliberations on the subject, besides participating in the intellectual delights of ' Lustenburg ' (Lützenburg), the Society of Sciences was, in July, 1700, actually called into life, with Leibniz as its perpetual president.[1]

Danckelmann's fall had, however, not put an end to Sophia Charlotte's difficulties at her husband's court. Some of these were of much the same sort as those from which her mother had suffered so much at Hanover, and from which the more sensitive nature of her grand-daughter Wilhelmina was afterwards

[1] Curiously enough, on the day after the opening of this august institution, Leibniz took a prominent part in a ' Village Fair ' at the Court, of which a graphic description remains in a letter from him to the Electress Sophia. It seems to have been a revised edition of the *Wirthschaften* of her youth, and of similar Arcadian diversions of later days.—For an interesting survey of the relations—both personal and philosophical—between Leibniz and Sophia Charlotte, see A. Foucher de Careil, *Leibniz et les deux Sophies*, Paris, 1876.

to suffer at Baireuth.   The Elector Frederick III's
new minister - in - chief, Kolbe von Wartenberg,
had himself many attractive qualities ; but his
wife was of humble origin and undistinguished
manners.   It pleased the Elector, apparently only
for the sake of the completeness of the thing, to
confer on her the position of his mistress *en titre*.
Sophia Charlotte's pride long rebelled against receiving this lady at her private court.   Another
source of anxiety to Sophia Charlotte was the training of her son Frederick William, which, during part
of his fourth year, she had entrusted to the veteran
Frau von Harling at the court of her mother, the
Electress Sophia.   But the boy, both passionate and
obstinate, could not agree with his cousin George
Augustus, and had to be taken back to Berlin.   As
he grew up he seemed to care for nothing but
soldiering, while he detested the ceremonial dear
to his father's heart, and more distinctive than ever
of the Court of Berlin since the manœuvres for securing a royal Crown had assumed a definite shape,
and this project had come to absorb the entire
policy of the Brandenburg court and Government.
Neither Sophia Charlotte's nor her mother's intelligence could fail to grasp the situation.   The
Electress of Brandenburg made up her mind that
no personal grievance should interfere with the
maintenance of a good understanding between her
consort and herself, and received the Countess of

Wartenberg at Lützenburg, although, oblivious of her guest's imperfections of education, she welcomed her there with a few words of French. The Electress Dowager Sophia was willing to cooperate; and, partly with a view to procuring for the furtherance of the project the good offices of King William III and of the Elector Maximilian Emmanuel of Bavaria, Governor of the Austrian Netherlands, it was, in the spring of 1700, arranged that the two Electresses should, on the pretext of Sophia Charlotte's health, repair to the baths of Aix-la-Chapelle, and thence visit Brussels and Holland. They accomplished this journey, on which Leibniz was by his own ill-health prevented from accompanying them, but in the course of which they, at the Hague, made the personal acquaintance of another philosopher of European reputation—' *l'illustre Bayle, honneur des beaux esprits.*' And, in October, 1700, they were received at the Loo, where (as we shall see immediately) other matters were also discussed between the Electress Dowager and King William, and where he promised Sophia Charlotte to acknowledge her husband as the first King in Prussia. The desire of Sophia Charlotte's consort (rather than her own) was consummated by their coronation as King and Queen of Prussia at Königsberg on January 18th, 1701—the year which likewise proved her mother's conference with her host at the Loo not to have been held in vain.

To understand this result, it is necessary to go back a few years, and to recall the circumstances which, in 1696, had led to an earlier, but more transitory, visit on the part of the two Electresses to the Loo.   The year 1696 was one of some importance in the history of the English Succession question.   After the death of Queen Mary, on December 28th, 1694, some time had necessarily passed before even a conjecture could be formed as to the future intentions of King William, who was prostrated with grief. But he was only in his forty-fifth year, and his remarriage was therefore by no means an unlikely event.   In the course of 1695, speculation was accordingly rife on the subject, and, taking time by the forelock, Louis XIV provided that any overtures made on William III's behalf at Stockholm (for the hand of the Princess Hedwig Sophia) should meet with a cold reception.   The hopes of the House of Savoy were once more aroused.   The claims by descent of the Duchess Anna Maria, daughter of Henrietta, Duchess of Orleans, and grand-daughter of Charles I, and of her issue, were superior to those of the Electress Sophia and the House of Hanover ; and, in the twofold event of another son being born to Anna Maria and Victor Amadeus II, and of the boy being brought over to England and there educated as a Protestant, he might acquire a Parliamentary title.   William III was supposed to look favourably upon this scheme ;

and, though, already in the summer of 1695, there
were rumours of Savoy having entered into secret
negotiations with France, Victor Amadeus was one
of the Princes who, about this time, ratified the
renewal of the Grand Alliance. But, in the following year, after France had paid the price of the
restoration of Pignerol, the Duke of Savoy went
over to her side (thus executing a movement of
which he carried out the exact converse in 1703,
early in the great War), and thereby closed any
prospect of his House inheriting the English throne.

Meanwhile, King William's widowed state occupied the thoughts of the dynasty of whose close
connexion with the House of Hanover we have just
been treating. Immediately after the campaign of
1695 and the renewal of the Grand Alliance, the
Elector Frederick III of Brandenburg had begun to
sound King William, through the agency of his
favourite, Keppel (soon afterwards created Earl of
Albemarle), as to the royal intentions on the subject
of a remarriage, with a view to directing the King's
attention to the Electoral Princess Louisa Dorothea,
then fifteen years of age. In the following year,
1696, William had found himself the object of an
unprecedented popularity in England, owing to
the discovery of the Assassination Plot, at the time
when James II was known to be preparing an
invasion of these shores. The Jacobite interest,
which was to have benefited by the most gracious

proclamation ever drafted by the exiled King, experienced one of the most disheartening of its many rebuffs ; and, instead of reconquering his kingdoms, James II informed the Abbot of La Trappe, that ' all these attempts which seemed to be lost labour in the eyes of the world, were great advantages as he managed them in order to that great end which had now become his sole concern.' Still, the ' Prince of Orange's ' weak condition of health prevented King James from regarding the chances of his restoration as at an end ; and, in the event of his rival's death, he was resolved to ' return into England, though three men had not followed him.' [1] In May, 1696, King William resumed the command of the army in the Low Countries, but no military operations of importance took place ; and, in the course of the summer, the Elector Frederick III, with his family and court, took up their residence at Cleves, whither the Duke of Celle likewise found his way, and whence in August the Electress Sophia Charlotte, with her mother the Electress Sophia, paid an *incognito* visit to the Loo in the King's absence. He was then invited to Cleves ; but he preferred in the first instance to send two

---

[1] This was the time when James II refused Louis XIV's offer of aid towards securing for him the Polish throne, then vacant by the death of John Sobiesky ; on which occasion Sophia wrote to the Duchess of Orleans that King James might pass for a saint, since we are told to become as little children, or we shall not enter into the kingdom of heaven.

agents—an Englishman (Southwell) and a Dutch-
man (General Hompesch)—to report to him on the
personality of the Princess Louisa Dorothea.   Their
reports were unfavourable, and, the King's visit
having been deferred on the plea of difficulties of
ceremonial,[1] no less a personage than Portland was
sent by him to Cleves to make another report.
Though this again proved deterrent, William resolved to trust to his own eyes, and, in September,
paid a visit to Cleves, of which a full account
remains in a letter from Stepney, then in the royal
suite, to Sir William Trumbull.   The Princess stood.
during four hours, as a spectatress of the royal game
at *l'hombre*, while the favourite, Keppel, was accommodated with a seat.   But the visit led to no
result ; and, when it became known that the two
Electresses had abandoned their proposed tour
through Holland, it was understood that the
marriage project was for the present at an end.

Whether or not because of his own unwillingness
to contract a second marriage, as well as on account
of the secession of the House of Savoy from the
Grand Alliance, the attention of William III,

[1] These were of a kind of which the Electress Sophia had,
as we have seen, had some experience.   According to English
usage, the King was alone entitled to an arm-chair (*fauteuil*) ;
but, according to the German rule, the Electors were privileged
to occupy an arm-chair even in the presence of the Emperor.
Hence the King and the Elector could not *sit* in one another's
company ; and, when the King actually came to Cleves, the
Elector had to absent himself from the royal *partie.*

in the latter part of 1696, turned more decisively than before to the Electress Sophia and the House of Hanover. He interested himself directly in the still unsettled question of the admission of the Elector of Hanover into the Electoral College. About the same time (October), when George William of Celle had returned home from a long visit to the Loo, whither he had proceeded from Cleves, Leibniz (who, it must be remembered, was in the service of the entire House of Brunswick-Lüneburg) put forth one of those feelers by which he is henceforth found from time to time endeavouring to test the sentiments of the Electress Sophia on the Succession question. Though on this occasion he approaches the subject most cautiously, it may be looked upon as significant that he prophesies for Sophia's grandson a renewal of the historic achievement of William III. Nothing, however, could be more explicit than her reply refusing to act on his insinuation. Two months later, she wrote to her niece, the Raugravine Louisa, then on a visit to London, where she had met with scant courtesy on the part of the Princess Anne, that everything ' Palatine ' seemed to have quite fallen into oblivion in England, nor did anybody there remember her (the Electress') existence, inasmuch as there was no apparent intention of allowing the Crown to descend to her family.

During the period immediately ensuing, William

III was necessarily occupied by the task of securing his own seat upon the English throne, rather than by that of determining its ulterior devolution. The success of the peace negotiations which opened at Ryswyk, in June, 1697, was rendered more than doubtful by the avoidance of any direct communication between the representatives of the King of France and of the King of England, whom Louis had as yet refused to recognise ; and William III had accordingly taken the startling step of entering into a secret negotiation with France. Among the extraordinary rumours that hereupon spread as to the compromise contemplated by the two sovereigns, was one, wholly false, which contrived to make its way into ' history.' William, it was said, intended to purchase peace by promising to secure the Succession to the English Crown to the son and heir of James II. In the instrument of the peace, William was not actually recognised as King of England, Scotland, and Ireland by Louis XIV ; but he was mentioned as such in the preamble, and secured in his possession of these kingdoms by a formula binding Louis XIV to refuse any direct or in-direct assistance to William's enemies. Indeed, this indirect recognition, and the check which it implied upon the original designs of Louis, constituted England's chief gain by the peace. William's motives for seeking, in the period next ensuing, to remain on good terms with Louis XIV, cannot be discussed here ; but they help to account for a certain slackness on William's part in his dealings with the Succession question, at a time when it was becoming of the highest importance for the future of his kingdoms.

In the autumn of 1698, however, shortly after the secret conclusion of the First Partition Treaty between Louis XIV and William III, the latter took up this question of a Succession which concerned him more nearly than that to the Spanish monarchy. He was in the habit of annually welcoming to the Loo, at this season, his old friend and fellow-sportsman, Duke George William of Celle ; but on the present occasion they met in the hunting-castle of the Göhrde,[1] near Lüneburg. The Elector George Lewis also put in an appearance there, as did his son, the Electoral Prince George Augustus, and his daughter, Sophia Dorothea the younger, then eleven years of age. Although Count Tallard, the French ambassador at the Court of St. James, was thoroughly puzzled as to the purpose of the King's journey, it could be no secret to the members of the House of Brunswick-Lüneburg. In September, the Princess Anne, who stood next in the Succession so long as King William remained childless, had given birth to another

---

[1] This favourite seat of both George I and George II was in September, 1813—shortly before Leipzig—the scene of a Hanoverian success against a French division.

still-born infant ; and her only surviving child, the
Duke of Gloucester, was known to be in weak
bodily health. Nor could any reliance be placed
upon Princess Anne herself, who was in constant
communication with St. Germains, and who, had her
father but given his assent to her mounting the
throne in due course, would have been glad enough
afterwards to play it into the hands of her half-
brother. King William must, therefore, manifestly
have visited the Brunswick-Lüneburg territories
with at least a predisposition towards placing
the House of Hanover in a more satisfactory
position, in regard to the Succession, than it held at
present ; but he had no reason for supposing that
the members of that House were themselves eager
to meet him half-way. Strangely enough, the
personage who now came forward to urge upon him
a decisive course, was the Duchess Eleonora of
Celle—perhaps with a view to thus recovering some
of the influence lost to her through her daughter's
catastrophe, perhaps in the hope of mitigating
the effects of that catastrophe for the unhappy
Sophia Dorothea herself, or simply from an inborn
love of diplomatic action and a general desire
to make things pleasant. Leibniz afterwards
assumed to himself the credit of having given her
the first hint of speaking to the King. This she
did before he quitted the Göhrde, representing
herself as obeying an inspiration from Hanover,

and begging her royal guest—now that the House of Savoy was out of the question—to promote the placing of the Electress Sophia and her descendants in the Succession. When the King pointed out that the Duke of Gloucester, though in delicate health, might imitate him by growing up into manhood, Eleonora further suggested that her grand-daughter, Sophia Dorothea the younger, would be a suitable match for the Duke. George William of course agreed *ex post facto* to the step taken by his wife, but stipulated that it should be mentioned to his nephew, the Elector, who gave vent to his annoyance that the King should be led to suppose him to have sanctioned this manœuvre. But, when the King met the Electress Sophia at Celle, he referred to the question of establishing her and her descendants' claim, and, as Leibniz expresses it, made considerable advances in this direction. Sophia, we may be sure, received these advances discreetly ; but that she should have rejected them, or have met them with coldness, is a conjecture unwarranted by her conduct either before or after. Neither can she be shown to have viewed with displeasure the activity, restless though it undoubtedly was, of Leibniz, who about this time corresponded with London as frequently as possible and encouraged the efforts of a Hanoverian agent there. Had Sophia taken up an attitude of indifference, King William would hardly, in June, 1699, have informed her in writing that he had used his best endeavours to bring the business to a conclusion satisfactory to her, and that he felt assured of effecting his purpose within a very short space of time. It is, moreover, significant that the two branches of the House of Brunswick-Lüneburg were acting in perfect harmony with one another ; in May, Gargan, the Electress' secretary, declares it impossible to listen without emotion to the conversations between the two illustrious ladies (Sophia and Eleonora), whom he describes as related to one another not less closely by blood than by friendship.

The reason why the Celle interview led to no immediate results in England lay, not in Sophia, but in the discordant relations between King William and his Parliament, caused mainly by his policy with regard to the Spanish Succession, into which of course the Electress and the House of Hanover had not been initiated. So late as July, 1700, she wonders what interest England and the United Provinces could have in seeking to cement the power of France. The unfriendliness of Parliament to the King had been heightened when, about a month earlier, the substance of the Second Partition Treaty had become known in this country ; and, as matters now stood, there was little or no chance of the House of Commons in particular agreeing to any proposals concerning the Succession that should emanate from the King. In the midst

of this trouble, less doubt than ever remained as to
the decrease of his physical strength, at no time
anything but precarious ; so that, after Anne,
the only hope for the Succession depended on the
feeble vitality of the young Duke of Gloucester.
Suddenly, on July 30th, 1700, the frail thread of his
life was snapped, and the prospect had vanished
of a successor who would have been generally acceptable, and, in all probability, have proved both an
intelligent and a kindly ruler.   In announcing the
news to the Electress Sophia from Berlin, her vigilant
monitor, Leibniz, promptly pointed out that it would
now more than ever be time to think of the English
Succession.   But it so chanced that already, three
days previously, she had written to him on the same
subject from Hanover, exhibiting her usual perfect
self-control. Though she took very coolly the news of
the young Duke's ' decampment '—as she called his
death, perhaps in cynical allusion to his innocent
military tastes,—she by no means showed herself blind
to the importance of the event.   Were she younger,
she told Leibniz, when informing him that, in
October, 1700, the Duke of Celle was to visit King
William at the Loo, she might fairly have looked forward to a Crown ; as it was, had she the choice, she
would rather see her years increase than her grandeur.
But she well knew that persons in her station rarely
have a choice, if they are resolved not to fall short
of their sense of duty.   She could hardly be aware

of the fresh intrigues that were being carried on by the Princess Anne, or of the hopes, still entertained by certain of William's most loyal English subjects, that he would marry again, perhaps this time choosing a Danish princess. But she could not have remained unaware that the thoughts of a wider circle of Englishmen were taking the direction of Hanover. Partly, however, under the influence of the regrets caused by the recent death of the young Duke of Gloucester, partly because of the wish to secure an heir to the throne young enough to be Anglicised and, more especially, *Anglicanised* before his advent to it, politicians, and Tory politicians in particular, were as yet intent rather upon the ultimate succession of the Electoral Prince than upon that of his father, the Elector, or that of his grandmother, the Dowager Electress.

At the meeting of King William with the Duke of Celle at the Loo, it was arranged that he should receive there the Electress Sophia and the Electress of Brandenburg, on the occasion of the visit to the baths of Aix-la-Chapelle on which the latter had persuaded her mother to accompany her. Burnet insists that now ' the eyes of all the Protestants of the nation turned towards the Electress of Brunswick ' ; but the arrival in Holland, as his mother's and grandmother's visit drew to a close, of the young Electoral Prince of Brandenburg (afterwards King Frederick William I of Prussia) seems to have vividly suggested to William III the notion of placing the heir of the Hohenzollerns in the position left vacant by the Duke of Gloucester. This passing fancy may be regarded as the sequel of a not less transitory ambition which appears to have flitted through the mind of the Elector Frederick III, of taking advantage of the Princess Anne's unpopularity to endeavour himself to find his way to the English throne. The idea of including the Electoral Prince of Brandenburg in the Succession could not of course be welcome to the House of Brunswick-Lüneburg ; and we accordingly find Bothmer, who was in the Celle service as envoy at Paris and was soon to play an important part in the progress of the Succession question, complaining to Ilten (August 31st, 1700) that the Berlin Ministry were preparing for their young Prince the plurality of King of Prussia, Stadholder, and King of England. Count Platen afterwards stated that he had heard it suggested that the Calvinism of Berlin might suit King William better than the Lutheranism of Hanover. Nor is it at all unlikely that he recognised in the Electoral Prince the germ of administrative powers to which full justice has only very tardily been done.[1]   But, however this may

[1] It may be noted that Borkowski, *Königin Charlotte als Mutter und Erzieherin* (in *Hohenzollern-Jahrbuch* for 1903), defends the Queen against the charge of having insufficiently cared for the education of the heir to the throne, and cites in proof letters addressed by her to Alexander von Dohna,

have been—and perhaps something might be said as to the religious influence noticeable in this period of Hanoverian history—there is no proof that William III seriously thought of adopting the Electoral Prince of Brandenburg, or of introducing him in any other way into the English Succession. Moreover, even had this been on his part more than a passing wish, he of course possessed no right of nomination.   No doubt, he would more speedily have dismissed the fancy, had he believed the House of Hanover to be very eagerly intent upon the prospect now opening before it. But, at all events, it is neither proved nor probable, that at the Loo the Electress Sophia once more rejected the overtures of her host on the subject of the Succession. The question possesses so much significance, if we are desirous of forming a judgment as to the whole tenor of her conduct in this matter, that it must needs be dwelt upon at some length. What actually passed between her and the King on the occasion is unknown ; and her behaviour can only be conjectured from the attitude which she maintained during a journey undertaken by her, it must be remembered, in the first instance at all events, in her daughter's interest rather than in her own.

At Aix-la-Chapelle Sophia had received a remarkable letter from Stepney, written from

·whom she selected and maintained against all opposition as the supervisor of her son's education.

London about the middle of September, in which he reviewed the entire situation. Remembering that in her veins ran the blood of the Stewarts, and that her personal reminiscences mounted back to the days of Oliver Cromwell, he excused himself from offering a decided opinion of his own as to the genuineness of ' *le Fils*,' but pointed out that there was no chance of his ever abandoning the religion of Rome, or escaping from the political leading-strings of France. On the other hand, he assured the Electress that the English were not Republicans at heart, and that among them there was nobody capable of playing Oliver's part over again as ' Captain-General.' In response to his modest appeal for a reply (by means of which he no doubt hoped to be able to clear up the situation at head-quarters), Sophia wrote the letter, undated, in which, from Lord Hardwicke downwards, so many critics have found indications of her Jacobite tendencies. In this letter she declares that, were she thirty years younger, she would have sufficient confidence in her descent and in the religion pro-fessed by her, to believe in her being thought of in England. After her death, which in the natural course of things would precede the deaths of the King and his appointed successor, her sons would be regarded as strangers. Moreover, the eldest of them was far more accustomed to sovereign authority than was the poor Prince of Wales, who was so young and would be so glad to recover what his father had thrown away that they would be able to do with him what they liked. After referring to her hope of shortly seeing the King in Holland, whither she had been induced by her daughter to accompany her, she added that she was of course neither so philosophical nor so foolish as to dislike hearing a Crown talked of, or as to refuse full consideration to her correspondent's extremely sensible and obliging remarks on the subject, though the number of factions apparently existing in England made it difficult to feel sure about anything.

Such is the substance of what is sometimes cited as the 'Jacobite letter' of the Electress Sophia. Clearly, it is nothing of the kind; but at most shows that, while primarily desirous of deferring all discussion till she should meet the King, she desired to apprise him, through a safe channel, that she was alive to the *cons* as well as the *pros*—the uncertainties as well as the opportunities—of the situation. Above all, she wished to show herself aware of the possibility of that situation being fundamentally changed by the conversion to Protestantism of the 'Prince of Wales,' as—assuredly without any *arrière pensée*—she naturally called the kinsman whose claim to this title she had never professed to doubt. Nor is any 'Jacobitism' on her aunt's part proved by the Duchess of Orleans' nearly contemporary graphic account of King

James II's tender sentiments towards the Electress, who, as he stammered, ' *m'a tou-toujours aimé.*'

The visit to the Loo was succeeded by a brief meeting between the King and the two Electresses at the Hague, just before his departure for England. It was on this occasion that Sophia Charlotte was accompanied by her son Frederick William, for whom the King manifested a sudden personal fancy.   Whether under its influence, or because he had resolved to respond to Sophia's guarded attitude by maintaining a reserve of his own, or, as is most probable, because English opinion was in his judgment, as well as in hers, still unripe for action —certain passages in the Electress' correspondence with the Raugravine Louisa, a few months later in date, show that William III had not arrived at any immediate decision as to naming the Electress and her descendants in the Succession, though he had held out to her the prospect of such a result being brought about.   This implies that she had by no means refused to entertain such a proposal. In a word, the attitude of cautious expectancy maintained by her and her House, was confirmed by her brief personal intercourse with the actual occupant of the English throne.

Before the end of this year, 1700, all hesitation vanished from the policy of William III.   His hopes of securing the peace of Europe by an international agreement based on the Second Partition

Treaty were finally extinguished, when the death of
Charles II of Spain, on November 1st, was followed
by the acceptance of his will, bequeathing the
whole of the Spanish monarchy to the Duke of
Anjou, by that Prince's grandfather, Louis XIV.
In February, 1701, French troops surprised the
Dutch garrisons in the Barrier fortresses ; and
the States General recognised King Philip of Spain.
The question whether England would follow suit,
or declare war, would have to be decided by the
new Parliament, summoned for February, 1701, ' in
respect of matters of the highest importance ' ;
which expression, as de Beyrie, the Hanoverian
resident in London, informed the Electress, unmistakably applied to the choice of the Duke of
Anjou, and to the English Succession. Stepney,
or some other correspondent, had previously apprised her of the course which events might be
expected to take in Parliament with regard to the
Succession. The Whigs would press for a further
limitation in the Protestant line, and, if necessary,
for the exclusion of any child or pretended child of
James II except the Princess Anne. An effort
(proceeding from the Marlborough interest) in
favour of the Princess Anne's consort, Prince George
of Denmark, would serve to lead Parliament to the
direct Protestant line, beginning with the Electress
Sophia, and going on to the Elector and the Electoral
Prince. Early in the same month (November) the

Electress, who was accompanied by Leibniz, conferred with her brother-in-law at Celle. The
Elector George Lewis was not present ; and the
confidential memorandum on the rights of the House
of Brunswick-Lüneburg in respect of the English
Succession drawn up immediately afterwards by
Leibniz for the use of Cresset, then at Celle, contained a significant passage. The Succession, it
was observed, could much more easily be secured
by the House, while King William, Duke George
William, and the Electress Sophia were still '*pleins
de vie.*' Soon afterwards, Sophia herself drafted a
letter, which was approved by the Duke of Celle,
asking the King's advice as to the course of action
to be pursued ; and Leibniz, who thought this
insufficient, was permitted to compose a supplementary letter to Stepney, for the information of
Baron Schütz, who represented the House of Brunswick-Lüneburg at the Court of St. James.' [1]   In this
it was suggested that, while the Electress wished
not to appear at present to be taking any active
steps, a further limitation of the Act of Settlement
might advantageously be promoted in England by
means of private overtures and of pamphlets not

---

[1] She told Schütz, about this time, that she was very sensible
of the kindness shown her by the English people, but very
sorry that she was so old that she would never be of any use
to them, and much annoyed that her son had not the same
inclinations on this head as she had herself, and made no secret
of his sentiments.

purporting to emanate from Hanover. The Electress once more showed a judgment superior to that of Leibniz, who, in his zeal, offered, if called upon, to proceed to London in person, but whom, in May, 1701, Stepney informed that, in his opinion, the English nation was so well disposed towards the Hanoverian Succession that neither pamphlets nor men of talent were needed to push it.

In the meantime, Parliament, which sat from February to June, had nearly concluded its session. The Speech from the Throne had duly recommended the further limitation of the Succession in the Protestant line ; and a proposal for carrying this recommendation into effect was, without loss of time, brought forward by the Whigs in the House of Commons (March 3rd). But, though the Tory majority in the House was not as a whole un-friendly to the Hanoverian claims, the opinion prevailed that it would be well to postpone the naming of any further successor, until certain additional securities had been obtained for the rights and liberties of the subjects of the Crown. It was generally understood that the Electress Sophia should be named; but some desired to name the Elector and the Electoral Prince likewise, in the expectation that the Electress Dowager and the Elector would waive their claims. On the other hand, it was felt that such an arrangement would involve a difference between the English and the

Scottish limitation, which latter had, already in 1689, been made to include Sophia's name ; and this could not have been easily set right until the anti-English feeling excited in Scotland by the Darien Settlement affair should have had time to subside.

Thus, after the eight articles had been agreed upon which were to take effect from the beginning of the new limitation to the House of Hanover, and some of which were, as a matter of fact, dictated by jealousy of the rule of a foreign line, the name of the Electress Sophia was inserted without opposition ; and by the *Act for the further Limitation of the Crown, and better securing the Rights and Liberties of the Subjects*—called in short the *Act of Settlement* —the Crown of England was, in default of issue of the Princess Anne or King William III, settled upon the Electress and her posterity, being Protestants. A protest, inspired by the Duke of Berwick acting under instructions from Louis XIV was, indeed, raised by the Duchess Anna Maria of Savoy, and communicated to both Houses of Parliament by the envoy of Duke Victor Amadeus II ; but no notice was taken of it.[1] On June 12th, 1701, the Act of Settlement received the royal assent, and, in his Speech from the Throne, King

[1] ' I do not see,' writes Sophia in April, 1701, ' how he can claim the English Crown before King James and his two sons, being himself as much a papist as they are ; but perhaps he is offering to have his son educated in the Anglican religion.'

William, after thanking the two Houses for further securing the Protestant Succession, passed on to the subject of the Grand Alliance. The answer of the House of Commons was an Address promising to support the King in sustaining the alliances deemed necessary by him for upholding the liberty of Europe and the welfare of England, and for reducing the exorbitant power of France.

The Act of Settlement, which secured the Hanoverian Succession, accordingly at the same time imposed certain fresh restrictions of the prerogative, which had an important bearing upon the nature of the royal authority exercised by Sophia's posterity. Furthermore, the Act, in which both the great English political parties concurred, secured the Hanoverian Succession at a time when the critical struggle was about to open between France and the renewed Grand Alliance ; and thus, at the very moment when the House of Hanover acquired a Parliamentary title to the expectancy of the English throne, it was, again with the assent of both parties, identified with the adversaries of France in the great European conflict. Nor is it without significance that at this very time a Pope (Clement XI) had been seated in St. Peter's Chair, who, in a far greater measure than his predecessor—for Innocent XII had on the whole disappointed the hopes of Louis XIV—served the interests of

France.   The letter addressed by Clement XI on his
election in November, 1700, to James II, had,
in its ' beautiful terms of paternal tenderness,'
drawn tears ' more from the heart than from the
eyes ' of the exiled King.

Throughout these transactions, the conduct of
the Electress Sophia had been uniformly judicious
—observing a wise mean between the adoption, as a
matter of course, of the advice readily given to her
by Leibniz, and an absolute impassiveness like that
maintained by her eldest son.   It seems unwarranted to regard her as having energetically defended
her rights up to the time when policy and the condition of affairs in England imposed upon her a
certain reserve, and having at the last enjoyed the
satisfaction of seeing both King and Parliament
sue for her acceptance of their offer.   On the other
hand, her conduct is misunderstood when she is
supposed to have resisted so long as possible the
unwelcome necessity of securing the inheritance of
a throne to which she believed her kinsman, the
Prince of Wales, to have had a just claim.   She
had frankly accepted the situation, and done her
best to promote a solution in the interests of her
dynasty, without going further than would have
been either seemly or judicious.   Her letter written
on June 22nd, 1701, to Burnet (who describes himself as in more or less continuous correspondence
with her from the death of the Duke of Gloucester

onwards) exactly expresses her point of view. Though sensible of his affection to her in the matter of the Succession, which excluded all Catholic heirs, ' who had always caused so many disorders in England,' she felt herself ' unfortunately too old ever to be useful to the nation.' Yet she wished that ' those who were to come after her might render themselves worthy of the honour awaiting them.'

On August 14th, 1701, the Earl of Macclesfield arrived in Hanover, in order formally to notify to the Electress Sophia the passing of the Act of Settlement, of which, kneeling before her, he presented her with a splendidly illuminated copy, still preserved in the Hanover Archives. Macclesfield appears to have been chosen for the office at his own request, as the son of a cavalier closely associated with Prince Rupert and a visitor at the Hague in Queen Elizabeth's days, and therefore likely to be *persona gratissima* to the Electress [1]—though his own antecedents rather associated him with the Mohocks. He was accompanied by three other Whig Lords, Say and Sele, Mohun (Macclesfield's intimate, who is stated to have taken care to be on his best behaviour) and Tunbridge. In their suite was the ingenious Toland, with his enquiring

---

[1] She writes that Macclesfield's father had been most friendly to her as well as to Prince Rupert—' *car il voulait me donner au roi Charles.*'—Macclesfield died shortly after his journey to Hanover.

eyes wide open, and in his pocket, according to Luttrell, a ' treatise lately wrote in relation to the Succession, intituled *Anglia Libera*, or The Limitation and Succession of the Crown explained and asserted,' for presentation to the Electress. With them were also ' Mr. King the herald,' who brought the Garter for the Elector, and Dr. Sandys, the ambassador's chaplain, who read the common prayers of the Church of England before the Electress in her ante-chamber. ' She made the Responses, and performed the Ceremonys as punctually as if she had been us'd to it all her life.' These and other details may be read in Toland's *Account of the Courts of Prussia and Hanover*, which he published after his return. He was particularly anxious to recount the honours which he had received at Hanover and Herrenhausen, including that of conversing with the Electress, who, on one occasion, had told him that ' she was afraid the Nation had already repented their Choice of an old Woman, but that she hop'd none of her Posterity wou'd give them any Reason to grow weary of their Dominion '— much the same words as those which she had used to Burnet.

We need not dwell upon the solemnities at Hanover and Celle, whither the special embassy proceeded in due course, nor upon the lavish munificence bestowed upon the ambassador,[1] nor

[1] The Electress bestowed on him a golden ewer and her

upon the medals distributed in honour of the event, among which none was more remarkable than that which exhibited the portrait of the English Matilda, the consort of Henry the Lion, and, on the reverse, that of the Electress Sophia, '*Angliae princeps ad successionem nominata.*' But it may be worth our while in our next chapter to return to Toland, and to his account of the Court of Hanover, as giving an interesting, though no doubt rather rose-coloured, picture of the Electress and her surroundings, at a point of time which may be described as the climax of her fortunes.

portrait in a jewelled frame—the total expense amounting to 20,000 dollars—rather more than two-thirds of the sum spent during twoscore years on the maintenance of the palace buildings at Hanover. No wonder that this profuse expenditure was looked upon without much satisfaction in the long years of waiting that ensued.

V

THE HEIRESS OF GREAT BRITAIN

(HERRENHAUSEN, 1701–1714)

GREAT BRITAIN was never to see the face of its
heiress, and the widowhood of the Electress Sophia
was almost entirely spent in the tranquillity of
Herrenhausen. More than any other place associated with her name, this palace and its still delightful gardens, in the midst of which her statue now
stands, recall her regal personality. The building
of the palace that was so long her home, and the
laying-out of the gardens where Leibniz was so
frequent a companion of her long daily walks, were
begun by Duke John Frederick as early as the
year 1665, when the old hunting-box of Lauenstädt
was transferred hither. Herrenhausen Palace seems
to have been reconstructed, under the superinten-
dence of Sartorio, in imitation of the new palace at
Osnabrück, of which, as has been seen, the younger
brother, Ernest Augustus, had more or less borrowed
the design from the Luxembourg at Paris. Ernest
Augustus and Sophia elaborated John Frederick's

beginnings, considerably enlarging the gardens, which were designed by the elder Charbonnier, and carried out by him and his son, in 1697, though it was not till 1705 that the Elector George Lewis caused them to be completed in their present form, which suggests Dutch influences. Thus a pleasing mixture of styles and associations is presented by the solid clipped hedges, some of which in the garden theatre serve as side-scenes and conceal dressing-rooms (these are attributed specially to Quirini), by the prim summer-houses and the wilderness, by the grottoes and the cascades with their stalactites and shells, and by the profusion of statuary in gilt lead among the hedges and in cool marble by the artificial water. It was in these gardens that, during her married life, when she was already accustomed to solitude, Sophia consoled herself with the company of the nightingales, and here that, in 1700, she is found amusing herself with her ducks and swans, and with the new lodgings erected by her for their convenience. She had a genuine fondness for innocent open-air delights ; at Lützen-burg she speaks of her promenades with her daughter as affording her the greatest delight, while her sons disported themselves at the opera and at comedies played by ' noble ' comedians ; and on the gravelled paths of her Herrenhausen gardens she indulged her love of walking almost literally to the moment of her death. No fine day was allowed to pass without an hour or two—or even more—of her favourite pastime ; and her persistency tired out all her attendants, except, as Toland elegantly puts it, when they had the honour of enjoying her con-versation.[1]

Among the buildings at Herrenhausen, where Sophia spent the greater part of her life from 1698 to 1714, the Orangery, one of the largest of its kind in Europe, ought specially to attract the visitor, since a portion of it was the residence, modest in dimensions, but decorated in a florid Italian style, of the Electress Dowager.   It had been erected in 1692 ; its great hall was painted by Tommaso Giusti and stuccoed by Dossa Grana.   The Elec-tress' rooms are small and narrow, but overloaded with decorations, and not in the most perfect taste, with the exception of the fine portal into the little garden.[2]   There seems no reason for crediting her with an artistic taste transcending that of most of her contemporaries, or sufficiently formed to main-tain the Dutch preferences of her younger days against the more debased French and Italian, but more especially Italian, modes favoured by her husband and his brother.[3]   Clever with her hands

[1] Sophia's love of walking seems to have been inherited by her eldest son. Marshal Schulenburg, when on a visit to his sister, the Duchess of Kendal, at Kensington, in 1727, describes his life there as fatiguing, inasmuch as he had to promenade with the King in the gardens every evening for three or four hours.

[2] See A. Haupt, *u.s.*

[3] She expresses extreme delight with the changes effected

as in every other way, she understood the use of the brush [1] as well as of the embroidery needle; [2] but neither artistic industry nor art, although as a descendant of the Stewarts she had doubtless inherited some love of both, was a sphere in which she sought to shine. Her husband consistently treated art as a mere handmaid to luxurious self-indulgence ; thus, while he devoted nearly 25,000 dollars to the furnishing and adornment of his new opera-house, he wasted an even larger sum in the expenditure of a single carnival season.

Sophia had never shown much sympathy with what may be called the Venetian tastes of her husband ; and, after her youth had ebbed away, had more and more come to live an intellectual life of her own. Perhaps, before recalling the political incidents of her last thirteen years in connexion with the question which invested them with an European significance, we may pause for a moment to summarise our impressions as to the most im-

by Count Rochus Quirini zu Lynar, who directed the building operations of the Hanoverian Court, in the hunting-box of the Göhrde.

[1] A copy of a portrait of her nephew, Raugrave Maurice, is attributed to her.

[2] The coverings of the chairs in the presence-chamber at Hanover, as well as those of the altar in the palace chapel there, were embroidered by her hands. She also embroidered a chair-cover for Baroness Kielmannsegg—an attention bearing out the statement as to the relations between that lady and the Electoral family given above. King Frederick I of Prussia mentions his mother-in-law's beautiful cabinet of china at Herrenhausen.

portant features of her mind and character, as they present themselves to us more especially in these final years. The tragic part of her life was now over; but, as has been well said by the finest of the modern critics of her career, Professor Kuno Fischer, she had herself never played the part of a tragedy queen. Even a panegyric like that pronounced upon her by the old Hanoverian historian Spittler—by no means an undiscerning flatterer—seems too highly strung. He speaks of the ' *Teutschgründliche überfürstliche Aufklärung*'—as who should say, the enlightenment above the ordinary enlightenment of princes, and one in its depth and thoroughness possible only to the Germanic mind —that rendered her deserving of the friendship of Leibniz. Beyond a doubt, Sophia was distinguished by an intellectual curiosity that was still uncommon, though much less so than is often supposed, among the women of her age. This curiosity her linguistic attainments (she was, as has been seen, from her youth up mistress of half a dozen languages) had long enabled her freely to satisfy. To the excellent system of education under which she had been trained she owed her acquaintance with various elements of theology, philosophy, and history. This knowledge she had improved in the course of a long life, abounding in (often involuntary) intervals of leisure, and bringing with it not a few special opportunities of learned intercourse. She had spent

some years at Heidelberg, once more a fountain-
head of learning ; and, already at Osnabrück, she
had been ambitious of converting that modest
episcopal city into a centre of philosophical speculation, holding colloquies there with Francis Mer-
curius von Helmont, the interesting son of the
great physicist.[1] At a later date she read at least
one of Spinoza's works, towards which she seems to
have been drawn by ideas of moral philosophy in
which some resemblance to his has been thought
traceable.[2] Yet it may be doubted whether either
here or afterwards at Hanover and Herrenhausen
she was ever a profound student, or even so much
as an ardent reader of books. She was fond of
reading memoirs—such as those of Pierre Chanut,
French ambassador at the Court of Christian of
Sweden, or the celebrated autobiography of Marshal
de Bassompierre. She had, also, a *penchant* for
novels, preferring to the fashionable long-winded
romances of her youth works enlivened by a
humour congenial to her own. She asked Leibniz

[1] He seems to have frequented her society up to a late date.
In 1696 the Duchess of Orleans expresses her pleasure that her
aunt should have his philosophy to amuse her—though, for her
part, she ' does not see how one can understand anything of
which one knows nothing.' The younger Helmont's doctrine
of metempsychosis was not in the long run satisfactory to
Sophia, who had once said that it might account for her unlucky
son Maximilian's resemblance to the ' seven old Dukes of
Brunswick,' who called all their servants ' thou ' and occupied
themselves with making nets and drinking warm beer.

[2] See H. Forst, *u.s.*, p. 378.

to draw up for her a list of all the novels she had read ; for she had come to an end with *Don Quixote* and *Don Guzman d'Alfarache*, of which she preferred the former. Of German romances, it is almost equally to her credit that she mentions *Simplicissimus*, while avoiding the stagnant fashionable bombast of her age.[1]   A still more striking testimony to her critical insight may be found in the remark, which the admiring Duchess of Orleans states to have been confirmed by the Elector Palatine Charles Lewis, that nobody in the world better possessed Michel de Montaigne better than her aunt Sophia. Nor was she afraid of even more potent draughts ; for, during her return journey from Italy, the *Gargantua* was read to her by Ezechiel Spanheim, divine and diplomatist. On the other hand, she does not appear to have greatly cared for historical reading on its own account ; according to Leibniz, the reason why she took pleasure in Clarendon was ' because she was acquainted with many persons mentioned by him.' Yet she had no personal acquaintance with the Emperor Justinian, whom, as known to her from the Byzantine historian Procopius, she compares with Louis XIV. She certainly had a liking for moral theology and philosophy, which were, in general, more in the way

---

[1] Of course, she had to read the *Mesopotamian Shepherdess* of the interminable Duke Anthony Ulric ; but she compendiously set it down as a burlesque on the Bible.

of the ladies of the period than the historical sciences. She had read Boëtius, and was invited by Leibniz to read the Jesuit Friedrich von Spee, a leader in the crusade against that long-lived form of bigotry—the persecution of ' witchcraft.' Dogmatic theology had no charms for Sophia ; and even the faithful Bishop Burnet's book on a theme which ought to have interested her, namely, the Thirty-nine Articles, she put aside as ' *bon à feuilleter, mais non pas à lire,*' flippantly adding that the good binding of her copy would make it an ornament to her library. Philosophy, like religion, seems to have interested her primarily on the ethical side ; the stoical maxims of Seneca and Epictetus had impressed her mind before it had opened itself to more comprehensive problems under the influence of Spinoza, whom, as we know, her favourite brother had sought to domesticate at Heidelberg, and afterwards, and, above all, under the influence of Leibniz. She can at no time have been very well seen in metaphysics, the study of which is held to contribute so largely to the formation of ideas on religion ; she shared her eldest son's somewhat crude notions on the origin of ideas, and would not —or could not—understand Leibniz's argument about monads. Possibly, like many clever people of both sexes, she was rather too fond of startling her interlocutors; and the excellent Molanus respectfully shakes his reverend head at ' *Serenissima nostra, quæ a paradoxis sibi temperare nunquam potest.*' On the other hand, the diplomatist Thomas von Grote, another of her intimates, moved perhaps by a not unnatural jealousy, opined that the learned companions of her Herrenhausen walks would in the end take her a little out of her depth, though he had no fear that for her the consequences would be what they had been for Queen Christina of Sweden. As for the mathematical and physical sciences, she took that casual interest in them which, in the case of great personages, and of great ladies in particular, alternately makes the delight and the despair of *savants ;* Leibniz distinctly states that works dealing in detail with such subjects are not among those which the Electress was fond of reading. When, in the last year of her life, the Czar Peter came to Hanover and talked mathematics to her, ' she held her tongue.'

And yet, though neither a profound philosopher nor a phenomenally accomplished blue-stocking, Sophia was the very reverse of a commonplace personage. She was a woman of the world, but a very wise one. In age, as in youth, she sparkled with wit and intelligence, and in her both these gifts were interfused with that third and greatest gift of humour, which is a property of the soul as well as of the intellect.[1] Of her conversation we

[1] In *The Freeholder*, No. 30, April 2nd, 1716, Addison quotes, *à propos* of offensive French criticisms of the English and other

can only judge from her letters, of which we fortunately possess a quite extraordinary quantity ; but, if her speech was like her writing, its style must have been equally far ' *esloigné de l'aigreur*,'—to borrow a phrase from Madame de Brinon, to whom she told not a few home truths. Her letters combine with the supreme charm of perfect naturalness a pungency in the choice of expressions superior, in the opinion of the Duchess of Orleans, to any minted by the academies ; ' for to write agreeably is better than to write correctly.' Occasionally, her wit was singularly incisive, as when she called the same Madame de Brinon ' *une religieuse qui passe pour bel esprit*,' and her eloquence extraordinary ' *car elle parle toujours* ' ; or when, Toland having *more suo* taken it upon himself in argument to whitewash the cannibals, she commended him for his prudence, in that, with all Christendom against him, he had provided himself with protectors. Not unfrequently, however, frankness and cynicism did

---

nations, a passage from *Chevreana*, the amusing anthology of Urban Chevreau mentioned on another page, in which the very sensible proposition that ' one ought not to judge well or ill of a nation from a particular person, nor of a particular person from his nation,' is illustrated by the assertion that there are Germans, as there are Frenchmen, who have no wit, and Germans who are better skilled in Greek or Hebrew than either Scaliger or the Cardinal du Perron—' there is not in all France a person of more wit than the present Duchess of Hanover, nor more thoroughly knowing in philosophy than was the late Princess Elizabeth of Bohemia.' ' Prejudiced ' witnesses are not always in the wrong.

duty for wit.   Her jests spared neither Leibniz, nor
the House of Hanover, nor ' *le bon lord Winchilsea*,'
whom she found so heavy in hand, nor Queen Anne's
husband, Prince George of Denmark, of whom, when
it was proposed to create him King Consort, she
observed that he would be a King like Jove among
the frogs—and perhaps popular for that very reason.
She had, too, a good deal of fun as well as wit—as
when, in acknowledging the courtesy of an unknown
Mr. Smith in sending a descriptive account of England and the English (among whom she had ' been
brought up till she reached the age of twenty '),
she says that he describes London and St Paul's
and the '*pantquitinhouse*' as if she had never heard
a word about them.   De Gourville, whose qualities as a butt possibly remained a secret to his
sublime self-consciousness, suspected her of a
natural inclination to criticising any fellow-mortal
brought into her presence, though he allowed that
the person bantered by her was sure to be the first to
laugh.   She was a good hater, and could even hate
at second hand, as in the instance of Madame de
Maintenon, the bugbear of the Duchess of Orleans.
But her aversions were, like all her feelings, kept in
constant check by the dictates of reason as well as
by her care for the interests of her family and
House ; and we have seen how even her sentiments
towards Eleonora d'Olbreuze underwent a gradual
mitigation which outsiders judged to be a complete

z

change. It may, too, be doubted whether sarcasm was really natural to her, though her sense of humour always responded to the irony of things. She was alike open-minded and open-handed, and had nothing of the stinginess which sits so ill on high rank and position. Though towards the close of her life she was desirous that an income should be granted her by the British Crown and Parliament, it was only for political purposes that she desired this. She had quite money enough, she said, to keep up her German establishment. When she found that the distinguished services of the Bruns-wick-Lüneburg officers and men were left unnoticed in the *Gazette*, she was anxious to pay for a proper mention of them out of her own pocket. The geniality of her disposition shows itself in an affa-bility which was the same to both great and small, and in her power to interest herself with the same readiness in the discourse of philosophers, the con-versation of ministers of State, and the gossip of country ladies on domestic thoughts intent. It also showed itself in a hospitality which made everyone welcome at Hanover and Herrenhausen, and a tact which put all at their ease there ; at no court in the world, wrote the Brandenburg states-man Paul von Fuchs, are *les étrangers et les gastes* treated better than at the Hanoverian. Though, during her later years, she lived chiefly in retirement at Herrenhausen, she by no means secluded herself, but received a large variety of visitors, both princely,

personages and political and literary celebrities.
Above all, it was always a delight to her to see
Englishmen at her Court, as indeed it had been even
before the passing of the Act of Settlement ; and in
welcoming them she carefully eschewed any and
every distinction between parties—divided as these
were in England with a severity unknown at the
time to any other country. Occasionally, when
the Elector was away on his campaigns, she took his
place at Hanover in the reception of distinguished
guests.[1] Amiable to all, she reserved the treasures
of her affection for those who were nearest to her—
not only for the survivors of her own passionately
loved brood, but for all the younger members of
her family, in which she included the children of
her favourite brother.[2] The Duchess of Orleans
comically avows her annoyance that everyone who

[1] It seems right to observe that, though the tone of refinement
characteristic of the Hanoverian Court was largely due to the
Electress Sophia, the Elector George Lewis was by no means
insensible to her example. Toland speaks of the liberty of conversation, ' that nobody who deserves it will abuse,' allowed
at the Elector's table. And (which is a more entirely trustworthy statement, and one which Toland would hardly have made
had there really been no contrast observable on this score
with contemporary English habits) he adds that the vice of
drinking, for which the German nation is so much branded, is
so far from reigning at the Hanoverian court, that he never
knew greater sobriety than is to be found there.

[2] I have already touched on her grief at her son Prince
Christian's death by drowning in 1703 ; but the passage in
which she refers to it in a letter to the elder Schütz should be
read as giving proof not only of her maternal affection, but of
the deep religious feeling at the bottom of her heart. (See *Briefe
an Hannoversche Diplomaten* (1905), p. 175.)

has had the privilege of living with her aunt should be brought to entertain towards her the very sentiments of love and affection cherished by Elizabeth Charlotte herself. Yet she was quite impervious to flattery, and, when told by a diplomatist that the court of Versailles was full of her daughter's praises, remarked that these were the usual talk to which an envoy was treated when there was nothing else to say to him. In her later years, Sophia seems never to have indulged herself either in outbursts of temper or in moods of discontent ; although she allows that her vexation about the vagaries of her son Maximilian had proved to her that her philosophy was only skin deep.

Those, wrote Elizabeth Charlotte, who thought her aunt incapable of being of use in affairs of State, could have little knowledge of her intellectual powers. We have seen, however, that during her husband's lifetime she had been allowed little direct interference in state concerns, though on several occasions Ernest Augustus had benefited both from listening to her advice and from utilising her personal influence. Her eldest son was not the kind of man to concede, like a sultan at Constantinople, a position of acknowledged control over his Government to his mother, the Electress Dowager. When unable to render to Leibniz a service solicited by him, she wrote rather bitterly that there were times when she found silence best.

But, apart from the Succession question, towards which she, of course, occupied a distinct position of her own, a considerable sphere of political influence remained open to her in the last period of her life. More especially, she rendered excellent service by maintaining a good understanding with the court of Berlin, and by restoring it when the relations between the two courts had become strained, and her daughter proved unable to manage them. The influence which had been established over King Frederick I of Prussia by his ' *gnädigste Mama*,' she contrived, though she saw through him, to exercise even after her daughter's death.

But even Sophia's ' nimbleness of mind,' to use another expression of her favourite niece's, was not so marked a characteristic of her as was the reasonableness which proceeded in nearly equal proportions from intellectual enlightenment and from a beneficent disposition towards humanity. She was, wrote Leibniz about 1701, ' entirely on the side of reason ; consequently, all measures calculated to make kings and peoples follow reason, will meet with her approval.' A rationalist in the stricter sense of the term she can hardly be called ; though her wholly unembarrassed way of expressing herself on any subject in heaven or earth at times resembles a want of reverence.[1] She was irritated

[1] Among such passages can hardly be excluded her finding fault with the Apostles, none of whom had been at the pains of

by Toland's restless tongue ; but, while thanking
Burnet for putting her on her guard, indicated that
she was too old for Toland to give her another twist
(perhaps this may be a coarse translation of ' *pli* ')
in religion than that to which she had been long
accustomed. For the rest, it was not, she said,
her habit to ' catechise ' English visitors. Anthony
Collins' plea for ' Free-thinking ' struck her as both
mischievous and ridiculously superfluous—' more
especially in England, where there was such a
multitude of factions'; 'Free thinquers,' she observed,
when complaining of his insolence in sending her
the book, ' are against all religions.' All men, she
allowed, might like to think as they choose so long
as their conduct was honourable ; but in a well-
governed State all men ought not to be free to
publish their opinions. Herein her conscientiousness as a German Princess no doubt counted for
something. Thus, when she was asked to lend her
aid towards inducing the East Frisian Government
to proceed against the spreading eccentricities of
the Pietists, she upheld the rights of authority.
' Lutheran Princes,' she declared, ' are the Popes
of our Church, and must be obeyed.' For herself, she had a thoroughgoing dislike of anything
' enthusiastic,' and would not hear of shoemakers

eliciting from Lazarus his experiences after death. Had anyone
brought him to court, her own natural inquisitiveness would
certainly have prompted her to ask him so obvious a question.

(like Jacob Behmen) becoming inspired prophets instead of sticking to their lasts.[1] More than this : Kuno Fischer rightly says that ' to her clear practical intellect the mysteries of religion remained obscure and alien '; and, when he asserts that she was at bottom a deist in her opinions, this is in so far true, that, while she avowed her belief in a personal Creator, she cannot be shown to have gone further in any declaration of her convictions. In 1709, Leibniz informed Toland that the Electress ' was accustomed to quote and give particular praise to that passage of Scripture which demands whether it be consistent with reason that He that planted the ear should not hear, and He that formed the eye should not see ? ' At the same time, her latitudinarianism was perfectly candid. She certainly (in 1702) encouraged the notion which had occurred to her son-in-law, the King of Prussia, of introducing the English Church liturgy into the Calvinistic services, telling him that he might then call himself Defender of the Faith. On the other hand, she had

---

[1] It has been seen earlier in this volume how she declined to be edified by the peculiarities of Labadie and Labadism, and how sceptical she had proved as to some new method of ' healing ' imported from Holland at the time of her husband's final illness. Both she and Leibniz, however, showed some interest in the vagaries of Rosemunde von Assing, a young lady whose pretensions caused a good deal of trouble at Lüneburg, and whom Molanus and the orthodox clergy proposed to clap into prison. Leibniz thought the case worth attention, though its phenomena might be ascribed to natural causes.

no sympathy with the views of what in one of her letters she calls ' *Heyschortz* ' men ; [1] she laughed at an English clergyman who refused to set his foot in a Calvinist ' temple,' and she seriously blamed the early attempts of Queen Anne, as she interpreted them, to force the Presbyterians into conformity both in Scotland and in England. It was as a declared adherent of the Reformed or (as in England alone it was called) Calvinist confession, in which she had been brought up, that, as Toland notes, she built a ' pretty church ' in the New Town of Hanover for the French Huguenot refugees, to which in his day King William III liberally contributed ; and she seems to have at least intended to build a church for the German members of the same religious body. ' You must know,' she humorously wrote to Leibniz on this occasion, ' that I am *une dame fort zélée*.' It was probably no mere commonplace of shortsighted criticism when, in 1700, about which time the idea of seeking to evangelise the heathen was first taking root in Germany, she pronounced it ' a fine enterprise indeed ' to send out missionaries to India. ' To me it seems,' she remarked, ' that the first thing ought to be to make good Christians at home in

---

[1] ' They say,' she writes in 1711, ' that the Bishops are busily preaching Passive Obedience, although they had much better hold their tongues and not interfere in matters of State.' Thus, notwithstanding her Stewart blood and her own protestations of impartiality, she had something of the Whig in her, after all.

Germany, without going to so great a distance for the purpose of manufacturing them.' In a word, she should be credited with genuine religious feeling ; though demonstrativeness, whether on this or on any other subject, was altogether out of her way. And she hated religious factiousness, which she thought domesticated in England.[1]

We have spoken of the Electress Sophia's profession of the Reformed faith—a fact as to which, although it has been called into question, there cannot really be any doubt. As we saw, she was, according to her own account, in her childhood taught the Heidelberg Catechism ; and, when she married the Lutheran Ernest Augustus, it was arranged that, though she was to take no Calvinist minister with her to Hanover, one should visit the town three or four times in each year, in order to administer the Sacrament to her. Toland explicitly states (as de Gourville, who in 1687 had a little scheme of his own for bringing over her husband and his family to Rome, had also stated at an earlier date) that the Electress was a Calvinist ; but he adds, in illustration of the tolerance prevailing at the Court of Hanover, that ' most of her women and other immediate servants were Lutherans, just as her son the Elector, though himself a Lutheran,

---

[1] ' In all countries of the world,' she wrote in 1703, ' religion serves the ends of morality. It is only in England that religion, I am sorry to say, serves to create cabals.'

had many Calvinists belonging to him ; and both
their Highnesses, to show a good example and their
unfeigned charity in these lesser differences, do often
go to church together.'[1]   Their only daughter married
a Calvinist,[2] and Sophia herself steadily adhered
to the confession in which she was born, though her
latitudinarian tendencies fell in easily enough with
the tolerant principles prevailing in the Lutheran
Church of Hanover, and represented by the head
of its ecclesiastical administration, the worthy
' Abbot ' Molanus.[3]   Nor is there any reason for

[1] Perhaps it may be well not to enquire too closely as to
their behaviour when they got there. Sometimes, we are told,
the Electress fell asleep ; occasionally, she wrote letters to her
brother, taking care, however, not to disturb her husband when
engaged in reading a play, which he did audibly.

[2] Owing, however, to the different forms of faith professed
by Court and people in Prussia, the tolerance practised at
Berlin was even ampler than that prevailing at Hanover ; and
the subsequent marriage-treaty between the Prussian Crown
Prince Frederick William and Sophia Dorothea the younger,
the only daughter of the Elector George Lewis of Hanover,
provided for her being allowed to adhere to the Lutheran form
of faith.

[3] Gerhard Wolter Molanus, who held the Abbacy of the
secularised Cistercian foundation of Loccum, situate in the
forest solitude near Rehburg and the celebrated Steinhuder
Lake, plays a considerable part in Sophia's correspondence. He
exercised a great influence in the direction of toleration and
irenic ideals, more, however, by his hierarchical position and
personality than by his writings. The motto of his life, ' *Beati
pacifici*,' admirably accorded with Cistercian principles. He
lived to an advanced age—so advanced, that his mental powers
at last collapsed, and the good old man is said to have fancied
himself a barley-corn. At the small watering-place of Rehburg,
the Hanoverian Court held a *villeggiatura*—or rather a sojourn
under tents—as early as 1691.

supposing that, had she been actually summoned to ascend the English throne, she would, in the matter of religion, have failed to do what was expected of her. Early in 1713, she wrote to Leibniz that Molanus had so well explained to her his Lutheran creed, that there had been some talk of putting his exposition into print for publication in England. Clearly, it was not any question of this kind which would have interfered with her accession to the throne. She had sufficient confidence in herself to shrink from no step approved by both her reason and her conscience. Moreover, there are indications that she by no means regarded the Church of her mother and her brother's native land with coldness ; and, had Leibniz apprehended any objection on her part, he would hardly have proposed that the English establishment which he desired for the Electress should include an Anglican chapel. Indeed, in 1703, she is found expressing a wish that Queen Anne would carry her ecclesiastical zeal as far as Hanover, and contribute to the English church there ; ' in which event we would call it the English Church, and read the Book of Common Prayer in both tongues.'

The one change, however, to which she would at no time have consented,—not even, whatever de Gourville may have believed, when her husband was entertaining some such thought in connexion with his long effort for the Ninth Electorate [1]—was conversion to the Church of Rome. In her old age, when Princess Caroline of Ansbach, for whom she cherished a particular affection, was systematically tempted to qualify herself by conversion to Rome for the hand of Archduke Charles, afterwards the Emperor Charles VI, there can be little doubt that the Princess was encouraged in her resistance by the Electress as well as by Leibniz.

Sophia was no stranger to one of the loftiest among the lofty conceptions which occupied the great mind of her friend and counsellor, Leibniz,— that which aimed at the reunion of Christendom. The correspondence on this topic between Leibniz and Bossuet, which took place in 1691–5, and after a pause was renewed in 1699, was brought about through the joint mediation of Sophia and her sister, the Abbess of Maubuisson. Mixed up in the transaction was Madame de Brinon, who found a refuge at Maubuisson after the sudden termination of her rule at Saint-Cyr. This good lady, whose ardent temperament was in glaring contrast with Bossuet's

[1] The scheme tempted him, not only as likely to approve itself to the Emperor and the Catholic Electors, but also as one which would practically have secured the see of Osnabrück in perpetuity to his House. It illustrates the popular ignorance in England concerning the House of Hanover, that, if Toland is to be trusted, a report was current that this House ' was so indifferent in point of religion, as generally to breed up one of their sons a Papist, in order to qualify him for Bishop of Osnabrug.'

imperturbable calm, made repeated attempts to
bring the Electress of Hanover back into the fold,
en attendant its enlargement by means of the Reunion.
But Sophia was not at all flattered by these high-
minded efforts. She trusted—so she told Madame
de Brinon—in the goodness of God, who could not
have created her in order that she should be lost ;
for the rest, she could not reconcile herself to the
persecutions of the Protestants in France.[1] But
her aversion from Roman Catholicism went further
than this. Although at times she spoke of such
doctrines of the Church of Rome as the Inter-
cession of Saints with nothing more than con-
temptuous indifference, she occasionally assumed
an attitude of open hostility towards a creed which,
as a child, she had been taught to hate. Of all
religions, she told Lord Strafford, there was none
that she abhorred so much as the Popish ; for there
was none so contrary to Christianity. Other
passages to much the same effect might be cited.
For the rest, in an undated letter to Madame
de Brinon, Sophia, with her characteristic humour
and perhaps her characteristic want of external
reverence, so clearly explains her general religious
position, that we may conclude our attempt to

---

[1] To these persecutions she repeatedly returns. In 1709,
we find her expressing the opinion that the ' poor ' French
' galley-slaves ' should not be forgotten in the peace negotiations
then on foot.

indicate it by extracting from this letter the
following passage :—

The tranquillity of mind which God has granted to
me on this topic, I take to be so great a blessing, that
He would not have bestowed it upon any person whom
He had not chosen to be among the number of His
elect.   David wished to be only a door-keeper in the
house of the Lord ; and I lay claim to no more important charge.   Those who are more enlightened than
I am will perhaps fill higher places ; for we are told
that in the Father's house there are many mansions.
When you are in yours and I am in mine, I will not
fail to pay you the first call ; and I fancy that we
shall agree very well ; for there will then no longer be
any question of religious controversies.

Leibniz, whose name has already so often
occurred in this chapter and in this volume, was
consulted by the Electress Sophia in other matters
besides religion, philosophy, and science.   Both as
enjoying her confidence and on his own account,
he was a welcome guest at several courts, including
the Imperial ; and to the Houses of Hanover and
Celle, in whose joint employment he stood as
historiographer, he rendered invaluable service,
not only in that capacity, but also as a publicist,
on important occasions, demanding a comprehensive as well as effective treatment of the problems
handled by him.   But his direct influence upon
the policy of the dynasty seems practically to have
been limited to the question of the English Succession,
which, as we have seen, had, up to the passing

of the Act of Settlement, been regarded as more
or less personal to the Electress, and which, after
that date, continued to be largely, though by no
means entirely, dealt with in the same way.   Thus
his position at the Electoral Court, where there
is no sign of his having been consulted in matters
of general politics by either Ernest Augustus or
George Lewis, was perhaps occasionally misunderstood at the time, and has certainly been misunderstood since.   He was never the Electress' secretary,
or even her quasi-official political adviser ; he was
only her trusted personal friend and servant, whose
function in such matters was to suggest rather than
to advise, and whose influence upon the conduct
of affairs in which the Electress took an interest
accordingly varied at different times.   His exertions as to the English Succession, before 1701,
have been already noticed.   After the passing
of the Act of Settlement, the Electress Dowager
appointed, as her confidential agent to England,
a diplomatic adventurer of the name of Falaiseau,
who had come over to Hanover in Lord Macclesfield's suite ; and his reports seem, as a rule, to
have passed through the hands of Leibniz.   From
1702 onwards, as will be seen, the conduct of the
relations of the House of Hanover began to fall
largely into the hands of Bothmer ; and, in 1705,
on the union between Celle and Hanover, Bernstorff, and with him Robethon, passed out of the

service of the late Duke George William into that
of his nephew, the Elector. The more regular
system of diplomatic representation at the Court
of St. James of itself diminished the influence
of Leibniz on these relations, more especially as
Sophia never seems to have had much personal
liking either for Bernstorff (perhaps because of
his ineradicable ill-will against Brandenburg-Prussia,
perhaps for other reasons) or for Robethon, who
became invaluable to the Elector as his private
secretary. The credentials of the Hanoverian
envoys—the Schützes, Bothmer, and Grote [1]—and
residents at the Court of St. James—de Beyrie
and Kreyenberg—were made out in the joint
names of the Elector and the Electress Dowager,
and all the official letters sent to England from this
time forward in the name of either were drafted
by Robethon. Thus, notwithstanding the active
interest taken by Leibniz in a question the progress
of which had owed much and continued to be
indebted to his assiduity, its threads were no
longer continuously in his hands. Whether this was
a misfortune for its ultimate development and
solution, need not be here discussed. From his

---

[1] Besides these, Count Ernest Augustus von Platen came over
on two ceremonial occasions. (See the *List of Diplomatic
Representatives and Agents, England and North Germany*, 1687–
1727, contributed by J. F. Chance to *Notes on the Diplomatic
Relations of England and Germany*; ed. C. H. Firth. Oxford,
1907.)

earlier days onwards he had exhibited something of the defect habitual to politicians more exclusively academical than himself, who had a considerable experience of affairs—the defect of excess, which includes the mistake of not letting well alone. Not only, however, did the force of his genius enable him to find out the heart of every political problem to which he addressed himself, but the universality of his insight made clear to him its various aspects, and the energy of his mind supplied the impulse which converts design into action.[1] Finally, his literary skill,[2] added to his gifts of finding his material and disposing it according to the leading ideas with which he approached it, made him in the times in which his lot fell, as it made Gentz, an infinitely inferior personality, in another period of even deeper national humiliation, the foremost publicist of his age.[3]

---

[1] See E. Pfleiderer, *Leibniz als Patriot, Staatsmann, und Bildungsträger* (Leipzig, 1870), and, of course, Kuno Fischer's great work.—Perhaps the most signal instance of the way in which in the political thought of Leibniz past and future came into contact (he says himself : ' *le présent est chargé du passé et gros de l'avenir* ') is, as Ernst Curtius says (*Alterthum und Gegenwart*, pp. 219 *sqq.*), his famous Egyptian plan, of which an account was published in a pamphlet in London, *à propos* of the French invasion of 1803, and as to which see Guhrauer's *Life*, and K. G. Blumenthal, *Leibnizens Ægyptischer Plan* (Leipzig, 1869).

[2] Nothing need be said here of his minor literary efforts, such as his tributes in verse to the Electress Sophia.

[3] In 1688, Leibniz prepared the counter-manifesto to Louis XIV's declaration of war in that year.

That Leibniz, whose political services to the
Electress and her dynasty were, in any case, highly
important, should at the same time have become
her chosen intimate and personal friend, forms
one of his titles to the grateful remembrance of
those who believe this pair to have been worthy
of one another. From his conversation and correspondence, which, in her later years, became more
and more of a necessity to Sophia, her active and
receptive mind derived constant stimulus and
refreshment ; while his humane as well as lofty
wisdom, at no time seeking to avoid contact with
the actualities of life, but neither ever conceding
to them a larger claim than was their due, helped
to fortify her character against the risk of being
mastered by the element of frivolity inborn in most
of her mother's children. Leibniz' own activity
at Hanover, from the time when (as far back as
1673) he had first entered into the service of Duke
John Frederick, was remarkably varied. He held
the offices of librarian, archivist, and historiographer ;
fostered, among other activities in the dominions
of his patrons, the endeavours of technical science,
as in the instance of the mining industry of the
Harz ; and organised both scientific and literary
effort, in connexion with his onerous task as the
historian of the Guelfs, with his work as a philologer
and with the studies in mental and moral philosophy,
which were, in 1710, crowned by the production of

his *Théodicée*. His influence upon the foundation of academies as levers for the advancement of scientific research[1] was by no means limited to Berlin, where success had attended on his labours in consequence of the sympathetic support of Sophia's daughter. The hopes placed by him on the third of the illustrious ladies of the Hanoverian dynasty who felt themselves honoured by his intimacy, were, notwithstanding her loyal efforts at the outset, doomed to disappointment. The Electoral Princess (Caroline of Ansbach) had been solaced by his *Théodicée* in a season of great anxiety ; but, when the political consummation to which Leibniz had so actively helped to prepare had been actually achieved, he had to remain behind in Germany ; and she found herself unequal to the task either of impressing his claims upon her impassive father-in-law—or of reconciling his merits with those of Newton.

During the years of Sophia's widowhood, to which we must here confine ourselves, Leibniz was drawn nearer to her, not only by intellectual and moral sympathy, but also by the discomforts to which she was subjected by the Elector's coldness, and by that Prince's habit of expecting all services to be absolved as per contract. Sophia was unable to

---

[1] See L. Keller, *Leibniz u. die Deutschen Sozietäten des 17 Jahrh.*, in Jahrgang x. of *Vorträge u. Aufsätze a. d. Comenius-Gesellschaft* (Berlin).

secure the fulfilment of Leibniz's wish for a sinecure like that by which his friend, ' Abbot ' Molanus, was recompensed for his ecclesiastical services. But her friendship with Leibniz was not dependent upon favours given or received. Not only was the encouragement which he derived from his intimacy with her and from that which through her he enjoyed with Sophia Charlotte and Caroline, of high value to him in the labours and in the trials of his life ; but in the Electress Sophia's case, at all events, her nature was in many respects supplementary to his own. Their correspondence thus furnishes a memorial of a friendship alike sincere and productive ; and their names will always remain inseparable from one another.

Sophia Charlotte, though her marriage had long since made it necessary for her to leave her mother's side, and though the trials to which she had since been subjected had greatly added to that mother's anxieties, and had often been mitigated by her tact and good-humour rather than by those of the Queen herself, remained Sophia's truest joy, till taken away by death in 1705. Mother and daughter had kept up a continuous correspondence with one another, besides interchanging visits when possible ; nor could the completeness of the confidence existing between them be better illustrated than by the treatment which, after Sophia Charlotte's death, it was thought judicious to apply to the documents of their mutual affection. At the instigation of Leibniz, the extant letters of the Electress Sophia to her daughter were committed to the flames at Berlin, so that only a small remnant of the series, copied out by him for his own use, have been preserved. Inasmuch as neither have any letters from Sophia Charlotte to her mother come down to us, they may be surmised to have been similarly destroyed by way of precaution. Possibly, these proceedings may have been in part due to evidence contained in these letters as to efforts made, in the Hanoverian interest, at the Court of Berlin by Leibniz or others. The chief trouble of Sophia Charlotte's married life—King Frederick I's infatuation for the Countess von Wartenberg—had been particularly acute in the period just preceding the Queen's death ; and her last visit to her mother (in January, 1705) could only be carried out by her submitting to the condition that an invitation to Hanover should also be sent to her detested rival. During this visit Sophia Charlotte died, the victim of a painful and incurable disease that befell her when her intellectual abilities were at their full height. Her death, even more impressively than her life, proved the justice of her grandson Frederick the Great's tribute to her strength of soul. The illness of the Queen had been concealed from her mother, who herself lay ill ; and thus, as she wrote, heart-broken, to her widowed son-in-law, she lost her darling child without even setting eyes upon her.[1]

Princess Wilhelmina Caroline of Brandenburg-Ansbach had, in her thirteenth year, been left an orphan by the death of her mother, who had been united to the Elector John George IV of Saxony as her second husband. In 1696, the child had been placed under the care of her guardians, afterwards the first King and Queen in Prussia. Thus Lützenburg became the home of Caroline's childhood ; and here she became familiar with the intellectual society which Sophia Charlotte loved to gather around her, and above all with Leibniz. The nature of their intercourse may be gathered from the letter, sublime in thought, which he wrote to her on the occasion of Sophia Charlotte's death. Only a few months after this event—in September, 1705—Caroline, lovely in person and richly endowed in intellect, had illustrated the saying of the Electress Sophia, that ' nowadays princesses are sacrificial victims.' After a proper interval had been allowed to elapse upon the breakdown of the project of marrying Caroline to

[1] After Queen Sophia Charlotte's death there was less love lost than ever between the King, her husband, and the Elector, her brother. In 1711, the Electress Sophia, speaking of a melancholy journey of her son-in-law's, observes that it was a Divine punishment on him that he should hate the Elector without any reason whatever.

Archduke Charles, the Electoral Prince George Augustus, to whom the thoughts of his grandmother, the Electress, had been directed already during the attempts made in 1704 to induce Caroline to change her religion, paid a preliminary visit to Ansbach. The rumour which had arisen in 1702, that the Electoral Prince was to find a consort in Sweden and Queen Sophia Charlotte's counter-suggestion of the Duchess Marie-Elizabeth of Holstein-Gottorp, had alike come to nothing. On September 2nd, 1705, the marriage between the Electoral Prince and Caroline of Ansbach was celebrated at Hanover. Here Caroline spent the following nine years of her life, beyond a doubt its happiest period; and, during the remainder of Sophia's own existence, she in a large measure filled the place in her affections which her daughter Sophia Charlotte had so long occupied. The congeniality of their tastes and dispositions made her a delightful companion at Herrenhausen to her grandmother-in-law; and thus a kindly fortune granted to Sophia, who was so singularly capable of enjoying it, the truest joy of old age. The Electress repeatedly speaks of the happiness of the marriage; nor can there be any doubt as to the genuine affection on both sides which constituted that happiness. Early in 1707, the Electoral Princess gave birth to her eldest son (destined afterwards to disappoint an indulgent world as Frederick, Prince of Wales), upon whom, a year later, his great-grandmother is found bestowing an infantine equipment for a fancy ball ; and three daughters were subsequently born to the young pair, before they accompanied King George I to England. The prospects of a permanent establishment of the Hanoverian dynasty upon the British throne were thus signally advanced by this marriage ; and to these prospects and their initial realisation we must now finally turn. They filled Sophia's last years with anxieties and un-certainties ; yet, on the whole, life flowed more easily for her in this final period of her existence ; although the joyousness of girlhood, which she so vividly recalls in her *Memoirs*, was a thing of the past, together with the experiences—some grotesque, some painful, some tragic—of her married days. The deep agitations of her life were at an end ; and she might pace the Herrenhausen gardens without caring too deeply even for the chances of the English Succession.

Thus we may imagine this spirited and sensible lady, at any time in these last thirteen years of her long life, exemplifying the old saw of ' *mens sana in corpore sano.*' In the main, she enjoyed excellent health ; and Leibniz' description of the day of her arrival at Lützenburg is certainly aston-ishing for a lady of seventy-four. It included, in accordance with her usual habits, two hours of walking exercise. Erect and handsome, with her mother's aquiline nose and abundant hair, she was, if not a Gloriana as imagined by poets, a princess worthy to mount a royal throne—or at least one who, if placed there, would of a certainty not lose the firmness of her footing by reason of such an elevation.

After, in 1701, a copy of the Act pledging King and Parliament to the new limitation of the Succession had been placed in the hands of the Electress Sophia, thirteen long years of expectancy awaited her, which might have made a less stout heart grow faint. Or, perhaps, it would be more correct to say that a nature less happily balanced, and uninured by experience, both inherited and personal, to the necessity of patience and resignation, might have fallen into mistake upon mistake, and have thus courted failure. Sophia, prudently choosing her own path, almost to the last did nothing to affront the approach of success. To suppose, however, that either her policy or that of her House was one of masterly inactivity, would be almost as contrary to fact as the converse assumption that, either before or after 1701, she was possessed by an absorbing desire to find herself seated on the English throne. The former supposition is confuted by the single circumstance that, by way of furnishing the necessary means in the event of a sudden crisis, a sum of not less than 300,000 dollars was secretly provided by the Committee of the Calenberg Estates, and placed in the hands of the Hanoverian envoy in London—the secret of this expenditure being kept for not less than seventy years.[1] The other assumption is simply irreconcilable with the whole tenor of Sophia's life.

The festivities at Hanover and Celle, on the occasion of the transmission of the Act of Settlement, were hardly at an end, when King William III had a meeting at the Loo with his old friend Duke George William. The Duke was accompanied by his grandson, the Electoral Prince George Augustus, whom, according to Toland, the King received as a son. This Prince certainly seems in his youth to have displayed attractive qualities, which were afterwards driven into the background by his master quality, self-conceit ; curiously enough, though he was a fair linguist, it had not been thought necessary to make him well acquainted with the English tongue. At this interview, the account of which shows how loyally the old Duke of Celle was working for the interests of the dynasty, King William promised to use his influence in order to obtain from Parliament an annual revenue for the Electress Sophia, and mentioned his intention of inviting her and the Electoral Prince to visit

[1] In a letter from the Electress to Bothmer (*Briefe an Hannoversche Diplomaten*, p. 319) she mentions some money of hers in England ; but the passage seems to refer to a private investment.

England in the coming spring. On his sounding
his next heir, the Princess Anne, at all events as
to the proposal of summoning the Electress, she is
said to have pretended to be still in hopes of an heir.
The Electress on her side seems to have trusted
in the fulfilment of the King's promise, not only
during the remainder of his reign, but for a few
months afterwards.

But no time was left to the King for carrying
out his design. On September 6th, 1701, nine days
after the conclusion of the Grand Alliance to
which William III had set the seal on his visit to
Holland, James II died ; and, by recognising his
son as King of England, Louis XIV once again,
and more completely by his own act than ever,
identified himself with the Stewart cause. His
grandson, King Philip of Spain, followed his example ; and Pope Clement XI publicly extolled the
action of Louis XIV, as entitling him to the gratitude of posterity. In the final form of the instrument of the Grand Alliance—which William III
was not to live to see actually concluded—a clause
was inserted binding the contracting Powers not
to conclude peace with France, until the King of
England should have received satisfaction for
the grave insult involved in the recognition of the
' pretended Prince of Wales ' as King. In other
words, the War of the Spanish Succession had
become a War of the English Succession also ; and,

to whatever extent this fact might be overlooked during the course of the conflict, it was certain to become prominent again so soon as a settlement began to be seriously discussed. Inasmuch as the first public suggestion of such a clause had been made by a prominent Tory politician (Edward Seymour), it can hardly have been inspired from Hanover, though in a letter to the Electress, written as early as 1701, Leibniz had stated such a stipulation to be desirable.

In England, the recognition of the Pretender by Louis XIV had an immediate consequence in the Attainder and Abjuration Acts, passed in January, 1702, by William III's sixth Parliament. The Act of Attainder had been criticised beforehand by the Electress Sophia, who, in October, 1701, told Leibniz that there was an intention of declaring the poor Prince of Wales a rebel, such as Monmouth had been declared to be before him, ' though his personal merit deserved a better fate.' Why should she have refused this modicum of sympathy to her kinsman, who, not more unfortunate in his fate than he was in his infatuation, was about this very time rejoicing that Pope Clement would manifestly ' leave no stone unturned to show how much he favours us ' ? The Abjuration Act, which led to long and warm debates in both Houses, provided both for abjuring the ' pretended Prince of Wales,' and for swearing fidelity to the ' rightful and lawful King ' and ' his heirs according to the Act of Settlement.' A motion in the Commons, carried by a single vote, made these engagements obligatory ; the opposition in the Lords ended in nothing but a protest, the list of whose signatories, including the names of Craven and Jeffreys, as it were mirrors the story of the downfall of the Stewart monarchy in England.

On March 8th, 1702, King William III died, after a fortnight's illness following on his fall from his horse. To Portland, the faithful friend for whom the King had asked, without being able to speak to him intelligibly, shortly before his death, the Electress Sophia, when the first shock of the blow had passed over, wrote in unaffected sorrow—

I assure you, Sir, that I have received with much pleasure the proof of your kind remembrance of me, and that, in the midst of the sad change which has come upon us, I called to mind that you would weep with us for the loss which the whole of Christendom has undergone. But when one does not die oneself, one has to see many others pass away ; and I cannot think that I shall live to see yet another calamity for England of the same kind ; for Queen Anne is much younger than I am, who have entered my seventy-second year. Nevertheless, I feel much happier than a Queen ; for, God be thanked, I am still in very good health, and have joined my daughter here, in order to enjoy myself with her here in her country-seat. [1]

---

[1] This letter is translated from one of the unpublished letters to the Earl of Portland mentioned in the Preface.

By the death, on March 8th, 1702, of King William III and the accession of Queen Anne, the prospect which the Act of Settlement seemed to have once for all thrown open to the House of Hanover was again clouded over. Queen Anne, indeed, at once sent an assurance to the Electress through the Hanoverian resident, the elder Schütz, that her sentiments towards the House of Hanover were the same as those of her predecessor,[1] and a few days afterwards repeated the message in writing. An Order in Council directed the Archbishop of Canterbury to insert the name of the Princess Sophia in the Book of Common Prayer ; and, as was usual in such cases, this Order was in due course sent on to Dublin.[2] It has been observed, nor is there great exception to be taken to the remark, that beyond the issue of this Order nothing was done by Queen Anne in the whole of the earlier period of her reign on behalf of the Hanoverian Succession. In other words, the proposals discussed at the Loo, which were to have resulted in the payment of an annuity to the Electress, and to her or the Electoral Prince residing in England, were not carried further.

[1] She also renewed the assent given by William III to the measures of force adopted at this time by the Elector of Hanover and the Duke of Celle against the Dukes of Brunswick-Wolfenbüttel.

[2] In September, Sophia writes that Lord Stamford has been good enough to transmit to her a dozen copies of the Prayer-book, with her name inserted in it ; but that there are not a dozen persons in Hanover able to join her in using them.

Interchanges of civility, however, took place ; and
the Earl of Winchelsea arrived at Hanover, in order
to return the congratulations brought thence by
Count Platen on the occasion of Queen Anne's
accession. But, though the special mission was
flattering, Sophia's wish, that the ambassador might
bring with him some money which she might apply
to the necessities of her sons Christian and Maximilian, remained unfulfilled. For the rest, she told
the Raugravine Louisa that, for all the compliments which had passed, ' time would show '
whether she was still wanted in England ; and she
continued to bear herself calmly, avoiding the
appearance of excessive zeal that some of her
partisans could not deny themselves. She had
thought it a piece of impertinence, when, after his
return to England, Toland had, early in this year,
followed up his *Anglia Libera* by another publication provocatively entitled *Reasons for addressing
His Majesty to invite into England their Highnesses
the Electress Dowager and the Electoral Prince of
Hanover ;* which, soon after Queen Anne's accession,
was duly censured by the House of Lords. The
Electress had reasons for disliking a championship
which under King William would have been superfluous and was now inopportune. She could not
consider Toland so ' *infâme* ' as Cresset painted
him ; and she took care that in her presence he
should not say a disrespectful word about Queen

Anne. But, when, in 1702, Toland found it convenient again to quit England for Germany, he left
the court of Hanover unvisited ; nor does he seem
to have reappeared there till 1707.

The Elector's instincts as to the doubtfulness of
Queen Anne's real sentiments on the subject of the
Hanoverian Succession were justified by what
ensued. The hope of an immediate grant to the
Heiress Presumptive out of the ample Civil List
good Queen Anne frustrated by the highly popular
step of making over to the Exchequer £100,000
towards lightening the burdens of the nation. The
claims upon the national resources were many and
urgent ; and Parliament could perhaps hardly be
expected to consider how much a subvention was
needed by the Electress, more especially in view
of the presents which, in accordance with the usage
of the times, she as well as the Elector had to make
to a succession of English special ambassadors.
There can, however, be no doubt but that, already
in this early part of Queen Anne's reign, and even
before the Toryism of her first Parliament had
encouraged in her the tendency which her choice
of ministers had implied, deliberate attempts had
been made to influence unfavourably her attitude
towards the Succession of the House of Hanover.
Moreover, her nature was so peculiarly prone to strong
personal attachments, and her gift of insight into
the motives of men was so unmistakably accompanied

by an absence of all real power of political judgment, that she could hardly but be dominated by
a strong prepossession against the line so likely
to succeed her on the throne of her ancestors. Yet,
hitherto, neither the Electress Sophia nor any of
the members of her House—and least of all her
impassive eldest son, who at one time had been supposed to have a chance of the hand of the Princess
Anne—had been on unfriendly terms with the new
Queen ; nor is there any reason for supposing her
to have imparted to any of them a share in the wild
scheme rumoured to have been set on foot for
ousting her from the Succession. When, however,
in May, 1702, the Whig Earl of Carlisle, the First
Lord of the Treasury, carried in the House of Lords
his demand for an enquiry into the scandalous
rumour which asserted that King William had
intended by a kind of posthumous *coup d'état* to
raise the Electoral Prince to the throne, Queen
Anne showed no desire for the vindication of her predecessor's good faith towards herself, and pointedly
dismissed Carlisle from office. Nor is it probable
that, at this early stage, the Queen was much intent
upon the interests of her half-brother, the Pretender.
The favourite advisers by whom she was swayed—
Marlborough and Godolphin—could have no wish
to hurry her intervention on behalf of either of the
two sides, with both of which they desired to stand
well ; and the Tory majority in the Commons,

typified by the Speaker, Harley, were certainly not prepared to unsettle the Act of Settlement. The Act for the further Security of the Protestant Succession passed in December, 1702, which declared it high treason to seek to defeat the Succession to the Crown as now limited by law, or to set aside the next Succession, followed the precedent of a similar Act passed in the previous reign, and accordingly encountered no resistance. Thus Queen Anne was slow to take up any definite attitude towards the political problem which overshadowed the whole course of her reign; and she was consequently all the more unwilling, and remained so from first to last, to listen to any suggestion of carrying out William III's promise and inviting the Electress Dowager and the Electoral Prince, or either of them, to England. The probability of this plan being brought forward, either as a practical proposal or by way of testing the sincerity of her own views on the subject, acted as a perennial irritant upon the Queen. Neither she nor her advisers are to be blamed for leaving without response the suggestion, pardonably enough made by Sophia, that the un-English title of ' Hereditary Princess ' should be conferred upon her. Other signs were noticeable of the uncertainty prevailing at the Court of St. James. At Hanover and Herrenhausen, Cresset watched the Electress with a suspiciousness that could not escape her

attention, though she commented on it with her
usual *insouciance ;* and Stepney even left off corresponding with her and her intimates, in order not
to give offence nearer home.   In conversing with
the Englishmen and Scotchmen who attended the
Court of Hanover, anxious to promote its fortunes
or their own, the Electress naturally sought to
emphasise her confidence in her august relative, the
Queen.   But in her intimate correspondence she
was fain to strike a different key.   She told the
Raugravine Amalia that Queen Anne had no desire
to be survived by her, although (quoting a Dutch
proverb which she has made classical) she allowed
that *' creaking wagons go on for a long time,'* and
suggested that the Queen's real preference was for
her brother.[1]   Matters continued very much in
this stagnant and unsatisfactory condition during
the first three years (or thereabouts) of Queen Anne's
reign.   In March, 1694, Sophia writes with some
bitterness, that Queen Anne ' seems to have more
friendship for the King of Prussia than for us, inasmuch as she speaks of the ' [Prussian] ' and says
nothing of the Brunswick troops, without whom the
battle ' [of Blenheim] ' could not have been won.
This is a sample showing what is to be expected in
that quarter.'   And she adds that the statement in

[1] This, too, was the impression of Queen Sophia Charlotte
at Berlin.   (See her letter to Bothmer, May 27th, 1902, in *Briefe
an Hannoversche Diplomaten*, p. 10.)

the *Gazette* of the great presents sent by the Queen to Hanover is untrue, whoever caused it to be inserted.

It may, at this point, be noted that the violence of public feeling which about this time disturbed Scotland had very seriously endangered the prospects of the Succession of the House of Hanover in that kingdom. Here, it was universally believed that Queen Anne cherished the secret wish of securing the Succession to her brother ; and no declarations to the contrary exercised the slightest effect upon the stubbornness of preconceived Scottish opinion. At the same time, a strong belief that she meditated a Prelatic as well as a Jacobite reaction, led to the anti-Episcopalian legislation of the last Scottish Parliament, which met in 1703.[1] The Act of Security brought forward in this Parliament provided that the Estates of the Realm should meet within twelve days after the present Queen's death, and should proceed to name a successor professing the Protestant religion. A proposal to insert the name of the Electress Sophia was rejected ; but the ministers, besides frustrating an attempt at inserting

[1] In June, 1702, Sophia had written that Scottish affairs seemed in a troublesome state, but that she could hardly doubt that the Queen would be prudent enough to leave the Scotch their *extempore* prayers . . . and that there would be no attempt to impose upon them bishops and ' common prayer,' by which means Charles I had spoilt everything.—For an elucidation of the religious condition of Scotland as affecting the question of the Hanoverian Succession, see Mr. Rait's paper in Appendix C.

a series of limitations calculated to take away
the last vestige of authority from the Crown, also
defeated a proposal to limit the Protestantism of
the successor to ' the true Protestant religion as by
law established within this kingdom,' which would
have excluded the Lutheranism of the House of
Hanover. On the other hand, the Government
could not resist a clause, proposed by the Earl of
Roxburghe, precluding Parliament from naming, as
successor to the Crown of Scotland, the person who
was successor to the Crown of England, unless conditions should have been previously settled securing
the interests of Scotland against English or foreign
interference. The Act of Security, with this clause
inserted in it, passed by large majorities ; but the
Duke of Queensberry refused to give to it the royal
assent. In 1704, however, the national and religious
agitation remaining unalloyed, the Marquis of
Tweeddale touched the Act with the royal sceptre :
and a condition of things was thus legalised which
might at any time put an end to the personal union
of the two countries, or actually provoke war between them. But time often provides its own
remedy ; and, in January, 1707, the Act of Union
became law, whose Second Article, limiting the
Succession to Sophia and her heirs, had met with
only a feeble opposition upholding the provisions of
the Act of Security. When the Union was on the
eve of actual accomplishment, the Electress Sophia

expressed herself as well satisfied, adding that, though she had never supposed the Scottish lords against her, she thought it quite natural that conditions should be imposed—another illustration of the way in which she looked upon constitutional questions. In Ireland, the Succession had already in the previous year been regulated by a measure modelled upon the English Act of Settlement, but subjecting all officials and magistrates to a rigid Church of England test.

Even in this early period of Queen Anne's reign, the Electress Sophia, though, according to her wont, she abstained from all restless manœuvring, was by no means without thought for the future. On June 4th, 1703, she signed three powers for Schütz, the envoy extraordinary in London, authorising him, in the event of the Queen's death, to bring forward her lawful claim to the throne ; and she kept up a correspondence with friends in England, both directly and through Leibniz. In November, 1703, she put it to Schütz that, if Marlborough resigned the command in the Low Countries, it would be right to appoint the Elector in his place ; ' for if it is wished that the Elector should have a good opinion of the English, they ought to do something towards making him entertain such an opinion and enabling him in any court to support those who were in his favour.' As for Leibniz, though indefatigable and full of initiative as ever, he naturally

enough occasionally fell short of the necessary
familiarity with English persons and affairs.   Thus,
about this very time, the Electress had to comment
on his approval of a scheme for marrying the Electoral
Prince to one of Marlborough's daughters, by reminding him that the Duke had no more daughters
in the matrimonial market.   Marlborough, however, gained the goodwill of the Elector, above all
by commending the behaviour of the Hanoverian
troops at Blenheim ; and, on a visit to Hanover in
December, 1704, while the laurels of his great
victory were still green, he completely won over
the Electress by the fascination of his manner.   She
declared that she had never seen anyone ' *plus aisé,
plus civil, ny plus obligeant,*' and that he was as
good a cavalier as he was a captain.   The extraordinary civility shown to him on this occasion,
when a special household was provided for him and
other courtesies were multiplied,[1] was not thrown
away.   His   correspondence   with   the   Electoral

[1] The Duke, we learn *inter alia*, played a game at cards with the
Electress and ' Madame Bellmont.'   This Lady Bellmont or
Bellamont, whom Leibniz in vain begged the Electress not to
admit into her intimacy, was no other than Frances Bard, who
claimed to be the widow of Prince Rupert, and whose relations
with him had certainly been of the most intimate kind.   She
justified Leibniz by misusing her position at Hanover to engage
in Jacobite intrigue, thereby giving much trouble to Cresset
and to Edmund Poley, who succeeded him as envoy extraordinary
in 1703 ; and it is just conceivable that she may have in some
measure influenced the Electress in favour of the Pretender and his
cause.   She died in 1708.

court—and with the Elector in particular, whose admiration for the military genius of the great commander was genuine—now became continuous.

The year 1705 marked an epoch in the history of the Succession question, as we saw that it did in the personal life of the Electress Sophia, who, during its course, lost not only her beloved daughter. but also her old admirer and constant friend, Duke George William of Celle. All the dominions of the Brunswick-Lüneburg line were now at last united under the single rule of the Elector George Lewis, and into his coffers flowed most of the great private wealth of his late uncle and father-in-law, which had materially contributed to the high consideration enjoyed by George William. About the same time the long-standing quarrel with the elder (Wolfen-büttel) branch of the House of Brunswick was brought to a close, and the House of Hanover stood stronger than ever before the world. No season could have been more opportune for taking up the question of the Succession with renewed earnest-ness. Its vigorous prosecution was further favoured by the circumstance that the late Duke of Celle's prime minister, Baron Andreas Gottlieb von Bern-storff, now passed into the Hanoverian service, and, on the death of Count Platen in 1709, became prime minister at Hanover. He was already a statesman of proved ability, trained in the school of his father-in-law, Chancellor Schütz, whom he describes as one of the greatest and most capable ministers ever known to him. While he always kept his political ends clearly in view, Bernstorff's political action was marked by ruthlessness that is apt to make a statesman of his type cordially hated where he is not eagerly followed ; and his bitter jealousy of Brandenburg-Prussia in particular was unlikely to commend him to the goodwill of the Electress Sophia. Her faithful echo at Versailles allows us to make a guess as to the sentiments of the Electress concerning him ; and they were afterwards reproduced by Queen Caroline, who, like Elizabeth Charlotte, was unwilling to differ in her opinion of men or measures from their venerated senior. Bernstorff's activity in the last stage of Sophia Dorothea's catastrophe proves that he had not been captivated by the influence which had so long been dominant at Celle ; and the Duchess Eleonora doubtless held the same opinion of him as the other ladies. He devoted himself with indefatigable zeal to advancing the greatness of the Hanoverian dynasty ; but he laboured in no narrow spirit and with no petty aims, as an adequate survey of his statesmanship in the earlier years of George I, should it ever be made, could not fail to show. With Bernstorff (to mention no other name) Jean de Robethon had passed from the service of Celle into that of Hanover—a perfect type of the sort of man and the sort of mind whose destiny it is to be *a secretis* of those whose grasp is

on the wheel of State.   After the Revocation of the
Edict of Nantes had driven him, like so many other
capable Frenchmen, into the service of the foes of
France, he had served his apprenticeship under no
less a master than William III.   During Queen Anne's
reign he became one of the most assiduous and useful
instruments in the transactions connected with the
Succession.   For a time, he in Bothmer's absence
attended to affairs at the Hague ; but he then
returned to Hanover, where as confidential secretary
he was of infinite service to both the Elector and the
Electress, and played a political part not the less
important because it was to a great extent played
behind the scenes.   Bernstorff trusted no man more
implicitly than Robethon, who, in the end, was said
to have acquired an unbounded influence over him ;
and by Robethon were drafted all, or virtually all,
the despatches and letters sent to England by the
Electoral family from the date of his entrance into
their service to that of George I's landing in England.
All the more important of these documents likewise
passed through the hands of Hans Caspar von Bothmer, whose services to the dynasty had likewise
begun at Celle ; whence he had been sent as envoy
to Vienna, passing on, after he had acted as a plenipotentiary at Ryswick, to Paris.   Unlike Bernstorff,
and unlike Bernstorff's master, Bothmer united
political insight of a high order with remarkable
diplomatic ability and tact ; and, after he had, when

the crisis came, shown perfect prudence in the supreme moment of success, he was perhaps the only one of the Hanoverians of the early Georgian period who attained to personal popularity in London. But this was later. On the accession of Queen Anne, it had been thought desirable that he should in the first instance take up a post of observation at the Hague, since the Queen was at present unlikely to welcome so prominent a Hanoverian diplomatist to her Court. Thus it was from the Hague that he actively helped to bring about the English legislative enactments, which we shall immediately notice, and which signally improved the prospects of the Hanoverian Succession. We shall see that, though his first and second stay as envoy in London were but short,[1] he returned thither in time to direct the final stage in the transactions connected with the Succession, and to apply to this task a consummate skill and an equally conspicuous courage.

The ministerial arrangements made after the death of his uncle by the Elector George Lewis, who was at no time wont to delegate to others any part of what he had clearly recognised as his own bounden duty, might seem to imply that, from 1705 onwards, the conduct of the Succession

[1] He was accredited to London after the death of Schütz in August, 1710, and remained certainly till March, 1711. He reappeared there in October, and remained till January, 1711. He came back in June or July, 1714. (Chance, *u.s.*)

question was more and more taken out of the hands
of his mother. It is true that the Elector had,
as the head of his dynasty, become more vigilant ;
but her interest in the question had remained the
same. And, as a matter of fact, at no previous time
had her name been bandied about between the
political parties in England as it was now and
during the remaining years of her life. To the
close of the year 1705 belongs that strange episode
in the party history of the reign, the attempt on the
part of a section among the Tories to bring the
Electress over to England.

Hitherto, she had wisely refrained—nor is there
any indication that her eldest son and her grandson
had done otherwise—from identifying the interests
of her House with either of the two Parliamentary
parties, both of which had had a part in the Act
of Settlement. No doubt it was the Whigs who
had most warmly supported the insertion of her
name in that Act ; the embassy which had brought
it over to Hanover had been exclusively made up
of Whigs ; and, writing to Leibniz towards the close
of 1701, Sophia, apparently with reference to the
approaching English elections, excusably lets slip
the phrase : ' *le parti des Whigs qui est le nostre.*'
But, already in the following year, when annoyed
by the officious importunities of Toland and that
other *grand fâcheux*, Sir Peter Fraiser, she confided
to her niece Elizabeth Charlotte her resolution not

to mix herself up with the manœuvres of the
Presbyterians and Whigs, which, as we have seen,
were at that time agitating Scotland. ' Besides,' she
observed, with a fastidiousness not inexplicable
when the composition of Macclesfield's embassy
is remembered, ' the Whigs that came to me here
I found anything but charming.' And, again in
1703, she ordered Baron Brauns not to answer
one of Toland's long diatribes against the Tories
by more than a simple acknowledgment. There
was no fear, she remarked, of their supporting the
Pretender ; no person of substance, in fact nobody
but Catholics and adventurers set on making their
fortunes, were on his side ; for the rest, she found
as many honest men among the Tories as elsewhere.
She had, as a matter of fact, certain affinities with
this party ; while some of their opponents in
the House of Commons offended her, as a true
Stewart who remembered the excesses of the
Commonwealth days, by comparing the Prince of
Wales to Perkin Warbeck and branding him as a
bastard—all in order to tickle the ears of *le petit
peuple*. There could be no question, she told
Leibniz in the same letter, as to the Prince's claims
interfering with her own ; her right was based on
her Protestantism ; except for this, many others
stood between the Crown and herself. While, then,
she adhered to her determination to place herself
in the hands of neither party, there was no reason

why the Tories should not in their turn seek to make her listen to their charming. When, about the end of 1704, it had become known through Marlborough that the Electress would be pleased to receive a formal invitation to England, both parties seem to have risen to the occasion ; but, while the Whigs returned to the notion of bringing over the Electoral Prince, some of the Tories became intent on the Electress herself being invited. Partly to ingratiate themselves with her, partly to spite Queen Anne, who preferred to their guidance that of the moderates of both sides under the leadership of Marlborough, Godolphin, and Harley, the malcontent Tories, led by Rochester and known as the ' High-fliers,' resolved on an attempt to take the game into their own hands. With Rochester she had been on friendly terms from the first ; in June, 1702, she writes that he was among the first to vote for the Act of Settlement, and that she had always mentioned this to those who wished to set her against him.[1] Towards the end of September, 1705, a correspondent informed Rochester of the cordial response returned by the Electress to certain overtures made on his behalf ; he declared himself convinced that, whenever the Queen and Parliament called upon her, the Electress would,

[1] On Rochester's sudden death, in 1711, Sophia expresses her deep regret for him as her friend—' he had plenty of *esprit*, and was in no way a republican.'

in the face of all difficulties, wait upon Her Majesty in England ; and, more than this, she had told him, and those in attendance on her, that, so soon as the Parliament summoned her, she was ready to obey. (In a letter to Schütz of about the same date, Sophia, however, qualifies this consent by requiring a proviso that she should be supplied with means of living in England as became a Princess of Wales.) Though, Rochester's correspondent added, the Elector was exceeding modest on the subject of some of his family coming to England, the Electress spoke as the Elector thought. Sophia was on friendly terms with other members of the Tory party besides Rochester. With Ormonde, for instance, she kept up a correspondence both in this and in the following year. But the task of moving an address to the Crown, in which it was proposed that the Heiress Presumptive should be invited to England, was committed to a quite recent convert to the ranks of the High-flyers, Lord Haversham. He displayed a proper zeal by hazarding the suggestion that it would be of the greatest advantage for the Electress to make the personal acquaintance of the Bench of Bishops. The comedy ended in the rejection of Haversham's motion by a majority of Peers ; but he returned to the fray in a pamphlet. In the Commons a letter advocating the proposal, hinting that it was approved by the Electress and censuring the Whigs

for opposing it, was voted libellous. This much-
vext letter was signed by Sir Rowland Gwynne,
who was at the time residing at Hanover; but
its real author was Leibniz. Towards the close
of 1705, Marlborough made use of the opportunity
of another visit paid by him to Hanover for explaining the situation to the Elector. Marlborough,
who, while anxious both to please the Queen and
to keep the game so far as possible in his own hands,
was more and more identifying his own interests with
the ascendancy of the Whigs, easily succeeded in
making clear to the Elector, how it was not in his
interest that his mother should at present proceed
to England; and he was able to add effect to his
arguments by exhibiting an official notice of the
intention of the English Cabinet to introduce
Naturalisation and Regency Bills in the interests
of the Electoral House. The understanding between the Elector and Marlborough now became
better than ever, while the Elector's confidence
in the Whigs steadily grew. It is impossible to
say whether this was the time when Marlborough
proffered at Hanover a loan of £20,000 in return
for a blank commission signed by the Electress
Sophia, which conferred on him the supreme command of the military and naval forces of the three
kingdoms after the death of Queen Anne.

The High-fliers had thus merely played into
the hands of the Whigs, who were in the majority

in the new House of Commons that met in October, 1705. The Address to the Queen had warmly thanked her for her great care and endeavour to settle the Succession of the kingdom of Scotland in the House of Hanover ; and soon afterwards the Bills were brought in which Marlborough had announced at Hanover. By the first of these, the Princess Sophia, Electress and Duchess Dowager of Hanover, and her issue were naturalised as English subjects ; and it is strange that the legal status thus secured to her should have been so persistently ignored in English national biography.[1] The second of these Bills, purporting to provide for the better security of the Queen's person and Government, was introduced in the Lords with much eloquence by the ever-young Lord Wharton. This Bill made it high treason to assert in writing, and attached the penalties of a *præmunire* to the assertion by word of mouth, that the Queen was not a lawful Sovereign, or that the Sovereign in Parliament could not limit the descent of the Crown ; and it further appointed seven great officers of State, and certain other persons, to

[1] She told Schütz (January 1st, 1706) that she thought the naturalisation unnecessary, as it had been held to be in the case of King William III and in those of her late brothers, but that she was quite prepared to act as the Queen and Parliament wished. She would have preferred the name ' Brunswick-Lüneburg ' to be substituted for ' Hanover,' and the style ' *Sérénissime* ' in lieu of ' Excellent.' The former of these criticisms, at all events, was perfectly just.

administer the government of the realm in the
event of the Queen's demise and the absence from
England of her lawful successor. The Bill met with
no opposition in the Lords, though Rochester
contrived to carry a limitation, supposed to safeguard the Act of Uniformity ; but in the House
of Commons it lay long on the table. The High-
fliers, putting forward as their spokesman Sir
Thomas Hanmer (who up to the last professed
the deepest devotion to the interests of the Electress
Sophia), were once more attempting to take the
game out of the hands of the Whigs by proposing
that the Electress should be brought over. Much
use was made, as appears from a passage in Burnet's
inaccurate narrative, of a letter written in November
by the Electress Sophia to the Archbishop of
Canterbury, in which she had reiterated the position
consistently maintained by her, that she was prepared to come to England, should both the Queen
and Parliament desire it. This position was alike
logical and appropriate ; but the letter did not
suit the Whigs, who were well aware that Queen
Anne would never be brought to express such
a desire. On the rejection of Hanmer's motion
the Electress informed Burnet with much dignity
that, should it prove to be in the interests of State
and religion, she remained ready to cross to England if invited, provided she were created Princess
of Wales. But, at the same time, she expressed to

Marlborough her conviction that her intentions had been so misrepresented to the Queen that her coming to England now would be superfluous. There is no reason for accepting Burnet's statement that her letter to the Archbishop of Canterbury had been instigated by the Tories ; but neither did she show any disposition towards encouraging the Whigs. In truth, though Sophia was not destined to mount a royal throne, and though what might be termed her monarchical apprenticeship had been served in a State that had but recently ceased to be petty and whose system of government was to all intents and purposes absolute, she displayed a higher capacity for constitutional rule than Queen Anne, who could only maintain a balance between factions by subjecting herself to their leaders in turn. It cannot be satisfactorily shown that the Electress definitely preferred the Tories, while the Elector favoured the Whigs. In fact, she remained on good terms with both the leading parties ; although she did not turn a deaf ear even to overtures from so unsafe a politician as Buckingham, who, after taking a leading part in the attempt to bring her over to England, tried to engage her in a fresh intrigue to that end.[1] The

[1] I have modified some expressions in my first edition, after comparing the account of F. Salomon, *Die letzten Regierungsjahre der Königin Anna*, pp. 276–7 ; but I cannot come to the conclusion that the attitude of the Electress as between the parties was even at this time incorrect,

Regency Bill, as it was shortly called, in the end became law ; and Parliament, which had further shown its goodwill to the House of Hanover by voting a modest subsidy for the payment of additional Hanoverian and Celle troops, was prorogued in March, 1706.

In the following May, Lord Halifax, who as Charles Montagu had been a leading Whig statesman already under William III and had quite recently been appointed one of the Commissioners for the Union with Scotland, was chosen, no doubt on account of his position and accomplishments rather than because of any personal attractiveness, to proceed to Hanover, there to present the Naturalisation and Regency Acts to the Electress Sophia, now the first subject of the English Crown.[1] Halifax was also the bearer of a Garter for the Electoral Prince, on whom a few weeks later the Queen conferred the title of Duke of Cambridge. On his way Halifax had secured the inclusion of a guarantee of the established Succession in future treaties with the United Provinces. In his suite was Addison,

[1] This visit synchronised very nearly with the coming of age of the Pretender (June), who seized the opportunity to assure Pope Clement XI that ' no temptation of this world, and no desire to reign, should ever make him wander from the right path of the Catholic faith.' The anecdote must go for what it is worth, which was said to have been related by Halifax to Lady Mary Wortley Montagu and her husband : how, at his first formal audience with the Electress, she ran across the room in order to place herself in front of a portrait of the Pretender, and thus screen it from the ambassador's eyes.

now one of the Under-Secretaries of State ; but the reticence of this celebrated personage seems to have disappointed the Electress.

From a later remark of Leibniz we gather that, on the occasion of Halifax's embassy, the Electress made no secret of the view held by her and the Elector with reference to the Succession. It rested, she considered, on hereditary right ; though, in the interests of the nation, certain persons possessed of claims prior to her own had been excluded. In other words, she acknowledged that Parliament had a right to exclude Catholics from the Succession, but declined to regard her title to the Crown as primarily a Parliamentary one. As a matter of fact, neither the Electress nor the Elector was much edified by the embassy of Halifax. He submitted to her a list of twenty-one persons, whom according to the Regency Act she was called upon to appoint as Lords Justices, in addition to the great officers of the Crown, for carrying on the government after Queen Anne's death in the event of her own absence from England. Of these twenty-one names, as it afterwards appeared, she struck out seven, one of which was that of Halifax himself.[1] As to the titles

[1] It was said that, when, after the death of Sophia, it fell to the Elector, her son, to substitute his nominations of additional Lords Justices for hers, and the original document was accordingly produced in London, the cover enclosing it was found to have been broken open. It was further reported that, after much wrangling with her ministers, Queen Anne cut the

conferred upon the Electoral Prince (which, Sophia said, were so many that she had to write them down in her almanack lest she should forget them), the grant of an annual income to herself as Heiress Presumptive would have been more to the point ; inasmuch as the titles were given to enable the Prince to take his seat in Parliament, from which Hanover was a long way off.

The elements of satisfaction contained in the Acts brought to Hanover by Halifax were not over-estimated by the Electress, to whom it must by this time have become clear that the real difficulty in placing the House of Hanover in its proper position towards the country with which it was to be inseparably connected, lay with Queen Anne herself. More especially after the publication of Sir Rowland Gwynne's unfortunate letter, the Queen thought that explanations were due to her from the Electress, who in truth had none to give. Marlborough had been wise enough to abstain from delivering at Hanover a letter written by the Queen in this sense and entrusted by her to him, and, instead, had held conciliatory language, advising both Electress and Elector to declare themselves absolute strangers to the obnoxious manifesto. The advice was judicious ; for, as Marlborough

discussion short by taking upon herself the blame of having opened the cover.

had predicted, the original proposal did not die
out.   In 1707, one Scott, an Englishman or Scotch-
man in the service of the Elector, entered, according
to Marlborough with the cognisance of the Electress,
into a negotiation with the High-fliers ; but he was
stopped by the Elector himself.   In July of the same
year, the Earl of Peterborough, when returning
to England from Spain to give an account of his
proceedings there, spent some days at Hanover and
Herrenhausen, where he addressed a letter to the
Elector and another to the Electress, in which he
insisted on the necessity of the residence of a
member of the Electoral House in England.   Sophia
handed the letter intended for herself to her son,
who, in the plainest terms, expressed his determination to take no steps in this direction, unless
with the approval of the Queen and her ministers.
Meanwhile, though perfectly prudent in her own
conduct, the Electress could not altogether conceal
the annoyance caused to her by the cold and suspicious attitude maintained by Queen Anne towards
everything connected with the Succession.   Sophia
complained repeatedly that from England came
nothing but titles and compliments, and declared
that she would not be made to pay for any more
special ambassadors from the Court of St. James.
(Her present of gold plate to Halifax had cost
her some 30,000 florins.)   For the conveyance of

honours that cost nothing she was, she said, perfectly content with Mr. Howe.[1] When Leibniz
reported to her as to prospects of the Union between
England and Scotland, which was actually achieved
early in 1707, she rather sharply replied that she
had no wish to discuss the affairs of either kingdom :
' *comme je n'en tire rien, je n'y suis point intéressée.*'
She can, however, hardly have been so indifferent
to the subject as she pretended to be ; since a
clause in the Act of Union definitively settled the
Scottish Succession upon herself and her descendants.
Nor can she have remained unaware that, as Queen
Anne's reign continued and the apprehensions
excited by the growing intolerance of the Church
of England more and more endangered the maintenance of the Union, Scottish Presbyterianism was,
irrespective of this consideration, obliged to look
to the Hanoverian Succession as the best guarantee
of its own security.

We know for certain that the Electress was well
informed as to the existence of a secret sympathy
on Queen Anne's part with the Pretender ; since
we have the explicit statement of the Duchess of

---

[1] Brigadier-General Emmanuel Scroope Howe was English
resident at Hanover from 1705 till his death in 1709.   He was,
as mentioned on a previous page, the husband of Ruperta,
Prince Rupert's daughter by Margaret Howes.   Ruperta seems
herself to have helped to embroil matters by writing some highly
indiscreet letters to England, in which she dwelt on the apathy
of the House of Hanover towards the Succession.

Orleans that her aunt believed the Queen to be secretly desirous of the accession of her half-brother, and further believed ' that she would some day bestow the Crown upon him.' Nor can we regard the latter clause a mere phrase, when we remember the earlier communications in this sense between Anne and her exiled father. But it by no means follows from this that this solution was one desired by the Electress Sophia herself. According to a fairly well authenticated anecdote, a bundle of letters was, some time in the reign of George III, found in Kensington Palace, endorsed in William III's own handwriting ' *Letters of the Electress Sophia to the Court of St. Germains* ' ; and a plan which had been formed for publishing these letters was frustrated through their being destroyed by George III's orders. But as to the contents of these letters there is no satisfactory evidence at all. Again, it is no doubt true, and of a piece with George I's habitual method of dealing with inconvenient evidence, that, in 1714, he requested the Duchess of Orleans to destroy all the letters received by her from the Electress which contained any reference to the House of Stewart ; and, though the Duchess of Orleans, who made no secret of her own sympathies, and whose portrait quite appropriately found a place in the Stewart family museum at Caillot, says that her aunt did not obey this wish, no such letters have been found, with a single exception.

In this letter, dated March 21st, 1708, after mentioning that the ' Prince of Wales ' was at Dunkirk
(whence he afterwards started on his brief expedition to Scotland), the Electress Sophia indulges in
the reflexion : ' Who knows whether God will not
elevate him who suffers so innocently ? ' But
though, in matters concerning the line from which
she was descended, as well as with regard to her own
immediate family, Sophia's nature was very far
from being untouched by sentiment, she never
allowed herself to be subdued by it. In her tenderness of feeling towards the House of Stewart she set an
example followed by the Hanoverian dynasty when
in possession of the British throne—from George I
downwards, of whose kindliness of feeling towards
the exiled House instances might easily be cited.[1]

Thus, in this period Sophia returned to Queen
Anne coolness for coolness, and though at times she
might almost have seemed to herself indifferent to
her prospects and those of her posterity, while at
other times she thought of herself as ' a candidate
for Sion ' rather than as the heiress to a throne, she
was content to avoid any false step, and to leave
unjeopardised a future which she could not control.

---

[1] The same feeling notably descended to George III, who
granted an ' apanage ' to the Cardinal of York in his last years ;
to George IV, who as Prince Regent provided a solemn sepulture
for the remains of James II, and erected a monument to the last
of his descendants ; and, as is well known, to the last and most
illustrious sovereign of the Hanoverian dynasty.

As late as September, 1708, in mentioning the visit of
Lord Hereford and two Whig M.P.s, she writes that
she found them very warm for the Succession, and
that she supposed they would always continue of the
same mind, so long as it paid them ; at present it did
not seem to pay *her*, for she was not treated as its
Princess of Wales. But, in the course of this year,
the Whigs were fully established in power ; and,
when the death, in the autumn, of Prince George of
Denmark, together with the subsequent refusal of
Queen Anne to remarry, had removed the last
possibility of issue from the reigning sovereign, the
Hanoverian prospects of course grew brighter. The
House stood well at this season in the eyes of Europe
and of England. George Lewis' envoy at Ratisbon
in this very year at last gained admittance into the
Electoral College ; and in the previous year (1707)
the Elector had assumed the command of the army
of the Lower Rhine, though his unswerving loyalty
to the cause of the Grand Alliance had met with an
incomplete response of confidence on the part of its
military leaders. Courtiers and others cultivating
a consciousness of coming events began to recognise
the necessity of turning their faces towards the rising
sun. Mrs. Charles Howard, for instance, had the
honour of being (with her husband) presented to the
Electress Dowager, and of receiving particular notice,
both from her and from the Electoral Princess—as
one of whose bed-chamber women she was in later

days to play so conspicuous a part at the British Court. But Queen Anne persisted in the attitude which she had assumed, and in the autumn of this year frankly told Lord Haversham that she could not tolerate the notion of the presence in this country of any successor, even were it to last no longer than a week.

When the approach of the great ministerial crisis of 1710 first announced itself by the dismissal of Sunderland, the Elector was moved to perhaps the most distinct expression of political opinion in British affairs to which he committed himself at any time before his accession to the throne. In a spirited re-monstrance addressed by him to the Queen, he gave words to the hope that she would enter into no further changes in the present Ministry and Parlia-ment. The Electress in the meantime remained mistress of herself ; and George Lewis followed her example, when the crisis reached its height, and the wheel of fortune once more brought the Tories upper-most. Neither Sophia nor her confidential counsellor Leibniz looked with fear or even with disfavour upon the transactions which seemed to have put a new face on the entire scheme of British State policy. The leading spirit of the new combination was Robert Harley, who possessed many valuable political qualities, but who was above all a born intriguer. The moderation of his conduct was set off by his personal merits, among which, in a brilliant literary age, his genuine love of literature was by no means the least important.[1]   Leibniz, whose own political influence at Hanover had of late visibly declined, was much gratified by the marked civility shown to him by one of his London correspondents, Dr. Hutton, a follower of Harley.

Queen Anne herself lost no time in communicating to the House of Hanover her own view of the political changes which opened the concluding period of her reign.   In the autumn of 1710, Earl Rivers (by whose appointment to the constableship of the Tower these changes had been heralded) made his appearance at Hanover.   His personal reputation was far from immaculate ; but he had been a successful general.   At the time of his arrival at Hanover, Sunderland's dismissal had been succeeded by no further ministerial changes.   That Queen Anne should not have resented the protest against this step transmitted by the Elector through Bothmer at the Hague, indicates her hesitancy in the process.   But, when a further series of ministerial changes had been accomplished in England, Rivers, who had made himself very acceptable at Hanover even to the Elector, began to develop the ulterior purpose of his mission.   Unmistakably, it was intended to facilitate the overthrow of Marlborough, without   which   these   changes   would   remain

[1] The latest tribute to it is the conjecture crediting him with the original authorship of *Robinson Crusoe*.

incomplete, by putting the Elector in his place as commander-in-chief in the war, which, as Rivers assured him, the new British Government intended to carry on with undiminished vigour. The ambassador was instructed to state that the Queen could no longer suffer the insolence of those whom she had raised to the highest pitch of power and authority. But, before Rivers reached the Electoral Court, Marlborough had already conveyed to George Lewis assurances of his fidelity to the Hanoverian Succession ; and the House of Hanover was thus confirmed in the attitude of caution which it maintained in this very trying turn of affairs. There was no reason why Elector and Electress should remain deaf to the blandishments of the well-affected and reasonable Tories, whose theory of the Succession harmonised with Sophia's own. But, at the same time, it would have been not less unwise to court the goodwill of the Queen and her new ministers by cutting communications with Marlborough and the Whigs, than it would have been to yield to the Whig proposal, communicated through Robethon, to base the claims of the House of Hanover on the principles of the Revolution of 1688. Leibniz was able to demonstrate the perfect consistency of the course pursued by the House he served ; and the firmness and prudence with which the Elector resisted perhaps the single temptation which, in the whole course of these

transactions, he personally found it hard to with-
stand—the offer of the supreme command in the
war—deserves a fuller recognition than has usually
been accorded to it.

The final period in the history of the Hanoverian
Succession—though even during this period the
question had, as will be seen, still to pass through
a series of stages before it was solved—began with
the transformation of the British Ministry into a
Tory Government, and the overthrow of the Marlborough influence, which, with that of Godolphin, had
so long cast its spell over Queen Anne.   During the
last month or two of 1710,[1] Schütz having died in
the previous August, Bothmer was performing the
duties of envoy extraordinary in London, where he
remained till the following March.   The Electress
was extremely desirous that he should, unlike
Schütz and Kreyenberg, refrain from showing any
inclination towards either of the political parties ;
here in Hanover, she assured him in January, 1711,
' we do not know the meaning of the terms Whig
and Tory, and decline to distinguish individuals
under those names ' ; and she applauds him for
having already, as she hears, managed to create a
far more agreeable impression than that made by
his predecessor.   But this attempt on the part of
the Electress to hold the balance between the two

[1] The Electress wishes him a happy voyage on October 29th.

parties, and to make Bothmer do the same, could not be of long endurance. On April 17th, 1711, the Emperor Joseph I died ; there could be no reasonable doubt as to the succession of his brother, the titular King Charles III of Spain, to the Imperial throne ; and an irresistible impulse was given to the desire for peace, with which the new British Ministry was known to be in sympathy.

Henceforth, until the Peace had been actually concluded, the question of its conclusion dominated all others, and that of the Succession among the rest. It might suit the purposes of the Whigs, who were opposed to the Peace, to represent the desire of bringing it about as put forward with a view to covering Jacobite designs with regard to the Succession ; as a matter of fact, the Tory leaders, though they might amuse Berwick—or others who were as ignorant of England as he was—with proposals about bringing over the Pretender to reside in England on his half-sister's invitation, were very careful not to allow any premature Jacobite outbreak to interrupt the peace negotiations. When, in October, 1711, Bothmer returned to London as envoy extraordinary, the situation had, for better or for worse, cleared up ; and it would have been impossible for the most skilful of diplomatists, with the strongest wish to carry out the conciliatory intentions cherished by the good Electress, to avoid an early collision with the Queen's ministers, and, in consequence, to place in his own way an insuperable obstacle against securing her own good-will. For the Elector was, heart and soul, in favour of the continuance of the war ; and the immediate purpose of Bothmer's present mission was to over-throw the peace policy to which the Queen's ministers had made up their minds. He brought with him an elaborate memorandum from the Elector, dated November 28th, 1711, against the conclusion of peace with France ; and in January, 1712, this memorandum was supported by a letter from the Elector asking for a hearing for his envoy. These documents were presented to the Queen on February 14th. As a matter of course, they were ascribed by the ministerialists to Whig influence, and repre-sented as implying an attempt to bring about the continuance of Marlborough in the command. There was no warrant for either asumption ; and it may be added that the Electress instructed Bothmer to express to Ormonde, as a tried friend of hers, the particular gratification with which she had heard of his appointment.

Violent altercations in Parliament ensued ; and Bothmer clearly perceived that any attempt to renew at present the proposal of inviting over the Electress and the Electoral Prince, if not the Elector himself, could have no other effect than that of uniting with the Jacobite wing of the Tory party the followers of Harley, with whom it was a cardinal principle to 'use the Queen with all duty and respect imaginable.' On the representations of Bothmer, Somers, Sunderland, and Godolphin agreed not to move in the matter without the Elector's assent ; and this was sure not to be given, until an invitation should have been approved by Queen and Parliament. Thus a blunder was avoided which must have proved more disastrous to the prospects of the House of Hanover than that actually committed three years later.

Both in 1710 and 1711 the air was full of more or less unsubstantial schemes for bringing about, at what already seemed the eleventh hour, the succession of the Pretender ; and rumours were rife as to the gradual transformation of the Ministry into a Jacobite Cabal. Though Leibniz was no doubt right in saying that the question of inviting to England, or (as the Electress so consistently repeated) of granting an income to, one or more members of the Electoral family, was the touch-stone of the real intentions of the British Government, and though this may, as he asserts, have also been the opinion of the Elector, yet there was no question at Hanover of claiming any such concession. In April, 1711, the Electress declared herself wholly uncertain of what would happen even in the event of Queen Anne's death—for ' what Parliament does one day, it undoes the next.' Thus, when, in the autumn of the same year, Lord Rivers made his second appearance at Hanover, the letter which he brought with him from Queen Anne, and his assurances of her care for the interests of the Electoral family, were received by Sophia with proper expressions of gratitude, whatever she might privately say as to the expense which this mission entailed upon the Hanoverian Court, with little prospect of return. There was, indeed, some talk of the Elector being offered the chief command in Flanders after Marlborough's dismissal in December, 1711; but nothing came of the suggestion, and in January, 1712, the Electress is found expressing her satisfaction at the appointment of Ormonde, who had always been so friendly to her. But as to the main object of his mission Rivers completely failed; for George Lewis firmly declined to give his approval to the British overtures of peace to France, at the risk of deeply annoying the Queen and her ministers by thus falling in with the wishes of the Whigs. He took his stand on the principles of the Grand Alliance, from which he had never swerved; while his mother judiciously held the balance by refusing to accept the insinuations of her correspondent at the Hague, Lord Strafford, against the inclinations of her House and Bothmer towards the Whigs, and appealing with much dignity to her conviction that, beyond the devices of Whigs and Tories, the Protestant Succession could depend on the support of the nation. Meanwhile, the two parties were alike striving to apprise the Hanoverian Court of the direction in which to look for its friends. The anxiety of the Whigs to identify their party with the Electoral House is at the same time proved by the motion of the Duke of Devonshire to give precedence to the Duke of Cambridge over other Peers.[1] The Ministry overtrumped this modest effort by a Bill giving precedence to the entire Electoral family, which was passed in two days (January, 1712), and which the minister's kinsman, Thomas Harley, was in July specially sent over to present to the Electress. She took the announcement of this new visit very coolly, regretting the expense to which she was put by it, and observing that, if the British throne were for sale, France on behalf of its client could afford the purchase better than the House of Hanover, which had no intention of imitating the prodigality of Augustus II of Poland.[2] Her instinct was correct, for Thomas Harley had instructions which, while pretending to put the blame on Bothmer, seriously reflected on the

[1] He had been created a Knight of the Garter in 1706, but not installed till December, 1710, Lord Halifax acting as his proxy.

[2] À *propos* of the mention of this sovereign it may be noted that about this time Queen Anne thought fit to impose upon the Electress the task (specially disagreeable because she specially disliked him) of dissuading King Augustus from forcing his son and namesake to follow him into the Church of Rome. Augustus II actually promised Queen Anne to send his son to England ; but in the meantime the latter had been received into the Catholic Church at Bologna.

Elector's opposition to the peace policy pursued by the British Government. In the course of the negotiations carried on at Paris in August, 1712, between Torcy and Bolingbroke, the latter on one occasion even went so far as to hint at the despatch of a British fleet into the Baltic, with a view not only to controlling the northern troubles, but also to frustrating possible designs on the part of the Dutch *and of Hanover.*[1]

Meanwhile the Court of Hanover, while maintaining unchanged its attitude towards the general question of war or peace, had immediate interests of its own to watch besides such as might be involved in the question of the English Succession. The recognition of the Hanoverian Electorship, for instance, was demanded from France, *pari passu* with that of the Prussian Kingship. Early in the year, in the negotiations already in progress, Bothmer, whom Oxford and Bolingbroke persisted in treating as antagonistic to their Government,[2] returned to his post at the Hague. In December, 1712, Baron Thomas von Grote, who belonged to a family of high distinction in the

---

[1] O. Weber, *Der Friede von Utrecht*, p. 313.

[2] Bolingbroke hated Bothmer, and described him as, ' notwithstanding that air of coldness and caution which he wore, the most inveterate party man that I ever saw, and the most capable of giving *tête baissée* into the most extravagant measures that faction could propose.' (Cf. Salomon, p. 239, and note.)

Hanoverian service, arrived in London, nominally
with the special charge of returning thanks for the
Act of Precedence. His instructions, drawn up by
Robethon in the name of the Electress Sophia,
illustrate the penultimate stage in the final period
of the transactions concerning the Succession. He
was to be polite to all, and not to consider himself
debarred from taking counsel with the old friends
of the House—in other words, with Marlborough
and the Whig leaders—so long as this was done
privately and secretly ; and he was to avoid giving
umbrage to the Queen's ministers, and above all to
the Queen herself. The Elector furnished him with
a special commendatory letter to Oxford. He was
to make friends with the clergy, and to reassure
them by pointing out that the ecclesiastical system
of the German Lutherans was to all intents and
purposes an episcopal one. The everlasting delicate
question as to the summoning of the Electress or
another member of the Electoral family to England he was to treat as if this event might any
day come to pass ; and, at the same time, he
was to press for a proposal to Parliament on the
subject of an establishment—say at Somerset
House. The Elector, while of opinion that such
a proposal would furnish the best means of testing
the sincerity of the Queen's and her advisers' intentions, declined to influence Parliamentary opinion
by means of any expenditure of his own, though it

would seem that he had previously not objected
to Bothmer's attempting to gain over some noble
Lords against the Peace by similar inducements.
But, though he still abstained from any intervention
in British home affairs, his own instructions to
Grote were less carefully balanced than those of the
Electress, and left no doubt as to its being the
leading Whigs on whom he reckoned as the true
friends of the House of Hanover.

Both at Hanover and elsewhere, however, eager
friends of the dynasty advocated a more expeditious
procedure.   In September, 1712, the indefatigable
Leibniz submitted a scheme, concocted by busy
brains in London, for including the demand for
establishing the Electress in England among the
conditions of the Peace of Utrecht.   But, though
both in her correspondence, and in conversation
with Thomas Harley, she had given considerable
attention to the scheme, she ultimately declared
it impracticable.   The unsatisfactory action of
the English ministers in the matter of the Dutch
guarantee of the Hanoverian Succession had once
more rendered her diffident ; she was, she said, so
old that there was no reality in all her talk ; were
she younger, she added with a touch of her old
spirit, the sovereignty of England should not pass
by her.

The Peace of Utrecht, when actually concluded
in the spring of 1713, was in many respects

unsatisfactory to the Elector ; and as an Estate of the Empire, he must have been well content to withhold his signature from it. But it contained a very explicit recognition of the Hanoverian Succession by France and the other signatory Powers ; so that, in this respect at all events, Bothmer's exertions had been entirely successful. Yet the tone prevailing at court and in ministerial circles in London very imperfectly agreed with this result ; and in Hanover there was a growing disbelief in the sincerity of the sentiments entertained in these quarters. Grote found himself coolly received, and his attempts to obtain assurances baffled. Various suggestions offered by him were ignored ; and in a lengthy despatch which he sent home in February (a few weeks before his death) he drew the darkest picture of the political situation which had as yet reached Hanover. He considered that, in spite of the generalities in which Oxford shrouded himself, he had gradually gone over to the Jacobites in order to please the Queen, while Bolingbroke he regarded as an open Jacobite on his own account. He thought that, as to the Pretender, there was reason for fearing the worst; he had heard that the Queen had expressed a wish to see her half-brother in England after the conclusion of the Peace, while the question of inviting over a member of the Electoral family had been indefinitely postponed. Part of this report sufficiently tallies with the information with which about this time the Pretender was being constantly supplied by his illegitimate half-brother, the Duke of Berwick. Though sanguine as to methods of action, Berwick never minimised the chances of the Hanoverian Succession ; the first thing requisite, he wrote to James in November, 1712, was to checkmate Hanover ; the rest could then be easily accomplished without mentioning the name of the legitimate claimant.   Both Oxford and Bolingbroke, Berwick wrote in May, 1713, were heartily resolved to go forward ; in July, he reported them to be rather less ardent ; but these were mere fluctuations.   From all this it is tolerably clear that Oxford, in trying to deceive others, deceived himself.   Much of his political life had consisted in a successful endeavour to face both ways without laying himself open to the charge of double-dealing. He now persuaded himself that he was throwing dust in the eyes of the Elector and Electress and the friends of the Hanoverian Succession, while at the same time drawing as near to the Jacobite projects as safety permitted.   He was, above all things, a Parliamentary statesman, and nothing but the decision of Parliament would determine his ultimate choice of sides ; but, as the majority was at present constituted, while the great achievement of the Peace assured the advance of Tory ascendancy, and the Queen seemed less and less inclined to re-concile herself to the Succession of the House of

Hanover, he looked to the triumph of the Jacobite cause as the event towards which his course would be most safely shaped. With Bolingbroke, the case was wholly different. Oxford was prepared to be in the end guided by the Parliamentary majority ; Bolingbroke was prepared to educate it up to that end—only he used a more sportsmanlike phraseology. For himself, he made no secret whatever of his likes and dislikes ; kept up a constant intercourse with Jacobites and Frenchmen ; and at times, as Grote complained, did him the honour of treating him ' *de coquin ou de fou.*' [1]

Meanwhile, the Queen and the Lord Treasurer continued their *banales* expressions of friendship and goodwill at Hanover, where, on March 17th, 1713, the useful Thomas Harley presented a letter from the Queen, declaring her intention of treating the interests of the House of Hanover as her own. But neither this letter, nor the amicable phrases with which in April she opened Parliament after its adjournment, evoked any warm response at Hanover. Sophia, indeed, wrote to Strafford at the Hague, begging him to thank the Queen, and adding that, as she had no expectation of ever ascending the throne herself, she hoped that Her Majesty would entertain no aversion to her on that score. But, as she told Bothmer, she only paid back Strafford in the coin she received from England—

[1] Salomon, *u.s.*, p. 223, from the Hanover Archives.

words, not deeds ; and, on the whole, Leibniz's
epigram not unaptly summed up the situation—

> *'Hannoverana domus magnâ me gaudet amicâ,'*
>   *Anna refert; tacita est Hannoverana domus.*

An attempt had been indeed made, or suggested, to
utilise the Queen's friendly expressions for a bold
venture on the part of the House of Hanover ; but
it had been still-born. After Grote's death in
March, Kreyenberg had carried on the affairs of
the Hanoverian Legation in London ; and reports
were also from time to time sent to Hanover by the
Dutch resident in London, L'Hermitage. In one
of these (dated May 9th, 1713) [1] the very important
proposal was made that the Electoral Prince should
come over to England on his own account, inasmuch
as the Queen would never send for him. The notion
found the utmost favour with the Whig leaders,
who knew how much depended on the issue of the
approaching election, and who hoped that it might
be influenced by so bold a step on the part of the
Hanoverian family. But Bernstorff, who was in
favour of the scheme and without whose persuasion
there was no prospect at all of the Elector approving
it, was ill at the time ; and, when he recovered, the
Elector was found to be entirely under the influence
of advice against action. An attempt to bring about
the repeal of the Union with Scotland was defeated,

[1] Printed in Macpherson, Vol. ii. pp. 792–3. See on this
transaction Salomon, *u.s.*, pp. 225 *sqq.*

without the question of the Hanoverian Succession playing more than a subsidiary part in the dispute.

When, in the following July, Parliament, after approving a number of the Treaties which formed the Peace of Utrecht,[1] was prorogued, on the eve of a General Election, the Queen's Speech significantly omitted the usual announcement of her readiness to support the Protestant Succession. While the versatile intellect of Leibniz was still devising new schemes for bringing about the desired result, the Elector adhered more closely than ever to his original policy. In August, 1713, Baron von Schütz the younger (George William Helwig Sinold), the son of the former envoy of the Court of St. James and the grandson of the Celle Chancellor, arrived in London as envoy. The choice of this agent was at the time unfavourably criticised by some of the Whigs, who thought that a politician of greater experience should have been selected. Sophia would not commit herself to Bothmer on the question whether Schütz would be better liked than her correspondent had been in England ; ' at all events,' she said, ' nobody will be attracted by his appearance ' (*il ne payera pas de mine*). We shall have to enquire immediately whether, in the great diplomatic catastrophe which befell him, the

---

[1] By composing the *Te Deum und Jubilate* for the celebration of the Peace at St. Paul's on July 7th, Handel gave great offence to the Hanoverian Court ; nor was he readmitted to favour till some little time after the accession of George I.

younger Schütz was himself deserving of blame. He was instructed by the Elector in the sense of an absolute abstinence from interference in British affairs. Even as to the question of inviting a member of the Electoral family to England he was to take up a distinctly negative position; but, at the same time, he was to treat as indispensable measures the removal of the Pretender from Lorraine and a provision for the Electress as Heiress Presumptive of Great Britain. The envoy's reports were far from encouraging, and his information as to the views and intentions of the Queen and her advisers again agrees with that transmitted by Berwick to the Pretender.

The tide of danger was unmistakably rising. Parliament was dissolved in August, 1713; and a proposal was on foot to bring to bear upon Queen Anne at the opening of the new Parliament the direct personal influence of the presence of her half-brother in England. In the attitude of Oxford and Bolingbroke no hopeful alteration occurred. In defiance of the manifest irritation of the Queen, the Elector coldly declared himself unsatisfied with the guarantees which he had so far received, and declined to sanction any expenditure on pamphlets or newspapers, or on more direct means of influencing elections or gaining over necessitous Peers. Yet, to the amusement of Sophia, whose sense of humour never deserted her, Hanover and Herrenhausen continued to attract not a few Englishmen desirous of being found in this vicinity at the critical moment. They were, however, she thought, reckoning without their host in hoping to strew palms before her on her entrance into London ; she feared that she could not contrive to live as long as Queen Anne, so as to prove to them her gratitude. And yet, when in the last days of the year Queen Anne herself fell ill, and the agitation in England was raised to an unprecedented pitch, it seemed as if, notwithstanding what Sophia described as her ' incurable malady of having passed her eighty-fourth year,' her repeated prediction that she would never herself mount the British throne would after all be falsified. In November she had herself been ill, suffering so seriously from an affection (erysipelas) to which she was subject, that fears were entertained for her life. But she soon recovered sufficiently to write to the Duchess of Orleans, and with her usual spirit she insisted on following the Elector to the Göhrde.

The situation was now coming to be one of a very high tension. On the one hand, Strafford, who never ceased from trying to persuade the Electress that the Tories were her friends, and that there was not a Jacobite left in the party, assured her that what he had observed during the Queen's illness had convinced him of the strength of popular opinion in England in favour of the Protestant

Succession.   And Steinghens, the Elector Palatine's
minister in London, who was on a footing of intimacy
with Oxford, declared to his correspondent, General
von der Schulenburg, that had Queen Anne died
during her illness the Princess Sophia would have
been proclaimed on the same day.   Assurances of
devotion poured in from every side ; in February,
Secretary Bromley laid himself at the Electress'
feet ; and Archbishop Dawes entreated attention
to his own humble endeavours and to the faithful-
ness and zeal of the whole body of the clergy.   On
the other hand, the demeanour and utterances of
those in power were not growing more propitious as
the new year came in.   Cautious as Oxford was in
his utterances, perhaps the most striking of all the
self-revelations reported of him at this critical time
was that which, in December, 1713, he made to the
Abbé Gaultier, according to the statement of the
latter to De Torcy : ' So long as I live, England
shall not be governed by a German.'   Except
through Gaultier, however, Oxford was inaccessible
on the subject, and though, in January, 1714, he
was said to have sent a private messenger to the
Pretender, in the following month Berwick heard
that the Lord Treasurer's intentions were still quite
unknown, and suggested to James to make sure of
the Queen and Bolingbroke by writing to them
himself.   Berwick's scheme of the Pretender coming
over to England in secret, so as to enable the Queen

to declare in his favour at the opening of Parliament, was quite visionary ; for Louis XIV was not inclined to make any move in his support, except by placing two men-of-war at Havre at his disposal ; and the Tory leaders were wholly intent upon removing, in the first instance, the insuperable obstacle to any chance of the Pretender's success by inducing him to come over—to the Church of England. As for Bolingbroke, who must have known that such a solution was not to be looked for, he seems to have been willing to depend on the double chance of something unexpected happening at the critical moment, and of the Hanoverian successor proving unable to maintain herself—or himself—on the throne even after mounting it. Thus, as the crisis drew nearer and nearer, the Tory leaders were becoming less and less prepared to meet it.[1]

And so it came to pass that, when, in February, 1714, the new Parliament met, with a Tory majority in the Commons outnumbering their opponents by at least two to one, the Queen's Speech could hardly have been more ambiguous in tone than it actually proved. She, like her ministers, had no wish for the House of Hanover, and saw no present chance for the Stewarts. While, therefore, discrediting all reports

---

[1] These conclusions seem irresistible in view of the documents, especially the despatches of Ibberville, collected by Grimblot and reviewed by Salomon, *u.s.*, pp. 235–64.

implying that the Protestant Succession, as settled in the House of Hanover, was in danger, the Speech also referred to the attempts ' to weaken the Queen's authority or to render the possession of the Crown uneasy to her '—obviously alluding to the design of bringing over a member of the Electoral family. While Bolingbroke may have been prepared to make use of this design so as to bring about a complete rupture between the Queen and the House of Hanover, Oxford could not but directly oppose a step which would have forced the hands of the Government, and removed the ultimate use of the situation out of his own wary hands.   Yet nothing could have been more distinctly double-faced than his action in the early months of 1714.   He dangled before Schütz the offer of a revision of the Regency Bill of 1705, which was to enable the court of Hanover to name the whole body of Regents, but which also might have furnished an opportunity for giving the *quietus* to the entire Bill.   Not long afterwards, in March, he expressed his intention to bring in a Bill declaring the introduction of foreign troops into England an act of high treason.   But ' under which King,' or under what Government, could the foreign troops whose arrival was thus to be prevented have been levied ? [1]

---

[1] Salomon, *u.s.*, p. 272.   Klopp, vol. xiv. p. 540, gives a summary of the discussion of Oxford's announcement from the Lords' Debates.

Though the calculated untrustworthiness of Oxford, and the reckless speculativeness of Bolingbroke, had by this time become as much of an open secret as had the consuming desire of the Secretary of State to supplant the Lord Treasurer, there was even now no disposition on the part of the court of Hanover to commit itself by any rash act. There had never been any real divergence of policy between the Electress and her son, the Elector, though his consistency of conduct had perhaps been the more formally complete, and we cannot follow him, as we can the Electress, in his private comments on the angular points which from time to time presented themselves in the situation. Now, they were more than ever at one in their determination to abstain from precipitate action. Robethon's memorandum of *Reasons for not sending the Electoral Prince to England* (January, 1714), whether or not the Elector's dislike of his son had anything to do with the conclusions reached, reiterated the old objection of the Electress to a course which would appear to be dictated by a desire to gratify the Whigs by offending the Tories, instead of uniting the moderate men of both parties in support of the Succession. Sophia had, by this time, come to have so little faith in either of the English political parties that, as she told Strafford, she disliked the very names of Whig and Tory ; and, as an octogenarian, she was inevitably indisposed to run any great personal risk or court any serious personal change. She gave Schulenburg to understand that she would never consent to proceed to England without the Elector. Yet neither she nor her son, who might be depended upon not to start for England a day too soon, affected indifference towards the Succession ; and even on the question of sending the Electoral Prince to England, there were signs that, in deference to Bothmer's advice, this course might after all be adopted, so soon as the Emperor should have concluded his peace with France.[1] It is no doubt in this connexion that, in the very last letter to Leibniz preserved from the hand of the Electress Sophia—which bears the date of May 20th, 1714 (N.S.)—she refers to a step which, as we shall see, she had just taken, and which Queen Anne had chosen to regard as a provocation offered to herself.

We must go back for a moment to the previous month of April, in which the relations between Queen Anne and the House of Hanover seemed to have become rather easier. Had she and her advisers—Oxford in particular—gained some special insight into the fundamental weakness of the Jacobite position ? Though the secret was open enough, one is almost inclined to some conclusion of the kind, in view of a communication from Berwick

---

[1] Bothmer to Robethon, January 2nd, 1714. (Cited by Salomon, *u.s.*, p. 232, from the Stowe MSS. in Brit. Mus.)

to James, dated April 11th, which describes the
situation so lucidly that it seems worth while to
extract from it the following passage (substituting
real names for the transparent pseudonyms) :—

I discours'd de Torcy about the King [James]'s
resolution to be taken in case Queen Anne should
break. I find he knows not what to advise; and in
truth it is to be wish'd one could have some newse of
Ormonde [now Commander-in-chief], and see what
disposition the Parliament will be in, before one comes
to a positive determination. The point is very nice ;
on one side it would look odd in the world that King
James should see the Elector of Hannover quietly gett
Queen Anne's throne without making the least opposition ; on the other side to beginn an expedition there
must be money, provision of arms, and all many other
things which I fear the King [James] wants, besides
that there can be no hopes of success unless one can
gett some officers of the army. A great many of the
Scotch will oppose the business and 'tis much feared
the Highlanders will have but very small means for so
great an undertaking. The Elector has actually the
law for him; the United Provinces are engaged to
support him; the Kings of France and Spain have
promis'd not to meddle in it; and I find the English
[i.e. the English friends of the King] so very slow and
cautious that 'tis much to be doubted their giving
any helping hand.

Not long afterwards, Berwick had no better
advice to give his royal kinsman, than that he
should keep his own counsel as to the point on which
he had made up his mind, and not allow his friends
in England to think the desired consummation (his

adoption of the Protestant faith) an event altogether
out of the question.   When the signs of the times
seemed so unpromising to those who watched them
with the most direct and personal interest, and
when, as to the problem on which chances mainly
turned, they could only advise a policy of temporis-
ing and dissimulation, Oxford may well have been
more desirous than ever to safeguard his own
future by seeking to maintain a good understanding
with the other side.   In this month of April, he is
accordingly found tendering assurances not only
of his own devotion, but also of Lady Masham's, to
the Hanoverian Succession, and declaring his conviction that the Queen was for it ; though, as
towards her, he again guarded himself by deprecating
the establishment of a second Court in England.
About the same time, his kinsman Thomas Harley
again arrived at Hanover, with a letter from the
Queen to the Electress, blandly enquiring whether
there was anything which in her judgment would
further secure the Succession of her House.   Should
she have no suggestion of further guarantees to
offer, this would be taken as implying that the
existing guarantees were regarded as sufficient.
At the same time, the House of Hanover was warned
against giving any encouragement, directly or
indirectly, to a faction which was working for its
own advantage only.   Harley brought no message
from the Queen inviting any member of the House

to England ; and the above-mentioned enquiry, as Bolingbroke's comments on it to Strafford implied, suggested a defiance rather than an invitation. He was specifically instructed to offer her on the part of the Queen an annuity (*pension*) for herself ; but this the Electress, with her usual quickness of insight, declined. The revenue desired by her was, she said, one that should be granted to her in due form as Heiress Presumptive by Queen and Parliament, in accordance with the precedent of the allowance made to Queen Anne herself, when Princess of Denmark in the preceding reign. Either before or after the Electress sent this reply —on May 7th—both she and the Elector attached their signatures to a formal answer to the enquiry brought by Thomas Harley. In this important memorandum they reiterated the view which had been expressed in Schütz's instructions, that the Succession could not be held to be really assured unless an end were put to the danger of invasion by the Pretender by his being made to leave his present residence in Lorraine, and that it was desirable to secure a revenue to the Electress by Act of Parliament. They further declared it to be desirable that a member of the House of Hanover should be established in England, in order to watch over the important interests at issue. There can be no doubt but that the Electoral Prince was the member of the family whom the memorandum had

in view. The document was signed and sealed by
both the Elector and the Electress ; and a covering
letter from the former to the Queen thanked her in
the most conciliatory tone for her continued care for
the Protestant Succession. This memorandum,
for which the Elector was directly responsible in
conjunction with his mother, takes the bottom out
of the supposition that he was at this time ready,
if he could do so with honour, to relinquish his
claims.

But before the memorandum was actually
transmitted, a cold blast had suddenly blown
athwart the relations between the House of Hanover
and Queen Anne. In the ordinary course of things
the Electoral Prince, as Duke of Cambridge, would
have, like any other English Peer, received his
writ of summons to attend the Queen in Parliament.
Aware, however, of her sensitiveness on the subject
of the presence of a member of the Hanoverian
family in England, the Lord Chancellor (Lord
Harcourt) had thought proper to delay indefinitely
the issue of the writ. The demand for it had
originally been suggested to Schütz by the Earl
of Nottingham, who, though a High Church Tory,
had long broken with the court ; and, though an
attempt to obtain the writ from the Lord Chancellor
made at the instigation of the Whig Lord Cowper
had failed, Schütz had naturally felt uneasy at its
issue being delayed. When, in a letter to him, the

Electress Sophia had given vent to her astonishment at the fact that the patent of the Duke of Cambridge had not been in due course followed by a writ, and had expressed her opinion that the Lord Chancellor would not object to Schütz's '*asking for it and the reason*' (of the delay), he had interpreted this expression of opinion as a command. The Whig leaders, including the Duke of Somerset, to whom Schütz had shown the Electress' ' order,' had, according to his own account, been delighted with it, and had approved of his proposal to take action upon it. In the Electress' letter to Leibniz of May 20th, already mentioned, she explicitly states, not, as Schütz puts it, that she had ' ordered the writ,' but that she had directed him to enquire from the Lord Chancellor whether the Electoral Prince ought not to receive it—which is not quite the same thing. But her letter to Schütz, on which the whole matter turns, cannot be said to be ambiguous, or to allow of any interpretation but that put upon it by him.[1] Even if it be the case that the memoranda of Hoffmann, the

---

[1] It seems necessary to quote the actual text of this much-vext letter : ' *Je vous prie de dire à Monsieur le chancelier Mylord Harcourt qu'on est fort étonné ici qu'on n'a pas envoyé un writ à mon petit-fils le prince électoral pour pouvoir entrer au parlement comme duc de Cambridge, comme cela lui est dû par la patente que la reine lui a donnée. Comme il a toujours été de mes amis aussi bien que son cousin, je crois qu'il ne trouvera pas mauvais que vous le lui demandiez et la raison.*' (*Briefe der Kurfürstin Sophie an Hannoversche Diplomaten*, p. 213.)

Imperial resident at the Court of St. James', imply that, so far as he knew, there was no intention at Hanover of actually demanding the writ till the meeting of the next Parliament, this would not make it necessary to place a forced interpretation upon the Electress' letter, with which in any case the Elector had no concern, and which can hardly have referred to the next Parliament, when the present was little more than two months old. The Hanoverian court had been pressed both by Marlborough and by Prince Eugene (who never believed in a policy of masterly inaction) to do what it could to obtain a summons for the Electoral Prince, and the Electress is known to have had this matter at heart, while the Elector's feelings towards his son made him from first to last averse to carrying it into execution.

Schütz, who, it must be remembered, was accredited from the Electress as well as from the Elector, had acted in accordance with his instructions; but he can hardly be acquitted of precipitancy, and of an excessive readiness to listen to the opinion of the Whig leaders before assuring himself of the approval of the Elector. In any case, the die had now been cast. Harcourt had replied that the writ was quite ready, but that it was not customary for Peers to demand their writ except when on the spot; he would, however, mention the subject to the Queen. The Cabinet, summoned

to deal with the envoy's demand, decided that
the writ could not be refused, though, according
to Gaultier's information, Bolingbroke had supported the Queen's opinion in favour of refusing it.
On April 17th, it was handed to Schütz by the Lord
Chancellor, or in accordance with his orders. Being
requested to state by whom he had been directed to
demand the writ, Schütz seems to have mentioned
the name of the Electress ; but this is not attested
by evidence at first hand. Schütz was speedily
informed by Oxford that he would do well not to
show himself at Court, and was afterwards formally
prohibited from appearing there ; but, as a matter
of course, there was no question whatever of breaking
off diplomatic relations, these being carried on for the
time by Kreyenberg. Presently—on April 22nd—
the envoy took his departure. On his arrival at
Hanover, the Elector made a point of declining to
receive Schütz ; censured him for having obeyed
any orders but the Elector's ; and told Thomas
Harley, who, before taking his departure from
Hanover, waited on him, with his whole *posse* of
Englishmen, that Schütz had never been instructed
to demand the writ, and that he (the Elector) had
never intended to send his son to England without
the knowledge of the Queen. This formula may
perhaps be reconcilable with the information given
by Robethon to Lord Polwarth,[1] according to which

[1] Lord Polwarth, eldest son of the Earl of Marchmont and
member for Berwick-on-Tweed (who afterwards became an

the Elector, though he knew nothing about the demand for the writ, would have sent the Electoral Prince to England in the end, had it not been for the Queen's letter to be mentioned immediately, which ' changed the entire system.' There seems to have been a good deal of feeling at Hanover—a feeling shared both by the Whig leaders in England and by Bothmer at the Hague—that, the writ having been now secured, the Electoral Prince should be sent over. But this the Elector refused to do ; and the success with which he had thus kept out of the whole of this transaction—the single wrong move made on the Hanoverian side in the whole course of the game—must be placed to the credit of his judgment, whatever course he may have intended to take at a later date. But how far both he and the Electress were from being intimidated by the displeasure of the Queen, is shown by the fact that at Thomas Harley's farewell audience the Elector placed in his hands the outspoken memorandum signed by the Electress and himself on May 7th. As for Sophia, the tone of her letter to Leibniz containing a narrative of the entire trans- action is perfectly cool ; and in it she as usual expresses the belief that, in spite of her recent illness, Queen Anne will outlive her Heiress Pre- sumptive, and cites the proverb, ' *krakende Wagens*

intimate friend of Bolingbroke), had kept up a correspondence with the court of Hanover since his visit there in 1712.

gân lang.[1]   Her reply to Strafford's letter entreating
her to signify her disapproval of Schütz's action
is unfortunately lost, though its purport was said
to have been the same as that of the Elector's
parting declaration to Thomas Harley.   The situation seemed far less terrific at Hanover than
it did in London, where the Queen's wrath was
visibly ablaze, so that the House of Commons
deferred voting payment of the arrears due to the
Hanoverian troops, and where it was believed that
if the Electoral Prince were after all sent over an
invitation to the Pretender would follow.   Moreover (though this is a matter into which it is impossible to enter here), the opposite views taken
by Oxford and Bolingbroke as to the final issue
of the writ undoubtedly helped materially to hasten
the fleeting triumph of the younger over the older
minister.

From what has been said it will appear how
greatly the facts of the case are exaggerated and
distorted in the tradition attributing the death of
the Electress Sophia, which took place at Herrenhausen on June 8th, 1714, to the agitation caused by
the letter addressed to her by Queen Anne in connexion with the affair of the writ, and accompanied
by two letters from the Queen on the same subject

---

[1] I do not know whether anything on the subject is mentioned in the fifteen letters from Sophia to Lady Colt, said to
range from 1681 to May 15th, 1714, and to have been sold by
auction in 1905.

to the Elector and the Electoral Prince. Undeniably,
the Queen's letter to the Electress Sophia, though
taking a less severe form of reprimand than the companion missive to the Electoral Prince, was both
offensive and insolent ; for Queen Anne, who (with
the exception of the Prayer-book Order) had taken
no step towards admitting the Electress and her
descendants into the royal family, could not lay
claim to any formal authority over them.   That
this view was widely taken of the letters may be
gathered from the fact that Boyer (Swift's ' Whig
dog '), who had been taken into custody on a warrant from Bolingbroke for publishing them, was,
a few months after the accession of George I,
discharged—so that their publication was evidently
regarded as having proved serviceable towards that
result.   Nor was the effect of the letters likely to be
mitigated by the honeyed protestations of Oxford,
whose system of procedure the letters almost hopelessly traversed, in a communication to the Elector
accompanying them.   The sharp wit of the Electoral Princess Caroline suspected that it was not
he, but Bolingbroke, who was their draughtsman ;
and there can be little or no doubt as to the correct-
ness of this surmise.   It cannot but have been shared
by the old Electress, and must have contributed
to make her stand firm against a blow contrived
by an all but avowed adversary of the lawful claims
of herself and her House.

Yet there can be no doubt that at the time the death of the Electress Sophia was very generally connected with, if not directly attributed to, the advent of the Queen's letters. The very straightforward account transmitted to Marlborough by Molyneux, who had been sent to Hanover by the Duke to counteract the effects of Thomas Harley's mission, shows the Electress to have been much agitated on the evening of the day (Wednesday, June 6th) on which, about noon, the letters had been delivered to her at Herrenhausen. On the following day, though Molyneux was told she was not well, she ordered him to send copies of the letters to Marlborough ; [1] on Friday, June 8th, she seemed well, but was still occupied with the subject and ordering fresh copies of the letters ; she dined with the Elector, and in the evening was, according to her habit, walking in the gardens, when rain suddenly fell. As she quickened her speed in order to find a shelter, she dropped down and rapidly passed away. The letters of the Countess of Bückeburg [2] to the Electress' niece and constant companion during the last fifteen years, the Raugravine Louisa, corroborates this account, and

[1] It was through these copies that the letters seem afterwards to have become known.

[2] This appears to have been the Countess Johanna von der Lippe-Bückeburg, who, on being divorced from her husband, was besieged by him in her residence at Stadthagen near Bückeburg, from which he thought himself entitled to expel her. She appears to have been a welcome visitor at Herrenhausen, where she told the story of this siege ' *fort joliment*.'

adds one or two significant touches.   On the Wednesday the Electress said to the writer of the letter :
' This affair will certainly make me ill—I shall never
get over it' (*j'y succombrai*).   ' But,' she added, ' I
shall have this gracious letter printed, so that all
the world may see that it will not have been by
my fault, if my children lose the three Kingdoms.'
And, on the Friday, though to all appearance in
her usual strength, she continued to talk of English
affairs with the Electoral Princess.   And, since the
Electoral Princess Caroline herself informed Leibniz,
on June 7th, that the Electress and the Electoral
Prince intended to send the Queen's letters to
England, it may be concluded that this high-
spirited but rather venturesome design still further
excited the old lady.   Although the outer world
had continued to believe her to be as full of
vigour as ever, she had of late begun to take
some thought of her health—a notable sign, inasmuch as ordinarily she set no high value on medical
advice, being of opinion that no doctor can pre-
dict anything with certainty except that a person
who died in February will not be ill in March.   Probably, she was aware of the tendency to apoplexy
which, already thirteen years earlier, her faithful
friend Leibniz had observed in her.   On the whole,
the natural conclusion appears to be that the agitation produced in her by the Queen's letters, together with her own resolution not to sit still

under the affront, contributed to the collapse
of a frame enfeebled by advanced old age, but
that this trouble was the occasion rather than the
cause of her decease. For her epitaph seems to
tell the truth when, in perfect agreement with the
Countess of Bückeburg's statement that 'never
was there seen a death more gentle or more
happy,' it describes the Electress' death as having
been not less peaceful than sudden. Her character
lies almost open to us in her private letters, and, as
she told Leibniz in April, 1713, she had made it a
principle to keep her mind tranquil, and not to
allow it to be affected by either public or private
troubles. As to her death, she had written to him
a little later, it would no doubt be a finer affair if,
in accordance with his wishes, her remains were
interred at Westminster ; 'but the truth is that
my mind, which hitherto has managed to rule my
body, at present suggests no such sad thoughts to
me, and that the talk about the Succession annoys
me.' Read in the way in which so many of her
letters ought to be read, as half-ironical, the
words just quoted attest the self-control and self-
possession that were on the whole the most
noteworthy features in the character of this remarkable woman. But neither this passage, nor
anything else that remains from her hand, con-
tradicts the belief which is derived from a review
of her entire career, that from first to last she

proved herself equal to the responsibilities of her life, and that, had she been actually called to the throne, she would have been not less ready than worthy to reign as a Queen.

We possess a minute official account of the proceedings after the Electress Sophia's death—of the sealing-up of her personal effects by the Elector's orders ; of the embalming of the corpse, the night-watch over it, and its transportation on the evening of the following day to Hanover.[1] Unfortunately, the list of those who paid her the last honours at Herrenhausen does not include the names of the ladies and 'cavaliers' who had been in personal attendance upon her.[2] Her remains were deposited in the chapel of the royal palace—the old church of the Minorites—at Hanover, with proper care and decorum, but, as is formally stated, 'without ceremony,' i.e. without any religious service. A record likewise exists of the Court-mourning ordered, and the black draping of the chapel and of the apartments of the late Electress and the members of the Electoral family at Herren-hausen. To make the formal announcement of his mother's death and of his own assumption of her claims to the British Succession, the Elector George Lewis once more sent Bothmer to

[1] Malortie, *Der Hannoversche Hof*, &c., pp. 225 *sqq.*
[2] The continuous series of the letters addressed by her youngest son, Duke Ernest Augustus, to his friend J. F. D. von Wendt, breaks off in November 1713.

London, the real object of the choice being of course the intention that this most capable diplomatist should, while keeping on good terms with the Queen's ministers, concert further action with the Whig leaders. On June 15th, the Elector signed certain powers for the event of the Queen's death, which would have given to his envoy an authority superior to that of the Lords Justices ; but, as theirs rested on an Act of Parliament, the special authority entrusted to Bothmer was really as futile as that which had in similar terms been previously conferred on the elder Schütz, Grote, and the younger Schütz in turn. Bothmer's reports show that Bolingbroke was believed to be acting in the interest of the Pretender; and of the truth of this charge, after he had succeeded in ousting Oxford from office, the latter, who had himself continued to be suspected of Jacobitism, personally assured the Elector's envoy. On the part of Queen Anne, the Earl of Clarendon, a Tory Peer of high connexion, but of marked incapacity,[1] arrived at Hanover on July 7th to express to the Elector the Queen's sympathy with his loss. Clarendon, who had been entrusted with an extraordinary mission to Hanover before the occurrence of the Electress' death, also brought with him an answer to the Electoral memorandum

[1] He had, as Lord Cornbury, been Governor of New Jersey and New York, where he left no honoured name behind him.

of May 7th, drafted by Bolingbroke, which declined
all the demands made in the memorandum.   Clarendon was charged with some polite explanations ;
but the Elector had no intention of trusting either
to these or to the chapter of accidents.   With an
alertness rarely shown by him before his mother's
death in regard to matters connected with the
Succession, he promptly caused a fresh instrument
of Regency comprising his own nominations of
Lords Justices to be prepared : and from this
revised list Marlborough was omitted—either because he was not in England, or in consequence
of a knowledge on the part of the Elector of the
double game which even now the Duke was
playing.   At Hanover things seemed to be taking
their usual course ; but the visit paid to the
Elector early in August by his nephew, the new
King Frederick William I of Prussia, was not
without its significance.   For George Lewis was
already taking thought of the safety of his
Electorate in the event of his being called to
England, and welcomed the assurances of support
received by him from the King of Prussia and
other German Princes.   They could not know,
but they might well suspect, the secret offers of
assistance which Louis XIV had made to Queen
Anne through Bolingbroke, and which the latter
had contingently accepted.   It was a few days

after the termination of the King of Prussia's visit that the news arrived in Hanover of the death of Queen Anne on August 1st.

The events which had crowded on one another between the death of the Electress Sophia and that of Queen Anne belong, not to Sophia's biography, but to that of the sovereign whose Heir Presumptive was now Sophia's son. That this heir was a ruling foreign prince, whom no immediate descent or early associations connected with the House of Stewart, and whose own dealings (apart from his mother's) with English politicians had been to all intents and purposes entirely with Whigs, could not but intensify the aversion from the Hanoverian Succession entertained not only by the Jacobites but also, though in a less degree, by those of the Tories whose political sentiments were in nearest touch with theirs. The bonds of party union had just been drawn closer among the Tories at large by the Schism Act, and the Church had been more decisively than before rallied to the Government. But even so, Oxford was still unable to make up his mind to risk everything by inviting or allowing the Pretender to appear on English ground. Hence, not quite a fortnight after the Electress Sophia's death, the proclamation against the Pretender was issued, and, a fortnight later (July 9th), Parliament was prorogued to an early date in August.

During the interval, it was manifest, the Queen must make up her mind between her two chief counsellors, of whom one still thought it possible to tack and tack about, while the other was still hoping for a wind so strong and straight that he might drift before it into the desired port. The Queen decided for Bolingbroke, and, on July 27th, Oxford was dismissed from office. Bolingbroke's moment had come, but he was unequal to its call. Instead of bringing the Pretender to England, he thought that even now there remained time for him to weld the Tory party still more closely together, by means of his Church policy above all, and to form a Jacobite Ministry that would be in readiness at the critical moment, while in any case the Whigs must be prevented from bringing over the Elector or the Electoral Prince in the interval. Bolingbroke and those in his confidence were very hopeful in this their brief day of authority ; but the Whigs were more than hopeful—they were prepared.[1] The organisation set on foot by their leaders overspread the country, and the very symbol or token of action was agreed upon, while Marlborough was waiting at Ostend to resume the command of the army. And, throughout the great body of the middle classes in England—among the

[1] The Whig ' plot ' to which Mr. Sichel refers in his *Life of Bolingbroke*, p. 351, as revealed by Chesterfield at a later date, seems to belong to March 1714, when the Queen had (on the 11th) a sudden attack of erysipelas.

Nonconformists in particular—a ready expectancy awaited the accomplishment of the Protestant Succession.

At last, and with a most extraordinary rapidity in the sequence of its events, the end came. The malady to which Queen Anne was to succumb announced itself on July 27th. By July 30th the anxiety had become so grave that, at a meeting of the Cabinet and of a few Privy Councillors not forming part of it, presided over by Shrewsbury, orders were issued to close the ports, to hold twenty men-of-war in readiness, and to make the Lord Mayor responsible for the safety of the City of London. On the following day, the control of affairs finally passed out of Bolingbroke's hands, when, after a meeting of the whole Privy Council, at which Bothmer and Kreyenberg were present, the Queen, in accordance with the Council's recommendation, placed the Lord Treasurer's staff in Shrewsbury's hands. A courier was sent to Strafford at the Hague, to remind the authorities there of the guarantee to which they were bound by treaty ; and the British troops were recalled from the Netherlands. Early in the morning of August 1st, the Queen lay dead. Everything was in readiness. Kreyenberg made his appearance with a box containing the commission of the Lords Justices ; and of the eighteen names included in it thirteen were found to be those of Whigs. During the morning, Peers,

Privy Councillors, and Members of the House of Commons flocked in to append their signatures to the proclamation notifying the death of Queen Anne and the accession of King George. It was read by the heralds at Charing Cross and Temple Bar, and within the City ; and a few days later the King was again proclaimed there, as well as at Edinburgh and Dublin. The Houses of Parliament, which had assembled for formal business on the day of the Queen's death, four days later voted loyal addresses to her successor.

Bothmer, who had controlled the entire process of these transactions,[1] had promptly despatched his secretary, Goedeke, to carry to King George the great news of his accession. He arrived at Hanover on the morning of August 6th, just a day after Secretary Craggs, who brought, with other missives, a letter addressed to the Elector on the day before the Queen's death, and informing him that everything was in readiness for his immediate journey to England so soon as that death should actually have taken place. On August 8th, the Earl of Dorset— a young Whig Lord, described, in his later days, by a severe critic as ' a perfect English courtier '— arrived from England with his suite, to make the

---

[1] It was Bothmer who advised the destruction of a packet of letters found in the Queen's private apartments by the Lords Justices and himself, and who, during the burning of them, thought that he recognised the handwriting of the Pretender.

official announcement on behalf of the Lords
Justices. Doubt has been thrown on the statement that Goedeke, having reached Hanover,
communicated the news to Clarendon, who had
returned from dining with the Elector and Baroness
von Kielmannsegg at her villa, Fantaisie, and who
at once bore the tidings to George I at Herrenhausen.
In any case, the formal announcement to the new
King was made by Dorset on August 9th, when he
was received by George in the flower-garden of the
Orangery at Herrenhausen. Inasmuch as, on that
very day, the Earl of Berkeley assumed the command of the imposing naval squadron which, a
little more than a week afterwards, anchored off
the Dutch coast, there was no reason why the new
King should delay his departure. Whether, however, because of his confidence in the circumspection
of his English friends, or because of his attachment
to his Electorate, George I was in no hurry. To be
in no hurry may be accounted one of the minor
virtues in a monarch. He left Herrenhausen on the
morning of August 31st, bidding farewell to his
and his mother's favourite place of sojourn in words
which, if the court chronicler is to be trusted, betray
more of sentiment than he was in the habit of
expressing, but at the same time show him to have
had no intention of breaking with the traditions
of the past. 'Farewell, dear place, where I have
spent so many enjoyable and tranquil hours.

I leave you, but not for ever ; *for I hope to see you again from time to time.'*

In the same spirit, George I's departure was left unmarked by any solemnity or ceremonial whatever. He was accompanied on his journey by his son, with whom the death of the old Electress seems to have furnished him with an opportunity of placing himself for the time on seemlier terms. The Princess (Caroline of Ansbach) followed rather later, with her children.[1] The King's favourite brother, Prince Ernest Augustus, remained behind in Hanover, chiefly, no doubt, in order that he might fill the Elector's place at the Privy Council there, and also for the purpose of taking care of his expectations at Osnabrück, which were realised a year later, when he succeeded to the bishopric formerly held by his father, his elder brother, Maximilian William, being, as a convert to Rome, left out in the cold. Six months later, the Bishop[2] was created Duke of

---

[1] So late as a fortnight after Queen Anne's death, the Duchess of Orleans mentions a report that the English people were quite contented to have George I for their King, but on condition that the Electoral Prince should never be his successor. Probably, Elizabeth Charlotte's personal prejudices inclined her to give credit to this ridiculous rumour ; for she is unable to forego the opportunity of alluding to George Augustus' ' ill ancestry.'—O. von Heinemann, *Geschichte von Braunschweig und Hannover*, vol. iii. p. 228, mentions, without reprobating, the mendacious ' Court scandal,' explaining the quarrel between father and son by a supposed passion of the former for his daughter-in-law !

[2] His letter describing his early days in his episcopal city

York. At the Hague, the royal party was joined by Baroness von Kielmannsegg; Melusina von der Schulenburg followed in due course. With the King were his prime minister, Bernstorff, and Baron von Schlitz-Görz, who was to succeed Bernstorff in the same capacity at Hanover, besides three Privy Councillors, of whom Robethon was one, and a small Chancery staff. The chief officers of the Hanoverian Court, and a fairly ample household, including ' Mr. Mehmet and Mr. Mustapha,' live remembrances of the King's Turkish campaigns, raised the royal retinue to the moderate total of something less than one hundred persons.

Bolingbroke afterwards asserted that King George, though he had quitted Hanover in the apparent resolution of leaving the Tory Government in England unmolested, had during his stay in Holland, in consequence of earnest importunities on the part of the Allies, and particularly of Heinsius and some of the Whigs, come to a contrary decision. How far this assertion, and the belief that the impeachment of the Tory leaders was due more particularly to the inspiration of Bothmer, are correct, the present is not an occasion for enquiring; but enough has been said in the course

gives a delightful picture of still life. ' I have allowed myself the pleasure of taking a walk along the ramparts, in which all the small boys of the town have accompanied me.'

of this narrative to indicate that George I was not easily led, or easily turned.

On September 16th, 1714, the new King of Great Britain sailed from Oranie Polder; on the 18th he landed at Greenwich; and two days later he held his entry into London. His Coronation took place at Westminster Abbey on October 18th. Few men who have laid claim to so dazzling and so elusive a prize as that which fell to his lot have maintained their claim with so calm a resolve and so consistent a self-restraint. Whether or not circumstances—such as an armed landing on the English coast by the Pretender, or merely his personal appearance on English soil—might have led to a counter-attempt on the part of the Heir Presumptive to assert his claim to the throne in person, who shall say ? And who will lay it down whether in putting his right to the test, even at the risk of civil war, he would have done wrong ? Such a step he had not been called upon to take ; and his course of conduct had remained consistent throughout. Although he had little personal inclination for the change which his accession to the British throne involved, this should not detract from the tribute due to his conduct before that accession. As his claim descended to him from his mother, so he had inherited from her some, though not all, of the qualities which, in her, well became the Heiress of Great Britain. True to the friends of his House, and without fear of its enemies, he professed no feeling which he did not entertain, and shrank from no duty that was imposed upon him.

The princely sense of honour to which the Electress Sophia and her son were true in accepting the great responsibility to which they were called by the Act of Settlement was beyond a doubt their primary motive in meeting it. But, at the same time, they were alike fully conscious of the significance of the cause embodied in the Protestant Succession ; nor was the triumph of that cause, to which Sophia looked forward with hardly a thought of self, merely or mainly the fulfilment of a great dynastic ambition.

APPENDIX A

GENEALOGICAL TABLES

I. Family of Frederick V, Elector Palatine.

Frederick V (1596–1632) m. Elizabeth (1596–1632).

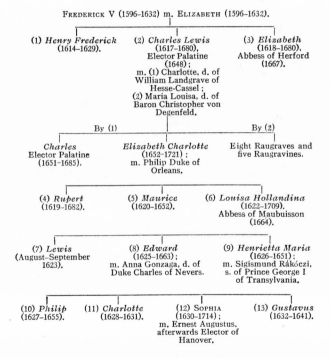

(1) *Henry Frederick* (1614–1629).

(2) *Charles Lewis* (1617–1680), Elector Palatine (1648); m. (1) Charlotte, d. of William Landgrave of Hesse-Cassel; (2) Maria Louisa, d. of Baron Christopher von Degenfeld.

(3) *Elizabeth* (1618–1680), Abbess of Herford (1667).

By (1)

Charles Elector Palatine (1651–1685).

Elizabeth Charlotte (1652–1721); m. Philip Duke of Orleans.

By (2)

Eight Raugraves and five Raugravines.

(4) *Rupert* (1619–1682).

(5) *Maurice* (1620–1652).

(6) *Louisa Hollandina* (1622–1709). Abbess of Maubuisson (1664).

(7) *Lewis* (August–September 1623).

(8) *Edward* (1625–1663); m. Anna Gonzaga, d. of Duke Charles of Nevers.

(9) *Henrietta Maria* (1626–1651); m. Sigismund Rákóczi, s. of Prince George I of Transylvania.

(10) *Philip* (1627–1655).

(11) *Charlotte* (1628–1631).

(12) Sophia (1630–1714); m. Ernest Augustus, afterwards Elector of Hanover.

(13) *Gustavus* (1632–1641).

Cf. Voigtel-Cohn's *Stammtafeln zur Gesch. d. deutschen Staaten u. d. Niederlande* (1871), *Tafel* 51. Feder, pp. 3–4, has gratuitously shortened the lives of not less than three of the Palatine children.

445

II. Descendants of Duke George of Brunswick-Lüneburg.

George (1582–1641) m. Anna Eleonora of Hesse-Darmstadt.

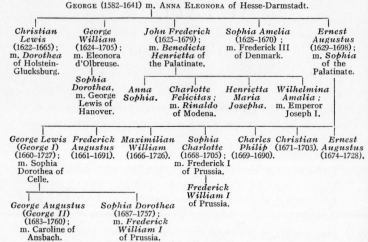

*Christian
Lewis*
(1622–1665) ;
m. *Dorothea*
of Holstein-
Glucksburg.

*George
William*
(1624–1705) ;
m. Eleonora
d'Olbreuse.

John Frederick
(1625–1679) ;
m. *Benedicta
Henrietta* of
the Palatinate,

Sophia Amelia
(1628–1670) ;
m. Frederick III
of Denmark.

*Ernest
Augustus*
(1629–1698) ;
m. *Sophia*
of the
Palatinate.

*Sophia
Dorothea*,
m. George
Lewis of
Hanover.

*Anna
Sophia.*

*Charlotte
Felicitas ;*
m. *Rinaldo*
of Modena.

*Henrietta
Maria
Josepha.*

*Wilhelmina
Amalia ;*
m. Emperor
Joseph I.

George Lewis
(George I)
(1660–1727) ;
m. Sophia
Dorothea of
Celle.

*Frederick
Augustus*
(1661–1691).

*Maximilian
William*
(1666–1726).

*Sophia
Charlotte*
(1668–1705) ;
m. Frederick I
of Prussia.

*Charles
Philip*
(1669–1690).

Christian
(1671–1703).

*Ernest
Augustus*
(1674–1728).

George Augustus
(George II)
(1683–1760) ;
m. Caroline of
Ansbach.

Sophia Dorothea
(1687–1757) ;
m. *Frederick
William I*
of Prussia.

*Frederick
William I*
of Prussia.

APPENDIX B

THE original French text of the Letters which the
liberal courtesy of the authorities of the Royal Secret
Archives of State at Berlin enables me to reproduce in
this place is here printed as supplied by their copyist.
The packet containing the Letters is inscribed in the
handwriting of Frederick the Great in the words of the
title here prefixed to them. The spelling of the words in
the Letters, the way in which those words are run into
one another, and the sequence of the Letters, have
(except in one instance in which there had been an
evident misplacement of manuscript) been left as they
stand in the transcript. The words ciphered in numbers,
whether in whole or letter by letter, have been deciphered—each deciphered word, whether proper or
common, being distinguished by italics. The nicknames
(or designations applied to particular persons by the
writers of the letters, in accordance with a mutual
understanding between them) are left as they stand;
their equivalents, so far as known, being mentioned at
the end of this introductory note.

An English translation is appended, in which an
attempt has been made, besides assigning the Letters to

their respective writers, to supply dates, where possible, to those which are undated, and to place them in their probable chronological sequence. This attempt is based in the main on a comparison of the Berlin with the Lund Letters. It could not be carried very far without establishing beyond all possibility of doubt the fact that the two series form an organic whole, and that each of them proves incontestably the genuineness of the other. A few brief notes have been added, identifying names of persons or places, where this could be done.

The original (French) letters are numbered consecutively (1—34); the English versions are arranged so far as possible chronologically, and numbered so as to correspond with the originals (F 1—F 34).

Nothing is actually known as to the way in which the Berlin Letters, whose number is less than one-tenth of that of the Letters preserved at Lund, came into the hands of King Frederick II of Prussia, the son of Sophia Dorothea's daughter and namesake and of her consort King Frederick William I. It is proved by fragments of the proceedings for a divorce against the Electoral Princess that letters which had passed between the lovers had been seized already in the course of the two months (May and June, 1694) preceding the disappearance of Königsmarck, and had thus come to the knowledge of the Electoral Government. (One of the letters here printed shows how apprehensive the guilty pair had been of such an occurrence.)

In Cramer's *Memoirs of Countess Maria Aurora Königsmarck and the Königsmarck family* (1837), a book which, notwithstanding the addition of a great deal of second-hand matter, is beyond a doubt largely based upon original documents, will be found an apparently authentic report of Auditeur Rüdiger (dated July 1, 1695). He states that after Königsmarck's disappearance on July 1, 1694, a certain von Metsch (who was married to the sister of Eleonora von dem Knesebeck, and had served as intermediary at some stages of Königsmarck's secret correspondence with the Princess) was frequently in the company of Königsmarck's secretary, Hildebrandt. In reply to an enquiry from the latter, Metsch stated that on the Count's journey to Dresden he had seen in his possession a packet of letters tied together with yellow ribbon in a little box, of which the Count took particular care. This packet, by Hildebrandt's advice, Metsch now sent unopened by the hands of a servant to Celle. If this statement is correct, there is much probability in the conjecture that these were some of the letters which found their way to the sisters of Königsmarck, and ultimately into the library at Lund.

Two days later, again according to the statement ot Rüdiger, who had it from Hildebrandt, the latter was ordered by an official personage (Secretary Zacharias) to open Königsmarck's apartments for a thorough examination of them and of all the furniture. In the course of the examination of the Count's bedroom (*Cabinet*) Rüdiger was called to summon a locksmith to open the writing-table ; but during the actual opening of it he remained in an ante-room. After this the rooms were sealed up, and the flow of talk began.

Possibly this was the way in which the Hanoverian Government obtained possession of the letters which, in the opinion of Leibniz, brought home conviction of Sophia Dorothea's guilt to her parents at Celle ; though after the divorce the Elector Ernest Augustus refused either to allow the letters to be kept at Celle, or to have them burnt *instanter*. In any case, there would thus be no difficulty in accounting for the preservation of evidence which could afterwards be sent by the Hanoverian court to that of Berlin, in order to convince Sophia Dorothea's daughter, who is said to have desired the liberation of the 'Duchess of Ahlden' from her imprisonment, of her unhappy mother's guilt.[1]

I subjoin so much of Count Schulenburg's key to designations and numerical ciphers for names, as applies to the Berlin Letters; it is supplemented in their case by Dr. Geerds and myself:

100 = Elector (Duke) of Hanover.

101 = Duke of Celle.

102 = Electoral (Hereditary) Prince (George Lewis).

103 = ? Fieldmarshal Podewils.

112 = Prince Maximilian.

120 = Königsmarck.

200 = Electress (Duchess) of Hanover.

201 = Electoral (Hereditary) Princess (Sophia Dorothea).

202 = Countess Platen.

214 = Fräulein von dem Knesebeck.

227 = Duchess of Celle.

300 = Hanover.

301 = Luisburg.

305 = Celle.

La Romaine . . = Electress (Duchess) of Hanover.
Le Reformeur . = Electoral (Hereditary) Prince.
L'Incommode . = Electoral (Hereditary) Prince.

---

[1] In the above, which it will be observed hardly passes out of the region of conjecture, I have followed the argument of Dr. G. R. Geerds, comparing Cramer as to the basis of fact.

Le Pédagogue . = Duchess of Celle.
Le Grondeur . . = Duke of Celle.
La Boule . . . = Electress of Brandenburg (Sophia
                   Charlotte).
L'Innocent . . = Prince Ernest Augustus.
Léonisse . . . . = Electoral (Hereditary) Princess
                   (Sophia Dorothea).
Le Cœur Gauche = Electoral (Hereditary) Princess
                   (Sophia Dorothea).
La Confidante . = Fräulein von dem Knesebeck.
La Marionette . = A sister of Landgrave Ernest Lewis
                   of Hesse-Darmstadt.

The titles ' Elector,' ' Electoral Prince,' ' Electoral
Princess,' could not have been formally used until after
the date of the Electoral Investiture, December 19, 1692.
(Cf. Königsmarck's sarcastic letter *ap*. Wilkins, p. 258.[1])
Before the Investiture the titles were ' Duke,' ' Hereditary Prince,' and ' Hereditary Princess,' and these
designations have accordingly been adopted in the
original and in the translated letters belonging, or
held assignable, to earlier dates.

Wilkins (p. 218, note) thinks that La Marionette was
' probably a Princess of Hesse.' Her brother is said
(by Sophia Dorothea) to be ' with the army,' and by
Königsmarck to be ' near ' Sophia Dorothea, also at
Wiesbaden, and ' in his own country.' The only Princess
of Hesse whom these indications would fit would be
one of the three surviving elder sisters of Landgrave
Ernest Lewis of Hesse-Darmstadt, who served under Mar-
grave Lewis William of Baden. They were Magdalena
Sibylla, Duchess Dowager of Würtemberg, Maria

[1] The edition of *The Love of an Uncrowned Queen* edited by
me is the revised edition of 1903. Dr. Robert Geerds' article, as
already stated, appeared in the *Beitrag zur Allgemeinen Zeitung*
for Friday, April 7th, 1902.

Elizabeth, Duchess of Saxe-Römhild, and Sophia Maria, Duchess of Saxe-Eisenberg.

The above list leaves unexplained the following numerical ciphers used in the Berlin Letters: 20, 110, 127, 131, 307, 308, 2000—seven in all, as against sixteen left unexplained by Dr. Geerds. Resort is now and then had in these Letters to the extraordinary notion (it can hardly be called a cipher) of disguising a word in a crowd of *jllj's* or *illy's*, thus:

jlljlandjlljgrajllivejlli = landgrave.

The letter-key, with which a large proportion of the words in the Letters have been deciphered at Berlin, is as follows:

22 = a		41 = n	
24 = b		42 = o	
25 = c		45 = p	
27 = d		46 = q	
29 = e		47 = r	
30 = f		50 = s	
$\left.\begin{matrix}32\\37\end{matrix}\right\}$ = g		51 = t	
33 = h		53 = $\begin{cases}u\\v\end{cases}$	
35 = i		54 = $\begin{cases}v\,^1\\w\,^1\end{cases}$	
31 = j ^{1}		55 = x	
37 = l		56 = y	
39 = m		50 = z	

^{1} See letter F 16 below.

LETTRES D'AMOUR DE LA DUCHESSE
D'ALLEN AU CONTE KÖNIGSMARC

1

voiage
de   brod   mardi
hausen

Princesse héréditaire a bien jmpatience de sauoir si
Königsmarck est *arivé* hereusement il sest passé bien des
choses que *Princesse héréditaire écrit sur le feuillet qui
est tout blanc* ie ne peus me consoler *d'avoir si tost perdu
Königsmarck* labsence en paroist mille fois plus cruelle
ie suis *abatue* a ne pouuoir me *soutenir l'exes des plaisirs*
et la douleur de ne plus uoir ce que j'aime me mette en
cét estat quil est cruel de *se separer* de uous uous estes le
plus aimable de tous les homme plus on uous uoit plus
on uous descouure de charme que ie suis heureuse d'estre
aimée de vous et que ie connois bien tout mon bonheur
tout ma felicité

la continuation
dépend de cette tendresse charmante

si elle uient a me manquer ie ne ueus plus uiure uous
me tenez lieu de tout et tout le monde ensemble ne
mest rien ie souhaitte que uous soyez aussi content de
moi que ie le suis de uous uous mauez enchantée et ie me
sens plus tendre que jamais sojez de meme et il ne
manquera rien a mon bonheur ie ne uous dirai point
que toutes les actions de ma uie uous marqueront mon
attachement uous deuez en estre persuadé et le tems uous
fera connoistre que ie ne ueus uiure que pour uous
Princesse héréditaire part demain.

J'ay donne ordre a 220 de m'envoier vos lettre par
nienb.

2

Brockhausen.   Jeudi 22 Juin.

Princesse héréditaire ariva hier au soir elle est contente du *Duchesse de Celle* ie ne doute point quelle ne fasse
tout ce que lon voudra *Duc de Celle* est bien plus difficile ie
nai point encore eu de vos nouuelles dont ie suis bien
triste ie me flate pourtant quil ne sest rien passé puis que
ie nai rien apris *Duc de Hanovre va lundi a Hanovre* cela
sest *resolu hier* si ie lauois seu plustost *ie ne serois pas
partie* et iaurois peu uous uoir encore quelque jours ie suis
persuadée quil a attendu Expres et cela me donne un
urai dépit car ie hais plus que la mort tout ce qui ueut
mesloigner de uous jl faut estre bien malheureux pour
passer la uie comme je le fais cependant ie ne voi‧point
de fin a mes peines iai fait milles reflexions hier seule
dans *ma chaise* qui mont desesperée ie ne saurois penser
que ie vai estre tout un mois sans vous voir sans une
douleur mortelle toutes *les mesures* quil *me faut garder* me
. . . ie ne saurois me passer de uous ie ne uoudrois uoir
que uous dans le monde cependant ie ne uous uoi point jl
faut a tous momens men separer jl mest impossible de
uiure dauantage dans cette contrainte elle me desespere
ma passion augmente tous les jours ie ne sai ce que uous
mauez fait mais vous mauez enchantée la derniere fois
que ie vous ai ueu et ie ne uous ai jamais aimé auec tant
dardeur que ie le fais jl est seur que uous me ferez tour-
ner la teste jai fait hier une chanson et cela me fait uoir
que lamour fait des miracles ie ne saurois mempecher
de uous la dire cest sur lair dans mon malheur . . .

> sans mon . . . tout le monde mennuye
> luy seul fait mon bonheur et mes plaisirs
> il est lunique charme de ma uie
> et en luj seul ie borne mes desirs

cest mon coeur tout seul qui parle jespere que ie nen

demeurerai pas la et quauec le temps ie pourrai uous le disputer 101 [or 201] va mardi a *Celle* cest pourquoi ne mescriuez plus que ie ny sois *Duchesse de Celle* a promis *au pauve* 2000 *escus si Prince héréditaire ne revient poit* cela redouble mon amitié *Princesse héréditaire* a parlé hier a *Luisburg* a 110 il en a cherché loccasion cest pour lexhorter a ne *doner aucune prise a ses ennemis* et a se défier sur tout de *Comtesse Platen Princesse héréditaire* la fort prié de lauertir de tout ce qui la regarderoit jl lui a promis ie ne say si tout cela ne regarde point *Königsmarck,* ie ne saurois vous parler que de la douleur ou ie suis destre si loin de uous ne uous consoler point de mon absence ie uous en conjure et najez point de joye que ie ne sois auec uous grand dieu quel charme et quels delices destre toujours auec uous plus on uous void plus on uous trouue au dessus de tous les hommes du monde je ne suis occupée que du souuenir charmant de la derniere fois que ie uous ai ueu jl ne sortira jamais de ma memoire ha mon cher enfant que uous estes tendrement aimé et quil mest jnsuportable de ne uous point voir je vai me mettre au lit jespere que mes songes uous representeront aussi charmant que uous lestes si ie ne crojois uous uoir en dormant ie ne uoudrois point dormir du tout car tant que ie suis esueillée uous moccupez entierement et ie nai dagreable dans ma uie que le tems que ie passe a penser a uous bon soir le plus aymable de tous les hommes uous estes adoré et uous le serez toute ma uie adieu encore une fois pourquoi ne suis je *pas entre vos bras* jen mourrois.

mecredi *Princesse héréditaire* a esté a table et parla a 110 ensuite a *Feltma* elle *ariva tard Prince Max* la *receut* et *lui dona la main* elle lui a parlé fort peu *Duc de* Celle vint dans la chambre *Prince Max* ny entra point du tout *Duchesse de Celle* estoit allé *au devant dele* et

reuint tard car elle ne trouua point *Princesse héréditaire*
on soupa ensuite *Princesse héréditaire Duchesse de Celle*
et *Duc de Celle* ont esté ensemble tous seuls *Duchesse
de Celle* mene Princesse électorale *chez elle* et personne
ny a mis le pied.

3

Que ne soufertong cant jl faux se separrer de vous,
tous les tourmens du monde, ne pove pas tans faire
soufrir, mais je me remais de mon schagrein, puisque
vous voules que je ne dois poins avoir de la jalousie, je
vous avoue qui laÿ difisile, dan avoir poin cant on aÿt
elonjé, de l'objaÿ que lon adore, mais mon anje vous
m'aves tans promis de garder unne bonne condouite que
je me fie à vous, et je vous pos assurer que dans se
moment je suis san jalousie, mais non san schagrein, et
vostre depars me schagrine plus que jamais je ne com-
prens pas se que je deviendraÿs a lafein, je say bien que
je ne pos pas toujour aistre à vostre veue, et sependans,
je san que tros que je ne peus plus me separer de vous,
vojes en quelle étas vos bos sieux mon mis. je vous énvois
la copie de la lestre dong je vous aÿ parlée sait most en
most comme l'orriginal, je vous demande pardong de la
main barbouliose dong je me suis servis, je lay fais copié
par mon page, qui ne saÿ se qui l'ecrist. M. Gor ma fais
un compliment de la par de la Deuschaise d'Essenack elle
ma fais dire que quois que j'avas éviter de luis parler,
elle monstreray qu'elle sonje plus a moÿ que je ne sonje
à Elle, je vous jureraÿ que se compliment ma pas fais
solement plaisir, aux contraire il me fasche quelle me la
fais faire je ne suis poin sortis de ma schambre toust
auxjourduis et je crois que je feraÿ demaime demain ;
mande moÿ pour me consoler comme vous vous governes

et can vous seraÿ de retour, je mor dannuis et de schagrein si je ne vous vois pas bientos ; adieux mon Emable
coeur, sonjes à vostre fidail amang et ne l'oblie pas parmis
tous saite foule de monde, éncor unnefois adieux

jodis à 12 hor apres minuit mon mal de
postrine me continue mais je naÿ point
eus de fiavre.

4

jodis

il me fallais vostre lestre pour me soutenir dans le desespoir aux j'aistois, voila se que saÿ cant on agit auxver-
tement et si vous mavié pas parlé de . . . je crois que
je nauraÿ peus tenir plus longtemps, je me suis pourtang
gouverné forbien, et j'ay voulus auxparavang savoir, se
que vous me dirie, et je me suis point émporté, sassché
dong que je fus aventhier à Linde, Mad: la Comtes:
aitois fort étonné que je ne jouaÿ avec vous, je luÿ dis
qui fallaist avoir permission, elle disaÿ Mad: Leonis m'à
fais demander á l'Elect: et j la repondus positivement
quelle pouvaÿ bien faire venir ses jouors, hiair avang que
de resevoir la vostre, ji su par oberg qui avois veus M.
Weÿ à Linde que S: Alt: vous l'aves dis a vous maime,
le Preince Ernest august me dist avec ses mos, que M.
l'Elect: vous avois dis, vous vous ennujé Mad: jl faux
faire venir vos jouors, j l'auraÿ depandu de vous, si jl
vous l'avois dis de la sorte, mais Mad: je fus bien soulagé,
can je lus la vostre, aux vous me parlié de sait affaire,
j'aÿ fais ma moralle, qui ais de ne me jamais plus énborté
sur des vapors, mes ma divine, pourié vous poin nous
laisser venir, afein que j' aÿe la joÿ de vous regarder et
que mes sieux et mon coeur puisse apprendre des vostres
comment je suis avec os, et si vostre passion aÿ telle
comme vous me l'ecrivie la vostre d ihair aÿ scharmont,

an suis si tousché que je me san plus enflamée que
j'amais. vous dite que vous ne voje personne, cela aÿ le
plus obligan du monde, mais vous vojes autang plus le
Ref: ses qui me fais craindre que vous vous acoutumeraÿ
pos à pos à ses mediocres carraisses et jl vous ém-
brasseras si souven que je more de schagrein dÿ sonjer
solement, pour lamour de vous maime, ne vous ÿ
accoutumes pas, sonje toujours de qu'elle mainere j vous
traite, vous qui merites tous les manieres honeste, obligant
et respectouose, mais je vois le defos daustruis es je ne
vois poin que sait en cela que je suis le plus criminel, vous
m'aves dis vous maime que le Re: en . . . en de temps
n'avois pas eus les maniere si disobligante que moÿ, je
more dÿ sonjer, que je suis malhoros de vous aimer si
tendremens et que saite passion si éxtraordinare, me rans
si odieux, ne sonjé plux aux passé je vous en conjure,
adieux, adieux, helas adieux.

5

je suis bien à plaindre, et mon malhor me persecuste
tros pour pouvoir l'endurer plus longtemps, les laistres
d'yair nous donne poin d'esperanse que le Ref:puisse partis,
et san se depar je ne puis ni dois vous voir, qu'elle cruelle
destiné, oh malhor insuportable appres des schoque si
terrible poje éncor respiré, la vie me devien insuportable,
je ne puis, ni ne dois plus aistre aux monde, car qu'i
ferage sans vous voir, j'ay eus auxjourduis dos malhor
dong le dernie me paraist à présang le plus cruel mes le
premié pos devenir le plus terrible, je me suis brulje ave
nostre vieux bon homme, et Gor aussÿ, et comme jl vous
à dis, si je redisaÿ a sos de qui S. Alt: aÿ mal contemps,
jls seraÿs bien étonné, san ma passion je saÿ le partis que
j'aÿ à prandre, mais ma schere comme je vous aÿ promis
de ne rien faire san vostre consentemens, je vos vous en

faire pars auxparavang, mon dessein aÿ de luÿ ecrire, et
luÿ dire que j'aistois for fasché que mon devoir mavoit
éngagé dans unne dispute, avec la personne du monde que
j'honore le plus, mais comme j'avois pris garde aux mos
qu'il m'avois dist jÿ aÿ observé qu 'il disaÿt (si je redisaÿ
à tous sos de qui nostre maistre aÿ mal contemps, j lian
auraÿ beaucoup de detrompé, je crus que vost : Exce⁚ⁿᵉ ne
le prandras pas mal, si je luy priaÿ d'avoir la bonté de
m'avertis soux main, si j'aÿ assaÿ de malhor à deplair à
Monsg : L'Elector, afein que je puisse prandre mon
partis, car jusques ici, je lay servis que par affection, et
sans aucun intaeraÿ, aÿ si j'avois le malhor d'aistre mis
mal dang son Esprit, jl me serais impossible de le plus
servir) voila a pos praÿ se que je vousdraÿ luÿ mander,
saschong vostre avis, je pos vous assurer que j'aÿ veus
positivement dans son émportement que cela s'adraissait
à moÿ, j'admire ma passianse, et je ne puis pas com-
prandre comme j'aÿ fais pour me possedé, car j'avois
forsouvang en beausche de luÿ dire, se que je vos luÿ
ecrire ; Le segon malhor aÿ bien plus schagrinang, j'aÿ
veus vos fenaistres auxvertes, le Ref : sortais de vostre
garderobe san vous j voir, quois que j 'aÿ parlé assaÿ hos,
passé et repassé, mais rien lon j vojaÿ ame vivante, je crois
comme j laistois tars vous fute deja sche la Romaine je
seraÿ inconsolable, si je n'avois l'ésperanse à vous voir
se soir à 6 hors a quois suje reduis, je conte pour le plus
grans bonhor du monde à vous voir de mille pas, Effective-
ment jl me seras dunne grande consolation, si je puis avoir
se plaisir ; seluÿ de vous écrire m'ais bien schaire, et ji
ne donneraÿ pas pour un Rauxjomme, je crains que ma
Diabolique destinée, m'en priveras, say seraÿt pour
maschevée, je vous conjure prenes si bien vos messure
que cela ne nous pos manquer, vous saves, j'aispaire par
vous maime que lon ne saurais vivre san cela, helas
pourquios ne suje pas Reden aux Hortanse tandis que

vous aites la niporte si vous me haisié, j'auraÿ pourtang la joÿ de voir selle que j'adore ; sai nostre passion
qui nouis éloinje lun de laustre, san mon amour, je seraÿ
partous aux vous aites, mes puis que je vous aime, je suis
en meschang credis l'on me regarde pas, l'on mauxblie,
mais n'importe, q'on me crage aux née je m'en fercheraÿs
pas.

6

dimanje :

auÿ Mad: je soufriarÿ pour vous, puisque vous me
l'ordonnes, mais can serage assay horos de me voir aux
poin aux j'aspire, sait éntre vos bras que je vos dire, mais
can aurage saite satisfaction, je pair tous l'ésperanse, car
de la maniere que cela vas, je m'én pos pas flatté, j'én
pair lespris et si je vous écris, san rime ni raison, ne vous
en prenes pas à moÿ, say, le desespoir aux je me trouve,
si vous ne croje pas je vous prie de regarde ses poils que
j'aÿ fais tire de ma taiste se matein, je ne pos pas vous
assurer qu'elle me song venus saite nuis, mais je pos
vous juré qui lia 8 jours, qui li en avois pas, croje moÿ
que mon desespoir ay grans, et que mon schagrein ait
extraime, je demore pour l'amour de vous, j'hasarde
honor reputation et émbisiong, car puis que je ne vas pas
en campanje, qu'es que lon dira de moÿ, et pourquois
aise que je l'hasarde, saÿ pour ne vous poin voire, je
suis venus a saite éxtremité, qu'il faux que le veinque
aux que je mors, emploÿe dong vos forse auxprais le Gro:
sais qui pos nous sauver uniquement aÿ j'appelle sas
veincre, je vos absolument vostre ordre, se que je dois
faire, demorer à Hanno. de la sorté ait inauÿ, car appres
trois semaine vous iraÿ avec le Gron. que ferage allors
dans un lieux aux vous naite pas, je vous prie d'ÿ faire
reflextion, et appres cela ordonnes, je suis prait à vous
montrer avec mon obeïssansse que ma passion n'écouste

poin de raisong. vous vojes à quois vous m'aves re-
duit, car je vous sacrifie mon Ambition qui aÿ la solle
schose, que j'usques ici j'avois conservé, vojes aux vas
ma passion, j'ugé dans quelle aitas je me trouve, ne me
rouiné pas de fons en comble, saÿe plus abitios que mois,
et éncourages un amang qui n'én à plus. je vous feray
pitié si vous connaissié bien les schagreins qui m'acable.
je vois bien le vostre aÿ ses qui me tue, car quois que
nous sajons bien énsemble, nous laisong pas que d'avoir
du schagrein, aÿ voila un mal san remaide ; la solle consolation aÿ de jouer avec vous, mes le plaisir de vous regarder mais poin permis car tantos, la 𝔰𝔠𝔥𝔴𝔞𝔯𝔷 𝔤𝔢𝔰𝔦𝔠𝔥𝔱
tanstos l'innossang tantos un austre des filjes vien nous
observé, tous cela aÿ pour en mourir, consolé moÿ je
vous en conjure, aux je me desespaire et ma desesparation
pouraÿ m'énporter à me servir des remaide indinge d'un
honest homme, vous m'attendes bien, mais mad. cant on
aÿ dans le Labourint comme je suis, jl nia blus d'honnesté
et plus de confianse, j laÿ bong de fenir aux je m'énporteray
davantaje.

7

a l hor de nuit

Le bon homme aÿ revenus de la conferanse et ma
faÿ ranvojer les Dragons de lordonanse sans ordre,
saÿ pourquois je crois que nous raisterons éncor saite
semainne et comme je vas demain diner sché luÿ je
sauray qu'elque schose, dong je vous feraÿ aussitos pars
énattandang prepare vous a éxecuter se que vous trouveraÿ ici jointe; *l'Électrice* a etté a *linde* faire *promener
Comtesse Platen*, Le Comte de Stenbock que vous aves
veus ici j lia 7 ans voulais faire la reveranse, comme aussi le
Comte Delagardy, je laÿ mennay la, et je trouvaÿ la bonne
Piesse, *eschoie*, et le *fahr* qui *coulai* de tous costé, *elle*
fus si decontenansé de voir arrivé tans d'éstrangé, qu'elle

fus toust a fais confus, le partis qu'elle pris aitois le
meiljor, car elle se *retira*, aussitos, pour se remaistre
en *ordre*, j lia bien de la malisse à *l'Électrice*, et elle pos pas
se vanier mieux. Sonjes je vous en conjure à *venir* et
crojaÿ que san vous *voir*, sait aistre morte, et je m'étonne
comme mong destein m'aist si cruel a me laisser sur vire
tous ses malhors, mais si je ne vous *vois bintos* j nia
ni guerre ni danger que je n'alje scherscher pour abrejer
mes jours malhoros ; je more de honte de naistre pas
mors deja, comment cela sacordetil de vous aimer eper-
duement, sans vous *voir* ni san vous parler, et vivre
encor, je crois que mon *foutus* destein, me preserve,
pour me schagriné davantage ; vous pouves sol me tiré
de ma desperation, *venez vite* me consoler, aux je ferais
un cous de desespoir dong je me repantiraÿ de ma vie,
car la vie que je maine m'aist insuportable, je la haÿ
a la mors, j'en suis las, et ne le pos plus suporté ; je
vousdraÿ que la foudre ecrasa tous sos qui énpesche
à nous *voir*, et à joindre nos fos, pardonne à mon
amportement que la tros violante passion me cause, jl
me semble, que si je ne *dois* voir se que *jaime*, j laÿ
juste de ne poin voir le jour, je seraÿ capable dans se
moment, a Masacre Paire, Maire, Frere, et soeur, si je
crojais q'os m'émpesche de *voir* mon *anje*. Leonis que
ta bosté me couste des tourments, tong scharme des
schagreins, *venez* me faire *auxblier*, tous mes mos, tu
le pos, par tais émbrassades, par taÿs caraisses, et jlia
que tois dans le monde capable de cela. je vous *attang*
auvec la plus grande *impatians* du *monde*, et ne souffres
que je dise, que vous aites promte *a partir*, et *mang* à
revenir aux L'amour vous *appemme*, j'auraÿ pourtang
tor si je me plainjaÿ *du depart*, car j laistois *tendre* et
seinsaire, mais je vous conjure, donne mois pas l'occasion
de me pleindre, du dernié adieux je tenbrasse mille aÿ
Mille fois. *Mlle. de Knesebeck* aÿ la meljore personne

du monde, je vous prie de lui dire, l'estimme que j'aÿ
pour elle je la salue avec vostre permission.

8

Atlenbourg 13me

Le 12me j'aÿ fais se que j'aÿ fais les austres jours,
sait a dire boire manjé, et visité les poste, le 13me de
maime ; M. le Duck de Zelle aÿ venus nous visiter,
vous vojé que je puis aisement faire mes journos, je crois
qu'il vous schoquerong gaire, car rien n'ay plus innossang,
et sos de Hanno : seraÿ de maime amoin que d'aller
souper avec les fammes ne vous deplust, se que je
m'engage de laisser aussÿ, vous assuran que saÿ la
moindre éprove que je vous donneraÿ, puis que je m'en
passeraÿ fort aisement, san que vous l'ordones. Dieu
volje que je puisse vous monstres par ma condouite,
que tous mes penses, tous mes pas, ne se fong que pour
vous, mais helas vous aves tans d'jnjustice, que vous ne
le voules pas voire, j'aÿ mon malhor, et saÿ se qui me
perdra un jour opres de vous. j'aÿ resu la 3me Lestre
daté le 5me d'ans, 8 jours appres selle marqué 4, je ne
conprans pas dous vien se delaÿ, mais je say bien, qui
laÿ danjeros qu'elle demore si lon temps en schemein.
je ne suis pas satisfais de vous et la meschante oppinion
que vous aves de moÿ comme si je vous neglijaÿ, me
schoque beaucoup, je sonje nouit aÿ jour qu'a vous, il
me vien poin d'austre pensé dan l'ésprit, et sepandans,
je vous oblie je vous neglige, je souis un inconstang,
aise que je merite ses titres sajes en le juge vous maime.
pouves vous m'accuser de ne vous plus aimer, aitil
passible que s'aÿ Leonis qui le croist et qui me reproche,
grandieux que vous aite plain d'injustice, et que vous
me faite gran tor, je vous aimes à la follie, je vous adore
san égale, ma passion surpasse tous les autres et sepandans vous douté de tous cela, vostre coeur parle gaire

en ma favor, j'aÿ raison de me plaindre de luÿ, saÿ se
coeur Barbare qui dois parlé pour, et saÿ luÿ qui m'accuse,
je laÿ veus tendre pour mois mais pos à pos tous sette
tendresse ait évanouÿ, ne revindratil poin à luÿ maime,
faiste luÿ des reprosches de ma par ; Le mien vous assure
unne éternelle attachement, jl vous jure qui vous sera
constang, et pourvos que vous dainje à sonjer à louis tous
les 24 hores unnefois, j laÿ Contemps, meritil vostre
souvenir je crois que sÿ, mais sait à vous d'en juger. Si
j'aÿ jamais le malhor de ne vous plus aimer (qui ait un
chose impossible) vostre souhaÿ me punira par, car je
vous jure, que je ne schergeraÿ plus de fidellite, et quois
que selle d'apresan mais plus schaire que ma vie, j'en
vousdraÿ jamais d'austre, souvene vous se q'un sertain
Espanjol à dis, je ne vos pas m'éncanaliser, j'apelle cela
éncanaliser si je quitaÿ le plus parfait objaÿ de l'univair
pour qu'elque austre, la qu'elle ne poura jamais se com-
parer en la . . .

9

vendredis à 8 hor du soir

dans se moment je vien de resevoir unne lestre trais
grande et comme je le demande de *Princesse électorale*
je naÿ pas eus le loisir de la lire, crainte que la poste ne
par, et san vous assurer qu'elle joÿ elle ma faite can je
laÿ resu ; Le bon homme vas demain à *Engsen,* à son retour
je sauraÿ ma destinée, se que je feraÿ dabor savoir a
Princesse électorale ; je ne fais que des vos pour ne poin
marscher afein que je puisse émbrasser selle que j'adore, et
pour la quelle je moureraÿ mille aÿ millefois Croje de mois
que je vous adore de la maniere la plus violante du
monde, plust aux siel davoir les aucasion à vous le bein
monstre, je n'obliraÿ pas un moment, pour vous en bien
persuader, quelle satisfaction seraÿ la mienne si par mon
obeissanse je pouraÿ vous monstrer combien je vous

aistime, et quelle plaisir je prans à aistre vostre éternelle
Esclave adieux mon incomparable Leonis que je te
Baiseraÿ petiste.   **K.**

10

Samdÿ.

j lait aisé à juger avec qu'elle satisfaction j'aÿ leus
vostre tres-scharmente lestre, jl me la vallaÿ telle pour
me tirer unpos de la profonde reverie aux mes malhors,
et *labsense* ma plonjé, elle aÿt grande tendre et comme
je la souhaite, n'en écrives poin de plus petiste, cela vous
dois soulager, et je vous jure qu'a mois aussÿ, vous ne
les sauries faire assaÿ amples Vostre passion m'ais si
agreable, que j'aÿ aucun plaisir dans *labsanse* que de la
voire peinte sur du papié, je conserve vos lestres comme
la schose du monde la plus pressiose puis qu'elle me
consolle de tous mes disgraces; j vojan que vous jure
de maimér, à maistre fidaille, et a me jamais abandonner,
que poje souhaiter plus de vous, vous voje dong que je
suis tous à fais contemps de vous, je vous conjure de
l'aistre aussi de mois et de me poin inputer que vous ne
reseves pas regoulierement tous les poste de mes lestres,
j'aÿ injoré un jour qui aÿ le *dimansche*, mais comme j'an
suis informé mon éxactitude vous feras connaistre que
j'aÿ pesché fauxte de le savoir mieux, et la neglijance
me vien pas des schagreins que j'aÿ, sait allors que je
sonje le plus a vous car vous me serves de consolation
et le plaisir de penser à vous surpasse tous austres
plaisirs que je connaisse Jdolo mio, can aurage la joÿ
de te tenir íntre mes bras, n'aisse pas pour desesperer
un Catong, que de voir que vous pouves *venir*, si *Prince
Max* ne l'anpeschaÿ pas, mais quois que l'anvie de vous
voir, me fist passer ma jalousie et que je vous priai, de
venir combien de temps pourage aistre avec vous, postaitre
que dos jours et appraÿ je vous voiraÿ parmis des jans

2 H

qui nous haisse, et d'austre qui volle sinsinuer, ne croje pas mon Ange que ma jalousie, me vien de la movaise oppinion que j'ay de vous, se seraÿ tros criminelle mais elle me vien de la violanse de ma passion, ainsi je me flátte que vous m'excuseraÿ toujours can saite follie me prans; que ne vous doige poin que vous prené tang de paine à me guerir de tous mes soupsons vos journos me console, vostre sermang me fait auxblié tous que j'avois dans la servelle, ha que ne *suige auxprai* de *vous* je me jaiteraÿ à vos pié, vous remersier de tous le soin que vous prenes à me randre horos et contemps, je suis persuadé de vostre bonne intasion, je ne doute pas de vostre fidailite, et je vois tres bien que si vous gouvernie la fortunne, tans d'inconvenian n'arriveraÿ pas comme je pouraÿ postaitsre recevoir ordre de marcher à Lunen: mande mois si je ne puis passer a *Celle*, san donner de lombrage si *vous ni aitte pas* la bien seanse le demande, mais apresan je ne saÿ se que je dois faire La reponse de la Boulle, ayt assaÿ pican et elle merite bien unne reponse, dans la quelle jl ne faux pas éparnier la *musique*. je ne saÿ si je me trompe mais en relisang 11me lestre je ne le trouve pas si tandre ni si sainsaire que la 10me mande mois si je me trompe, la 10me aÿ scharmente elle marque unne veritable passion que vous aves eus en l'écrivang, pour lamour de mois, saje toujous de la sorte, et me faite poin apersevoir de la froidor, que je fais pour le merité, dite le mois, afein que je me puisse excuser. aise postaistre que vous trouve pas tendre que je vous prie pas de *venir*, mais songes se qui m'émpesche de le faire si vous le voules pourtang je vous en priraÿ mais je seraÿ postaistre 2 jour ici et puis vostre voisein aura le schang libre jl vous à aimé, ai maime jl vous a pas étté indifferang, je le crains toujour quois qui laÿ gaire à craindre, mais jl soufit qui la étté sur un pié for famillié avec vous, pour avoir juste raison de craindre son

impertinanse, et maime jl seraÿ faschos, de voir un homme
aupraÿ de vous, qui pourait avoir 20 petistrous par aux
jl vous pouraÿ voir, austre que vous ne saurie dire un
most qu'il ne puisse entendre, mais tous ses raisons ne
son pas soufisang, et si j'avois l'ésperanse à demorer je
vous conjureraÿ toujour de *venir* dans l'ésperanse que
vous trouveraÿ le mojein de vous en defaire, car san
cela je ne pouraÿ vous voire, puisqu'il seraÿ toujour en
gaÿt à Espioner. Puis que je ne puis vous abandonner
saÿ pourquois je refuse tous les avantage qui se presante,
je pretans vous faire voir par la mon attachement et saÿ
la mon unique but pour quois je vous fais voire les
lestres que lon m'écrivois de tous costé, crojé pourtan
caucunne avantage aÿ capable à me faire quiter ici tandis
que vous auraÿ de la bonté pour mois ; je connaÿ le
pouvoir d'unne *maire* que lon aime, et can selle vous
donne loccasion jl fauxtaistre aussi saje pour pouvoir
resister, mon san se remus, can je pense que la vostre seraÿ
capable, pour se vanjer de *Prince électoral* que vous le *fisie
coqus* et cant jl me vien dans la taiste, si jamais vous faisié
ses caraisses, à qu'elcaustre qu'a moÿ tous mon sang se
tourne dans mes vaines et je ne puis demorer sur la
plasse, tans que saite pensé me donne de linquiettude,
ah bondieux si je vous vojaÿs émbrasser qu'elqun avec
autang de passion *que vous* me *lavez* faite, et *monter* à
scheval avec la maime énvie, je ne vos jamais voir dieux
si je n'en devein pas fous, tenes en l'écrivang ma main me
tramble aÿ j'aÿ de la painne à poursuivre. schangon
de matiere, les amis don je vous aÿ parlé song Busch et
hammerstain, l'aurié vous bien crus, se sont os qui on mis
Prince électoral tous les histoire de mon jos en taiste, mais
'aÿ écrit aux premié unne lestre, qui luÿ feras bien connaistre sa foseté je me flatte de reschef puis que *Duchesse
de Celle* et *Duc de Celle* se songt accomodé, faite dong

de vostre mieux La *gaire* ne durera pas si longtemps
que cela *rouinerai* le *paix*, saÿ pourquois saite excuse ne
pos longtemps passer pour unne defaite, vojes si vous
tiendraÿ vostre parole, puis que vous me promaité que
vous moureraÿ plusto, que de n'aistre pas *unis avec
mois*, continue dans ses santiments, et vous me rande
la vie, vous souije assaÿ schaire, que vous serié capable
a tenir se que vous maves promis, si cela aÿ, je vous
jure éncor unnefois par les astres, que rien aux monde
m'éloinjeras de vous, par le lestre <u>ici jointe vous</u>
verreraÿ comme de nouvos, lon schersche à me persuader
d'Épouser la Filje de M. Bielke, mais ma reponse à étté,
que je moureraÿ plusto de fein que de le faire et que je
le priaÿ for, de me plus parlé de mariage, car cela nous
pouraÿ bruljer ensemble je me flatte que vous seraÿ
contente de ma resolution ; puisque nous vojang si pos
d'apparanse à nous *voir*, il faux sonjer à des expedian,
<u>vous le trouveraÿ sur se biljaÿt</u>, je crois que cela se
pouras, pour vos que je ne parte pas, et que je vous
feraÿ savoir entre ici et se temps la ; si vous voules
attendre jusques à ce que *Prince Max* sannuis, je ne vous
voirai de longtemps, car cant j laÿt avec *l'Électrice* et sa
maigre divinité, j laÿ comptemps comme un Roÿ, je n'auraÿ
pas crus que se margos m'auraÿ donné tang de schagrein,
comme jl faÿ, je vousdraÿ qui fust aux *fong* de la *hongrie*,
jl me donneraÿ plus des mos de coeur comme jl faÿ pre-
santement. Lon ne sauraÿ plus obligament, parlé comme
vous le faiste sur le schapistre de mourir de fein, mais
croje vous que quois qu'il meseraÿ dunne grande consolation de vous voir toujour a mon costé, que je vousdraÿ
vous antrenner dans la misaire, non non ne le croje pas,
vous deves vivre horos et comptemps enattandans que
je scherge qu'elque mors gloriose, pour abrejer mes jours

malhoros, et mourir *lament* de *Princesse électorale*.
j'aispaire que vous auraÿ resu les dos lestres dong je
vous ay parlée, si non mande le mois, vous me feraÿ plus
l'injustice de croire que qu'elque consideration dans le
monde me post detascher de vous, l'avos ici desus vous
feras voir que je moureraÿs avec mon Amour, comment
pouraitong vous quiter, car tans plus que lon vous connais
tan plus que lon vous adore, lon decouvre tous les jours
des nouvelles merites, et vostre passion aÿ sol capable à
me faire plustos tranjer la taiste que de vous abandonner,
pour jamais; j'aÿ de la honte de mon pos d'exactitude,
je vous en demande pardong, saite unne foste que je
vous prie de ne point attribuer à la neglijance mes aux
pos de memoir que j'ay, mais ma divinne Leonis, avoué
à vostre tour que mes lestres son bien plus grande, et
que san vous en avoir avertis, vous les aurié pas fais si
émple, schaqun à son paquaÿ, ainsi je consantiraÿ jamais
que vostre passion aÿ plus grande que la mienne, aÿ je
seraÿ inconsolable si je ne vous en avais pas donner plus
des marques essansielle, car vous pourié croire que la
vanité, puis que vous *aite preincess*, ferait que je
m'attasche, non je vous jure si vous aitié *filie* du *bouro*,
et que vous eusié les merites que vous possedes à
presang, je vous aimeraÿ, avec autang d'ardor, vous
me trouveraÿ gaire delicas, mais je me flatte que vous
trouveraÿ mes santimens tendres; onon des dieux continues, dans les santiments aux je vous vois, si ma dis-
grasse me voulaÿ pouser si loin, que vous eusie de
l'aversion pour mois, je me donneraÿ assurement un
cous de pistolaÿ . . .

11

Quo que j'avois pris la resolution de vous ecrir
demain, et de vous repondre émplement sur vois lettre
que j'aÿ reçu à la fois, du 13me 14me et 15me je me vois

privé de se plaisir, par la resolution que le Roy à pris,
d'ataquer demain l'armée de Franse, la quelle aÿt à 2
hors de nous, le lieux se nomme Engein; Dans tout
austre temps sette nouvelle m'auraÿ donné de la joÿ,
mais je vous avoue qu'a lors qui laÿ elle me chagrinne,
je suis aimée de vous l'unique objaÿ que j'aÿ trouvé
dinje d'aimer, je me suis poin trompé dans mon opinion
de croire que vous possedié, toute les Belle calité, que
lon puisse trouver aux monde, mais ma chaire je dois
hasarder la vie, et postaitre vous revoire jamais, à paine
aije sus que vous aitié innossante, et que je vous aÿ
soupsonné en fos, que je vous dois postaitre jamais plus
revoir, j'aÿ hasardé ma vie sant fois, par sottise aux par
geté de coeur, et je me connaÿ assaÿ, que je saÿ que
lamors ma jamais éffrajé, mais ma divinité se que me rans
poultrong aÿ la crainte de ne vous plus revoire, adieux
dong émable jllÿdojllÿrojllÿadieuxjllÿ, que je suis a
plaindre, et je suis pourtang horos, mais je ne pos
profiter de mong bonheur. ne croje pourtang poin que
vous aves un galang poltrong, non ma chaire, puis qu'il
faut aller aux combat, je mÿ comporteraÿ comme j faux,
et si je pos, j'aispaire de mi sinjaler; mais mon coeur
permaitemoÿ, de vous faire unne priaire la quelle aÿ,
que si mon destein me vost assaÿ de mal, d'aistre
éstroppié, d'un bras, aux d'unne jambe, ne m'oblie poin,
et ajé unpos de bonté pour un miserable qui, à fais son
unique plaisir de vous aimer, non ma chaire ne l'oblie
pas, sait un homme qui à eus un veritable attaschemens
pour vous, et qui l'auras tous le reste de sa vie, quoÿ
qu'estropié, mais sieux qui ont aité charmé par les
vostres, ne les vairerongs postaire plus, je ne pos penser
en cela, sans verser des larmes, ah que je profite bien
pos, d'aistre aimé de vous, et que vous me causé bien
des tourmens. jl sonne 12 hors; aux closjé de Halle; lon
apporte des balles poudre, et maisches saÿ le prologue

pour la saine que nous devons jouer demain, jl faux me
rendre à mon devoir, adieux emable enfang, ah que je suis
à plaindre du cang de Halle le 23me

12

mais Maistresse m'aurais émpesché de sonjer à vous,
aux Dieux est il possible, que vous croje cela, et si je
vous avois poin écris de tous (quo que celci est la 4me
lettrere) vous devries jamais avoir eus telle penses, ce
postil que vous croje que j'aime quel auître que vous, non
je vous proteste qu'apres vous je n'aimeraÿ jamais plus,
il ne seras pas for difficile de tenir parolle, car appres con
vous à addorer, post on trouver d'auître Famme jolie,
vous vous faite tors, decroire telle schose, et comment
pourie vous faire une comparaison de vous et les autres
et se post il c'apres avoir aimé une Deessé, lon pusse
regarder les Mortels, non énverité je suis de tros bong
gous, et je ne suis poin de ses jang qui voilje s'en-
canailjser ; je vous addore scharmante brunetté, et je
moureray avec ses sentiment, si vous m'oblije pas, je
vous jure que je vous aimeraÿ toute ma vie je n'atten
plus de vos lettres, parceque, je pretemps d'aistre bientos
aupres de vous, et mon unique occupation allors seras de
vous montre, que je vous aime à la follie, et que rien
m'ay plus schaire que vos grace, adieux, $\frac{\text{le 3me}}{23.}$.

13

Crainte de ne vous pouvoir parler je prens la liberte
à vous montre mong schagring du malheur, qui vous est
arrive Dieux sait que mon coeur me la predit, mais mon
companjon na schamais voulu attendre, quo que je luÿ
en aÿ pries, mais par comble de malheur jl faux que
j'éttande que mon amÿ intime à eus le plaisir avec
son faschos conpanjoin à vous éntretenir, jl me semble

que j'ay beaucoup de raisong de me plaindre des Dieuxs,
puisquil sont assay injuste de m'oter tous les mojengs
à vous rendre service et én meme temps le Donne, en
main à sos de qui j'ay le plus à craindre, depuis cet
axcidemps je me suis mis en teste, des étranje schose,
et je suis assay sos de croire que l'axcidemps arrivé,
hier, cet un prognostique de mon malheur, et que cela
sois le meme homme qui me coseras tous ses schagrings
cela feras que je le feraÿ observer de plus pres, à mon
absence et si j'attang la moindre schose, crojé moy en
honesthomme que je vous reverrerai jamais, et que
j'vaÿ plustos scherjé le fong de la Laplende, que de
parraistre devang ses sieux qui mon scharmée. je deteste
mon companjong, car sen cela j'auray éus le plaisir de
vous servir, aux lieux que je vois cette joÿ dans le sains
d'un homme, que j'abhorre, et qui est assay impertinang
de me le venir conter luy meme, m'apprenang dans
l'étas aux vous aviéz étté, voître deshabiljemen, sans
cornette les schevos pandus sur votre inconparable sain,
aux Dieux je ne pos plus ecrire de raje.

14

En faisang reflextion sur la miserable condiction dans
la quelle je me trouvois lon mapporte la voître pos
attendu de moy, ma joy estois si grande que j'ay oblijé
d'avoir du mal, en me lensang sur la lettre comme si
rien me manques vous avez tous fais ce que je souhaites
à vous voir faire, jl reste dong à moy à vous remercier
de vos bontée, et a vous bien persuader de ma fidellite

Jo ti saro fedele,
  Ne mai ti tradiro.
Se ben mi sei crudel,
  sempre t'adorero';

si vous m'en croje pas, je suis prest à abandonner Mere,

Parang, Amy, Biens, et la Patrie, pour vous en mieux persuader, et il dependera que de vous, si je dois faire le vojage que vous saves bien, mon malheros étas me fournit une bonne excuse, je pouray faire le malade bien longtemps, si vous aite d'acor avec moy je vous prie à me le mander car je prendray mes messure ladesu, say la plus grande éprove que je puis vous donner à présan, acceptele dong, et rende moy par la horos car le bien de vous voire surpasse de beaucoup à Lembition que jay de faire ma fortune, je n'an sauraÿ trouver de plus considerable et seluy de vous posseder may si jaire que je ne fais plus de reflextion sur tous les autres. Vous avez par votre lettre tellement purifié mon coeur que le moindre soupsong de jallosie ni reste pas, l'empressement que vous me temoinje pour savoir l'état de ma senté, me persuade assaÿ que vous maime pour contenter à votre desir je vous diray que je soufre éxtremement sepandang la douleur de ne vous voir poin surpasse en beaucoup, selle de la schutte, je pouray me porter mieux en 4 jour, mais si vous accepté ma proposition, je garderay éncor 10 jour la chambre cela n'émpescheras pas qu'ossitos que je pouray marscher je pouray vous embrasser aux lieux connue ; pour avoir de vos nouvelles, je crois que le plus sur mojen, est q'un de mes jangs (sur le quelle je pos me fier). . . .

15

Un autre que moy vous metteray sur l'éprove pour voire, si votre amour vous pouseray si loin que de venir sche moy, mais moy je vous aime trops pour vous pouvoir voire dans set hasar, et votre offre me sufit, cepandan pour ne poin perdre l'occasion de vous voire (puisque j'aÿ si pos de temps à rester avec vous) je viendray se soir sche vous, si vous j consente, et jattang de vous leur du rendevous, si vous trouve bong que je parraisse à la cour je le feray, mais sans cela poin.　La joÿ de vous revoir me fais oublier tous les schagrins que ma maladie ma attiré, je suis aureste assay contemps de vous, sepandang je ne pos oublier le pos d'opposition que vous faitte aux sujet de mon vojage, ajan une bonne éxcuse pour men dedire, je ne say se que j'an dois juger, Dieux volje solement que cette absence ne soy funeste pour moy.　Vous m'accusé que je vous aime pas assaÿ, comment pouve vous aistre si injuste, mais je passeray se poin sans j repondre saschan bien que vous aitte tros persuade de ma passion, qui est la plus pure que jamais à étté, et qui dureras tandis que je viveray, je vous l'ay contesté souven en prosse, permaite que je le fasse pour le presang en vers.

> So lang mein herҿ noch ohten ſpüret
> Wiel ich votre non lieben,
> Solange ſich mein blut noch rüret
> Bleibt ſie mir darrein geſchriben,
> Und ſol mit meines läbens lauf
> Bey mir die liebe nicht hören auf.

a 6 hors mon homme seras devang la schambre de la bonne bonne amÿ.

16

Le 1^{mer} de septemb.

Pardonnes si le schagrein et le desespoir m'a fais faire la foste à ne vous point écrire depuis dos jour cant on aÿ dans l'état aux je souis lon ne saÿ se que lon fais. je commenseraÿ par vous dire que j'aÿ schangé dos schifres dans nostre Clée, qui ay, j, se marque 31/ i, se marque 35, u, se marque 53, v, se marque 53, v, se marque 54/ je vous d'opserver sesÿ ; Appraÿ cela je vous diraÿ que vous aves marqué dos lestres, 10me ainsy que la 14me devraes aistrÿ la 15me mais continues solement

apresan, car j lia poin d'austre mal, que la segonde, aux
premiere 10me auray peus se perdre san que lon eus seus,
solement, que lon en eus perdue unne.   J'aÿ éncor à vous
dire, que je vous aÿ écrit dos lestres, adraissé, à 131,
que j'aÿ crus à *Celle*, jl faux savoir si vous les aves reseus ;
3 lestres ont été adraissé, aux *maistre de poste de Celle*
qui son daté le 20me et aÿ la 9me lestre, le 26me et aÿ la
12me lestre elle aÿ de *consequense* le 30me et ay la 14me
lestre ; j laÿ bong aussÿ de regarder si vous aves la 13me
lestre, je vous prie manques pas à me repondre ici desu,
vous pouves tous voir par la souite car je souis bien sure
que j'aÿ ette exacte saite fois ici.   Vous seraÿ surpris de
me voire faire des reflextions pareilje, dans l'état aux je
souis, mes ma schere nous avons tant des malhors, qu'il
ne faux pas s'en faire sois maime ; j'aÿ resu la vostre
daté le 26me mais vous saves quelle accidans m'ayt arrivé,
en prenan unne boutelje pour laustre, je vous laÿ mandé
dans mes presedantes je vois pourtang, dans vos daté
28me 29me et la 30me se que vous m'aves voulus dire
dans la 26me, j'ay unne joÿ tres grande de vous savoir,
hor *de crainte* et je me vos du mal d'aistre cause, de
vostre inquiettude, qui a contribué *beaucous a votre mal ;*
presantements que vous aites *hor de crainte* j'aispaire
que *la fievre vous quitera aussi ;* Que je vous plain
d'avoir tant soufer, *sis hors l'axaÿ* je ne comprans pas
comme *vous aves asay* de *forse* à *m'ecrire* éncor, je le
reconnaÿ comme je dois, et je souis persuadé que l'amour
vous, en rang ; mes a quelle poin vous souige point
obligé pour se marque de vostre tendraisse, j'amais
j'obliraÿ des telles bonté.   Si mes *lestres* avois assaÿ de
forse à *soulajer vos mos ;* je feraÿs en sorte que vous
en eusie, tous *les hores,* mes je prans se compliment
pour un aiffaÿ de vostre bonté, sepandans je pos vous
jurer que les vostres me consolle beaucoup, et san les
trois derniés daté 28me 29me et 30me je seraÿ aux tombos

à lheur qui laÿ. Se seraÿ la plus grande sottise appraÿ
tous que je pouraÿ faire, car quois que cela seraÿ tendre,
je vous perdraÿ; et vous dite forbien dans unne des
vostre qu'elle desespoir de ne se poin voir pour jamais,
vivons dons énsembles, aimons nous éternellement et
jurong nous de nouvos, unne constance à ne jamais finir,
et qu'aparÿ le trepas si nous avon le sang, que cela dois
durer aussÿ; Pour vivre énsemble prenes tous les soins
imaginable, à vous *conserver*, sonjes que mon repos en
depans; Si vostre *mal continue*, j laÿ seure que je
deviendraÿ fous. La fievre rainje beaucoup ici, nous
avons praÿ de 200 malades, de nos troupes mes domes-
tique le devienne un appraÿ l'austre, j'aÿ etté obligé,
d'anvojer mon valaÿ de chambre à Zelle, les austres sont
à Lunenb: si cela continue, le tous viendra à moÿ aussÿ.

17

Le 3me

jaÿ pensé tumber en apoplexie can j'aÿ auver vostre
lestre, san voir vostre mains j'aispairaÿ d'attendre *que
vous vous porterie mieux*, et vous faite tous le contraire,
j'ay crus du comensemens, que *saitais fais avec vous* ne
croje pas que je souis fasché que cela ne soÿ de vostre
main, bien loin de la, je vous conjure de continuer, de la
sorte car je ne vos absoluments pas, que vous vous *fa . .
ge.* je vous plein autang qu'un . . . tendre aÿ passionée,
le pos faire, faut il que le plus parfaist ojaÿ de l'univair
soufre *si cruellament*, Dieuxs pour quois aites vous si
injuste, mes mon coeur, je saÿ pourquois, *se malhor
tarrive*, pour me randre plus malhoros, le destein te *rang
mallade*, lon *te fais suffrir* pour me crucifier, L'on j
reusit car on pos pas, m'envojer un plus grans malhors
vous m'ordonnes de me poin *inquietter*, jl faudrois vous
gaire aimer, pour ne le pas aistre à la mors; je souis
a tous moments à *genous* faire *des veux* pour vostre

éntiere *retablissements*, je me flatte qua la fein on aura pitié de mois, mes vos son tros devoste, pour ne pas aistre éxhosé, Dieux volje que *cla sois bintos* que vous seray *quite* . . . *vos mos* et moÿ de mes *crain* . . *s* et de mon *inquetude* avec qu'elle joÿ vous embrasserage, can j'auraÿ selouis de vous voir je ne saÿ can je le pouraÿs, mes mon dessien aÿ de *faire en sorte comme si un acsai de fievre me prenais*, je diraÿ os bon homme, que je vousdraÿ bien allé pour *tros jour* à 317 pour éviter que la fievre n'aye poin de prise, sait a dire prendre des remaides, aux Lieux de demorer à 317 je *prandray la poste* et je *voleray* à *Celle*, je pourais aistre *dos nuis avec vous* quelle joÿ qu'elle satisfaction je pouraÿs aistre à vos pié les beinger de mes larmes, vous voiraÿs dans qu'elle éttas pitojable, *votre mal ma mis ;* Mes je me flatte postaistre envein, car avan que je pouraÿ *juer* se *role* jl faux premierements que le bon homme se porte mieux . . . depans encor de la fortunne de la 9 . . . je n'aÿ rien de bong à Esperer , La rage le desespoir, le schagrein l'inquiettude la Passions, tous ses schoses énsemble font un aifaÿ sur moÿ, que je souis comme ses jans que lon voist à Amsterdam dans le Dulḥaus, Dieux sait qu'elle feins que cela auras ; Les maladie hogmante de jour en jour, mon vieux Lieute C: et dos Lietenang le song devenus aujourdoÿ, je ne saÿ comments j'an éschappe, sait un miracle car avec tous les schagreins, qui m'abastes je le devraÿs avoir ; adieux mon Ange je ne pouis vous Mander davantage, l'expraÿ qui m'a été envojé, du bon homme par, crojes que vous aves un amang, qui prang tang de . . . r à tous se qui vous tousche que vous le . . . ie faire vous maimes, j laÿ seinsaire vous adore, et à autang de Respect pour vous que qui que se soit ; je merite toute vostre tendraisse, et tous les soins oblijan que vous aves pour mois, si je ne vous donne pas assaÿ d'assuranses, de ma passion, et de ma fidelité, se n'aÿ pas ma fostre, saÿ que j'en aÿ pas l'occasion ; je vous annueraÿ avec mes protestations, car je le repaiste dans tous mes lestres, je me flatte que vous aite comme mois je ne les sauraÿ trop attendre et tous vos lestres fusetelles ramplis daustre chose elles me seray toujo . . . . . . reable et plus que comme si j liavois rien.

18

Je suis bien aise, que vous aites unnefois contemps de moÿ, mais jl me semble que cela vous rejouis poin car vous me donne toujours des mattiere, à vous faire des reprojes ; et par la vous m'oté la joy d'aistre satisfait de vous, vous vous plainjé que vostre passion vous trouble vostre repos, je le vos croire mes saite passion vous tient pas tang aux coeur, que vous retranjeraÿ les moindre plaisirs pour cela, non non sait a moÿ a me blaindre, ma passion me trouble poin solement, mais me desespaire, Dieux comme je fie les éndrois aux je saÿ que les divertissemens song, je vousdraÿ bien vous voir à la Porte de Brusels, aux de Gens sans j maistre le pie, plustos de faire cela vous m'abandonnerie, et dis austre galang, vous trouve vostre conduite bonne, moÿ aussÿ, mais je seraÿ hors deséspoir que la mienne ne fus pas meljor je suis bien aise que vous ne s'ajé, tombé malade, jen aurais etté inconsolable, quoÿ que je ne suis poin contente de vous, vous aves étté contente de ma lettre, j'en aÿ de la joÿ, vous j aves veus les santimens de mon coeur, sans faintes ; je vous remersie bien, humble-ment, que vous me promaistes, de ne poin donner vostre portraÿ, à la personne connue Pourquoÿ me flatté vous tang dans vos lettres, can vous sonjes si pos a me tenir vos promess, vous m'assurés que rien vous seras dificille et que vous feraÿ tous pour me plaire, saÿ for bien dis mes for mal tenus ; helas vous me dite flattong nous le

temps nous poura randre horos, mais saschés que le temps
me rendra le plus malhoros de tous les hommes, je naÿ
poin la hardiesse à vous dire se que je saÿ deja, mais ma
chaire je crois, que lon moblijera a vous quiter, je ne pos
finir saite lettre, de schagrein, tristesse et collaire adieux,
ne me haijsé dumoin pas, car sur mon dieux je ne le
merite en fason du monde.

19

14me.

Assurement san la vostre du 12me le Bastement de
Coeur que 127 m'avois causé, mauraÿt aschevé, mais
Pour mon bonhor, je laÿ resu dans le temps que mon
coeur allais craiver, et comme j'ÿ vois que sa nouvelle aÿ
traÿ fose, je commense aussi à me remaistre, jl me disaÿ
pour tres assuré, que *votre fievre* vous aves, *repris*,
assurement je n'auraÿ peus passer la nouit, avec saite
inquiettude san mourir, et alor que je vous écris, j'aÿ
encor lohs de la Raine d'hongrie sur le née, je crois
pourtang que cela se passera, je me san Pourtang alterré,
et éschofé, si cela se passe pas la nouit je me seinjeraÿ
pour prevenir le mal, qui pouraÿ m'en arriver; M. de
sporque Mourera selon tous les apparance encor aujour-
douis, j'aÿ 3 Captaine, 5 Lieutenans, et 4 Enseinges mal
à lamors, plus de 300, fantasein aÿ Dragons, de nos
troupes sol, son sur les dans, sait un air infecté, les plus
sain j deviene malade, toustefois je me flatte de ne le
poin devenir *vous saschang, hor daffaire.* Vous auraÿ
veus par ma lestre daté le 12me combien je souis contemps de vous, ne prene pas mal que je vous aÿ prié de
me marquer dos mos par vostre main, je savois que vous
vous portié unpos mieux san cela je ne l'auraÿ pas fais,
mais mon incomparable coeur vous en faite tros, car
vous m'écrives dos foiljes éntieres, se que je vous prie
tres instament de ne poin faire plus, ni plustos que vous

aites tout à fais bien. Le *sieje* de *Scharleroi* feras que *Prince électoral* seras pas si tos ici, gran Dieux fais que se *sieje* nous *delivre* des *faschos*. Lon dis pour sertein que les affaires s'acomode, mais les ordres que lon donne pour soinjer les malades, me fong trambler de pur, que nous quiteron pas sitos se poste ; je souis agité du maime desespoir que vous, de passer ma vie avec des jans pour les quelles j'aÿ unne aversion et de la passer si pos avec selle que j'adore, sepandans vous aites plus à plaindre car je pos forsouvang m'en dispensér, et vous poin, austre les *embrasades* que vous aites obligé à essujer, jl me semble si j'aÿtais obligé a soufrir la maime schose, je ne pouraÿ m'énpescher de vosmir tous les fois que cela m'ariveraÿt, ah qu'elle horor de *caraisser* se que lon hait mortellement, je crois fortement que le pourgatoire ne donne poin tans de tourments, que des pareiljes *caraisses.* si j laÿ vraÿ que *Électeur de Hanovre* vas pas a 308, je pouraÿ bein j venir, mes nous pouvons pas prendre des mesures avang, que lon sasche, se que deviendra *Prince électoral la Dujais d'Hanovre* n'*arrivera*, que *ver la fein du mois* qui *vient* et allors *Prince électoral* sera deja de retour, et les *schases* finÿ. Dieux volje solement que nous les comension bientos, et que *vous* fusies *en etas de vous rendre.* Je vous plains que vous *aites* tan *maigri* mes (avec vostre permission) je trouve redicule, et absourde, la question que vous me faite, si je n'aimes en vous que vostre bosté je vous le pardonneraj mes vous aites persuadé, que se n'aÿ pas solement cela que j'adore, se son vos merites vostre humor, je vous avoue que de vous voire belle cela aÿ scharmang pour la veus, mes je vous proteste que fusie vous laide comme Mad: Kopstein, je vous aimeraÿ pas un brein de moin ; du degous pour vous, ah postong faire unne question pareile à selle ici, à un amang qui vous aime tendrement, non non Leonis vous n'aite pas

persuadé de ma sainsaire passion, que fostil que je fasse
pour vous en bien conveincre je n'auraÿ du repos, que
j'usques à se que je sache que vous laite toust à fais ;
croje vous q'unne passion pareilje à la mienne, saÿ
formée sur unne schose si passaschaire que la bosté,
quois que vous en aje beaucoup, et plus coqunne de
vostre sexe, je vous pos dire que se n'ay pas elles qui
ma mis dans l'estas aux je souis, j laÿ vraÿ que la Bosté
que vous possedé, mas énflame, et sans elles je n'auraÿ
postaire pas étté si huros que je souis, mes se qui ma
randu comme je souis saÿ vostre ésprit, vostre seinserité,
vos maniere de vivre, et a lafein saÿ saite ame si bien
née, et si juste, la quelle prodouit en vous unne dousor
non pareilje, unne jenerosité sans égale, de la Clemanse,
au dela de l'imagination, se son saÿs vertues qui mon
mis dans saite aimable Esclavage dans la qu'elle je me
fois à sait hors, et dans la quelle je pretans mourir aussÿ.
En verité Leonis vous me schagrines beaucoup, avec vos
questions, vous crainjes que je deviendrays invidelle à
la plus grande Boté du siecle, et à la vertue maime, pour
qu'elque gose de *preinsaises* qui n'aurong poin d'austre
merite que selle de *venir de Paris* encore unne fois, je vois
que tros que vous n'aite pas éncor bien persuadé de mon
amour, je me flatte qu'a la fein je vous en donneraÿ
tans de marques que vous n'en saurie plus douster.
Pour prendre des messures juste jl faux se parler, nous
avon du temps jusques à *la fein* du *moi* qui *viens* et avang
se temps nous avons point à craindre le *retour* de *Prince*
électoral et de *la Dujaïÿse* vous entames encor des *preinsai*
crojes vous postaitre que j'aime tans la nouvosté, le
schangementes, et les jans qui vienne de *Paris* comme
vous, vous vous trompes beaucoup, je porte mes schaines
avec beaucoup de plaisir, et je ne les janjeraÿ pas, pour
le Raujome du grand mogol.   La lestre de la Lieutenan
Colonelle ay for sotte mes la personne aÿt assaÿ resonable,

elle à randus un for galant homme aux baÿ bas, de grande
Calité, fort amouros, jl sapelle le marquis de Spinosa,
saÿt un des galans de se paÿ la ; mais pouis que je vous
aÿ énvojes unne tres sotte lestre, je le recompenseraÿs
par unne qui aÿ forbien écrit ; si elle n'aitois écrit d'un
livre, on la doist, admirer particoulierement venan de
saite personne, mes sasche qu'elle se trouve mot en mot
dans un livre, sepandans elle ne laisse pas, que d'aistre
tourné assaÿ aprospos, je vous prie de me la ranvojé, je
vous l'envois parse que jè crois que cela vous divertiras
adieux.

20

je vois que le plaisir que je maitait fais à vous émbrasser s'évanuit entieremens puisque l'incomode à paru
si brusquement, je vous avoue que se visaje m'a bien
deplus can je lay appersu, un cous de foudre m'auray
pas plus pus surprendre, mais jl faux qui lÿ aÿe toujor
des faschos visajes qui empesche, un doux éntretien
comme celuÿ que nous devien croir, selong tous éppar-
ance devray aître, ouÿ j'an nay eus l'idé si remplis de
joÿ, que je naÿ pus dormir toute la nuit, mais helas tout
est vanuis, et il faux que je passe la seconde nuit sans
dormir, et avec du jagrein aux lieux que la premiere me
rejouissay, j laÿ sur qu'a moin que vous n'aje la bonté
de me consoler, je me beinjeray dans mes larmes, consolé
moy dong divine bosté, et soulajes un homme qui se
mor pour vous, et qui est si éntesté de vos merite que
la servelle luy en tourne.

> Pour unné joué merveilje
> je brule d'un fos si beaux
> que ma raison ma conseilje
> De l'aimer jusques aux tombos

Voila ma maxime, et vous me le vairreraÿ éxecuter
éxactement, ma plus grande satexfaction seras de vous

montrer, que la mort sol est sollement capable d'éfasser
mon amour. mais pour l'amour de Dieux sonjes à la
divise, rien d'inpure mallume, adieux.

21

à 6 heurs.

je ne sauraÿ partir dici sans vous remersier, de
l'ambaras aux vous maves tiré, assurement j'aitois
un homme fricassé sans la conversation d'hier aux soir,
je pars aussi contemps, q'un homme qui laisse ce qui
addore, le pos faire, mais se qui me consolle, ces que
je suis bien persuadé de vôtre amitié, et que mon absance
me fais poin de tors, j'ay lame si reposé que je suis tout
autre que je naÿs étté ; je vous prie, poin de tait à tet,
avec personne, particulierment avec M. R: je sauraÿ
tout, car j'ay des bons amÿ ici que vous soupsonne poin.
adieux Bella dea, sonjé autang à moy que je sonje à
vous, je vous émbrasse les jenous un million de fois, et
suis eternellement vôtre esclave.

22

ce 25 aoust
4 septembre

Je prens tant de plaisir a vous entretenir que dabord
que jai un moment de liberté je lemploÿe a vous assurer
de ma tendresse je vous aÿ escrit hier mais jl me semble
que ie ne vous aÿ pas assez marqué linquietude ou je
suis sur ce que vous me dites je nen aÿ pas dormi toute
la nuit j aÿ repassé toute mes actions et plus ie mexamine
et moins je deuine ce que vous pouuez auoir contre moi il
est seur que vous deuez estre content de ma conduite ma
passion la regle et cela suffit je vous conjure encore une
fois de me mander tout le plus tost que vous pourrez ce
que ce peut estre jl me sera fort aisé de me justifier
puis que ie naÿ jamais pense qua vous plaire et je vous
feraÿ auec plaisir tous les sermens les plus affreus sur

mon jnnocence mais je vous demande jnstamment de
me dire qui sont ceus qui vous disent de semblables
Calomnies jls ont sans doute leurs raisons pour nous
brouiller et selon toutes les aparences ils nen demeureront
pas la soẙez persuadé je vous en conjure que je suis
jncapable de rien faire qui vous déplaise mes manieres
vous lont fait voir jusques icẙ et jen feraẙ encore plus
a lauenir je suis au desespoir de ne pouuoir vous faire
connoistre au tant que ie le voudrois mon attachement
pour vous les occasions me manque et point la volonté
et je ne seraẙ point contente que ie naẙe fait voir a toute
la terre que vous me tenez lieu de grandeurs de plaisirs
et de tous les agremens du monde le seul que je souhaitte
est celuj de posseder vostre coeur je nen demande point
dautre et ce seul bonheur me rendra toujours tous les
autres jndifferens je suis persuadée que si jestois a han.
on me feroit bien des histoires de vous mais je me fie
trop a vous pour croire legerement ce que lon me
pourroit dire faites en de mesme et croẙez fortement
que rien nest capable de me faire changer je suis dans
un chagrin mortel on dit quil sest donné un combat
depuis peu et je ne saẙ encore ce qui en est je tremble
que vous ne vous exposiez sans necessité et quil ne
vous soit arriué quelque accident conseruez vous je
vous en conjure sil vous reste encore quelque tendresse
moẙ que deuiendrois je si japrenois que vous fussiez
blessé ie croẙ que ien mourois.

23

ce 2 septembre
12

Il estoit si tard quand ie vous aẙ escrit que ie naj
peu repondre a tout ce que uous me dites jaẙ releu
plusieurs fois vostre lettre cest un mélange de tendresse
et dairs railleurs que ie trouue fort plaisant et jl me
parroist quelque mine que uous fassiez que mon uoẙage

ne uous plaist point uous auez cependant tous les torts du
monde car selon toutes les aparances ie repartiraj dicȳ
sans auoir ueu une personne raisonable et je le souhaitte
de tout mon coeur. Je ne croȳ pas aller a la foire de
jllifrancjllifortjlli et ie ne dirai pas un mot pourȳcontribuer
il me semble que cela uous doit persuader que ie ne
cherche pas le monde et que ie suis jncapable de songer
aus plaisirs quand ie ne uous uoȳ point jespere partir
dicȳ en quinze jours le peda. a pris aujourdhui cette
resolution ie men retourne auec elle trouuer le grondeur
et je me rendrai à Han. un peu auant le retour du
Reformeur ie ne saurois encore uous dire rien de positif
pour ce qui regarde le *jlligörjlli* ie ne croj pourtant pas
ȳ aller car la saison sera trop auancée pour que le
Reformeur en puisse estre et je me flatte pourueu que
rien ne vous retienne ou vous estes que ie pourraȳ vous
voir bientost je jugerai de uostre tendresse par uostre
empressement mais je uous conjure de prendre si bien
uos mesures que ie uous uoje en particulier la premiere
fois. Jl me seroit jmpossible de soustenir uostre ueue en
public et mon transport me trahiroit, on dit que les
françois pourroient nous enleuer aisément cela fait que
ie souhaitte fort de men aller car je naȳmerois point du
tout a estre prise et ie ueus uous conseruer uostre con-
queste je suis charmée de uostre Careme et je uous en
fais tous les remerciemens que uous meritez jen suis
surprise et je ne mȳ attendois point cest en quoi la chose
est plus obligeante jl nȳ a point de sentinelle au monde
que uous deuiez craindre et le prisonnier doit Conter sur
la prison qui sera toujours ouuerte pour luȳ et fermée
pour toute la terre cest dequoi ie uous reponds et dune
passion qui seruira dexemple ie ueus uous en persuader
malgré que uous en aȳez et que ie ne trouue de bonheur
nȳ de satisfaction qua vous aimer et la Estre aimée uous
me paroissez si peu seur de cette uerité que ien suis

sensiblement touchée dites moÿ ce quil faut faire pour
que uous nen puissiez plus douter il nÿ a rien que ie ne
fasse auec joÿe pour vous faire uoir que vous me tenez
lieu de toutes choses et que tous mes desirs et mon
ambition sont bornez a uous plaire sil ne faut que cela
pour vous rendre heureus vous lestes plus que personne
du monde car ie ne ueus viure que pour uous seul et ie
renonce auec plaisir a toute la terre pour nestre jamais
qua uous.

24

ce 13 septembre
23

au lieu de lextresme plaisir que me donnent toutes
uos lettres celle que Jaÿ receue ce soir ma percé le cœur
Lon ne peut rien jmaginer de plus offensant que ce que
uous mescriuez ie ne le repeteraÿ point ie croÿ que uous
uous en souuiendrez bien encore et ie donnerois tout au
monde pour pouuoir loublier par quel endroit de ma uie
aÿ je peu meriter lopinion que uous me tesmoignez auoir
de moÿ si ie croyois ÿ auoir donné Lieu ie uoudrois estre
morte mais plus ie mexamine et plus ie me trouve es-
loignée de pareils sentimens et graces a dieu je me sens
le coeur aussi noble que ie le dois auoir ie ne ueus plus
uous rien dire sur ce suiet ie pourrois me facher et ie
hais fort laigreur mais pour repondre aus quatre points
qui uous ÿ tiennent si fort ie suis bien trompée si ie ne
uous aÿ mandé ÿ que jliisparrjllii a esté a L. et si je ne
laÿ point fait cest assurément par oublÿ et par ce
que ie naÿ pas trouué quil ualust la peine que ie me
souuinsse de luj. je puis uous faire tous les sermens
quil uous plaira quil nÿ a aucune raison que celle la et
de plus ie ne luj aÿ pas dit deus mots pour la joye que
uous me reprochez dauoir eue de trouuer jliiguljlljden-
jllyleujlii icÿ ie ne uous ÿ repondrez point car cest une

opinion ridicule, et rien au monde n'est si mal jmaginé a
lesgard de la foire ie uous assure que ie naÿ pas dit un
mot pour ÿ aller mais comme ie suis de bonne foÿ ie ueus
bien uous auouer que ie nen suis point fachée et pour
mon nouuel amant uous estes fou de uous jnquieter pour
luj car jl est loin dicÿ et selon toutes les aparences ie ne
le uerraÿ point et ses soeurs nÿ personne du monde
ne me feront jamais faire aucune demarche contre la
tendresse dont jaÿ le coeur si rempli ie uous aÿ déia
mandé que ie suis persuadée quil ne uiendra point a
han. mais si cela arriuoit pourueu que ie sois plus contente de uous que ie ne la suis ce soir ie brutaliseraÿ
plustost que de soufrir ces uisites ie suis bien sotte de
uous rendre raison sur toutes uos uisions uous qui en auez
peu sur tout ce qui me regarde et qui mauez desesperée
par uos tre belle lettre jl est uraÿ que uous uoulez
ensuitte reparer uostre faute mais cela ne suffit point et
ie ne suis pas contente car ie ueus uostre estime et uous
ne temoignez pas en auoir pour moÿ, la Confidente en a
receu hier une de laimé jlliketjllilerjlli qui lui escrit par
lordre du jljlandjlljgrajlliuejlli pour faire ses complimens a Leonisse puis que uous uoulez lappeller ainsi
et pour lassurer quil fera son possible pour la uoir icÿ ou
a la foire ie ne croÿ pourtant pas que cela se puisse par
ce que nous partons demain et lon nÿ sera quun seul jour
ie uous escriraÿ dabor, que ie seraÿ arriuée et ie uous
rendrai un conte sincere et fidelle de tout ie ne uous
diraj rien de tendre pour ce soir car uous ne le meritez
point ie crains bien que ie nauraj pas la mesme force
demain et que ie ne me souuiendrai plus de ma colere
car Jai furieusement du tendre pour uous et quoi que ie
ne uous le dise point ie sens bien que ie uous aime auec
une passion qui neut iamais desgale.

25

fra ce $\frac{14}{24}$

je suis ici depuis deus heures le peda. a esté descendre
chez la p. jllitajllirenjllitejlli ou ie naӯ ueu que de soste
figures de la nous auons esté a la foire ou ie naӯ pas ueu
une personne de qualité la Marionette est icӯ et sa belle
soeur ie ne les uerraӯ que demain dont ie suis bien aise
car ie pourraӯ me reposer dont jaӯ grand besoin naӯant
pas fermé loeil toute la nuit un aӯ passé la moitié a uous
escrire et lautre a me chagriner sur ce bel endroit de
uostre lettre, ie nous prie bien fort de ne me plus donner
de pareils suiets dennuӯ car ie suis fort delicate sur le
chapitre dont il est question hors ce uilain endroit que ie
ne saurois oublier et qui gaste tout uostre lettre est charmante et rien nest si dous que tout ce que uous me dites.
raccomodez cette affaire si uous uoulez estre bien auec
moӯ car elle me tient fort au coeur le mien est si rempli
de uous que quoi que jaӯe suiet de men plaindre ie ne
saurois mempecher de uous dire que ie me suis faite une
uiolence horrible hier au soir pour ne uous point parler
de ma tendresse jamais on nen a tant eu et jamais lon a
moin merité de reproches que ie le fais uous estes le
plus jnjuste de tous les hommes dauoir la moindre
défiance sur ce qui me regarde je suis trop ueritablement
auous pour que uous aӯez rien a craindre toute mes
actions uous en persuaderont car jl est certain que ma
passion pour uous ua jusqua lexces je uous conjure destre
bien persuadé de cette uerité et quil nӯ a rien au
monde que ie ne fasse pour uous faire uoir que ie suis
plus a uous qua moi mesme iespere que ie ne uerraӯ nӯ
le Land. nӯ personne et ie le souhaitte de tout mon
coeur si uous trouuez quelque chose qui ne nous plaise
point dans ce que ie uous aӯ escrit hier nen accusez que
le depit ou uous mauez mise.   Il a esté jusqua me faire

pleurer et tous les charmes de vostre lettre nont peu me faire pardonner larticle ofensant soÿez en repos sur ma conduite elle sera diuine ie uous en repons et pour le Riual.

26

au nom de dieu menagez vous ma uie est unie a la vostre jl me vient mille pensée desesperante dans lesprit et je suis accablée de douleur jaurois peine a vous parler dautre chose jaÿ tout loisir de nourrir mon chagrin et je suis auec une veritable joÿe dans cette solitude Jai oublié hier a vous rendre graces de ce que vous me dites au suiet de la boule rien nest si obligeant je consens a cette condition quelle deuienne ma riuale car je vous auoue que jaime le triomphe et quil est fort de mon goust adieu rien nest capable de me faire changer ie suis née pour vous aimer vous estes ma seule passion je nen aÿ jamais en auant de vous Connoistre et je mourraÿ en vous aÿmant plus que lon na jamais aime.

27

mecredi 24.

Il faut vous rendre conte de ce que jaÿ fait hier jai esté tout le jour seule il est venu un envoÿé du maistre de ce lieu faire compliment au peda. il sest si fort embarassé dans sa harangue que iaÿ eu peine a mempecher den rire jl en a fait un aussi au coeur gauche et sen est allé dabord lon sest promené a pied au retour lon a soupé et je me suis entretenue auec la Confidente cest le seul plaisir que jaÿe car nous parlons toujours de vous.

28

Quo que je vous aÿ ecrit hier aux soir je ne pos m'empescher, de vous dire que j'aÿ passé la plus meschante nuit du monde, j'ay sonjé a vous mais je vous aÿ veus infidelle, voila le sonje, il me semblais, que

je vous avois prie de ne poin voir un sertain grant
homme, et que malgre vos promesse vous lavie fais
entré ché vous pour luÿ dire adieux, j'en fus avertis, ne
pouvan énduré cette infidelité, je feinjis d'avoir une
lettre de Mad : voître maire pour vous donner j'entraÿ
prusquement dans vostre schambre, et je vis le spectacle
le plus affros du monde, ces grans M. vous tenais
émbrassé, et que pis aÿ, vous aitié sol dans vostre
schambre. vous faisie unpos la vasché contre vostre
adonus en luÿ disant qui laitois impertinent, je voulus
aussi me retire mais vous m'apellaté, je fus ravis de cela
parce que cela me donna lieux de vous dire en oreilje
que vous aitié la plus ingrate de tous les dames, et que
ce seraÿ la dernierefois que je vous parleraÿ, en
éffaÿ je fus trouver M. de Pude, pour luÿ prier de
m'envojer en Hongrie, ce qu'il fit. je vous demande
pardong du sonje criminel, mais je me croirais bien plus
criminel si je vous en avertissaÿ poin, ne croje pas que
je l'invante non j lay surmondieux vraÿ, pourlamour de
tous ce qui vous aÿ le plus schaire, aje soin de me
fortifier l'esprit, et tiremoÿ de ma crainte, j'ay por que
ce sonje saÿ qu'elque pressage funeste, et qui ne vos dire
rien de bong. Il seraÿ injuste q'un tendre amour
m'attiras des infidellites, je ne l'éspaire pas car pourquoÿ
voudrievous abandonner un coeur qui vous adore, et qui
vous jure de vous aistre fidelle, si des telles vos vous
pove attascher uniquemens à moÿ, je vous proteste devan
Dieux, que jamais je vous serraÿ infidelle, et que je vous
aimeray toute ma vie avec la maime passion que je fais
astor. Can j'auray l'honnor de vous éntretenir de la
debeausche faite hier vous riraÿ bien, la baronne si aÿ
sinjales et les grande barbe suedoise, on faite le meljor
. . . du monde, elle a tens aites fro . . . os que la
planjer de song tei . . . turel, à commensé à paraistre se
qui à fais le plus plaisans spectacle de monde ; Elle

ma demande pourquoÿ je me divertissaÿ poin je luÿ
respondis que j'aitois venus faire ma cour à M. Bil. et
non pour me divertir, en me quitans elle ma donné le
non de traiter, surquoÿ je louÿ ai repliqué, que je ne
laistas pas encor mais que je le pouraÿ bien devenir.
M. le Duck, a joué à l'homber hier au soir sches Elle,
voila le Diable, je finiraÿ en vous prians de vous preparer
à me tirer de l'inquiettudes aux je suis, et de me croire,
inviolablement attasches à vous et à tous sos qui vous
regarde, je vous émbrasse de tous mon coeur, et je paise
un milion defois vostre portrais, adieux.

29

venes sur un vendredis au soir ici, et attandes que
l'Elector vient ici, si lon oste pas *Prince Max* vous vous
pouves retourner, et cela vous servira de pretexte aupraÿ
Duc de Celle et *Prince électoral* mande mois si vous
agrees, ma pense, si vous le pouves faire faite que je
vous vois car franjement je ne puis plus vivre de la sorte,
pour la mour de mois de vous faite que je vous vois
et que je vous embrasse, car san saite satisfaction la
vie may rien.

30

La joÿ de voir le Ref: partÿ a étté interrompu par le
schagrein de vous voir malade, j'aispaire pourtang que
cela ne sera pas grans schose, car san cela je n'en pouraÿ
dormir toute la nouit, j'aispaire a vous émbrasser demain
aux soir, j'attemps le sinjal ordinaire, et le meschang
temps m'enpescheras pas de gouter du plaisir, de vos
scharmantes émbrassades, amoin que vous me l'ordonnié
austrement je me flatte du contraire et j'aispaire que
vostre émpressement reponderas aux mien ; si vous ne
sorte pas demain, sisi souffira pour vous assuré que les
momens me durerong des siecles, et que le temps que je
suis éloinjé de vous sont sos que je posse inutilement

dans le monde et que je suis prait a venir demain aux lieux connus, j'áttemps le sinjal et je suis vostre tres-obeissant valet.

31

Lon ne pos aistre plus contemps de vous que je le suis vos mamire obligante d'hiair, vostre tres-schere lestre, enfein tous me scharme, je commense à revivre, et la journé d'hiaire et unne de sos quil fos que je marque dans mon livre ; pour bien en profiter je vous prie que je vous vois se soir, j'attendraÿ le sinjal avec bien de l'impatiance car je mor d'anvie de vous temoinger ma joÿ elle ait axsaissive, et ne se post exprimer, pour lamour de vous de moÿ, et de tous se qui vous aÿ schaire, continue *de la* sorte, vous pouraÿ allors me persuader que je n'aÿ rien à craindre, que je seraÿ toujour horos et contemps, voila le plaisir de l'amour, son la les scharmes d'un attaschement seinsaire et veritable ; L'avos du Grond : me donne encor beaucoup d'ésperanse tasché de l'attendrir, vous le pouraÿ si vous voules, mais il faux vous j appliquer, et bien prendre vostre temps saye avec cela persuadé, que si le siel me destinne le bonhor de vous posseder, que j'auraÿ les maniere tous austre, que vous vous les immaginée, et je vous jure que je le regleraÿ sur les vostre, ajouté fois a set avos car j laÿ seinsaire et par d'un amme san fosseté, et san finesse ; Comme le temps aÿ bos je me flatte à vous voir a la volerie, j'aispaire de vous j trouver tendre, et contemps adieux jusque la, vous me diraÿ bien un petit mos, du quel je pos voir que vous accorde ma priaire.

32

le 2me

Vous me faite mourir can vous faite des complimens, parseque vous ne me reponde poin sur tous les poin des miennes je vous aÿ prié de ne poin écrire de tous, et à me fair solement savoir par *Mlle. von dem Knesebeck l'etas de votre santé* je le repaite éncor ici, et vous conjure de ne le poin faire si cela vous donne la moindre fatigue, jl soufit pourvos que vous me marques dos mos, affein que je voje saite devinne écriture la quelle aÿ capable a bannir tous les craintes que je me forme. La resolution que je dois prendre selong l'avis de tous mes amis, me mait à l'hasar, que can *joray quité*, je feraÿ resonner tous le monde, et postaistre me feraitong dire par un troisiemme, que *lon souhaite*, que *je me retire*, que deviendrage allors, crojé moy quil fos penser a toust avan que de prandre unne ferme resolution, la schose m'aÿ de tros grande consequence ; *Duc de Hanovre* trouvera mille jans comme *Königsmarck* mais je me flate que *Princesse héréditaire* n'én trouveras jamais qui sois si fidelle, et que aime avec plus d'ardor que moÿ, L'exaÿ de ma passion vas à la follie, helas ma tres schaire vous merites bien d'autres que *Königsmarck*, je souis tres persuadé que si lon vous devraÿ avoir donné un galang selong vos merite, je n'auraÿ pas eus le bonhor d'aistre vostre Esclave, mais si qu'elcun d'unné passion Extra-ordinaire d'une constanse sans Egalle auraÿ dus aistre vostre galang j lay juste que se soÿ mois, car je le desputeraÿs non pas oh Mortels, mais aux dieux maime, et je leur defie d'en faire un qui m'égalise ; Que les sermans on daifaÿ cant on aÿ dans l'estas, *aux vous aites*, jamais je naÿs etté plus contemps de vous, jamais je vous aÿ plus crus, qu'a presang, vous m'aimeraÿ dong toujour jan pos aistre assuré, car vous me iuré que tan que je vous aimeraÿ, vous feraÿ demaime je vous aimeraÿ touste ma vie, et vous me jures la maime schose, que poje plus pretandre, tous mes vos sont éxhausé, je souis l'homme du monde le plus horos ; *gerisse* vous, et je pos aistre aux comble de may joÿ, je souis poin contemps, que vous preferais á m'ecrire, plus qu'a prendre du repos, je vous conjure sonjes à *prendre vostre repos*, et pouis à vostre

amang. Que je vos du mal à vostre coeur, de son mauvaÿ
gous, vous quiter pour venir sché moÿ, jl ne connais pas
la diferance, laisse cela aux mien, jl faux pas schanger en
mal mes en bien. Vostre resit me fait tramblé, et je crains
que *la fievre* laustre *accidans* ne vous *abate tang* que vous
ne saurie vous remaitre si tos. je ne saÿ mon coeur me dis
que vous *aite hor de danje* je naÿ plus tans d'inquiettude
que j'aÿ eus du comensements, je pran cela pour un traÿ
bon sienge, dumoin je m'én flatte et je souhaite ardaments
que cela soit einsÿ, j'espaire que mes vos sont éxhausé, et
qu'a lor qui laÿ vous vous *portes mieux.* La resolution
que vous aves prisse, de prandre *se que je vous avois
laise* aÿ *grande*, je vous avoue que si je l'avois seus au-
paravang, j'an auraÿ tramblé, mais comme toust aÿ bien
allé, je souis enrepos, j lia que le schagrein, *daitre caus*
que vous *soufres bien plus* et si vous vous *trouvie astor
plus mal* je serais inconsolable. je souis obligé d'avouer que
les marques de vostre tendraise surpasse à presan beaucoup les miennes rien nay si touschang, que se que vous
m'écrives . . . de *devenir malade* je ne trouveraÿ pas
locasiong à vous faire voire combien de tendraisse j'aÿ
pour vous. Atil possible que *Duc de Hanovre* soit
assaÿ *baite de vous avoir refuser la pose* je feray plustos,
mourir 20 *feltmarescho* que de *refuser* unne fois à
Princesse héréditaire pareilje schose. Quois que *Prince
héréditaire* ne *revienne* pas si tos et sur les ordres que lon
avois devulgué con avois envojé, nous somme pourtang
deja dans le mois de *septembre et la campanjeay bintos
finnis* faite reflextion la desu adieux.

33

se tienne à 8 heure du soir aupres la porte de la grande
salle, aux la Pr: à cutume de jouer, jla poura recevoir
la en toute sureté, puisque personne j passe, Demain
éstang le Dimange.

34

j lÿ sera à leur sudite ne doute pas de sa fidellite.
Adieux inconparable Deesse je vous donne le bonsoir,
et souhaite que vous sonjé autang à moy comme je fais
à vous, appres avoir relus éncor une fois votre lettre, je
m'endormiray, avec l'esperane de songer d'autre schose
que de vous. je vous émbrasse un Million de fois, et
suis votre tres-obeissant ser.

CORRESPONDENCE OF SOPHIA DOROTHEA
AND COUNT KÖNIGSMARCK

F 3

[From Königsmarck to Sophia Dorothea]

[Spring of 1692.]

WHAT sufferings one has to bear when it is necessary
to separate from you ! All the torments in the world
cannot cause such suffering ! But I recover from my
trouble, since you are of opinion that I ought not to have
any feeling of jealousy. I must avow to you that it is
difficult to feel none when one is far away from the object
one adores. But, my angel, you have made me so many
promises of behaving well that I place confidence in you ;
and I can assure you that at the present moment I am
free from jealousy, but not without feeling troubled ;
and your departure troubles me more than ever. I
cannot understand what is to become of me in the end ;
I well know that I cannot always be in sight of you, and
yet I feel [only] too much that I cannot separate from

you. See in what condition your beautiful eyes have put me. I send you a copy of the letter of which I spoke to you, word for word like the original ; and I ask your pardon for the scrawling hand of which I have made use ; I had it copied by my page, who does not know what he writes.

M. Gor brought me a complimentary message from the Duchess of Eisenach ; [1] she sent word to me that, though I had avoided speaking to her, she would show that she takes more thought of me than I take of her. I will swear to you that not only did this compliment give me no pleasure, but, on the contrary, it vexes me that she ordered it to be delivered to me. I have not left my room all to-day, and I think that I shall do the same thing to-morrow. Let me know, by way of consolation, how you are faring and when you will return. I shall die with vexation and trouble if I do not see you soon. Good-bye, my beloved heart ; think of your faithful lover, and do not forget him [?] among all this crowd of people. Once more, adieu !

Thursday, at 12 o'clock after midnight.

My pain in the chest continues, but I have had no fever . . . .

---

[1] Amalia, Duchess of Saxe-Eisenach, a born Princess of Nassau-Dietz. Cf. as to her visit to Celle in March 1692, Colt *ap*. Wilkins, p. 163.—Königsmarck mentions a " M. de Goritz " as a brother-officer in the Flemish campaign, ib. pp. 216, 232 ; he appears to be identical with Count Frederick von Schlitz-Goertz, who afterwards became Marshal of the Court and President of the Chamber, and, after accompanying George I to England, died as Prime Minister at Hanover. See Vehse, *Gesch. d. Höfe d. Hauses Braunschweig*, Part I. pp. 116, 187, and Part II. p. 10.

F 6

[FROM KÖNIGSMARCK TO SOPHIA DOROTHEA]

Sunday, [*Spring of* 1692].

YES, Madam, I will suffer for your sake, as you command me to do so ; but when shall I be fortunate enough to find myself at the point to which I aspire—I mean in your arms ?   But when shall I have this satisfaction ? I lose all hope, for in the way in which things go on, I cannot flatter myself that it will come about.   My mind gives way over it all, and, if I write to you without rime or reason, do not find fault with me on that account —it is [because of] the despair to which I find myself reduced.   If you disbelieve me, I beg you to look at these [gray] hairs which I had pulled out of my head this morning : I cannot declare to you that they turned last night ; but I can swear to you that a week ago I had none.   Believe me that my despair is great, and that my trouble is extreme.   I stay on for the love of you ; I risk honour, reputation, and ambition ; for, since I do not join in the campaign, what will they say of me ; and why do I risk this, without seeing you after all ?   I have reached this extremity that I must either conquer [?] or die.   Use therefore your force [influence] with the *Gro*[*ndeur*] ; it is he who alone can save us, and I call this to conquer.   I absolutely must have your commands as to what I am to do.   To stay on in this way at Han[over] is out of the question ; for after three weeks you will go [away] with the *Gron*[*deur*].   What shall I then do in a place from which you are absent ? I beg you to reflect on that, and after that give your commands ; I am ready to show you by my obedience that my love does not listen to reason.   You see to what state you have reduced me, for I sacrifice to you my

2 K

ambition, which is the single thing that up to this time I had preserved. See to what length my passion goes ; judge in what state I find myself ; do not ruin me utterly—be more ambitious than I am, and encourage a lover who no longer has any [ambition] ! You would pity me if you quite understood the troubles that oppress me. I see clearly that it is your trouble which is killing me ; for although we actually are together we never have anything but trouble ; and this is an ill beyond cure. The only consolation is to play [cards] with you ; but the pleasure of looking at you is never allowed me ; for at one time the *Schwartz gesicht* [black face], at another the Innocent One, at another some one else among the maids [of honour], comes to watch us. All this is enough to make me die of it. Console me, I entreat you, or I shall despair ; and my despair may drive me to seek remedies unworthy of a man of honour. You wait for me, certainly ; but, Madam, when one is in the Labyrinth as I am, honour and trust come to an end. It is well to come to a close, or I shall be still more enraged.

F I

[FROM SOPHIA DOROTHEA TO KÖNIGSMARCK]

On the Brockhausen journey.[1]
Tuesday [1 *June* 1692].

THE Hereditary Princess is very impatient to know whether Königsmarck has arrived safely. Many things

---

[1] *Voyage de Brockhausen* may mean ' during the journey from ' or ' to Brockhausen.' This and the following letters appear to belong to the dates here assigned to them ; but it is possible that they belong to June 1693. The Princess left Hanover for Brock-

have happened which the Hereditary Princess has written on a quite clean half-sheet. I cannot console myself for having lost Königsmarck so soon ; this makes his absence a thousand times harder to bear. I am worn out to the point of being unable to keep up any longer. The excess of enjoyment and the sorrow at seeing no more what I love reduce me to this condition. How hard it is to take oneself away from you ! You are the most amiable of men. The more one sees you the more charm one finds in you. How happy I am to be loved by you, and how well I know all my happiness ! All my bliss depends on the continuance of this tender affection. If I am deprived of it, I no longer wish to live. You take the place of everything else for me, and I care nothing for the whole of the world besides. I wish that you may be as pleased with me as I am with you. You have enchanted me, and I feel fonder of you than ever. Be you the same, and nothing will be wanting to my happiness. I need not tell you that all the actions of my life shall declare my attachment to you ; for you must be convinced of this, and time will show you that I do not wish to live except for you. The Hereditary Princess leaves to-morrow.

I have instructed 220 to send me your letter by [way of] Nienb[urg].

---

hausen on June 21, 1692, see Wilkins, p. 180 ; as to her movements to and from that place in June 1693, see ib. pp. 256–76. After a careful consideration of dates, as well as of the general contents of the letters, I have come to the conclusion that the 1692 date is the more probable. Brockhausen, or Bruchhausen, was a country-seat of the Duke of Celle, situate, like the town of Nienburg, mentioned at the end of this letter, in the division of the old countship of Hoya, which had from the middle of the sixteenth century onwards belonged to the Celle branch of the House of Brunswick-Lüneburg. Brockhausen is about 18 miles N.W. of Celle.

F 2

[FROM SOPHIA DOROTHEA TO KÖNIGSMARCK]

Brockhausen,
Thursday, June 22nd [1692].

THE Hereditary Princess arrived yesterday evening. She is pleased with the Duchess of Celle. I have no doubt but that she will do everything that one wishes. The Duke of Celle is far more difficult [to manage]. I have as yet heard nothing of you, which makes me very sad. I flatter myself, however, that nothing has happened, inasmuch as I have heard nothing. The Duke of Hanover goes on Monday to Hanover. This resolution was taken yesterday ; if I had known it sooner, I should not have started, and I might have been able to see you for some days more. I am convinced that he waited on purpose, and this truly vexes me ; for I hate worse than death whatever seeks to separate me from you. It is a great unhappiness to have to pass one's life as I now pass mine. I cannot, however, see the end of my woes. Yesterday I had a thousand thoughts in the chaise which drove me into despair. I could not think of waiting a whole month before seeing you without mortal grief ; all the measures which I must take . . . me. I cannot do without you ; I do not care to see anybody in the world except you ; yet I do not see you ; and at every moment I have to be deprived of [the sight of you]. I can no longer exist in this constraint, it drives me to despair ; my passion increases day by day ; I do not know what you have done to me, but you bewitched me the last time that I saw you, and I have never loved you with so much ardour as I do. It is certain that you will [completely] turn my head. Yesterday I wrote a song, and this makes it clear to me that love works miracles.

I cannot keep myself from telling you my song ; it goes
to the air ' *Dans mon malheur* ' :

> ' Without my . . . I loathe all company : [1]
> He is my only bliss, my sole content,
> The one enchantment of this life to me,
> On whom the wishes of my heart are spent.[1]

It is my heart and nothing else that speaks ; I hope that
I shall go further, and as time goes on I shall be able to
prove it to you. The Duke of Celle [or the Hereditary
Prince] [1] goes on Tuesday to Celle; for this reason
do not write to me any more lest I be not there [?].
The Duchess of Celle has promised 2000 dollars if the
Hereditary Prince does not return ; this redoubles my
friendship. The Hereditary Princess spoke yesterday
at Luisburg [2] to 110 ; he sought for an opportunity for
it. It was to exhort him not to give any chance to his
enemies, and above all to be on his guard against
Countess Platen. The Hereditary Princess begged him
particularly to let her know about anything which
concerned her. He promised her to do so. I am not
aware whether all this does not concern Königsmarck.
I cannot speak to you except about the grief which it is to
me to be so far away from you. Do not console yourself
for my absence, I entreat you, and have no enjoyment
when I am not with you. Great God, what a charm and
what a delight to be always with you ; the more one sees
you, the more one finds you superior to all men in the
world. I occupy my whole time with the charming remembrance of the last time when I saw you ; it will never quit
my memory. Ah, my dear child, how tenderly you are
loved, and how insupportable it is to me not to see you !

[1] Cipher uncertain.
[2] A country-seat, not very far from Brockhausen, belonging to
the Duke of Hanover, where his Court seems to have been in
the earlier as well as in the later part of this summer. Cf. Colt,
ap. Wilkins, p. 215, *note*.

I am about to go to bed ; I hope that my dreams will
figure you to me as charming as you are. If I did not
think I should see you while asleep, I should not care to
sleep at all ; for as soon as I am awake you take up all
my thoughts, and there is nothing that is pleasant to me
in my life but the time which I pass in thinking of you.
Good-night, most amiable of men ; you are adored by
me, and so you will be all my life. Good-bye, once more
—why am I not in your arms ?—I shall die of this !

On Wednesday the Hereditary Princess appeared at
table and spoke to 110, then to the Field-Ma[rshal].[1]
She arrived late. Prince Max received her and shook
hands with her ; she said very little to him. The
Duke of Celle came into the room ; Prince Max did
not come in at all ; the Duchess of Celle had gone to
bring her in, and came back late for she did not find the
Hereditary Princess. Supper was afterwards served.
The Hereditary Princess, the Duchess of Celle, and the
Duke of Celle, were together, quite by themselves.
The Duchess of Celle took the Hereditary Princess to
her rooms, and nobody entered them.

F 12

[FROM KÖNIGSMARCK TO SOPHIA DOROTHEA.]

$$\frac{\text{The 3rd}}{\text{23rd}}[2] \ [1692 ?]$$

MY Mistresses are supposed to have prevented me from
thinking of you ? God, is it possible that you should

---

[1] Field-Marshal Henry von Podewils (1615–96) commanded
the Hanoverian troops in the campaign of 1688, and also in the
demonstration of 1693.

[2] The above dating is incomprehensible ; ' the 3rd ' may
possibly be a slip of the pen for ' the 13th.' There is nothing in
the letter to give any satisfactory clue to the time of writing.

believe this; and, even had I not written to you about
everything (though this is letter No. 4) you ought never
to have harboured such a thought. Is it possible that
you should believe that I love anyone but yourself? No,
I protest to you that after you I shall never love again.
It will not be very difficult to keep my promise, for after
one has adored you is it possible to think any other
woman pretty? You wrong yourself by believing such
a thing ; and how could you draw a comparison between
yourself and the others ; and is it possible that after
having loved a Goddess, one could bestow a look upon
Mortals? No, in truth, I have too good taste for that, and
I am not one of those people who wish to make themselves common. I adore you, charming brunette, and I
shall die with this feeling. If you do not forget me, I
swear to you that I shall love you all my life. I expect
no more letters from you, because I intend to be soon
in your company, and my sole occupation will then be
to prove to you, that I love you to distraction, and that
nothing is so dear to me as your person. Adieu !

F 18

[FROM KÖNIGSMARCK TO SOPHIA DOROTHEA]

[*July* 1692, from the Camp.]

I AM very well pleased that you are for once satisfied
with me ; but it seems to me that this does not delight
you, for you are always supplying me with matter for
reproaching you ; and thus you deprive me of the joy
of being satisfied with you. You complain that your
love interferes with your rest ; I am willing to believe it,
but this love does not touch your heart so deeply that
you would cut off the slightest pleasures for its sake

No, no; it is for me to complain: my passion not only troubles me, but brings me to despair. Oh, God! how I [hate] the places where I know the amusements are going on ; I should much like to see you at the Gate of Brussels[1] or of Ghent [?] without appearing there myself ; rather than do this you would abandon me and ten other *galans*. You find your conduct correct ; so do I ; but I should be beyond despair if mine were not still more so. I am very well pleased that you have not fallen ill ; it would have left me inconsolable. Although I am not satisfied with you, you were satisfied with my letter; this fills me with joy ; you find there the unfeigned sentiments of my heart ; I thank you very humbly that you promise me not to give your portrait to the person we know of. Why do you flatter me so much in your letters, when you think so little of keeping your promises to me ? You assure me that nothing will be difficult for you, and that you will do everything to please me ; this is very well said, but very ill kept. Alas ! you say to me, let us trust that time will be able to make us happy ; but know that time will make me the most unhappy of mankind. I have not the audacity to say to you what I already know; but, my dear, I believe that they will force me to leave you. I cannot finish this letter, what with trouble, sorrow, and anger. Adieu ; do not, at all events, hate me; for, I swear by my God, I do not deserve it in [any] way on earth.

---

[1] In July 1692 Königsmarck appears to have paid a visit from the Camp to Brussels, see the Princess's letter *ap*. Wilkins, p. 197. (Of the old gates of Brussels the Porte de Hal now alone remains.)

F 11

[FROM KÖNIGSMARCK TO SOPHIA DOROTHEA]

From the Camp at Hall [*August*] 2*nd*—3*rd* [1692].[1]

ALTHOUGH I had resolved to write to you to-morrow and to reply at length to the letters of the 13th,[2] 14th and 15th, which I received from you at the same time, I find myself deprived of this pleasure by the resolution which the King has taken to attack to-morrow the French army, which is two hours distance from us ; the place is called Enghien. At any other time this news would have delighted me ; but I confess to you at the present moment it troubles me. I am loved by you, the only object that I have found worth loving. I have not deceived myself in my belief that you possess all the fine qualities to be found in the world ; but, my dear, I must risk my life, and perhaps never see you again. Hardly was I made aware that you were innocent, and that I falsely suspected you, when I am perhaps never to see you again. I have risked my life a hundred times, by way of folly or high spirits, and I knew myself sufficiently to be sure that death never terrified me. But, my divinity, that which makes me a coward is the fear of not seeing you again. Adieu then, amiable Doro, adieu ; how much I am to be pitied—and yet I am fortunate, but I cannot take advantage of my good fortune. Do not, however, think that you have a coward admirer ; no, my dear, since to battle I must go, I will behave there as is right, and, if I can, I hope to distinguish myself.

---

[1] This letter is dated ' the 23rd,' but August 3rd, O.S., was the date of the battle of Steenkirk, on the eve of which this letter seems to have been written. I have adopted a very ingenious conjecture, which I can hardly describe as warranted by the transcript, but which may nevertheless be correct.

[2] See the Princess's letter of July 13th *ap*. Wilkins, pp. 193-6.

But, my heart, permit me to make a request to you,
namely, that, if my fate is so unkind to me as to leave me
crippled by the loss of an arm, or a leg, do not forget me,
and have a little pity for a poor fellow who has let it be
his only pleasure to love you ; no, my dear, do not forget
him : he is a man who has been really and truly attached
to you, and will remain so for the remainder of his life,
although a cripple ; my eyes which have been charmed
by yours, will perhaps never see them any more. I
cannot think of that, without shedding tears. Ah, how
little advantage I have from being loved by you, and
of how many torments you are the cause to me ! It is
striking twelve from the Hall [1] clock tower ; they are
bringing in cannon-balls, powder, and matches ; it is
the prelude to the scene which we have to play to-
morrow ; I must betake myself to my duty ; adieu,
beloved child ! Ah, how I am to be pitied !

F 22

[FROM SOPHIA DOROTHEA TO KÖNIGSMARCK]

[Wiesbaden], *August 25th*
September 4th [1692].[2]

I TAKE so much pleasure in conversing with you that, so
soon as I have a moment of liberty, I employ it to assure
you of my affection. I wrote to you yesterday, but it
seems to me that I did not sufficiently insist to you on
the disquiet in which I am about what you tell me. It
prevented me from sleeping all the night. I reviewed
all my actions, and, the more I examine myself, the
less I can guess what you can have against me. It is

---

[1] A small town between Brussels and Enghien. Compare
Wilkins, pp. 208 sqq.

[2] Cf. Wilkins, pp. 233 sqq.

certain that you ought to be content with my conduct ;
it is ruled by my affection, and this is sufficient. I entreat
you once more to let me know as soon as you are able
what it can be. It will be very easy for me to justify
myself, since I have never thought of anything but
pleasing you, and I will with pleasure take all the most
horrid oaths to you as to my innocence ; but I urgently
ask of you to inform me who are they that tell you such
calumnies. No doubt they have their reasons for
making a quarrel between us, and according to all
appearances they will not stop there. Be persuaded, I
entreat you, that I am incapable of doing anything that
could displease you. My behaviour has shown you this
up to the present time, and I will do even more in the
same way in the future. I am in despair not to be able
to make you perceive as much as I should like to do my
affection for you. The opportunities are wanting to me,
but not the will ; and I shall not be happy until I have
made the whole earth see that for me you take the place
of the grandeurs and pleasures of the world and of all its
charms. The only one which I desire is that of possessing
your heart ; I demand no other, and this one happiness
will always make me indifferent to all others. I am
convinced that if I were at Han[over], I should be told
plenty of stories against you ; but I trust you too much
to listen easily to what I might be told. Do you act in
the same way, and believe firmly that nothing is capable of
making me change ! I am in mortal trouble. They say
that an engagement was fought a short time since, and
I do not yet know the rights of it. I tremble lest you
should expose yourself without need, and that some
accident should have befallen you. Take care of yourself, I entreat you, if there remains in you any affection
[for] me. What would become of me if I were to learn
that you were wounded ? I think I should die of it.

F 32

[FROM KÖNIGSMARCK TO SOPHIA DOROTHEA]

[September] 2nd [1692].

YOU make me [wish to] die when you pay me compliments.   Since you do not reply to me on all the points
of my letters, I have begged you not to write at all,
and simply to let me know through Fräulein von dem
Knesebeck the state of your health.   I repeat it again
here, and entreat you not to do it if it causes you the
slightest fatigue.   It is sufficient that you should write
me two words, so that I may see that divine handwriting
which is able to banish all the fears that I imagine to
myself.   The resolution which I must take, according to
the opinion of all my friends, exposes me to the risk that,
when I shall have taken my leave, I shall set all the
world arguing about it ; and perhaps I might be told
through a third party that it is desired that I should
retire.   What will then become of me ?   Believe me that
it is necessary to think of everything before taking a
fixed resolution.   The matter is of too great importance
to me.   The Duke of Hanover will find a thousand
people like Königsmarck, but I trust that the Hereditary
Princess will never find anyone who is so faithful and
who loves her with more ardour than myself.   My
passion is so beyond bounds as to rise to madness.
Alas ! my dearest, you deserve [lovers] far better than
Königsmarck.   I am quite convinced that if they had
given you an admirer according to your deserts, I should
not have had the honour of being your Slave ; but if some
one with an extraordinary affection and an unequalled
constancy was to have been your admirer, it is right
and just that this should be myself ; for I would dispute
the place not with Mortals, but with the Gods themselves,

and I defy them to create anyone to equal me. What an effect vows have when one is in the condition in which you are ; never have I been more satisfied with you, never did I believe you more implicitly, than at present. You will, then, always love me, I may rest assured of it, for you swear to me that, so long as I shall love you, you will do the same. I shall love you all my life, and you vow the same thing to me ; what more can I desire ?—all my wishes are fulfilled, I am the happiest man in the world ; recover your health, and I can be at the height of my bliss. I am not pleased to find that you prefer writing to me to taking your rest ; I entreat you, think first of taking your rest, and then of your lover. How angry I am with your heart for its bad taste, to leave you in order to come to me ; it does not know the difference ; leave that to mine, one ought not to change for the worse, but for the better. Your account makes me tremble, and I fear lest the fever [and] the other accident tire you out so much that you will not be able to recover as quickly [as you ought]. I do not know, my heart tells me you are out of danger ; I am no longer so much disquieted as I was at the beginning. I take that for a very good sign ; at least I hope it is, and I ardently wish that it may be so ; I hope that my prayers are granted, and that at the present moment you are better. The resolution that you have taken, to take what I had left you, is great ; I avow to you that, if I had known it beforehand, it would have made me tremble ; but, since everything has gone off well, I am at rest ; and there is only the trouble of being the cause of so much more suffering on your part, and, if you found yourself still worse, I should be inconsolable. I am obliged to confess that the marks of your affection greatly surpass mine at present ; nothing could be so touching as what you write to me . . . of falling ill. I shall not find an

opportunity of enabling you to see how great an affection
I have for you.   Is it possible that the Duke of Hanover
is stupid enough to have refused you the appointment ?
I would rather put twenty field-marshals to death than
once refuse such a favour to the Hereditary Princess.
Although the Hereditary Prince does not return so soon
and in response to the orders which it was made known
had been sent, we are in any case already in the month of
September, and the campaign will soon be at an end.
Reflect on that !   Adieu !

F 23
[From Sophia Dorothea to Königsmarck]

[Wiesbaden], *September* $\frac{2nd}{12th}$ [1692].

It was so late when I wrote to you that I could not reply
to all that you told me.   I reread your letter several
times ;   it is a mixture of love and raillery which I find
very pleasing ;   and it seems to me, whatever countenance
you may assume, that my journey does not find favour
with you.   Yet you are altogether as wrong as possible ;
for, according to all appearances, I shall go away again
from this place without having seen any reasonable
person, and I desire it with all my heart.   I do not think
of going to Frankfort fair, and I shall not say a word
to help to bring this about.   It seems to me that this
ought to convince you that I am not in quest of society,
and that I am incapable of thinking of pleasures when
I do not see you.   I hope to leave this place in a fortnight.   The Peda[gogue] has to-day taken this resolution.   I return with her to join the *Grondeur ;* and I
shall proceed to Han[over] a little before the return of
the Reformer.   I cannot yet tell you anything positive
about what concerns the Göhrde ; [1]   I do not, however,

_____

[1] George Lewis' favourite hunting-box near Lüneburg, in the

think that I shall go there, for the season is too advanced for the Reformer to be able to be there, and I hope that, provided that nothing keeps you where you are,[1] I shall soon be able to see you. I shall judge of your affection by your eagerness, but I entreat you to take your measures so well that I may see you in private on the first occasion. It would be impossible for me to bear seeing you in public, and my transport [of delight] would betray me. They say that the French could easily carry us off. This makes me wish very much to get away, for I should not at all like to be taken prisoner, and I wish to keep your conquest safe for you. I am delighted with your [present ?],[2] and I offer you all the thanks for it which you deserve. It took me by surprise and I did not expect it at all, which makes the thing all the more obliging. There is no sentinel in the world that you ought to fear, and the prisoner may reckon on the prison which will always be open to him and closed to all the rest of the world. As to this you may depend on me, and as to a love which will serve as a model; I wish to convince you of it, although you have some of it, and that I find no happiness or satisfaction except in loving you and in being loved. You seem to me so little certain of this truth that I am sensibly affected by it. Tell me what should be done so that you should be unable to doubt it any more; there is nothing that I

eastern corner of the principality. There is a picture of it at Herrenhausen, with a meeting of the hunt in face of the *château*.

[1] In camp in Flanders.

[2] The significance of the word *carême* in this passage is obscure. Its ordinary meaning 'lent, fasting' gives no sense. Dr. Braun-holtz informs me that the word may also mean 'a collection of lent-sermons'; but, as he observes, this was not a very likely gift in the circumstances. And a 'lenten gift' of any kind seems out of season in September.

would not joyfully do in order to make you see that for me you take the place of everything else, and that all my desires and my ambition are confined to pleasing you. If nothing but this is needed to render you happy, you are more so than any person in the world, for I do not desire to live but for you alone, and I renounce with pleasure the whole world, in order never to belong to anyone but yourself.

F 24

[FROM SOPHIA DOROTHEA TO KÖNIGSMARCK]

[Wiesbaden], *September* 13th
$\overline{23rd}$ [1692].

INSTEAD of the extreme pleasure which all your letters afford to me, that which I received this evening has pierced my heart. One could not think of anything that could hurt one more than what you write to me. I shall not repeat it ; I believe that you will remember it still very well, and I would give everything in the world to be able to forget it. By what passage of my life can I have deserved the opinion which you show you have of me ? If I thought to have given cause for it, I should wish to be dead ; but, the more I examine myself, the more I find myself far removed from such sentiments, and, thanks be to God, I feel my heart as noble as it ought to be. I wish to say nothing further to you on this subject ; I might lose my temper, and I very much hate harshness. But, to reply to the four points on which you continue to harp. I am very much deceived if I did not tell you that Sparr has been at L.,[1] and, if I did not do so, it was certainly because I forgot to do

[1] I cannot offer any conjecture as to the identity of Sparr. He may have been a descendant of the celebrated Brandenburg Field-Marshal von Sparr. 'L.' may of course be Luisburg.

so and because I did not think that he was worth the trouble of my remembering him. I can swear to you all the oaths you please that there is no reason besides this; moreover, I did not say two words to him [about] the joy which you reproach me for having felt at finding Guldenleu [1] here. I shall not reply to you on the subject, for it is a ridiculous notion, and nothing in the world could be so ill-imagined with regard to the Fair. I assure you that I did not say a word in order to go there; but as I am quite sincere I am prepared to *confess to you that I was not vexed about it;* and, as to my new lover, you are mad to disquiet yourself about him; for he is far away from here, and according to all appearances I shall not see him; and [neither] his sisters nor anybody in the world will ever make me take any step against the affection which so fills my heart. I have already told you that I am convinced that he is not coming to Han[over]; but, if this should happen, provided that I am better pleased with you than I am this evening, I shall treat [him] with absolute rudeness rather than allow his visits. I am very foolish to give a reasonable explanation in reply to all your fancies—[to] you who are so far from reasonable as to anything that concerns me, and who have driven me to despair by your fine letter. It is true that you mean afterwards to repair your fault; but this is not sufficient, and I am not well pleased, for I desire your esteem, and you do not show that you have any for me. The *Confidante* yesterday received [a letter] from the beloved Ketler,[2] who writes to her by order of the Landgrave [3]

---

[1] 'Guldenleu,' if that be the true reading of the MS. (Wilkins, p. 229, spells the name 'Guldenlon'), might conceivably mean Ulric Christian Gyldenlöve, the natural brother of Charles XII.

[2] The Kettelers of Harkotten were Hanoverian Barons. (The famous Bishop of Mainz was a scion of this family.)

[3] The Landgrave is no doubt Landgrave Charles of Hesse-

to offer his compliments to Leonisse, since you wish to call her by that name, and to assure her that he will do what is in his power to see her here or at the Fair. I do not, however, think that this is possible, because we take our departure to-morrow, and one will only be there for a single day. I shall not write to you till I shall have arrived, and I shall give you a sincere and faithful account of all. I shall say nothing affectionate to you this evening, for you do not deserve it ; I am afraid that I shall not have the same strength of mind to-morrow, and that I shall have forgotten my anger, for I am furiously fond of you, and, although I do not tell you about it, I nevertheless feel that I love you with a passion of which there never was the like.

F 25

[From Sophia Dorothea to Königsmarck]

Fra[nkfort], $\overline{\frac{14th}{24th}}$ [*September* 1692].

I HAVE been here during the last two hours. The Peda[gogue] alighted at the house of the P[rincess] of Tarente,[1] where I saw nothing but silly faces. From there we went to the Fair, where I saw nobody of quality. The Marionette is here, and her sister-in-law. I shall not see them till to-morrow, with which I am well pleased, for I shall be able to take a rest, of which I have great

Cassel, of whom the Duchess of Orleans speaks as her cousin. His mother, the Landgravine Hedwig Sophia, was a daughter of the Elector George William of Brandenburg and his wife Elizabeth Charlotte, sister of the Elector Palatine Frederick V.

[1] Princess Emily of Hesse-Cassel, sister of Landgrave William VI, married Henry Charles, Prince of Tarente, and died in 1693. As to the 'Marionette', see the Introduction to this Appendix.

need, not having closed an eye all the night. I spent half of it in writing to you, and the other in worrying myself about the fine passage in your letter. I beg you very particularly not to give me any further such subjects of annoyance, for I am very touchy on the subject in question. Except that wicked passage which I cannot forget and which spoils all, your letter is charming, and nothing is more delightful than all that you say to me. Put this matter to rights, if you wish to be on good terms with me, for it goes very near to my heart. Mine is so full of you that, although I have reason to complain of you, I cannot bring myself not to mention to you that yesterday evening I had to make a terribly violent effort in order to keep silence to you about my affection. Never did one feel so much of it, and never did one less deserve reproaches than in my case. You are the most unjust of mankind to have the slightest mistrust as to what concerns me. I am too veritably yours that you should have anything to fear. All my actions should convince you of it, for it is certain that my passion for you exceeds all bounds. I entreat you to be fully convinced of this truth, and that there is nothing in the world which I would not do to make you see that I am more yours than my own. I hope that I shall not see either the Land[grave] or anybody, and I wish it with my whole heart. If you find anything which does not please you in what I wrote to you yesterday, lay all the blame on the vexation which you caused to me. It was enough to make me cry, and all the charms of your letter could not induce me to forgive the offend-ing passage. Rest tranquil as to my behaviour. It shall be divine, I promise you for myself and for the Rival.

F 26

[From Sophia Dorothea to Königsmarck]

[Ebsdorf,[1] *September* 1692.][2]

In the name of God, take care of yourself! My life is united to yours. A thousand desperate thoughts come into my mind, and I am crushed with grief; I should find it difficult to speak to you of anything else. I have plenty of leisure for nursing my trouble, and it is with a real joy that I find myself in this solitude. I forgot yesterday to return you my thanks for what you tell me about *la Boule*. Nothing could be so polite; I consent, on this condition, that she becomes my rival, for I confess to you that I love a triumph, and that it is very much to my taste. Adieu, nothing is capable of making me change. I was born for loving you; you are my sole passion; I never had one before I knew you, and I shall die loving you more than anyone has ever loved.

F 27

[From Sophia Dorothea to Königsmarck]

[Ebsdorf,] *Wednesday, the 24th* [*September* 1692].

I ought to give you an account of my doings of yesterday. I was alone all day. Then arrived some one sent from the master of this place to pay his respects to the Peda[gogue]. He got into such difficulties in his speech that I could scarcely stop myself from laughing at it. He also made a speech to the *Cœur Gauche*, and then took his departure. Then there was a promenade on foot, and on our return there was supper, and I had a conversation with the *Confidante*. This is the only pleasure I have, for we always talk about you.

[1] Ebsdorf, a hunting-box of the Duke of Hanover, about fifteen miles from Lüneburg.　　　　[2] Cf. Wilkins, p. 233.

F 28

[FROM KÖNIGSMARCK TO SOPHIA DOROTHEA]

[Hanover, *November* 1692.]

ALTHOUGH I wrote to you yesterday evening, I cannot stop myself from telling you that I have spent the worst night in the world ; I dreamt of you, but I beheld you faithless to me. I dreamt as follows : It seemed to me that I had requested you not to see a certain great man, and that, notwithstanding your promise, you had appointed him to pay you a visit so as to say good-bye to him. I was informed of it, and, not being able to endure this faithlessness, I pretended to have a letter from Madame your mother to hand to you. I entered your room abruptly, and saw the most horrible sight in the world : that great gentleman held you in his arms, and, what is worse, you were alone in your room. You pretended a little to be annoyed with your Adonis, telling him that he was impertinent. In my turn, I wished to withdraw, but you called out to me. I was delighted with this, because it gave me a chance of whispering into your ear that you were the most ungrateful of all ladies, and that this would be the last time that I should speak to you. In fact, I went to find out M. de Pude [Podewils] in order to beg him to send me to Hungary,[1] which he did. I beg your pardon for this criminal dream ; but I should think myself very much more criminal if I did not let you know of it. Do not think that I am inventing; no, by my God, it is a true tale. For the love of all that is dearest to you, take care to restore my peace of mind, and free me from my

---

[1] The Imperial campaigns in Hungary were still in progress, and, by the *Kurtractat* of 1692, Ernest Augustus and his brother were under the obligation of keeping up a military force there till the end of the war.

fear. I am afraid that this dream may be some melancholy presage, and something that bodes no good. It would be unjust that a tender affection should be requited by infidelities; I hope it may not be so; for why should you wish to desert a heart that adores you, and that swears to be faithful to you? If such vows can attach you solely to me, I protest to you before God, that never will I be unfaithful to you, and that I will love you all my life with the same passion that I do [at present]. When I shall have the honour of amusing you with an account of yesterday's debauch, you will laugh a good deal. The Baroness [1] [*sic*] distinguished herself on the occasion, and the big Swedish beard[s] made the best effect in the world; she was so much . . . that her natural colour began to appear beneath, which produced the most diverting spectacle in the world. She asked me why I did not amuse myself; I answered that I had come to pay my court to M. [Bielke] [2] and not to amuse myself. In leaving me she called me a traitor; whereupon I replied that I was not one yet, but might very possibly become one. M. le Duc played at ombre yesterday evening with her. That is the very Devil! I will conclude by asking you to prepare yourself to rescue me from the disquietude in which I am, and to believe me inviolably attached to you and to all those who have a regard for you. I embrace you from my very heart, and I kiss your portrait a million times. Farewell!

[1] The ' Baroness '—unidentifiable—not the ' Countess '; though Countess Platen was famed as an expert in the art of painting, and was even said to have invented a mysterious pigment called ' white rouge.'

[2] The letters ' Bil ' in the original no doubt stand for ' Bielke.' See note to F 10, below. ' M. le Duc ' is clearly the Duke of Celle.

F 29

[FROM KÖNIGSMARCK TO SOPHIA DOROTHEA]

[Hanover, *December* 1692.]

COME here some Friday evening, and wait till the Elector[1] comes here. If Prince Max cannot be got rid of, you can go back, and that will serve you as a pretext with the Duke of Celle and the Electoral Prince. Tell me if you agree with my notion ; if you can do it, arrange so that I may see you, for, frankly, I cannot go on living in this way ; for the love of me [and] of you arrange for me to see you and to embrace you, for without this satisfaction life is worth nothing to me.

F 30

[FROM KÖNIGSMARCK TO SOPHIA DOROTHEA]

[Hanover, *December* 1692.]

THE joy of finding the Ref[ormer] departed was broken by the trouble of finding you ill ; I hope, however, that it will not be of consequence ; for otherwise I shall not be able to sleep all night because of it. I hope to embrace you to-morrow evening ; I await the ordinary signal ; and the bad weather shall not prevent me from tasting the delight of your charming kisses ; unless indeed you give me other orders. I hope for the contrary, and I trust that your eagerness will respond to mine. If you do not go out to-morrow, this will suffice to assure you that the moments will seem like centuries to me, and that the times during which I am away from you are those which I pass to no purpose whatever ; and that I am ready to come to-morrow to the well-known place. I await the signal and am your very obedient servant.

[1] Of Hanover (on the point of becoming such).

F 31

[FROM KÖNIGSMARCK TO SOPHIA DOROTHEA]

[Hanover, *December* 1692.]

ONE could not be better pleased with you than I am. Your obliging ways of yesterday, your very dear letter, in a word everything, charms me ; I begin to revive, and yesterday is one of those days which I ought to mark in my book. In order to take full advantage of it, I beg that I may see you this evening ; I shall await the signal with great impatience, for I die with desire to prove to you my joy—it is beyond all bounds, and cannot express itself. For the love of you, of myself, and of everything that is dear to you, continue in the same way ; you will then be able to persuade me that I have nothing to fear, that I shall always be happy and contented—that is the pleasure of love, those are the charms of an attachment that is sincere and genuine. The avowal of the *Grond[eur]* further gives me much hope—seek to soften him, you will be able to do it if you try ; but you must take pains about it, and choose your time well. Be withal convinced that, if Heaven destines me the joy of having you for my own, my ways will be quite different from what you have imagined to yourself, and I swear to you that I shall regulate them according to yours. Put faith in this avowal, for it is sincere, and springs from a soul without guile and without finesse ; as the weather is fine, I hope to see you in the [falconry] [?].[1] I hope to find you there loving and happy. Farewell till then ; you will, I feel sure, say a little word to me, from which I can perceive that you grant my prayer.

[1] I cannot be sure about the ' falconry.' The list of the Elector's household in 1696, *ap*. Malortie, *Der Hannoversche Hof unter d. Kürfürsten Ernst August*, &c., p. 40, includes one ' bird-catcher,' and one ' ortolan-catcher.'

F 33

[From Sophia Dorothea to Königsmarck] [1]

[Hanover, *December* 1692 (?)]

LET [him] be at 8 o'clock in the evening near the door of the great hall, where the Pr[incess] is accustomed to play cards ; he will be able to meet her there in safety, since nobody passes there, to-morrow being Sunday.

F 34

[From Königsmarck to Sophia Dorothea]

[Hanover, *December* 1692 (?)]

HE will be there at the above-mentioned hour ; do not doubt of his fidelity. Adieu, incomparable Goddess ;

[1] What is here printed as two letters (F 33 and F 34) runs on without break in the Berlin manuscript. It is, however, difficult to believe that the earlier portion is not distinct from the latter, and that the former was not written by '*la Confidante*,' and the latter by Königsmarck ; and I have therefore, though with diffidence, ventured on the arrangement in the text. It must not be supposed that these two letters refer to the assignation which led to the catastrophe of the amour between Sophia Dorothea and Königsmarck. The day of Königsmarck's disappearance was, no doubt, a Sunday, and the place in which, according to tradition, he was struck down dead was by the door of the *Rittersaal*, in the *Leineschloss* at Hanover. But apart from the fact that, according to Rüdiger's statement (Cramer, vol. i. p. 69), Königsmarck did not leave his lodgings till between 9 and 10 p.m., the body of the letters in the Lund and in the Berlin collection appear to belong to an earlier date than that at which Königsmarck quitted the Hanoverian service (probably about the spring of 1694) ; and it can hardly be supposed that these two specially incriminating letters were left by the Secretary Hildebrandt to be seized, and that they found their way to Berlin with a series of which they formed no integral part. The Princess, it may be added, was in the habit of playing cards in the Grand Hall as early as 1691 (cf. Wilkins, p. 145).

I wish you good evening, and desire that your dreams may be as full of me as mine are of you. After having once more reread your letter, I shall go to sleep, with the hope of dreaming of [nothing] else than you. I embrace you a Million times, and am your very obedient ser[vant].[1]

F 9

[FROM KÖNIGSMARCK TO SOPHIA DOROTHEA]

Friday, 8 *o'clock at evening*. [*Summer*, 1693.]

THIS moment I have received a very long letter, and one of the kind I like from the Electoral Princess. I have not had leisure to read it, lest the post should leave, and without assuring you what joy it gave me when I received it ; *le bonhomme* goes to-morrow to Engsen [1] ; on his return I shall know my fate, which I shall at once make known to the Electoral Princess. I am continually offering up vows that I may not have to set out on the march, so that I may be able to embrace her whom I love, and for whom I am ready to die a thousand and a thousand times. Believe me that I adore you in the most violent way in the world. Would to Heaven I might have occasion to prove it to you ! I shall not forget for a moment, in order to convince you of it. What satisfaction it will be to me if by my obedience I shall be able to show you how deep a regard I have for you and what pleasure I take in being your slave for ever. Adieu, my incomparable Leonisse ; how I will kiss thee, my little one.[2]—K.

---

[1] Near Celle.

[2] *Ma petite*. For Königsmarck's use of the same term of endearment, cf. Wilkins, p. 162.

F 7

[FROM KÖNIGSMARCK TO SOPHIA DOROTHEA]

One o'clock in the night. [*Summer of* 1693.]

THE *bonhomme* has returned from his conference, and
made me dismiss the orderlies without commands. This
is what leads me to suppose that we shall still remain
[here] during the present week ; and, as I am to dine
with him to-morrow, I shall have some further information, which I will at once communicate to you.   In
the meantime, make ready to carry out what follows.
The Duchess has been to Linde,[1] to get rid of Countess
Platen.   Count de Stenbock, whom you saw here seven
years ago, wished to pay his respects, and Count de La
Gardie also.[2] I took them there, and I found the good
Plesse[?][3] at a stand [?], and the paint running down
everywhere—she was so overcome at seeing such a
number of strangers arrive that she was quite confused.
She chose the wiser part, for she withdrew at once, to put
herself to rights again.   There is a good deal of malicious
wit in the Electress, and she could not have revenged herself better.   Think of coming, I entreat you ; and believe
that without seeing you is to be dead, and I marvel that

---

[1] See note to F 4 below.

[2] Count Magnus Stenbock, afterwards renowned as a Swedish
general under Charles XII, and sympathetically remembered for
his tragic death, entered the Dutch service as a volunteer in 1690.
The Count de La Gardie mentioned here may be Pontus Frederick
who died in 1693. Stenbock was connected by descent with the de
La Gardies ; a Countess Stenbock, born de La Gardie, was with
Aurora von Königsmarck immediately after her brother's death.
The two Counts are mentioned as likely to come to Celle in July
1693, *ap.* Wilkins, p. 288.

[3] ' The good Plesse ' must have been the lady of General Pless,
formerly in the Danish service, like many other members of his
family, which was of ancient Brunswick descent.

my fate should have been so cruel to me as to let me survive all its misfortunes ; but, if I do not see you soon, there is no war nor danger which I will not seek in order to shorten my unhappy life. I die with shame at not being dead already. How does it agree with my loving you to distraction that I neither see you nor speak to you, and yet survive ! I believe that my confounded fate preserves me in order to trouble me all the more. You alone can rescue me from my despair ; come quickly to console me, or I shall commit some desperate act which I shall regret all my life, for the life I lead is unbearable ; I hate it like death, I am tired out with it and can no longer bear it ; I wish that the lightning would destroy all those who prevent us from seeing one another and joining our flames. Pardon the rage which my too violent passion calls forth in me : it seems to me that, if I must not see what I love, it is right that I should not see the light of day. At this moment I should be capable of sacrificing Father, Mother, Brother, and Sister, if I thought that they prevented me from seeing my angel. Leonisse, what torments your beauty costs me, to what trouble your charms give rise ! Come and make me forget all my woes ; thou canst do it, by thy embraces, by thy caresses ; and there is no one in the world capable of this but thyself. I await you with the greatest impatience in the world ; and do not allow me to say that you are quick to depart, while . . . to return where love calls [?] you. I should however be in the wrong, if I complained of our parting, for it was loving and sincere ; but I beseech you, do not give me reason to complain of a last parting. Farewell ! I kiss you a thousand, thousand times. Mlle. de Knesebeck is the best person in the world ; I beg you to tell her of my regard for her. I ask, with your permission, to be remembered to her.

F 10
[FROM KÖNIGSMARCK TO SOPHIA DOROTHEA]

[Hanover], *Saturday*, [*July* 1693].

IT is easy to suppose with what satisfaction I have read your very charming letter. This satisfaction was due to me, in order to take me a little out of the deep reverie into which my misfortunes and our separation have plunged me. Your letter is long, loving, and as I desire it to be ; do not write any more short letters ; this ought to relieve you, and I swear to you that for me also you cannot make them long enough. Your love is so agreeable to me that I have no pleasure while away from you but to see that love depicted on paper. I preserve your letters as the most precious things in the world, because they console me for all the disgrace I have to undergo ; as I see in them that you swear to love me, to be faithful to me, and never to abandon me—and what more can I desire from you ? You see, then, that I am thoroughly well pleased with you ; I conjure you to be the same with me, and not to impute it to me that you do not receive my letters regularly by every post. I did not know one day which was Sunday ; but, since I am now informed of it, my exactness will show you that I sinned because I knew no better ; and my negligence was due to the trouble which is upon me. It is then that I think most of you, for you serve as a consolation to me, and the pleasure of thinking of you surpasses all others that I know. *Idolo mio*, when shall I have the joy of holding thee in my arms ? Is it not enough to make a Cato despair, to see that you can come if Prince Max did not prevent it [1] ; but, although the wish to see you

---

[1] Prince Maximilian, who excited Königsmarck's jealousy so strongly, was staying at Brockhausen in June 1692 after his catastrophe at Hanover (cf. Wilkins, p. 136), Königsmarck being at Hanover. In June 1693 Maximilian was lodged at Luisburg,

took away my jealousy and I begged you to come, how long shall I be able to be with you, perhaps only two days, and then I shall see you among people who hate us, and others who wish to insinuate themselves. Do not believe, my Angel, that my jealousy springs from any bad opinion I have of you : this would be too criminal —it springs from the violence of my love ; so I flatter myself that you will always make excuses for me when this madness takes hold of me. What do I not owe you for taking so much pains to ease me of all my suspicions ! Your diaries console me ; your vow makes me forget all that I had in my brain. Ah ! why am I not by your side ! I would throw myself at your feet, to thank you for all the care you take to render me happy and con-tented. I am convinced of your good intentions ; I have no doubt of your fidelity ; and I see very well that if you ruled fate, so many worries would not occur. As I may perhaps receive orders to march to Lunen [Lüneburg ?], tell me if I may not go to Celle, without giving umbrage. If you are not there, politeness demands it ; but at present I do not know what I ought to do. The answer of the Electress of Brandenburg [1] is amusing enough, and well deserves an answer, in which the music ought not to be spared. I do not know whether I am mistaken, but, on rereading letter No. 11, I do not find it so sincere as No. 10 ; tell me if I am mistaken ; No. 10 is charming—it shows the real passion which you felt in writing it. For the love of me, be always like that, and do not let me perceive any coldness. What have

in rooms next to the Princess (cf. Wilkins, p. 259). In July 1693 he was at Herrenhausen (ib. p. 286). The letter, with its references to the contiguity of Prince Maximilian's rooms, and to the Duchess of Celle's encouragement of him, seems to belong to the later date.

[1] Sophia Charlotte.

I done to deserve it ; tell me, so that I may exculpate myself. Is it perhaps that you do not think it loving that I do not ask you to come ?   But remember what it is that prevents me from doing so. If, however, you desire it, I will beg you to come ; but I shall be perhaps two days here ; and then your neighbour will have a free field. He has loved you, and, indeed, he has not been indifferent to you. I am always afraid of him, though there is hardly anything to be afraid of in him ; but it is sufficient that he has been on a very familiar footing with you, for me to have good reason for fearing his imperti-nence, and it would even be annoying to see a man about you who might find twenty little holes through which he might see you, besides that you would not be able to say a single word without his hearing it. But all these reasons are not enough; and, if I had hopes of staying, I would nevertheless entreat you to come, in the hope that you would find out a way to get rid of him; for, apart from this, I shall not be able to see you, since he will always be looking out for spying [upon you].   Inasmuch as I cannot give you up, I for this reason refuse all the advan-tages which present themselves ; I intend to make you see from this how attached I am to you, and this is my sole reason why I make you look at the letters which were written to me on all sides. Believe, all the same, that no advantage is capable of making me leave this place so long as you will be kind to me.   I know the power of a mother whom one loves, and when she gives you an opportunity, you ought to be prudent enough to resist it. My blood curdles, when I think that your [mother] would be capable, in order to take vengeance on the Electoral Prince, of letting you make a *cocu* of him ; and when this comes into my head, if you ever thus caressed anyone but myself, all my blood flows back in my veins, and I cannot rest still, so long as this thought keeps me unquiet. Ah! good God! if I saw you kiss anyone with the same passion with which you have kissed me, and ride on horseback with the same pleasure —may I never see God if it would not drive me mad! Why, in writing it my hand trembles, and I find it difficult to go on. Let us change the subject. The friends of whom I spoke to you, Bussche and Hammerstein[1], could you have believed it, it is they who have put into the head of the Electoral Prince all the stories about my [game]. But I have written a letter to the first, which will make him see his falseness very clearly. I am in hopes, moreover, since the Duchess of Celle and the Duke of Celle have come to an agreement; therefore do your best. The war will not last so long as to ruin the country[2]; that is why this [excuse] cannot long be accounted a defeat. See if you will keep your promise; for you promised me that you would die sooner than not be united to me; continue in this way of thinking, and you will restore my life to me. Am I dear enough to you for you to keep the promise you made to me? If this is so, I swear to you once more by the stars, that nothing in the world shall separate me from you. By the letter *enclosed* you will see how they are once more trying to persuade me to Marry the Daughter of M. Bielke[3]; but my answer was, that I would

---

[1] Probably Christian William von dem Bussche, who became Adjutant-General of the Elector George Lewis, and died as a general in 1711. George Christopher von Hammerstein was Adjutant-General to the Hereditary (Electoral) Prince.

[2] The war, begun in 1688 by the French invasion of the Palatinate, lasted till the conclusion of the Peace of Ryswyk in 1697.

[3] Count Niels Bielke, the well-known Swedish politician (afterwards governor of Swedish Pomerania), seems already at this time as Swedish envoy to have furthered the French interest, with which he remained identified. See Colt *ap.* Wilkins, p. 176.

rather die of hunger than do it ; and that I begged him particularly not to speak to me any more of marriage, for this might cause a quarrel between us. I flatter myself that you will be pleased with my resolution. Since we have so little chance of seeing each other, we must think of expedients. *You will find it in this note ;* I think that it can be managed, provided I do not go away and that I let you know between the present time and that. If you wish to wait till Prince Max is tired, I shall not see you for a long time ; for when he is with the Electress and his thin divinity [1], he is as happy as a King. I should not have thought that this magpie would have caused me so much sorrow as he does ; I wish he were in the heart of Hungary, he would no longer cause me so much heart-ache as he does at present. One could not speak more kindly than you do on the subject of dying of hunger ; but do you believe that, although it would be a great consolation to me to see you always at my side, I should like to drag you down into misery ? No, no, do not believe it ! You must live happy and contented, while I seek some glorious death, to put an end to my unfortunate life and die the lover of the Electoral Princess. I hope that you have received the two letters about which I spoke to you ; if not, tell me ; you will no longer do me the injustice of believing that any consideration in the world could detach me from you ; my protestation on this subject will make you see that I shall die with my Love. How could one forsake you, for the more one knows you the more one adores you ; one discovers every day new merits [in you] ; and your love alone is capable of making me prefer to have my head cut off rather than abandon you for ever. I am ashamed of my want of exactness ; I beg your pardon for it ; it is a fault which I entreat you not to

---

[1] Can this have been Melusina von der Schulenburg ?

attribute to my negligence but to my shortness of memory. But, my divine Leonisse, acknowledge in your turn that my letters are much the longest; and that, had I not told you of it, you would not have made [yours] so large. So each has his due; hence I shall never concede that your love is greater than mine, and I should be inconsolable if I had not given you more substantial proofs of it; for you might believe that vanity, since you are a princess, is the cause of my attachment. No; I swear to you that if you were the hangman's daughter, and if you possessed the attractions which are actually yours, I should love you with as much ardour. You will think me not very polite; but I flatter myself that you will find my feelings tender and true; in the name of the Gods, continue in the sentiments in which I find you now! If any disgrace were to drive me so far that you conceived a dislike for me, I should certainly send a pistol-shot through my brain. . . .

F 16

[FROM KÖNIGSMARCK TO SOPHIA DOROTHEA]

September 1st [1693, from the Camp].

PARDON me, if sorrow and despair has made me commit the fault of not writing to you for two days. When one is in the state in which I am, one does not know what one is doing. I will begin by telling you that I have changed two ciphers in our key, namely, j means 31, i means 35, u means 53, v means 54. I [beg] you to note this. Next, I must tell you that you have marked two letters No. 10, so that No. 14 ought to be No. 15. But just continue for the present, for there is no other harm done, [except] that the second or first No. 10 might have been lost without one's having known at all that one had been lost. I must further tell you that I wrote to you two letters addressed to 131, whom I supposed to be at Celle; you must let me know whether you have received them. Three letters were addressed to the postmaster at Celle, which are dated the 20th, and [this] is letter No. 9; the 26th, and [this] is letter No. 12—this one is of consequence; the 30th, and [this] is letter No. 14. It would also be well to see whether you have letter No. 13. I beg you to reply to me without fail as to this. You can see everything by the way in which they follow on one another; for I am quite sure that I have been exact on this occasion. You will be surprised to find me making such reflexions, in the condition in which I am; but, my dear, we have had so many misfortunes, that one must not create any more for oneself. I received yours dated the 26th; but you know what accident happened to me in mistaking one bottle for another. I told you about it in my preceding letters; I see, however, in yours dated the 28th, 29th and 30th what you meant to say to me in [that dated] the 26th. It is a great joy to me to know you free from fear, and I am angry with myself for having been the cause of your disquiet, which has contributed greatly to your illness.[1] At present, now that you are free from fear, I hope that the fever will leave you also. How I pity you for having suffered so much—[a] six hours of fever. I do not understand how you have strength enough still to write to me. I am as grateful as I ought to be; and I am convinced that it is love which gives you strength; but to what extent am I not obliged by this mark of your affection? Never shall I forget such favours. If my letters had force enough to comfort you in your sufferings, I would arrange for you to have one every hour; but I take this compliment to be an effect of your kindness. However, I can swear to you

[1] Cf. Wilkins, pp. 313 sqq.

that your letters are a great consolation to me, and without the three last of them, dated 28th, 29th and 30th, I should be in my grave at this very moment. It would after all be the greatest folly I could commit, for, though it would be a sign of affection, I should lose you ; and, [as] you say very well in one of yours, what despair never to see each other again for ever·! Let us then live on, together, love each other everlastingly, and swear to each other afresh a constancy which shall never end ; and that [after ?] death, if we have sense enough, this may likewise endure. In order that we may live together, take all imaginable pains to preserve yourself; remember that my quiet of mind depends on it : if your illness continues, I am quite sure that I shall go mad. The fever prevails a great deal here ; we have nearly 200 on the sick-list among our troops ; my servants fall sick one after the other. I have been obliged to send my valet de chambre to Celle ; the others are at Lüneb[urg] ; if this continues, my turn [?] will come too.

F 17

[FROM KÖNIGSMARCK TO SOPHIA DOROTHEA]

The 3rd [September 1693, from the Camp].

I THOUGHT I should have an apoplectic fit when I opened your letter, without seeing your handwriting. I hoped to hear that you were better, and you are doing quite the contrary. I believed at the beginning that it was all over with you. Do not suppose that I am annoyed that it is not in your handwriting—far from that, I entreat you to continue in the same way, for I am absolutely against your fatiguing yourself. I pity you as much as an affectionate and tender . . . can do so— must the most perfect object in the universe suffer so cruelly ? Ye gods, why are you so unjust ? But, my heart, I know why this misfortune comes to you [1]—it is to render me more unhappy that destiny causes you to fall ill; you are made to suffer in order that I may be crucified. And the design succeeds, for no one could send me a greater misfortune. You order me not to disquiet myself—it would be necessary not to love you, in order not to be at the point of death. Every moment I am on my knees to offer up prayer for your complete recovery ; I flatter myself that in the end I shall find pity—my prayers are too devout not to find acceptance. May God grant that you may speedily be relieved of your sufferings and I of my fears and of my anxiety! With what joy shall I embrace you, when I shall have that of seeing you. I do not know when this will be possible to me ; but my design is to make pretence of an access of fever happening to me; I shall say to the *bonhomme* that I should like to go for three days to 317, to avoid the fever taking hold of me, that is to say, to take some remedies. Instead of staying at 317, I shall take the post and fly to Celle. I should be able to be two nights with you— what joy, what satisfaction ! I should be able to be at your feet, to bathe them with my tears : you would see into how pitiable a state your illness had driven me. But perhaps I am indulging these hopes in vain ; for before I can play this part it is in the first instance necessary that the *bonhomme* should be in better health . . . depends further on the future of the 9 [?] . . . I have nothing good to Hope for ; rage, despair, trouble, disquietude, Love—all these things together have such an effect on me that I am like those people one sees at Amsterdam in the madhouse. God knows what the end of all this will be. The sickness spreads from day to day ; my old Lieutenant-C[olonel] and two Lieutenants have

---

[1] The familiar second person singular is employed in this and the next two lines.

fallen [ill] to-day ; I do not know how I shall escape it ;
it is a miracle, for with all the troubles that oppress me
I ought to catch it. Farewell, my Angel, I can tell you
no more. The express that was sent to me by the *bonhomme* by [?] thought that you have a lover, who takes
so much [interest] in everything that concerns you that
you . . . do yourself [?]; he is sincere [and] adores you,
and has as much Respect for you as anyone in the
world ; I deserve all your affection and all the kind
interest you take in me. If I do not give you assurances
enough of my love and fidelity, it is not my fault—it is
that I have no opportunity for doing so ; I should weary
you with my protestations, for I repeat them in all my
letters. I fancy that you are like myself. I cannot
wait for them too long, and all your letters, were they
filled with anything else, would be to me always agreeable and more so than if there were nothing in them.

F 8

[FROM KÖNIGSMARCK TO SOPHIA DOROTHEA]

Atlenburg, *the* 13*th* [*of September*, 1693].[1]

ON the twelfth I did what I do on all other days: that is
to say, drink, eat, and go the rounds; the same on the
thirteenth. The Duke of Celle came to call on us.
You see that I can keep my diaries without difficulty ;
I do not think they will annoy you at all, for nothing could
be more innocent, and those from Hanover will be of
the same sort, at least if my going to sup with ladies
does not displease you. But I promise to leave this
alone also, assuring you that it is the very slightest proof
I can offer you, inasmuch as I shall be pleased to do

---

[1] Atlenburg (mis-spelt ' Altenburg ' *ap*. Wilkins, p. 314) must
be Artlenburg, in the part of the duchy of Saxe-Lauenburg on
the left bank of the Elbe.

without it, even if you send no orders to stop it. Would to God I could show you by my conduct, that all my thoughts, all my acts are only done for you ; but, alas ! you are so unjust that you refuse to perceive this. I hate my bad fortune, and it is this which one day will ruin me with you. I have received the letter No. 3 dated the 5th, within eight days after that marked 4 ; I cannot understand whence arises this delay ; but I well know that it is dangerous that the letter should be so long on its way. I am not satisfied with you, and the unkind opinion you have of me as if I neglected you hurts me very much ; I think only of you night and day ; no other thought enters my mind ; and yet, I am [supposed to] forget you, to neglect you, I am inconstant—do I really deserve these designations ; be you the judge yourself ! Can you accuse me of no longer loving you ? Is it possible that it is Leonisse who believes this and reproaches me with it ! Great God ! how full of injustice you are, and how great a wrong you do me ! I love you to madness; I adore you beyond compare ; my love surpasses all others—and yet you have doubts of all this ; your heart does not speak in my favour. I have reason for complaining of it—that barbarous heart, which ought to plead for me, instead of being my accuser. I have known it kind to me ; but little by little all that affection has vanished. Will not your heart recover itself ? reproach it on my part ; my heart promises an eternal attachment, it swears constancy to you, and, provided that you deign to think of it once in every twenty-four hours, it is content. Does it deserve to be remembered by you ? I think it does, but it is for you to judge the case. If I am ever unfortunate enough to love you no longer (which is an impossibility), your wish will be no punishment to me [? ?], for I swear to you that I shall never seek any other faithful attachment, and, though the present one is dearer to me than my life, I should never wish for another. Remember what a certain Spaniard said : ' I do not wish to make myself common '—I call it to make myself common if I were to quit the most perfect object of the universe for some other, who could never compare herself as to . . .

F 19

[FROM KÖNIGSMARCK TO SOPHIA DOROTHEA]

The 14th [of September, 1693. From the Camp].

MOST assuredly, without yours of the 12th the Beating of my Heart, of which 127 had been the cause, would have made an end of me, but, most fortunately for me, I received it at the time when my heart was about to burst ; and, as I see from it that the news is quite false, I also begin to recover myself. He told me, as quite certain, that your fever had seized you again. Assuredly I should not, with this disquiet, have been able to pass the night alive ; and now while I am writing to you I still have the Queen of Hungary Water [1] on my nose. I think, however, that this will pass away ; but I feel very much upset and exhausted ; if this does not go away in the night, I shall bleed myself to prevent any evil consequences that might overtake me. M. de Sporck [2] will, according to all appearances, die before

---

[1] This old-fashioned toilet-water has hardly gone quite out of use. Its name is said to have been derived from the fact that the original formula of the compound (of which the chief ingredient is rosemary) was presented by a hermit to a queen of Hungary. In his rapturous letter *ap.* Wilkins, p. 155, Königsmarck begs Sophia Dorothea to have *de l'eau de la reine d'Hongrie* in readiness.

[2] A member of the ancient family von Spörcken, which possessed numerous estates in Lüneburg, and from which sprang Field-Marshal von Spörcken. He was born in 1698, and his mother was a sister of Field-Marshal von der Schulenburg.

the day is over ; I have 3 Captains, 5 Lieutenants and 4 Ensigns sick to death, more than 300 foot-soldiers and dragoons, of our troops only, are quite down ; it is an infected air, the healthiest sicken in it ; all the same, I hope not to fall sick, knowing you to be out of the wood. You will have seen from my letter dated the 12th how well satisfied I am with you ; do not be offended that I begged you to [write] me two words with your own hand ; I knew that you were a little better ; otherwise I should not have done it ; but, my best beloved heart, you have done too much, for you have written me two entire pages ; I beg you very particularly not to do this any more, nor until you are quite well again. The siege of Charleroi [1] will prevent the Electoral Prince from being here so soon ; great God, may this siege deliver us from troublesome people ! It is said for certain that things are settling down ; but the orders that are given for taking care of the sick make me tremble with fear that we shall not so soon quit this post. I am agitated by the same despair as you are, to have to pass my life with people for whom I feel an aversion, and to be allowed to pass so little time with her whom I adore. However, you are more to be pitied, for I can very often get free of it, and you not, besides the embraces which you are obliged to undergo. It seems to me that, if I had to suffer the same sort of thing, I could not prevent myself from being sick every time it should happen to me. Ah, how horrible to caress what one hates mortally ; I firmly believe that purgatory does not inflict so many torments as do caresses of that sort. If it is true that the Elector of Hanover is not going to 308, I might well come there ; but we cannot take our measures before

---

[1] The siege of Charleroi by Vauban began on September 15, 1693, and ended with the capture of the place on October 11.

it is known what will become of the Electoral Prince.
The Duchess of Hanover [1] will not arrive till towards the
end of next month ; and then the Electoral Prince will
have returned, and the hunting will be over.   May God
only grant that we begin it soon, and that you are able
to put in an appearance.   I pity you for having grown
so thin ; but (with your permission) I find the question
which you put to me ridiculous and absurd.   If I loved
nothing in you but your beauty I would forgive it you ;
but you are convinced that it is not only this which I
adore—it is your merits, your [sweet] temper.[2]   I confess to you that to see you beautiful charms the eyes ;
but I protest to you that, were you ugly like Madame
Kopstein,[3] I should not love you a whit the less.   Tired of
you ?   Ah, is it possible to ask such a question as this of
a lover who loves you dearly !   No, no, Leonisse, you are
not convinced of my sincere affection.   What must I do
to bring the conviction of it home to you ?   I shall never
be at rest, till I know that you are quite convinced of it.
Do you believe that an affection like mine arose out of
anything so transitory as beauty ?   Although you have
much of it, and more than any one else of your sex, I
can tell you that it is not your beauty which has put me
into the condition in which I am.   It is true that the
beauty which you possess set me on fire, and that without
it I should perhaps not have been as happy as I am ;
but that which has made me as I am is your *esprit*, your
sincerity, your way of living, and, finally, it is your soul,
so high-bred and so well-balanced, which produces in you

---

[1] *Sic* in text ('*la Dujais d'Hanovre*' and, lower down, '*la
Dujaïÿse*,' Königsmarck's spelling), though the date of the letter
admits of no doubt.

[2] The remainder of this letter was misplaced in the Berlin
copy.

[3] Probably the wife of Court-Marshal von Koppenstein.

a sweetness beyond compare, an unequalled generosity, with clemency beyond all imagination. It is these virtues which have placed me in the dear slavery in which I find myself at this moment, and in which I also mean to die. In truth, Leonisse, you trouble me greatly with your questions ; you fear that I shall become unfaithful to the greatest Beauty of the age, and to virtue itself, for some unfledged princesses [1] without any other merit but that of having been to Paris. Once more, I see only too well that you are not well convinced of my love ; I hope that in the end I shall give you so many signs of it that you will no longer be able to doubt it. To take the proper steps it is necessary that we should speak to each other ; we have time up to the end of the coming month [?], and before this time we need not fear the return of the Electoral Prince, and of the Duchess. You still attack [me about] princesses [?]. Do you perhaps think that I am so fond as you are yourself of novelty, of change, and of people who come from Paris ? You are quite mistaken : I wear my chains with very great pleasure, and would not change them for the Kingdom of the Great Mogul. The letter of the Lieutenant-Colonel is very silly, but the person is reasonable enough ; she has inspired a strong affection in a very brave man, of high rank, in the Low Countries, whose name is the Marquis of Spinosa.[2] He is one of the fine gentlemen [*galans*] of that country. But since I have sent you a very silly letter, I shall make up for it by one that is very well written ; if it were not written out of a book, we

---

[1] *Gosses de princesses* in the original. I owe the following reference to Dr. Braunholtz : *Dans le jargon des voyous, une gosse, une gosseline, c'est une fillette de quinze à seize ans. . . .* (L. Rigaud, *Dictionnaire d'argot moderne*, n.e., 1888).

[2] I am unable to identify this nobleman. The spelling Espinosa seems the more common.

ought to admire it particularly as coming from this person ; but let me tell you that she found it word for word in a book. However, it must be allowed that it is phrased very suitably. I beg you to send it back to me ; I send it you because I think it will amuse you. Adieu.

F 4

[FROM KÖNIGSMARCK TO SOPHIA DOROTHEA]

Thursday [1693].

I NEEDED your letter to sustain me in the despair which had fallen upon me. This is what comes of acting openly, and if you had not spoken to me of . . . I believe that I could not have held out a day longer. However, I controlled myself excellently ; and I wished in the first instance to know what you would say to me ; so I did not give way to my anger. Let me tell you then that I was the day before yesterday at Linde.[1] Mme. la Comtesse was greatly astonished that I did not play with you. I said to her that this required permission ; she said, Mme. Léonisse made the Elector ask me ; and he replied positively that she might summon her players. Yesterday, before receiving your letter, I was told by Oberg who had seen M. Weyhe at Linde, that his Highness had said it to yourself.[2] Prince Ernest

[1] Linde or Linden, an estate in the immediate vincity of Hanover, purchased in 1688 by Count Platen, who built in its fine gardens a *château*, frequently mentioned as '*la cour de Linden*.'

[2] The Obergs were an ancient noble family, whose estates lay in the bishopric of Hildesheim and elsewhere. A Privy-Councillor von Oberg is mentioned *ap.* Malortie, *u. s.* pp. 193, 194. Christian Lewis von Oberg, a general of much distinction in the Hanoverian service, was not born till 1689. The Obergs were afterwards raised to the rank of Counts.—The von der Weyhe

Augustus said to me in these words, that the Elector had said to you, ' You are bored, Madam ; you ought to summon your players.' It would have depended on yourself, if he had spoken to you in this way. But, Madam, I was greatly relieved when I read your letter, in which you write to me about this matter. I have drawn my moral, which is never begin to fly into a passion about vapours. But, my divine creature, could you not [contrive to] let [me] come, in order that I might have the joy of gazing upon you, and that my eyes and my heart might learn from yours how I stand with them, and whether your love is such as you wrote to me. Your letter of yesterday is charming ; it touched me so that I feel more on fire than ever. You write that you see nobody ; nothing could be more obliging ; but you see the Reformer all the more ; which makes me fear that you will accustom yourself little by little to his mediocre caresses, and he will kiss you so often that I die with trouble only to think of it. For the love of yourself, do not accustom yourself to it ; always remember the way in which he treats you—you who deserve all proper, obliging and respectful ways. But I see the defects of another man, and I do not see that it is in this that I am the most criminal. You have told me yourself that the Re[former] . . . [at times ?] was not so unpleasant in his ways as myself. I die to think of it. How unfortunate I am to love you so tenderly, and that this excessive passion makes me so odious. Think no more of the past, I beseech you. Adieu, adieu, alas, adieu !

mentioned in the text was probably the same who afterwards became a General, and married the widowed Frau von dem Bussche, Countess Platen's sister.

F 5

[1693.]

I AM much to be pitied, and my ill-fortune persecutes me too much for me to be able to bear it any longer. Yesterday's letters give us no hope that the Ref[ormer] may take his departure; and until he has gone I cannot and ought not to see you. What a cruel destiny! oh, insupportable misfortune! Can I still breathe after such heavy blows; life becomes insupportable to me; I cannot, nor ought I to, remain any longer in the world, for what can I do in it without seeing you! I have to-day had two unfortunate experiences, of which at present the second seems to me the most cruel, but the first may prove the most terrible. I have fallen out with our old *bonhomme,* and with Gor too; and, as he told you, if I were to repeat it to those with whom his Highness is displeased, they would be much astonished. Apart from my passion [for you], I know what course I have to take; but, my dear, as I have promised you to do nothing without your consent, I wish to let you know about it beforehand. My intention is to write to him, and to say to him that I was very much annoyed that duty had involved me in a dispute with the person in the world whom I honour most; but, as I had carefully taken note of the words he addressed to me, I had observed at the time that he said [that] if I repeated [it] to all those whom our master holds in contempt, there would be many who would be unde-ceived; I thought that your Excellency would not be offended, if I asked you to be good enough to inform me privately, whether I am unfortunate enough to have dis-pleased Monseigneur the Elector—in order that I might

shape my course accordingly. For hitherto I had
served him from affection only, and without any interested motive; and, if I was unfortunate enough to have
incurred his disfavour, it would be impossible for me to
serve him any longer.[1] This was, in substance, what
I wished to say to him, being aware of your opinion.
I can assure you that I positively perceived that his rage
directed itself against me. I am surprised at my own
patience, and I cannot understand how I managed to
control myself, for I had it very often on the tip of my
tongue to say to him what I intend to write to him.
The second misfortune troubles me a great deal more.
I saw your windows open; the Ref[ormer] came out
of your dressing-room; without [my] seeing you there,
though I raised my voice tolerably high, and passed and
repassed; but there was nothing—one could not see a living
soul there. I suppose that, as it was late, you were already
in the room of the *Romaine*. I should be inconsolable, if I
had not the hope of seeing you this evening at 6 o'clock.
To what am I reduced! I count it the greatest good
fortune in the world to see you a thousand feet off. In
good truth, it will be a great consolation to me if I can
have this pleasure. That of writing to you is very dear
to me, and I would not give it up for a Kingdom. I fear
that my Diabolical destiny will deprive me of it; this
would be my finishing stroke. I conjure you, take your
measures so well that we may not miss this joy. You
know, I hope, through your own self that one would
not be able to live without this. Alas! why am I not
Reden or Hortense[2]; so long as you are there, it matters

---

[1] The meaning of this passage is hopelessly obscured in the
original by the wild use of brackets, and by a reckless interchange
between *oratio obliqua* and *directa*, and the second and third
persons.

[2] Von Reden was Chamberlain to the Electress Sophia.

not if you were to hate me. I shall, however, have the
joy of seeing her whom I adore ; it is our love which takes
the one far away from the other ; without my love,
I should be wherever you are ; but because I love you
I am in bad repute, I am disregarded, I am forgotten.
But never mind ; let them spit in my face, I will not
take offence at it.

F 13

[FROM KÖNIGSMARCK TO SOPHIA DOROTHEA]

[Hanover, *latter part of* 1693].[1]

IN fear of not being able to speak to you, I take the
liberty of expressing to you my concern at the misfortune which has happened to you. God knows that
my heart forewarned me of it ; but my companion was
never willing to wait, although I begged him to do so ;
but, by way of climax to my ill luck, I have to wait
till my intimate friend has had the pleasure with his
troublesome companion of an interview with you ;
it seems to me that I have great reason to complain of
the Gods, as they are unjust enough to deprive me of
all means of being serviceable to you, while at the same
time they furnish such means to those from whom I have
most to fear. Since this accident strange things have
come into my head, and I am foolish enough to believe
that the accident which happened yesterday is a prog-
nostic of my ill luck, and that this is the same man who
will be the cause of all these troubles to me. The result

' Hortense ' is the Abbé Hortensio Mauro, mentioned in Chapter
III. In her letters, the Electress often refers to him as ' Ortence.'

[1] This and the following two letters might belong to the
spring of 1692 ; but I think that they may with more probability
be assigned to the latter part of 1693.

will be that I shall have him watched as closely as possible while I am away, and, if I hear the slightest thing, believe me as a man of honour that I will never see you again, and that I would rather seek out the innermost parts of Lapland than appear before those eyes which [once] enchanted me. I detest my companion, for without this I should have had the pleasure of serving you, instead of my seeing this joy in the breast of a man whom I abhor, and who is impertinent enough to come and tell me of it himself, informing me of the condition in which you were, your *déshabillement*, without a cap, your hair loose over your incomparable bosom. O God, I am too furious to write any more.

F 14

[FROM KÖNIGSMARCK TO SOPHIA DOROTHEA]

[Hanover, *latter part of* 1693.]

WHILE I was reflecting on the miserable state in which I found myself they brought me your letter, which I had little expected. My joy was so great that I forgot my sufferings, throwing myself on the letter as if nothing were wanting to me. You have done everything that I wished to see you do ; it therefore only remains for me to thank you for your kindness, and to give you every assurance of my fidelity :

> *Io ti saro fedele,*
> *Ne mai ti tradiro.*
> *Se ben mi sei crudel,*
> *Sempre t' adorero.*

If you do not believe me, I am ready to abandon Mother, Kinsfolk, Friends, Possessions and Country, the better to convince you of it ; and it will only depend on you whether I shall take the journey of which you are well aware. My unhappy condition furnishes me with a good excuse; I shall be able to pretend illness for a long time. If you agree with me, I beg you to let me know; for I will take my measures accordingly; it is the greatest proof [of my affection] which I can offer you at present; so pray accept it, and thus make me happy; for the satisfaction of seeing you far surpasses the ambition which I have of making my fortune. I could not find any greater [good fortune], and that of possessing you is so dear to me that I do not any longer meditate on any of the others. By your letter you have so purified my heart that there no longer remains in it the slightest suspicion of jealousy; the eagerness which you show to know the state of my health sufficiently convinces me that you love me. To meet your wish, I will tell you that I suffer extremely; yet the pain of not seeing you greatly exceeds that of my fall. I expect to be better in four days; but if you accept my proposition, I shall keep my room for ten days longer. This will not prevent me, so soon as I shall be able to walk, from being able to embrace you in the well-known locality; to have news of you, I believe that the safest way is for one of my people (in whom I am able to place confidence). . . .

F 15

[FROM KÖNIGSMARCK TO SOPHIA DOROTHEA]

[Hanover, *latter part of* 1693.]

ANYONE but myself would put you to the proof, to see whether your love will carry you so far as to come to me; but, as for me, I love you too much to be able to expose you to this risk, and your offer is sufficient for me. However, in order not to lose the occasion of seeing you (since I have so little time for remaining with you) I will come to you this evening, if you consent ; and I shall wait to hear from you the hour of the *rendez-vous*. If you think it well that I should appear at court, I will do so, but not otherwise.   The joy of seeing you again makes me forget all the trouble that my illness has brought upon me ; for the rest, I am well enough pleased with you ; I cannot, however, forget how little opposition you have to offer on the subject of my journey, having a good excuse for dissuading me from it ; I do not know at what judgment to arrive on the subject.[1]   Only, may God grant that this absence may not prove of deadly import to me !   You accuse me of not loving you enough ; how can you be so unjust, but I will pass over this point without reply, knowing well that you are too fully convinced of my love, which is the purest that ever existed, and which will last so long as I live.   I have often protested this to you in prose ; permit me on the present occasion to do it in verse :

> While breath within my heart remains,
>   Beloved is *votre nom* by me ;
> So long as blood runs in my veins,
>   It shall retain the mark of thee ;
> And with the current of my days,
> Love shall remain with me always.

At 6 o'clock my man shall be in front of the room of the *bonne, bonne amie.*[2]

[1] The reference seems to be to his intention to quit the Hanoverian service.

[2] Fräulein von dem Knesebeck.

F 20

[FROM KÖNIGSMARCK TO SOPHIA DOROTHEA]

[Hanover, *latter part of* 1693.] [1]

I PERCEIVE the pleasure that I had taken in embracing you vanishes entirely since the Troublesome One has appeared so suddenly. I confess to you that this countenance displeased me very much so soon as I perceived it ; a thunderclap could not have surprised me more. But it is fated that there should always be disagreeable faces to prevent a tender meeting like that which all appearances allowed us to think ours was to be. Yes, my idea of it was so full of joy that I could not sleep all the night ; but alas ! all is vanished, and I have to pass a second night without sleeping, and with grief instead of the joy with which the first filled me ; it is certain that, unless you are so kind as to console me, I shall bathe in my tears. Console me then, divine beauty, and comfort a man who is dying for you, and who is so set upon your charms that his head turns :

> For a toy [?] of charming beauty
> Such flame me doth consume,
> That to love her is reason and duty,
> Till I am laid in my tomb.

Such is my maxim, and you shall see me carry it out exactly ; my greatest satisfaction shall be to prove to you that only death is alone capable of extinguishing my love. But, for the love of God, think of the motto, ' Nothing impure inflames me ' ; [2] adieu !

[1] This and the following letter ought possibly to be dated in the spring of 1692 ; but I think the date assigned the more probable one.

[2] The seal on some of Königsmarck's letters in the Lund Correspondence represents a flaming heart on an altar, the sun shining down upon it, with the circumscription, *Rien d'impure m'allume*. Wilkins, p. 123.

F 21

[From Königsmarck to Sophia Dorothea]

[Hanover, *latter part of* 1693] 6 *o'clock.*

I CANNOT go away from here without thanking you for having rescued me from such a difficulty. Surely I was a lost man without yesterday evening's conversation. I go away as happy as a man can do who leaves behind what he adores ; but what consoles me is that I am well assured of your friendship, and that my absence does me no harm ; my soul is so at ease that I am quite a different man from what I was before. I beg of you, no *tête-à-têtes*—not with anybody, in particular with M. R.[1] I shall know everything, for I have good friends here whom you do not in the least suspect. Adieu, *Bella dea*, think of me as much as I think of you. I kiss your knees a thousand times, and am eternally your slave.

[1] I cannot guess at ' M. R.' Prince Maximilian's second name was William.

APPENDIX C

NOTE ON THE RELIGIOUS SITUATION IN SCOTLAND, AS IT AFFECTED THE HANOVERIAN SUCCESSION

THE Church of Scotland was, in the main, well affected to the Union and the consequences which it entailed as regards the Succession. But the friends of the House of Hanover had to guard against two distinct sources of weakness within the Establishment itself.

(1) Episcopacy in Scotland had never been more than a compromise, even in the districts where it had not been violently opposed. The best instance of this is Aberdeenshire, where protests against the government of Charles II are late in date and are confined to verbal expressions of sympathy with the persecuted Presbyterians. But the *Records of the Exercise* [Presbytery] *of Alford* (New Spalding Club, 1897), dealing with the period 1662-1688, show clearly enough that the episcopal function was ordination, and that the government and, in many respects, the public worship of the Church was Presbyterian. The effect of this was that, at the Revolution, Episcopal clergymen were permitted to remain in their parishes on condition of their taking the oath to William and Mary, although they were forbidden to take part in Presbyteries, Synods, or Assemblies. The tendency was for such men to conform to Presbytery, but they formed a distinct ' left wing.' They were most numerous in the north-east, and they were well represented in the Universities. Both the Universities of

Aberdeen, for example, were Jacobite in sympathy. The result was that many ministers shared in, and urged their people to join, the '15. They were deposed in 1716, and the Universities were ' purged ' by the Commission of 1717.

(2) A section of the more robust Presbyterians in the Church sympathised with their brethren who had declined to accept the Revolution Settlement, and their feeling was accentuated by a gross breach of faith on the part of the British Parliament—the passing of the Patronage Act of 1712, which disturbed the Church for more than a century and a half. So strong was this tendency that, as late as 1745, the Provincial Synod of Moray considered it necessary to inform George II that ' with pleasure we reflect that very few of the people who hold communion with us have joined those enemies of your Majesty's crown and government.' (Allardyce, *Jacobite Papers.*)

Episcopalian Jacobitism within the Church practically disappears in 1716, and the clergy, as represented in ecclesiastical and academic records, were devotedly loyal to George I and II, from that date.

Outside the Church we have a body who were not Dissenters in the English sense, for they approved of the constitution of the Church, but objected to the establishment of Episcopacy in England, and the toleration of Dissenters in Scotland. They were the men who had suffered most in the ' killing time,' and their only associations with the functions of government were connected with Grierson of Lagg and Bloody Mackenzie. They considered it possible that James Stewart might be turned from the error of his ways, and take the Covenant as Charles II had done. Their attitude, in fact, was precisely similar to that of their predecessors, who had crowned Charles II after fighting against Charles I.

They declined to acknowledge the Revolution Settlement and the Union. They spoke of Queen Anne as ' that wicked Jezabel the pretended Queen,' and ' the late woman.' But even when they had little hope of the Pretender's conversion, they protested against ' the Prince of Hanover, who hath been bred and brought up in the Luthren religion, which is not only different from but even in many things contrar unto that purity in doctrine, reformation, and religion we in these nations had attained unto.' (*Protestation against the Union.*)

The Episcopalians, the largest section of Protestant Dissenters, were, almost without exception, High Tories. They had suffered for refusing the oath to William and Mary, and had undergone some trifling inconveniences as the defeated and unpopular party. The rising of 1715 was, therefore, very largely supported by Episcopalians, who found themselves ranged along with extreme Presbyterians and Roman Catholics. The religious aspect of the '15 and the '45 has never been satisfactorily examined. Mr. Blaikie said, not long since, that the '45 was much more Presbyterian than is commonly imagined. I hope he will work out the subject.

R. S. RAIT.

INDEX

PRINTED BY
SPOTTISWOODE AND CO. LTD., COLCHESTER
LONDON AND ETON